PEBBLES BY ZEBLOCKS

A MINTFACE GENERATIVE ART GUIDE

MintFace

"We are Ars0nic & Cheaterflums; blockchain enthusiasts who develop generative arts."

— ZEBLOCKS

"**NextGen** is an on-chain generative art NFT contract. It is also a tool to support the ambitious aspirations of the 6529 community."

— PUNK6529

"Whoah. This Pebble looks like a gooch!"

— PEBBLES COLLECTOOR

CONTENTS

PART III
FEATURED COLLECTOORS

PART IV
6529 CONTRIBUTIONS

AUTHOR NOTE

Blockchain technology has given generative art a 21st Century digital home. Artists share art with minted provenance, and can follow the journey of each artwork after it is generated on-chain. Art appreciators can enjoy the beauty of generative art on any device.

Pebbles are hardened from decay or destruction thanks to the distributed permanence of the Ethereum blockchain; a settlement layer for billions of dollars of transactions, assets and the art-led revolution that we are each contributing to.

Pebbles were released to the public as 'Creative Commons 0,' instantly freeing the art from copyright constraints. The artist Zeblocks now benefits from the network effects of distribution efforts, such as this book, as art value accrues at the token layer to all collectoors.

ARTIST PREFACE

Pebbles is a generative art collection that captures the organic diversity of stones as seen through a modernist lens. Against a backdrop that suggests the texture of woven fabric, each piece in the collection presents a playful scatter of rounded shapes and colors.

The collection's signature lies in its structured randomness, with certain artworks featuring a deliberate grid of circles that contrast with the free-form distribution of ellipses above. This juxtaposition of order and chaos mirrors the natural world's balance, evoking the varied forms pebbles take when tumbled by water and time.

Pebbles is a homage to the beauty of natural simplicity found in the most basic elements of our environment, reimagined through a digital medium.

Script at index 0 updated to: let e=document.createEle-
ment("style");e.innerText="body {background:
black;height:100vh;width:100vw;margin:0;padding:0;overflow:hid-
den;display:flex;justify-content:center;align-items:center;}",docu-
ment.head.appendChild(e);let traits={"Collection
Name":"Pebbles"},t=0|hash.slice(0,16);function a(){return
t^=t<<13,t^=t>>17,t^=t<<5,(t<0?1+~t:t)%1e3/1e3}let l=document.cre-
ateElement("canvas"),n=document.createElement("canvas"),r=win-
dow.innerHeight,o=r/1.294;o>window.innerWidth&&(o=window.in-
nerWidth,r=1.294*o),o|=0,r|=0,n.height=r,n.width=o;l.height=1294,l.

width=1e3;let i=r/1294,c=o/1e3;document.body.append-
Child(n);let f=n.getContext("2d"),d=l.getContext("2d");f.line-
Join="round",d.lineJoin="round";let s=!0;a()<.7&&(s=!1),trait-
s.Edge=s?"Yes":"No";let h=1.5/1300*r;f.lineWidth=h;let
u,p=!0,b=a(),g=!1;b<.05?g=!0:b<.9&&(p=!1),traits.Traced=p?
g?"No Fill":"Border":"No Border";let M=a();function m(e)
{return parseInt(e,16)}M<.1?(u=-.2,traits.Over-
lap="Fuse"):M<.15?(u=-.1,traits.Overlap="Blend"):M<.65?
(u=0,traits.Overlap="Harmonize"):M<.9?(u=.2,traits.Over-
lap="Disjoin"):(u=.4,traits.Overlap="Isolate");const w=
{};function D(e="#000000",t=0){let
a=m((e=e.slice(1)).slice(0,2)),l=m(e.slice(2,4)),n=m(e.s-
lice(4,6));const i=document.createElement("can-
vas");i.width=o,i.height=r;const c=i.getContext("2d");let
d=f.getImageData(0,0,o,r),s=d.data;for(let
e=0;e<s.length/4;e++)s[4*e]+=(a-s[4*e])*t,s[4*e+1]+=(l-
s[4*e+1])*t,s[4*e+2]+=(n-s[4*e+2])*t;c.putImageDa-
ta(d,0,0);let h=f.createPattern(i,"no-repeat");w[e]=h}function P(e)

```
{return e=e.slice(1),w[e]}let v,C=a();C<.16?(v=1+
(10*a()|0),traits["Color Density"]="Faint"):C<.28?(v=11+
(27*a()|0),traits["Color Density"]="Hush"):C<.58?(v=38+
(27*a()|0),traits["Color Density"]="Bloom"):C<.95?(v=65+
(26*a()|0),traits["Color Density"]="Vivid"):(v=91+
(11*a()|0),traits["Color Density"]="Drench"),v/=100;let S,q=
[{a:33.33,n:"summer.jpg",c:
["#fffff3","#0c8ecd","#0976aa","#075175",.85,
   "#00122c","#022346","#ff0962","#01408d"]},
{a:33.33,n:"Magma Mambo",c:
["#dca23e","#1b1f20","#111314","#414849",.85,
   "#080a0a","#2b3131","#1d2323","#aa1403"]},
{a:33.34,n:"Lunar Chuckles",c:
["#292929","#000000","#000000","#000000",.95,
   "#000000","#060b0b","#232323","#131313"]},
{a:31.66,n:"Blueprint",c:
["#f7f7f7","#2c52e5","#2a4edb","#3c69f7",.9,
   "#1d3aab","#4d6de9","#2341b5"]},{a:33.33,n:"Salsa
Blush",c:["#030303","#a70312","#8d0310","#56020a",.85,
   "#7b1315","#8c4353","#5b8c85","#6ccfa3"]},
{a:35.01,n:"Elephant Pajamas",c:
["#e9e6de","#c7c7bf","#c7c7bf","#dad7d0",.95,
   "#b5b5af","#d8d9d3","#cbc8bf","#bb-
b6ae","#c4c1b8","#b9b9ad"]},{a:100,n:"Sgt. Pepe",c:
["#5b8344","#472a2c","#472a2c","#311d1e",.85,
   "#211213","#e6c679","#e2dedd","#c29e84","#9d4c31",
   "#dbad3d","#e8773f","#6e6083"]},{a:5.8,n:"Shades of
Hey!",c:["#f3efe2","#1a1a1a","#131313"..........putImage-
Data(E,0,0),requestAnimationFrame(ne)):console.log("done")}
```

CODE AS ART

Seventeen Kilobytes of script generated the Pebbles collection. The code was split across two transactions to fit into Ethereum's transaction block size limits. Once the code is saved to the Ethereum blockchain, it gets distributed throughout thousands of nodes around the world.

The code creates the art on mint day, with the Pebbles collection allowing the code to run 1000 times. Each artwork is generated in sequence and numbered #0 to #999. All artworks are preserved on-chain, without any filtering or editing by Zeblocks. The code defines the boundaries and concepts within which it creates the art.

Index 0 Transaction

0xef1d33115a973d2e06964ef5b7268bfa47bb1284c1f5ec45a7ff4bd31072f9de

Index 1 Transaction

0x3a309d19cf8109c0ff1c5de-
b98234593696d467e23a41e8ab948c53bd75c478c

Artist Signature

AlL OuR PeBbLeS ArE BeLoNg To YoU - ZeBlOcKs

PEBBLES EXHIBITION

The Pebbles exhibition can be visited on The Line (theline.wtf), where over 1,000 artists exhibit their collections in one single connected line of artwork spanning hundreds of digital miles. The goal of The Line is to display one million minted artworks in a single line.

Visit Pebbles on The Line at oncyber.io/line808 to be immersed in Pebbles from this book. The Line is open 24x7 and free to visit. Art enthusiasts of all ages are welcome to walk amongst the Pebbles exhibition provided by The Line.

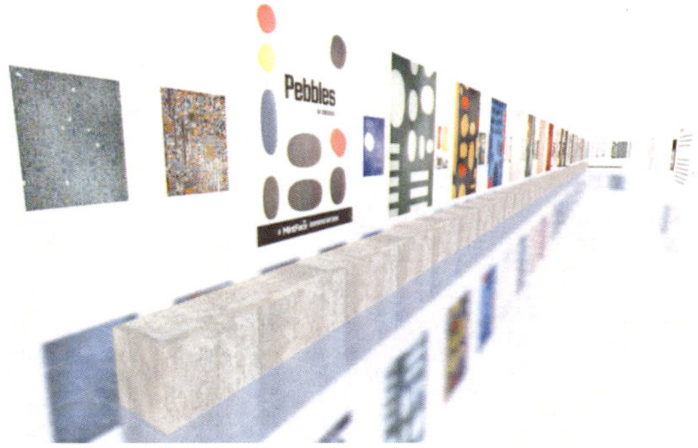

Visit The Pebbles Exhibition on The Line 808 oncyber.io/line808

INTRODUCTION TO PEBBLES

Digital Identity and Art

Our lives continue on an arc towards more digitization, not less, making owning our own digital lives critical to our digital being. Each Pebble is the first generative output built on a smart contract programmed that acknowledged the sovereignty of our individual identities.

The DNA Strands of Pebbles

To be introduced to the Pebbles collection, is to know the 'DNA strands' that contribute to each genetic expression visible to the eye. Some of these individual DNA strands, known as art traits; are obvious. Many traits are prominent only in the presence of other traits. A few traits are hidden in plain sight. Over the course of the Pebbles book you will learn how to spot all the Pebble traits.

The Traits

There are nine individual traits that could be called upon by the code to create the art. Some traits are persistent, like *Palette* and *Size* so these will be found switched on across all 1000 Pebble artworks. Traits like *Edge* and *Flow* may be switched on or off.

Mint Type

- The **Mint Type** rewards wallets with access to exclusive palettes, if their wallet can demonstrate a high level of 'Collectoor Provenance.' This might include collecting memes, gradients, 1/1 art from the artist or from Punk6529, Sgt. Pepe meme cards, amongst other desired collectoor behaviour.

Persistent and Obvious Traits

There are two traits you will find in all Pebbles and are easy to identify:

- **Palette** output decides which colors the Pebble artwork will draw from. Each *Palette* has a predetermined range of a few colors.
- **Size** output decides how big the Pebbles inside the artwork should be. The *Size* output range is broad. An artwork may show just one large Pebble or hundreds of tiny Pebbles and everything in between.

Amplifier Traits

There are two traits that are gradually turned up or down on a scale. For example:

- **Color Density** decides whether to use lots of colors from the *Palette* or very few at all on a scale of 1 to 100.
- **Overlap** decides to add a lot of spacing or bunch up the Pebbles by overlapping them.

Special Elements

- **None** presents the output of a 'pure' or 'raw' Pebble that contains no additional *Special Element* features or adornments beyond the Pebbles themselves.
- **One, Two, Three** and **All** determines how many of the four *Special Elements* appear in an artwork.

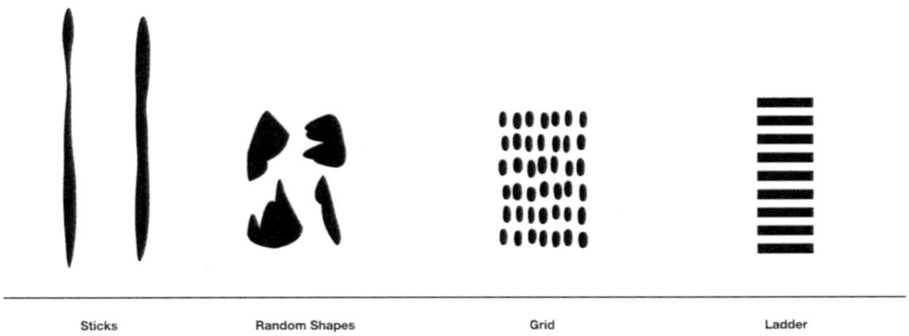

The four Special Elements illustrated in the Pebbles collection

There are four kinds of *Special Elements*:

- **Sticks** are long, vertical filled in blobs that appear at the same scale as the Pebble size
- **Random Shapes** are just that. They add variety and interest to small Pebble sizes and create unique, emergent properties at large Pebble sizes
- **Grids** are a group of similar sized Pebbles in the same color. They provide more area for the background color to shine through on smaller Pebbles and can create unique, emergent properties at the large Pebbles sizes
- **Ladders** show rectangles stacked on top of each other, creating a pathway effect. Ladders are the sharp end of Pebble aesthetics

Traits that Switch On and Off

There are three traits that are either switched on or off. *Edge* is easily spotted, while *Flow* has not strongly appeared in any part of the collection. *Traced* can add or remove elements within every individual Pebble:

- **Edge** decides whether to add an *Edge* frame around the Pebble or not.
- **Flow** creates an invisible focal point that gives the effect of magnetizing the *Flow* of Pebbles towards it.
- **Traced** can add an outline around each filled Pebble or remove the filling of each Pebble.

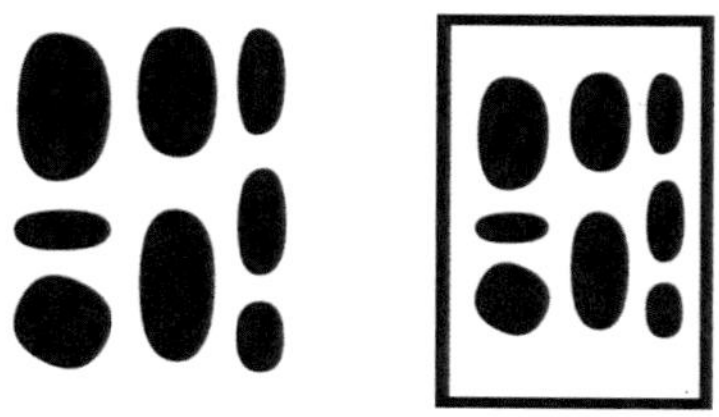

No Edge Edge

The Edge trait that adds or removes a frame

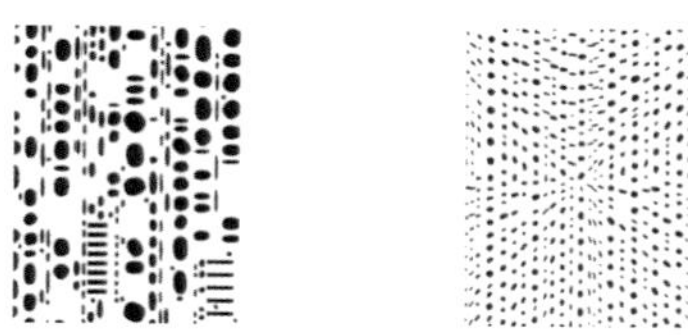

No Flow Flow

The Flow trait that moves Pebbles towards a focal point

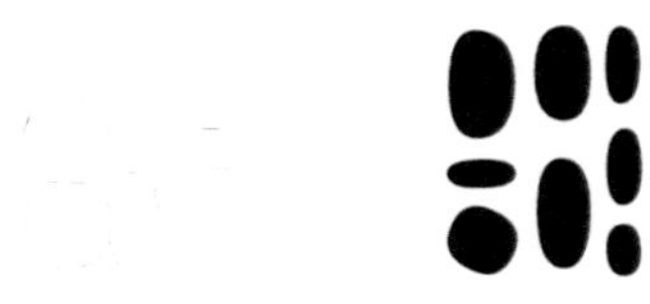

The No Fill trait that removes the fill from all Pebbles

The Variants

There are also traits, with variants more complex than a simple on-or-off switch. These variants give more granularity to the trait feature, allowing for its presence to be slowly dialled up or down. The *Overlap* trait variants can output Pebbles that are very close together or the Pebbles can be arranged far apart from each other. The *Color Density* trait variant can reduce the number of colors used in a palette or can select from the entire *Palette* color range.

The Outputs

Each selection the code makes on the fly at time of mint, beyond the control of the artist, can substantially influence the final code generated output. To the first time minter, the *Palette* and *Size* traits on their own provide 140 varying combinations to marvel at. To the trained eye, a combination of trait variants can often surprise and delight that even the artist might be surprised by the possible outcome.

The Aesthetic

From an aesthetic perspective, Punk6529 believes Pebbles 'hit all the high notes of long-form generative art.' Long-form can be translated as lots of artworks from a single source of code as art. There are three qualitative ways to measure the ability of the Pebble collection to reach the aesthetic 'high notes' including:

- Each individual Pebble looks great
- Each Pebble has its own personality
- The group of Pebbles looks like its from the same family

The Reveal

For many collectors of 'The Memes by 6529,' Pebbles mint day marked their first experience of minting unseen artwork, where the code uniquely generated their piece. The risk of buying art sight unseen contrasts with the randomised potential reward of a rare. The combination of these behavioural aspects is its own performance.

Allowlist holders eagerly watch as more artworks are revealed, trying to decipher the story told by the code. Some prefer to mint early and nab an early mint number. Others with zero skin in the game also get to participate in the fun without buying a thing.

The Performance

The performative aspects of minting generative art was well enjoyed by early Art Blocks Curated collectoors. It is encouraging to see the 'lucky dip' mint entertainment aspects being brought across to the NextGen contract for meme collectoors to experience.

As of June 20th, 483 people own at least one Pebble, with a substantial proportion minting their Pebble on mint day. How many of the 483 holders truly understand all the characteristics of their Pebble?

Vibe Check

Ask yourself 'do I vibe with this art?' or 'does this art hit different?' when viewing an artwork. These questions get to how you feel about the art, not what you might think about it after analysing the code.

MintFace provides a 'Vibe Check' for each Featured Collectoor Pebble providing additional context for the art. The Vibe Check is one opinion and one lens that you are welcome to adjust, adapt or flat out disagree with. The beauty of generative art is that while there is a source of truth to the math driven code, the source of truth for the vibe is for your heart to decide.

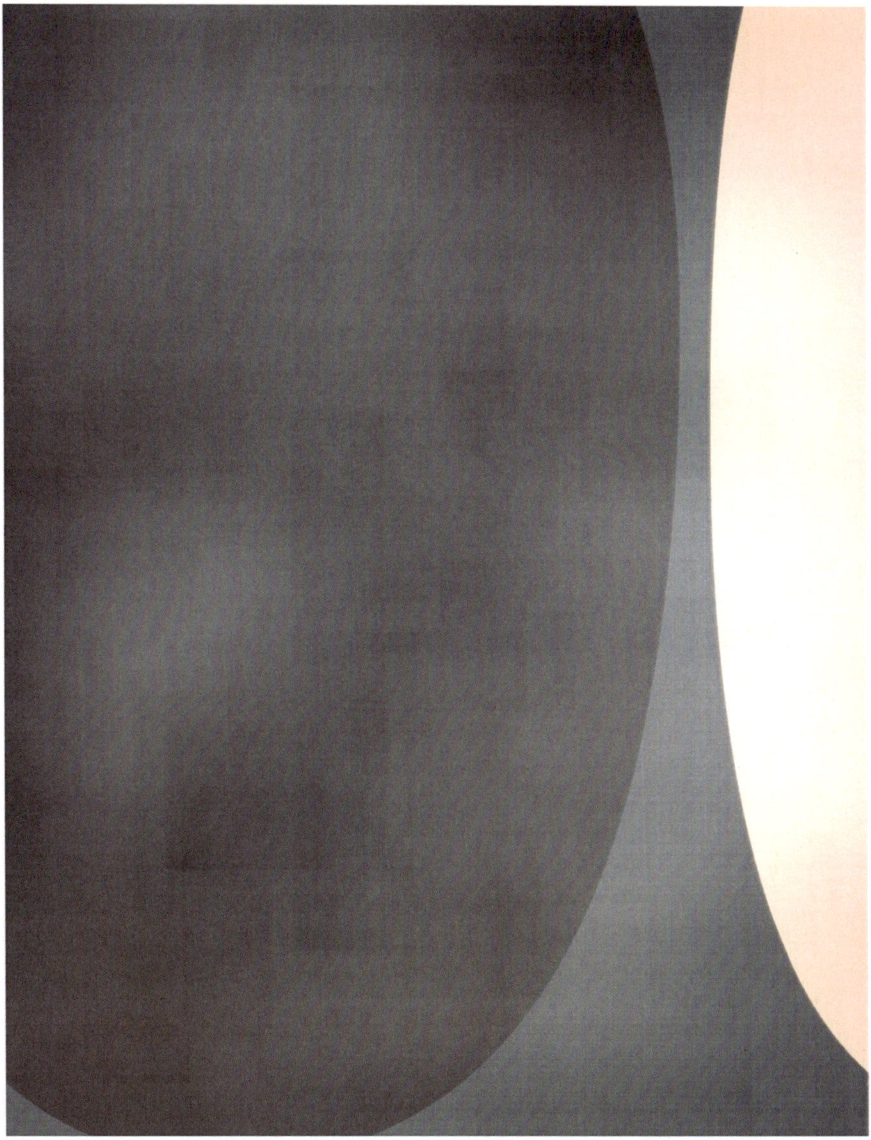

Pebble 286 with Mountlet size

MintFace Vibe Check Example

A gargantuan *Mountlet* Pebble minted by CaptainDerp. The *Harmonize Overlap* focusses the gaze of the viewer on the confined space between the two behemoths.

• • •

Selection for the Book

The Pebbles featured in the book were selected by their owners, who stepped forward by giving 10,000 rep to the MintFace profile as a signal that they would like their Pebble included in the book. 51 Pebble collectoors nominated between one and four Pebbles to participate in the book.

Book Goals

One of the goals of the Pebbles book is to help Pebble collectoors understand their own collection a little better by going beyond statistical rarity and raw trait rarity and explore the origins of each Pebble aesthetic.

A second goal was to capture the emotive aspect of generative art. Collectoors were invited to name and describe their Pebble with any lore imbued to their Pebble to date. The responses provided shows a broad range of emotion that generative art can evoke beyond 'number go up.'

> *"Pebbles is a homage to the beauty of natural simplicity found in the most basic elements of our environment, reimagined through a digital medium." Zeblocks*

Pebbles in Nature

Pebbles are found in the natural world in many locations including riverbeds, streams, lakeshores and even glacial deposits. Where does a Pebble come from? We get to learn a lot about the original rock, by studying pebbles in nature.

Pebbles originated from rocks or large slabs that are weathered and eroded away over time. As these former rocks are broken down into smaller shaped Pebbles, they become vulnerable to forces that transport them beyond their original creation point.

A generative art algorithm creates new permutations from an original source code, perhaps giving us clues as to how nature itself was generated.

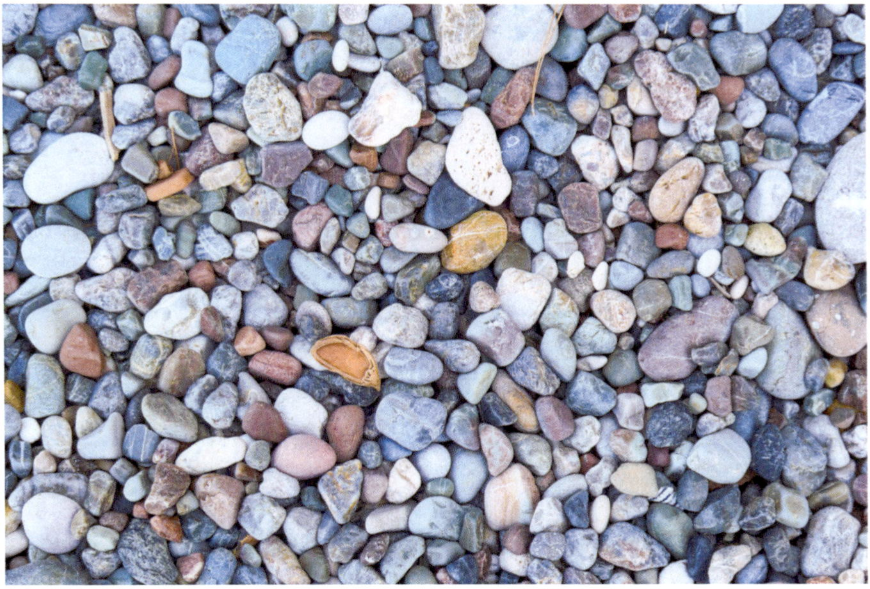

Photo by Engin Akyurt

Pebbles in nature travelling a long distance thanks to flows of water from the mountain tops to the beaches and lakes via meandering stream and rivers. Before I get carried away...remember that Pebbles are both an artwork and a larger metaphor for the role each of us plays collecting artworks minted immutably on the blockchain.

> *"Did you ever pick up a Pebble and skim it across the surface of a lake as a child?" MintFace.*

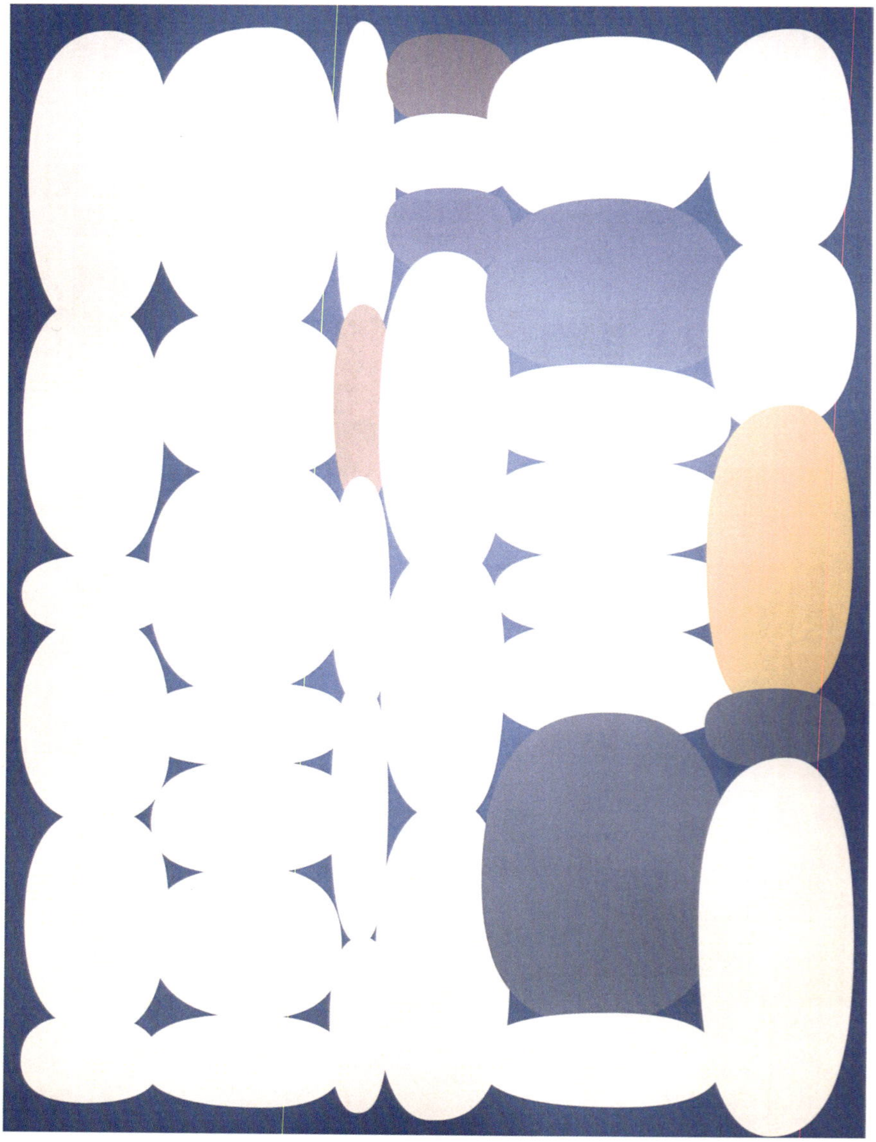

Pebble 441 with no Special Elements

MintFace Vibe Check Example

Pebble #441 minted by Ruskin, is a clarion call to minimalism in generative art and the pleasure that can be derived from the simplest of shapes. The absence of any *Special Elements* makes this 'pure' Pebble more special than most.

. . .

To begin to explore the Pebble collection, *Palette* and *Size* traits are the starting points. These each determine the most visually obvious aspects of the artwork.

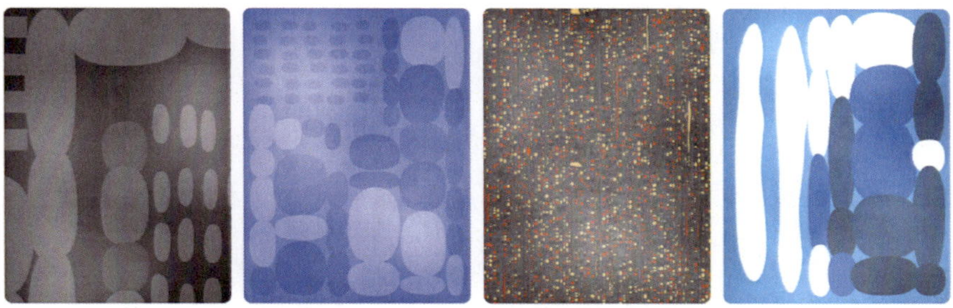

Pebble Palette and Size (from left to right) 927 Stonelet Dusk Riverbed, 37 Rockling Serenity, 115 Rockling Desert Mirage, 690 Boulderette Coral Reef

Size and Palette Overview

Every Pebble is given a *Size* and set color *Palette* by the algorithm that effectively paints and sizes each Pebble. The *Palette* trait lends a group of colors to the artwork and the *Size* trait determines how big or small each collection of Pebbles is within the artwork.

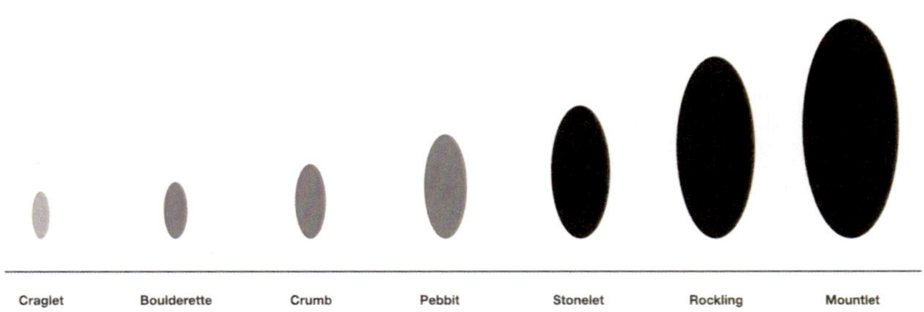

Pebble size comparison chart

Pebble 3 'Ghost of Nazca' with Mint Type HyperMaxis

MintFace Vibe Check Example

Squint your eyes to catch a faint glimpse of empty *No Fill, Rockling* sized Pebbles. Beyond the visible and into the code, *Elephant Pajamas* palette minted by chrisroc, is one of only 16. The first minted rare ever derived from on-chain collector behaviour.

PART I

PALETTE AND SIZE

SIZE

There are two *Size* aesthetic groupings that emerge around smaller or larger Pebble artworks. Individual collectoors have their own views on which *Size* is better. The Pebble *Size* trait chapter introduces you to the full spectrum of *Size* traits, allowing you to decide for yourself. There are many interesting outputs to explore. Let's take a deeper look at the seven Pebble *Size* traits, starting with *Craglet*.

Craglet

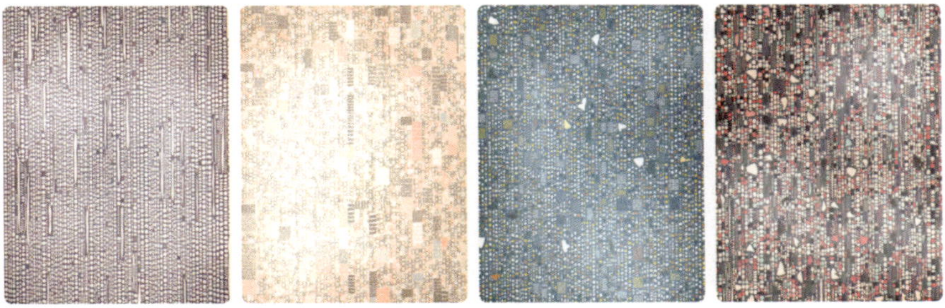

Craglet size Pebbles 864, 585, 510 and 949

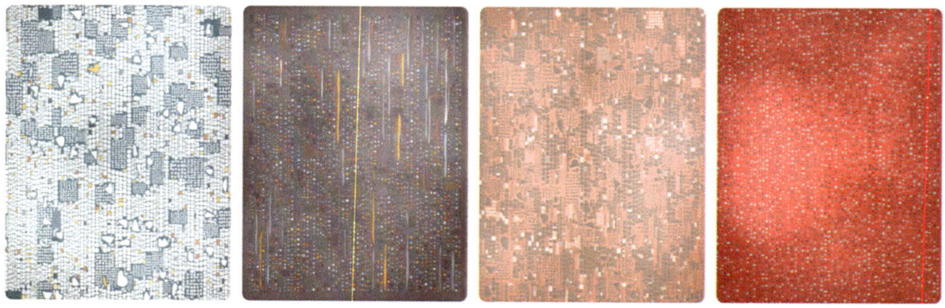

Craglet size Pebbles 110, 118, 143, and 15

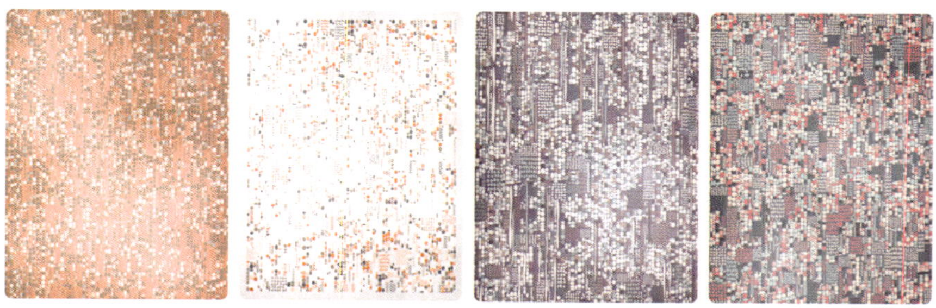

Craglet size Pebbles 163, 170, 177, 206

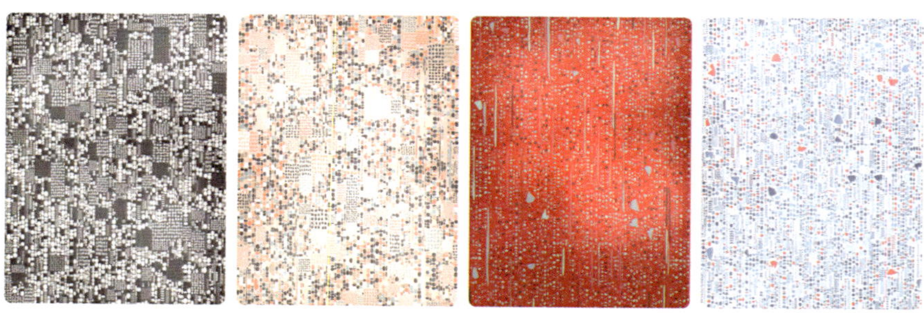

Craglet size Pebbles 34, 344, 346 and 347

Craglet adds the most Pebbles to each artwork because the *Size* of each Pebble is the smallest. Hundreds of tiny Pebbles create an intricate set of patterns, where the whole is greater than the sum of its parts. There are 85 *Craglet* Pebbles in the collection, making it the third rarest *Size* trait.

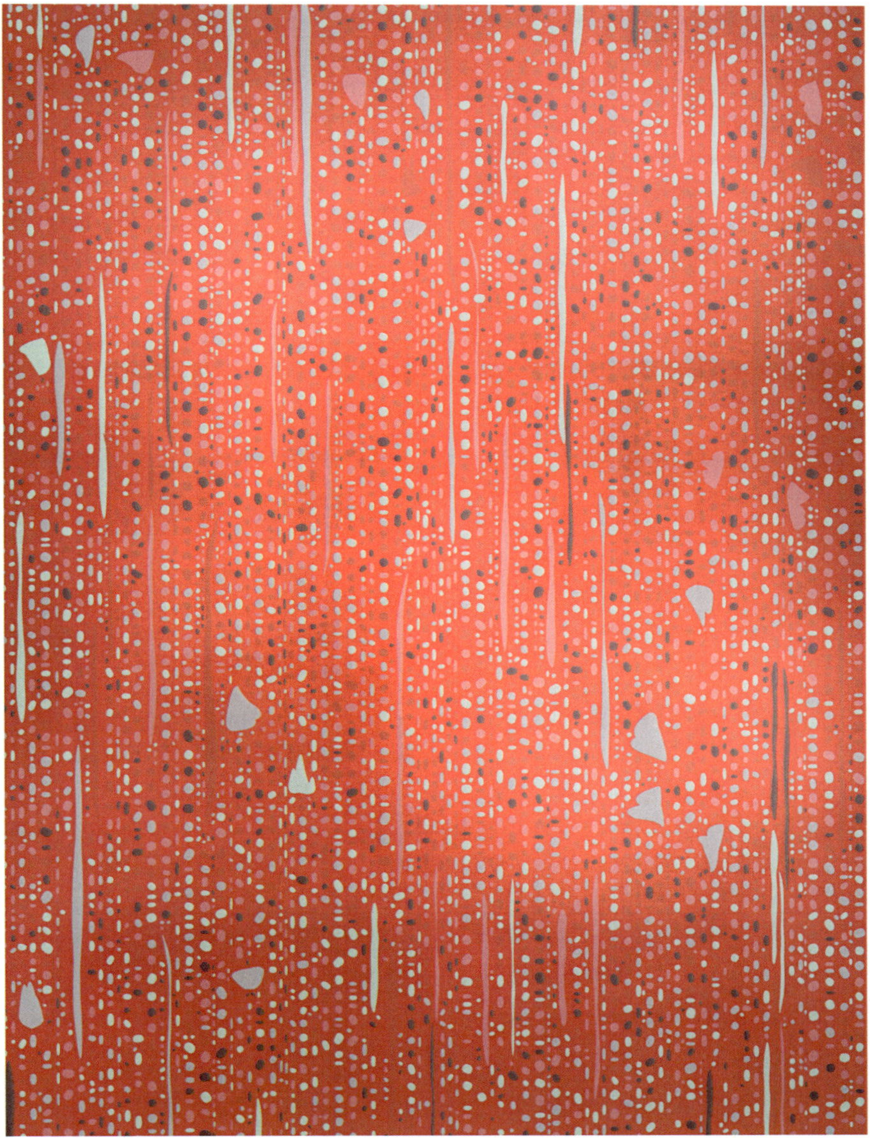

Pebble 295 with Craglet size

Salsa Blush Pebbles
Craglets and overlaps add flair
Playful and mature

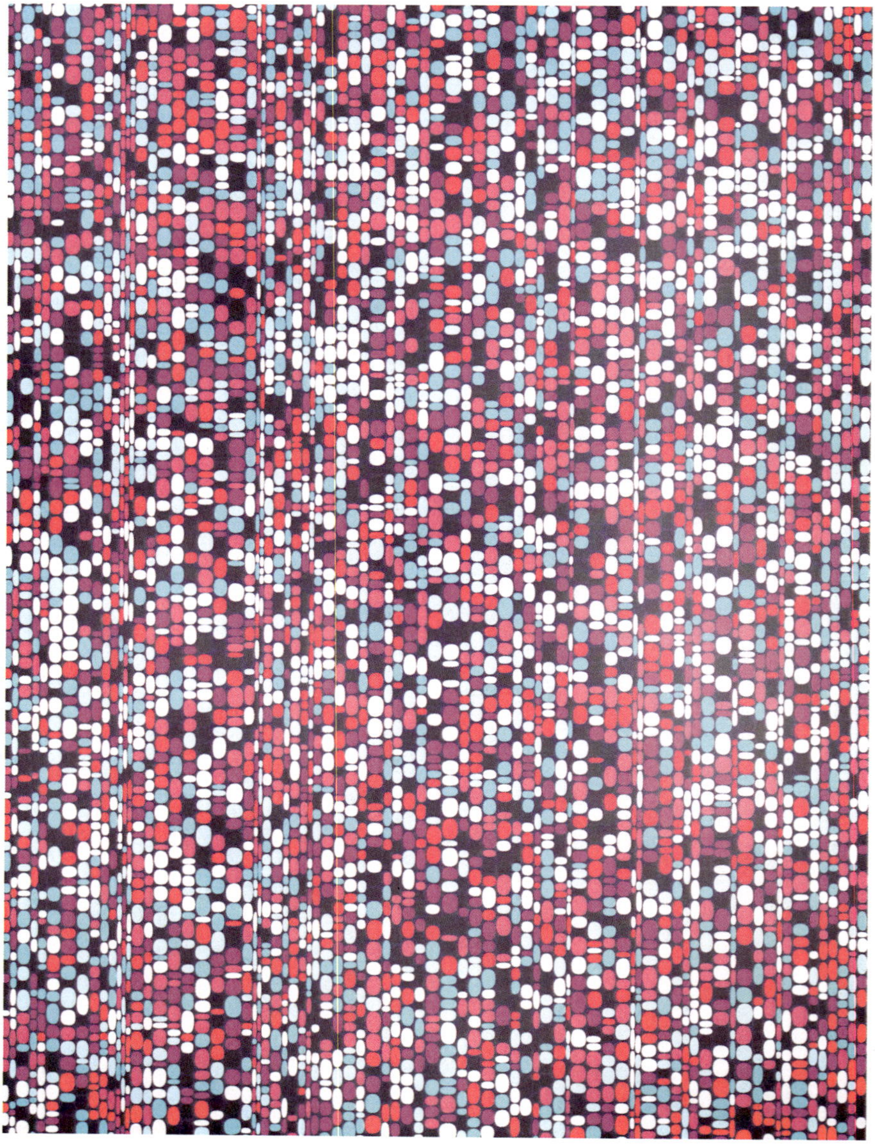

Pebble 716 'The Matrix' with Craglet size

'The Matrix' shows *Craglet* in its purest form. One of only 55 *No Special Elements*. Look a little more closely and you might begin to make out the outlines of three human shaped forms.

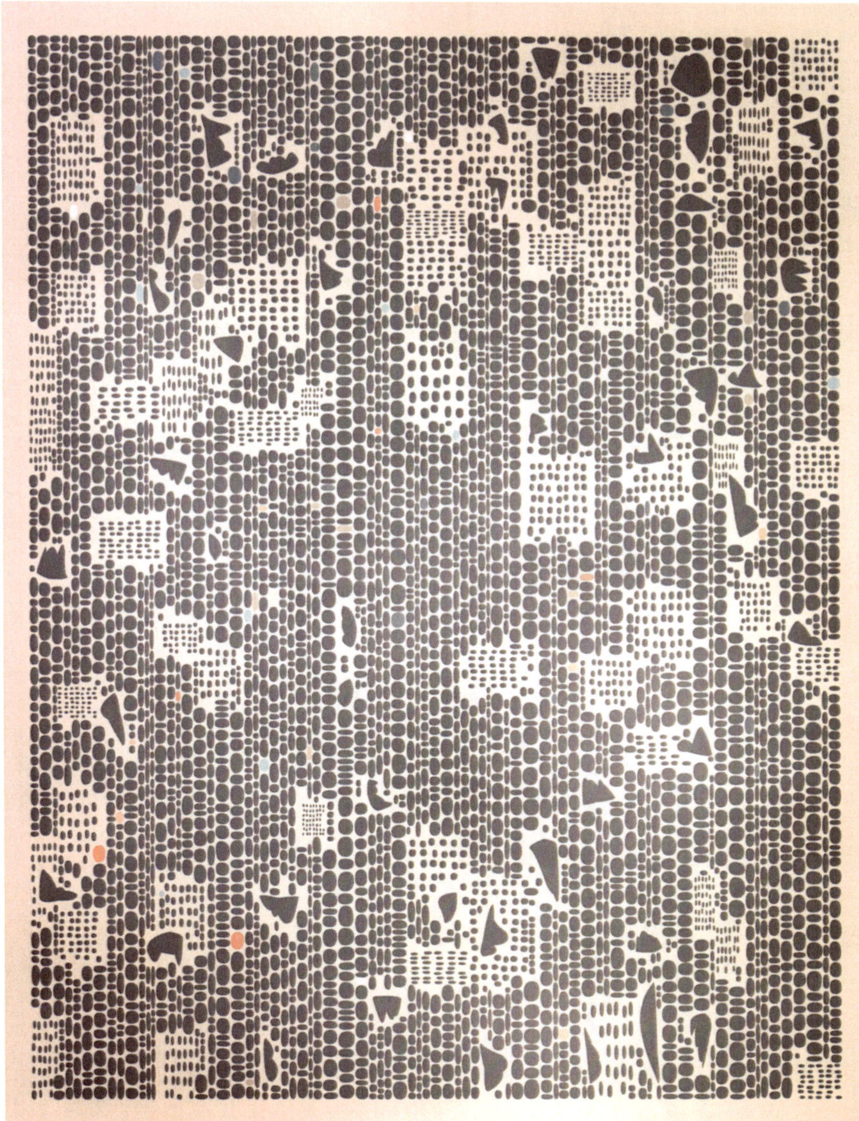

Pebble 81 'Shadow of Satoshi' with Craglet size

"'Shadow of Satoshi' - need we say anymore." OMDegen

Boulderette

Boulderette is the second smallest Pebble and fourth rarest *Size,* with 147 *Boulderettes* minted. The *Boulderette* treatment results in a highly consistent aesthetic across all of the Pebbles. Generative art that delivers a wide range of variety within a trait, while still being recognizable as from the trait, is the signature of a good artist.

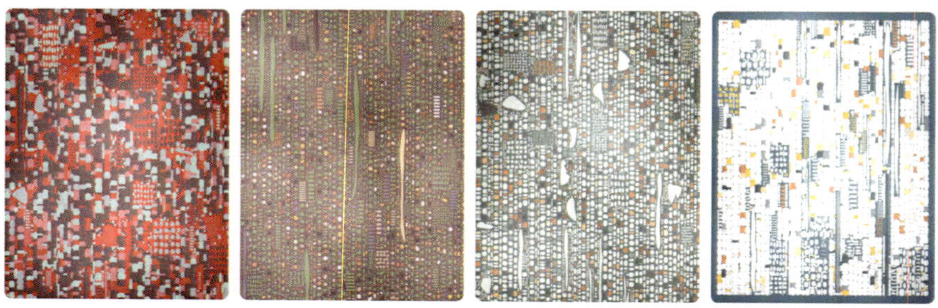

Boulderette size Pebbles 628, 573, 667 and 992

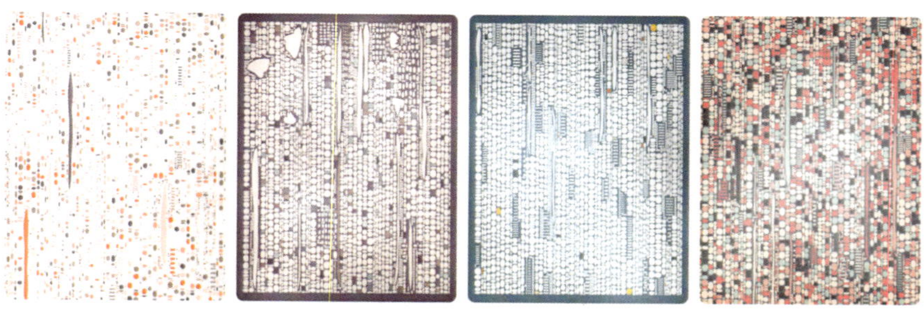

Boulderette size Pebbles 699, 484, 967 and 314

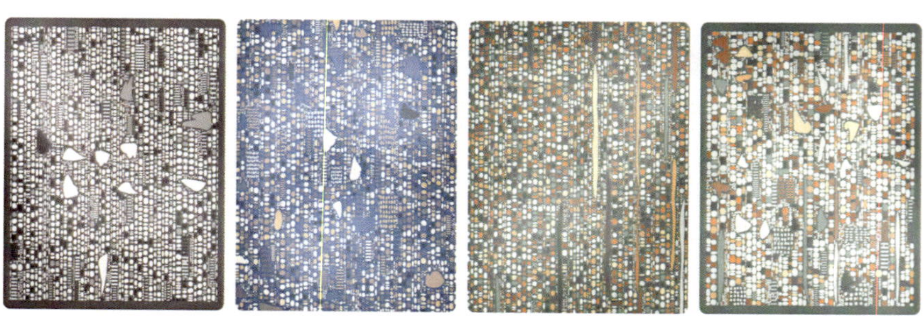

Boulderette size Pebbles 006, 470, 494 and 505

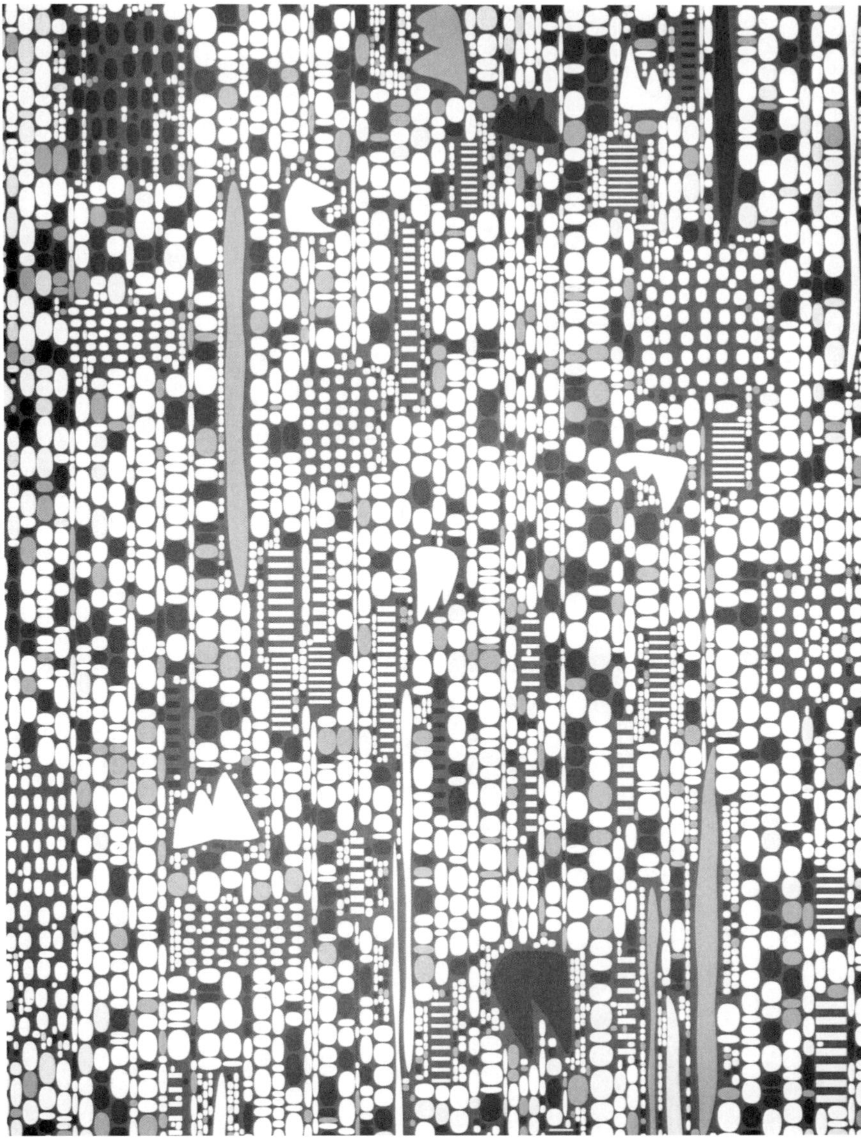

Pebble 155 'Carbon Copy' with Boulderette size

'Carbon Copy' got its name from the first Pebbles Race. I hope that it will be my legacy to my family and stay with us as long as ETH is still making blocks.' Regular Dad

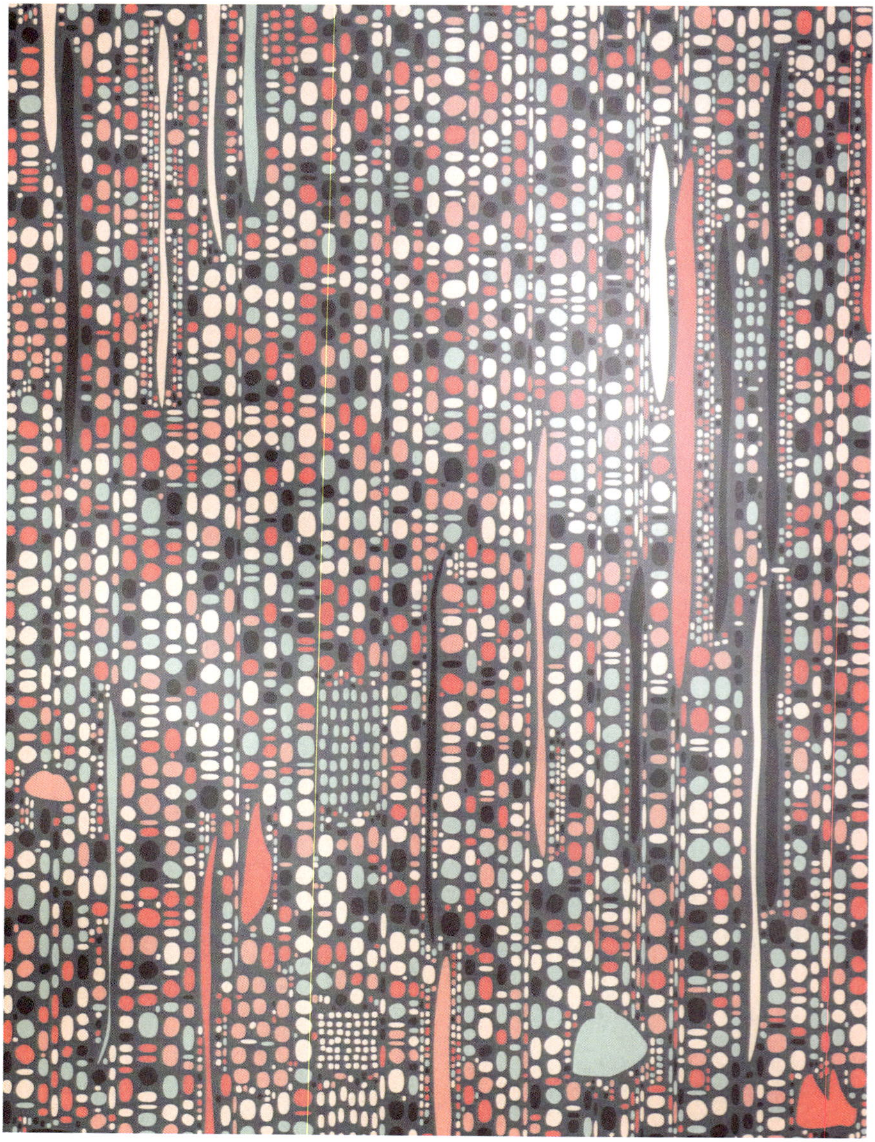

Pebble 590 with Boulderette size

Meme-numbered artworks are afforded elite status by collectoor communities and the applause for minting Pebble #690 goes to lapislight. This *Vivid Color Density* Pebble boasts plenty of exquisite details to be discovered throughout the *Boulderette* size array.

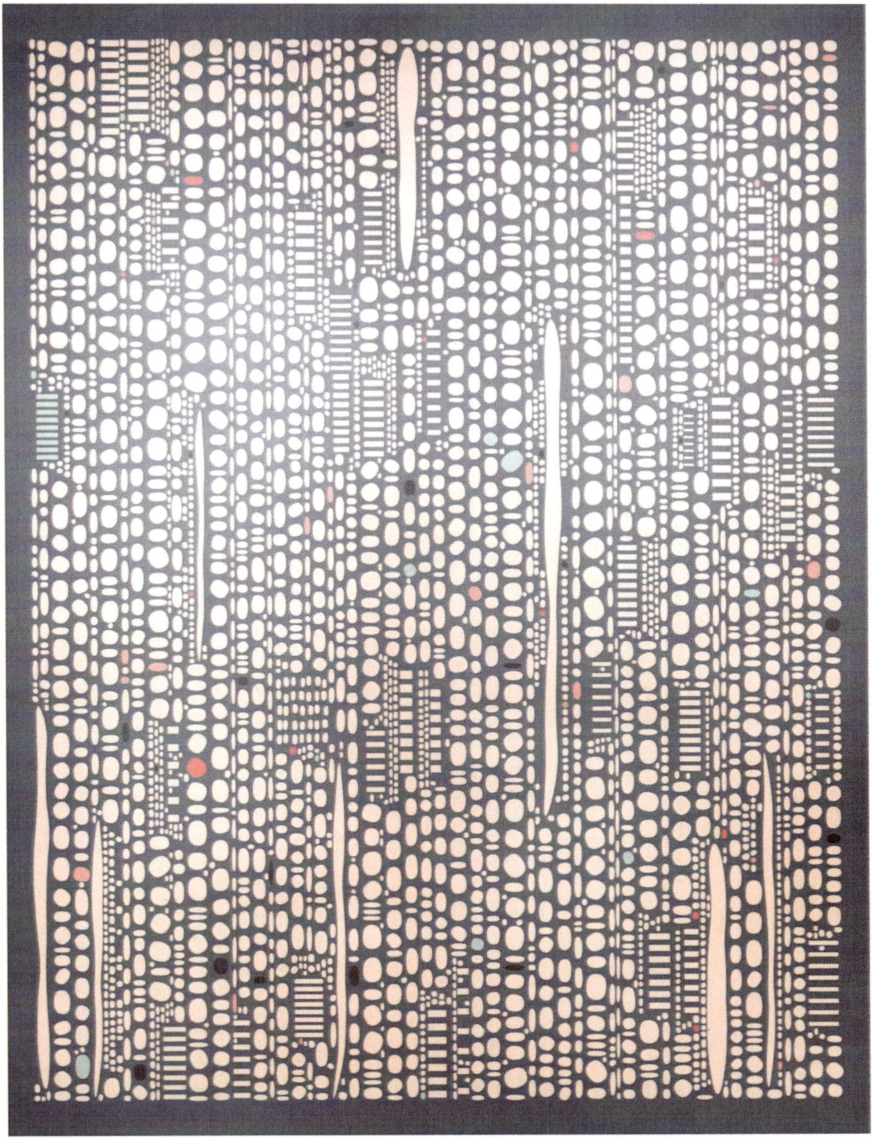

Pebble 43 'Metallic Shine' with Boulderette size

Pebble #43 is well framed in the olive green from the *Coral Reef* palette. The *Boulderette* Pebbles are tinted from top to bottom as the *Faint Color Density* remixes the formal *Coral Reef Palette*. Pebble #43 is a second *Coral Reef* owned by Animated, alongside #41.

Crumb

Crumb is the rarest *Size* trait present in only 72 of 1000 Pebbles. The Crumb trait is a mid-sized trait, being bigger than Craglet and Boulderette, yet smaller than any of these four larger traits. There are 72 Crumb Pebbles in the collection.

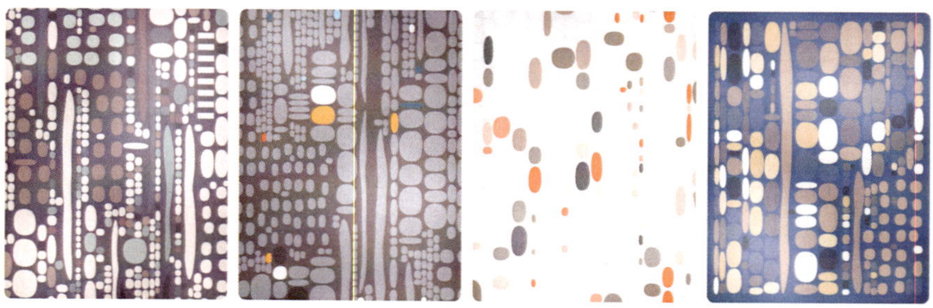

Crumb size Pebbles 561, 553, 647 and 260

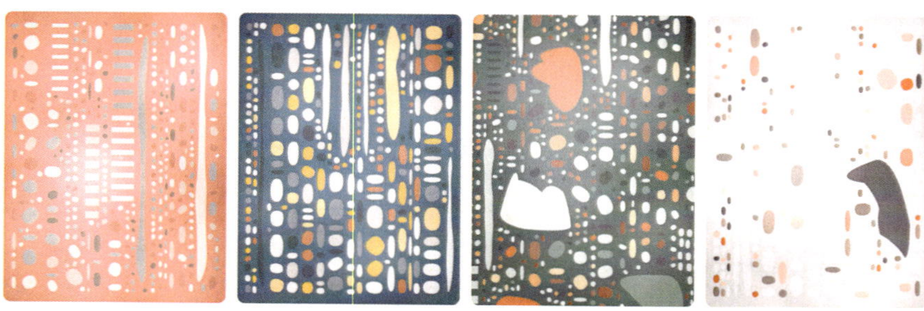

Crumb size Pebbles 977, 467, 653 and 563

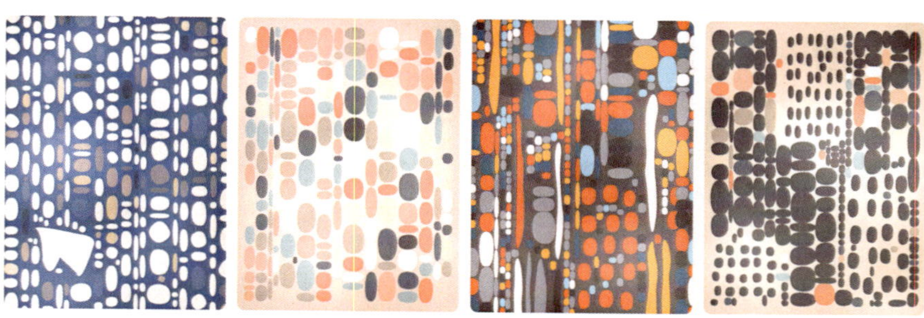

Crumb size Pebbles 203, 009, 780 and 588

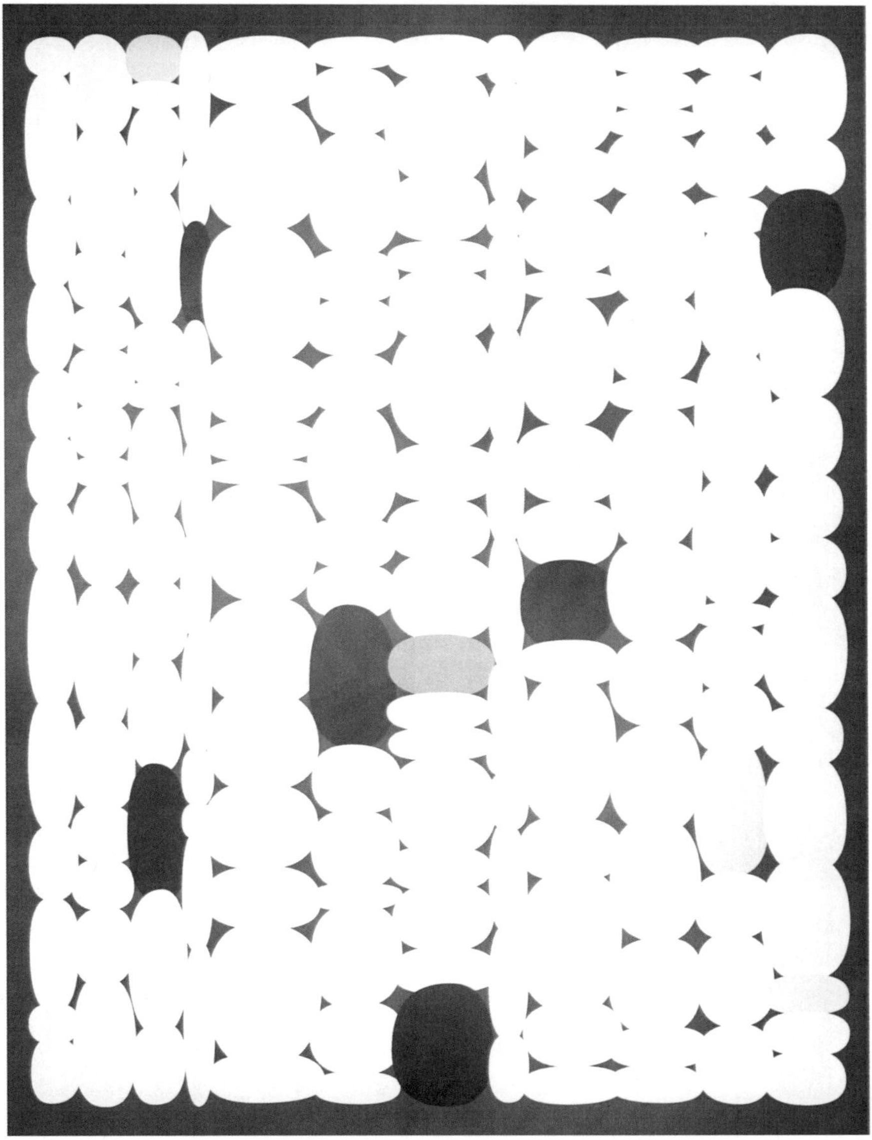

Pebble 312 with Crumb size

A *Crumb-sized* Pebble with *Shades of Hey!* palette framed with a stunning *Edge*. The *Fuse Overlap* pushes each Pebble on top of each other, while the *Faint Color Density* keeps the Pebble colors predominantly white.

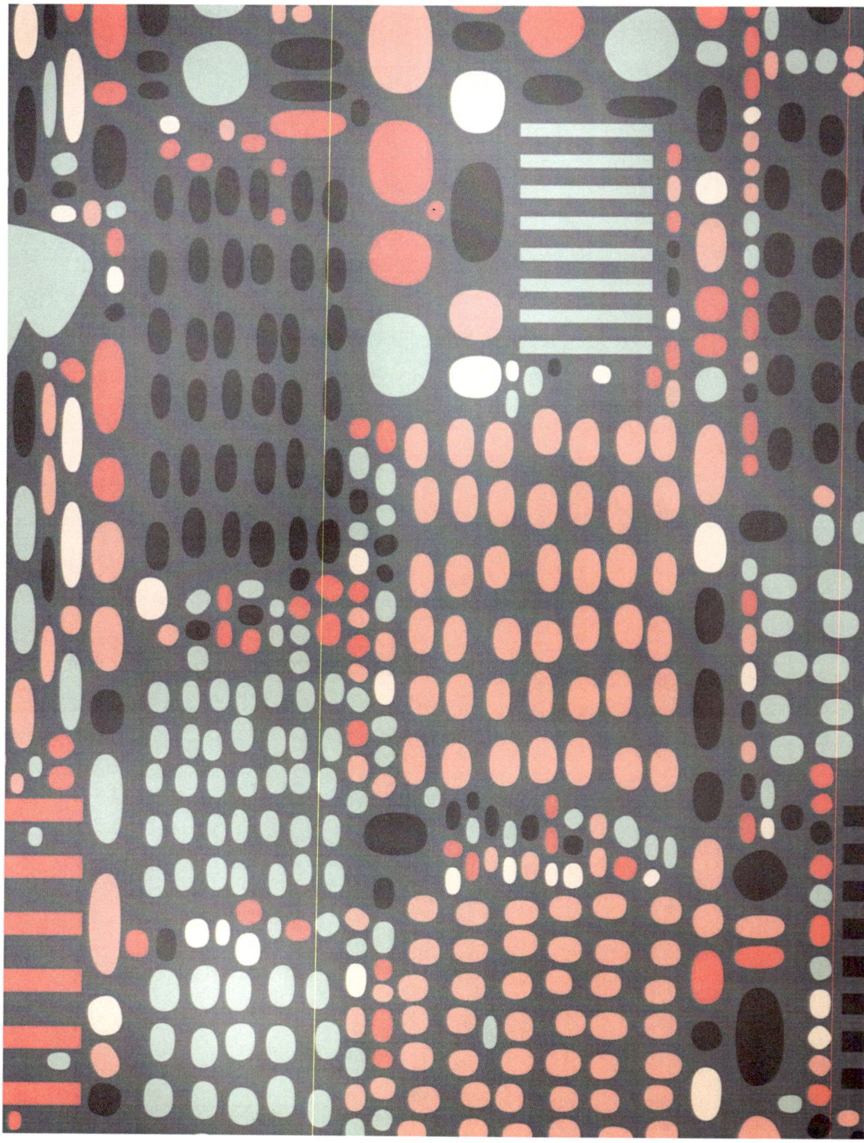

Pebble 431 with Crumb size

Seven super-sized grids of Pebbles are the hallmark of Pebble #431. There are also three rectangular pathways visible, a second hallmark of a *Special Element* making an appearance. The third *Special Element* is most obvious in the craggy-like Pebble in the upper right corner. The best aspects of *Coral Reef* palette are on display here.

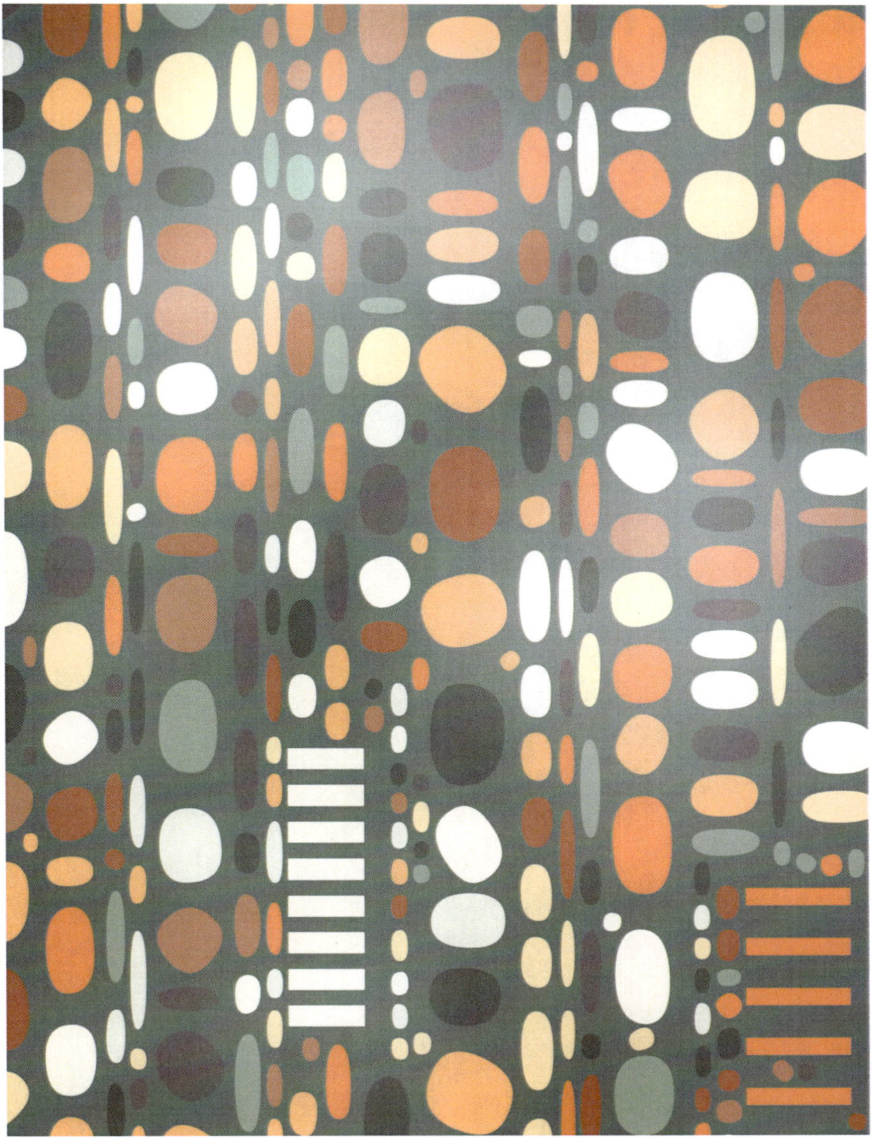

Pebble 805 with Crumb size

“ 'Pebbles' embodies the serene beauty of natural formations with its meticulously arranged ovals and rectangles." Pakal

Pebbit

Pebbit zooms the viewer in, making it possible to visualize individual elements in each work. The art begins to develop its own sense of a personality, making is possible to visualize them in your mind's eye; often a sign of remarkable work.

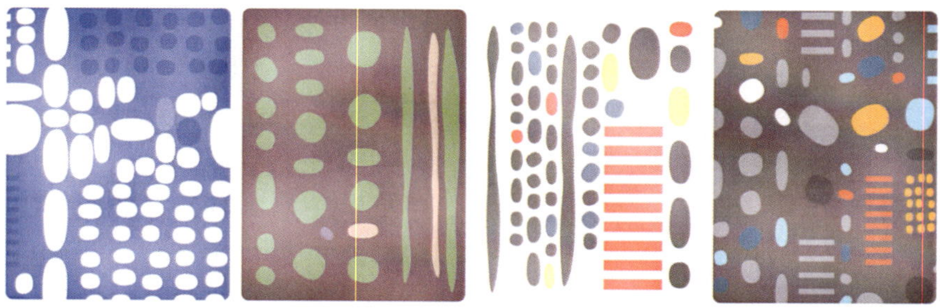

Pebbit size Pebbles 10, 12, 23 and 27

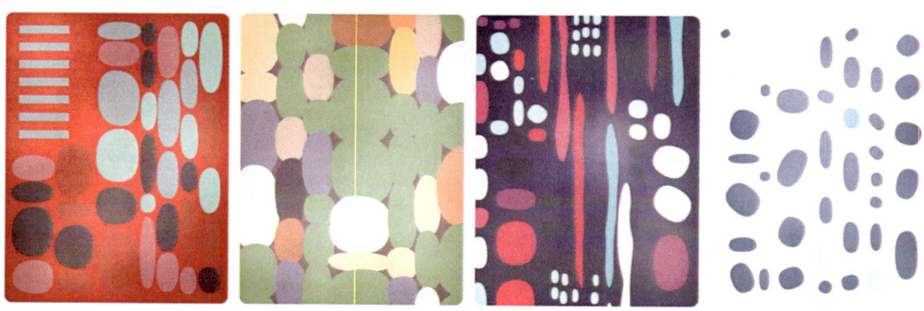

Pebbit size Pebbles 261, 121, 58 and 183

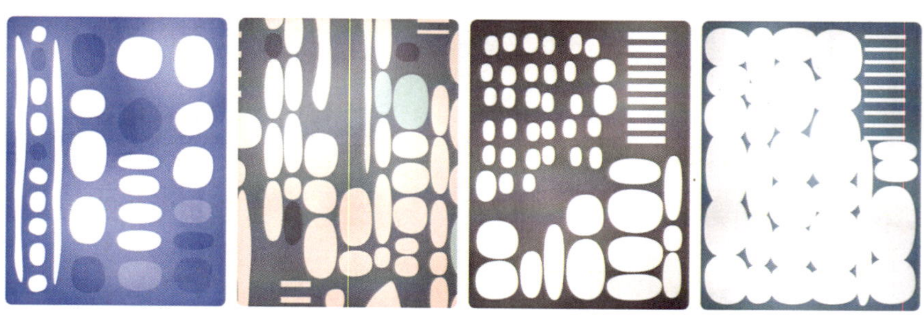

Pebbit size Pebbles 514, 518, 463 and 524

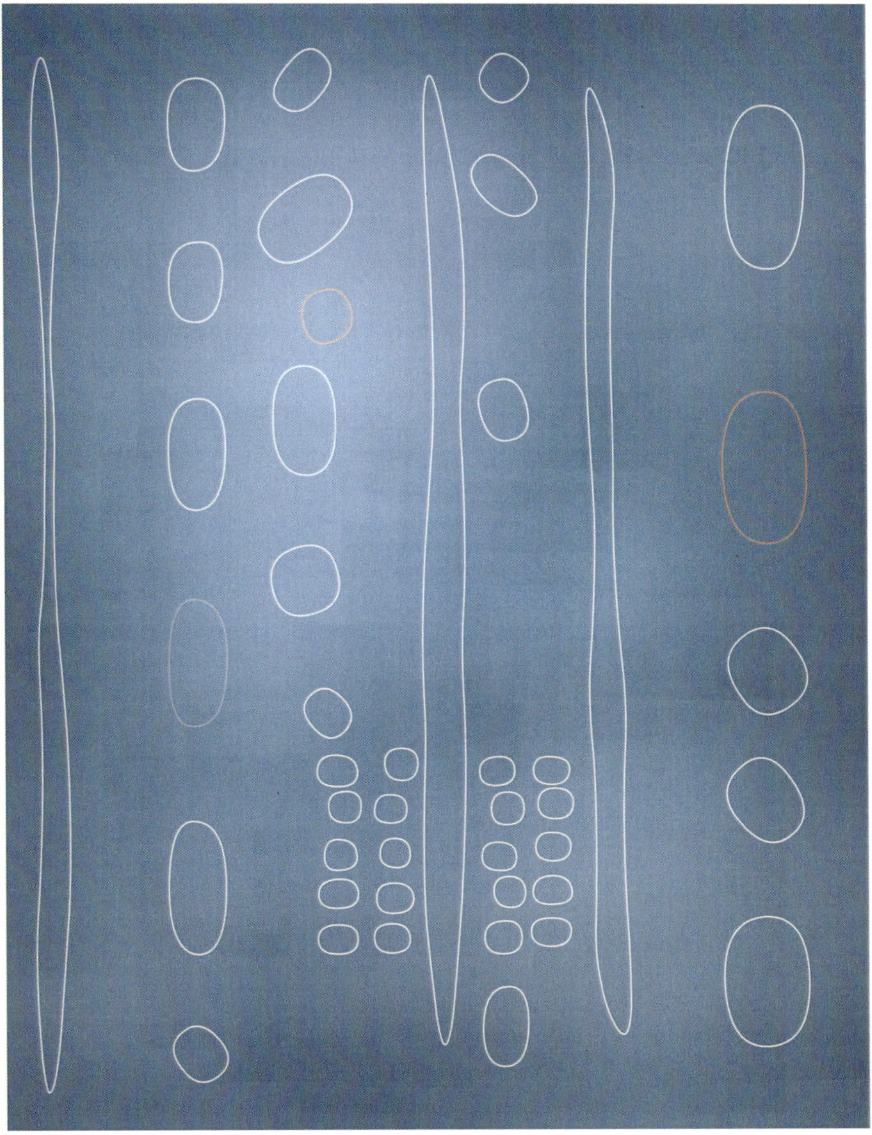

Pebble 962 with Pebbit size

"'Empty Threats' is a play on words. 'Sticks and Stones' alongside the *No Fill* trait makes the threats of violence empty." 4lteredBeast.

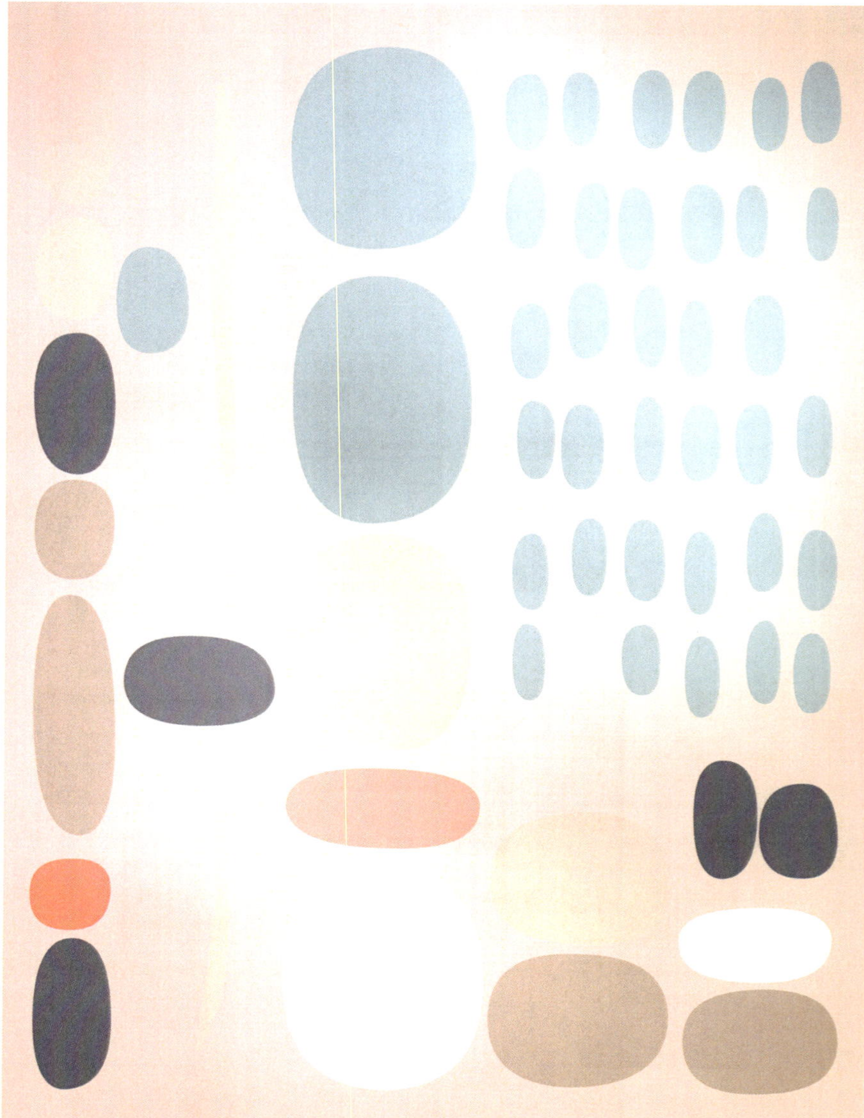

Pebble 724 with Pebbit size

The shimmering gold canvas lights up in the *Desert Mirage* landscape with *Drench Color Density* placing a varied range of colored *Pebbit*-sized Pebbles to relish. All *Special Elements* are present, some more easily spotted than others.

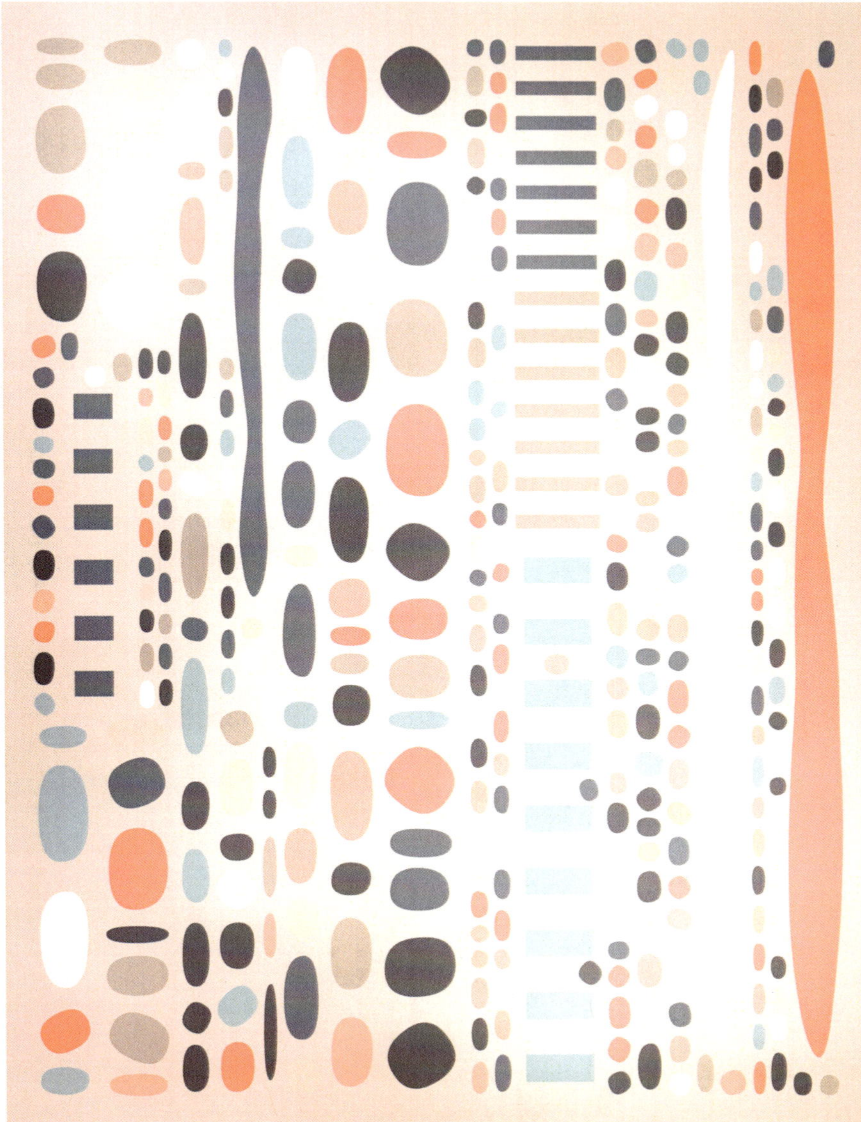

Pebble 275 'DNA Sequencer' with Pebbit size

"Reminds me of DNA sequencing, and how we all are unique in our own right. Favorite traits are *Crumb* and *Desert Mirage* for the time I've spent training in the desert and the solitude and serenity." Franklin Fit

Stonelet

Stonelet Size Pebbles offer a minimalist simplicity with a generous helping of Pebbles in each artwork. Every exception or *Special Element* is amplified more than in any of the four smaller-sized Pebble variants. We begin to realize how much can be communicated from so few visual elements.

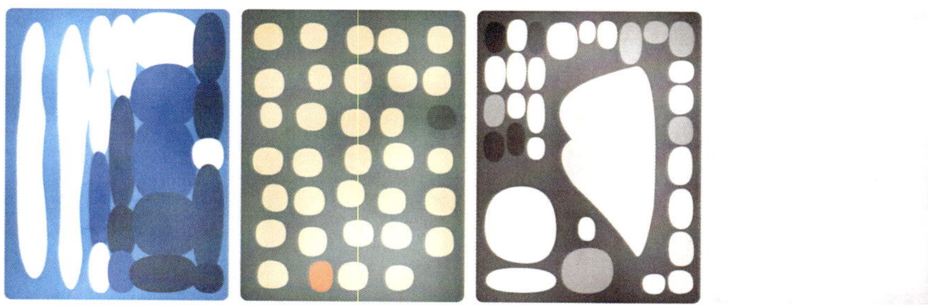

Stonelet size Pebbles 96, 815, 852 and 27

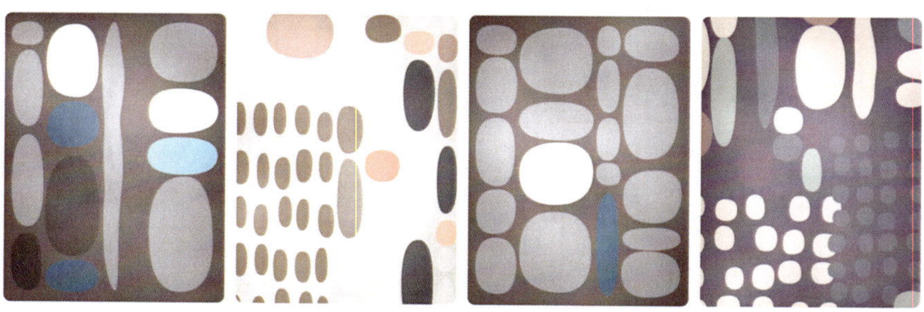

Stonelet size Pebbles 154, 546, 511 and 846

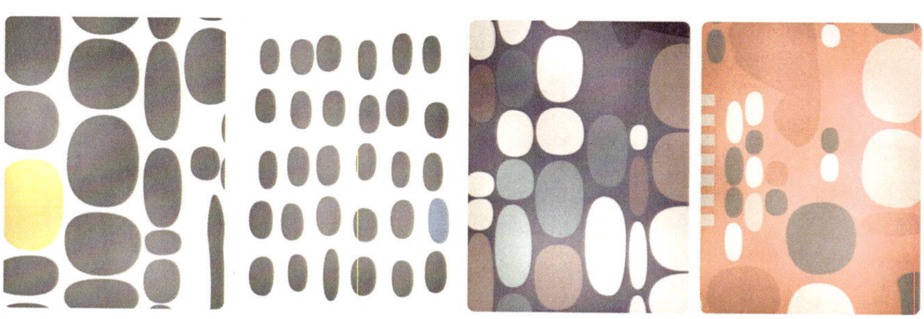

Stonelet size Pebbles 960, 850, 86 and 469

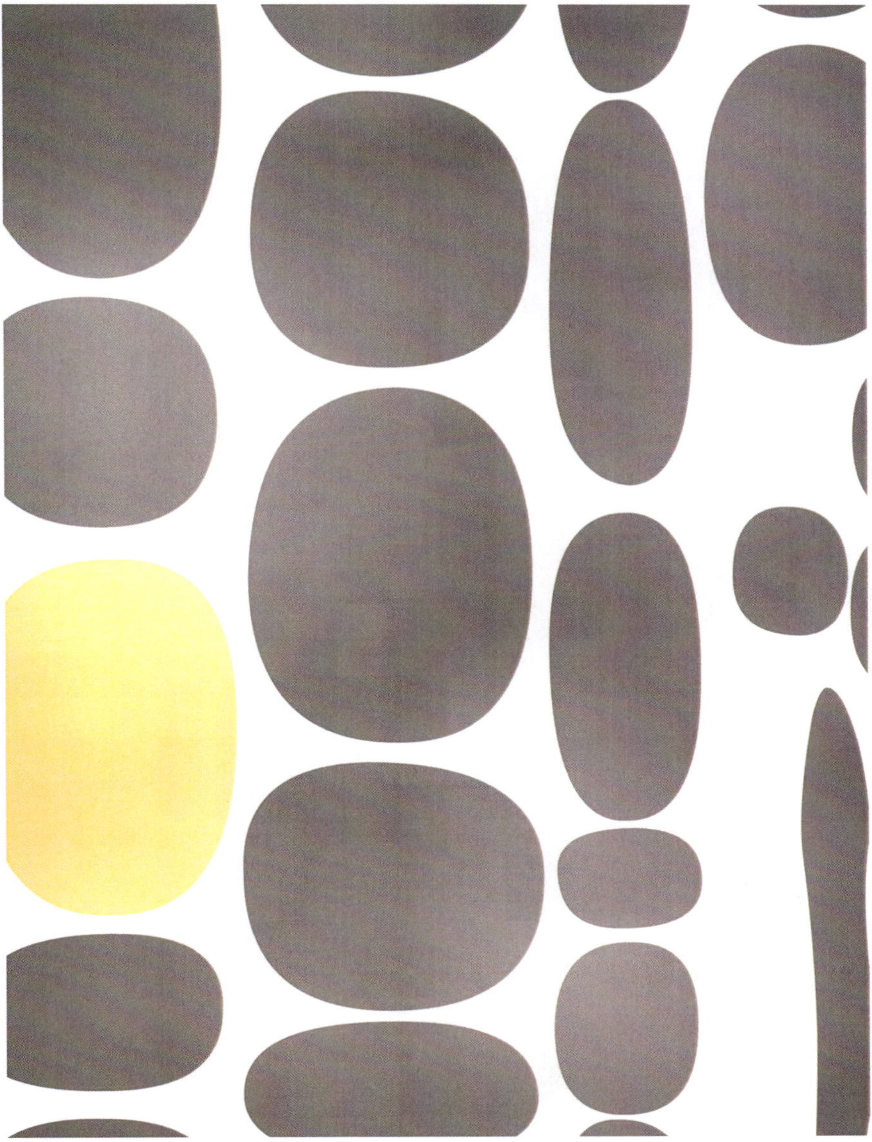

Pebble 960 'The Goose Egg' with Stonelet size

"'The Goose Egg' was first." gmmoney

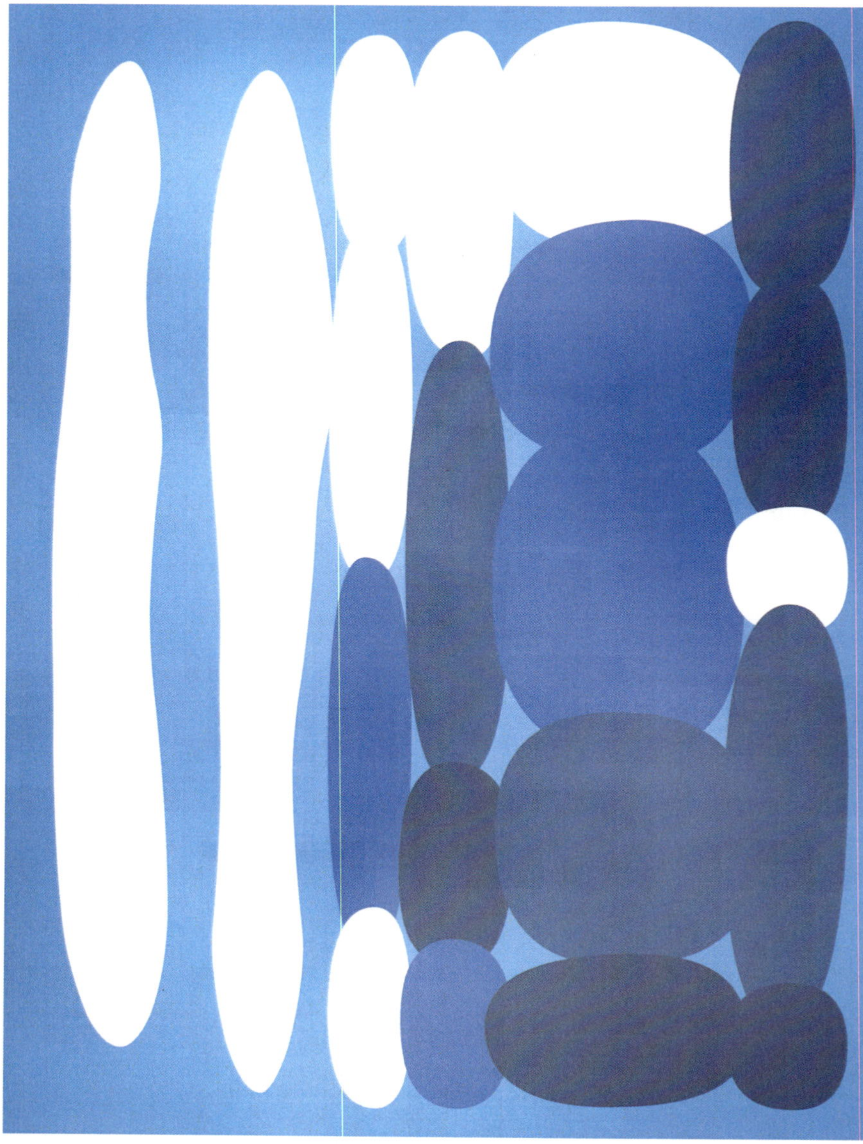

Pebble 96 'Onchain Summer Breeze' with Stonelet size

'Onchain Summer Breeze' is one of two *summer.jpg* palettes that also show *Fuse Overlap* of the Pebbles. *Stonelet Size* coordinates the Pebbles into an almost perfect *Rothko*-like rectangle. A fine *Vivid* that doesn't need the *summer.jpg* neon pink color to make a statement. Cool summer evenings of 'Onchain Summer Breeze' are on their way.

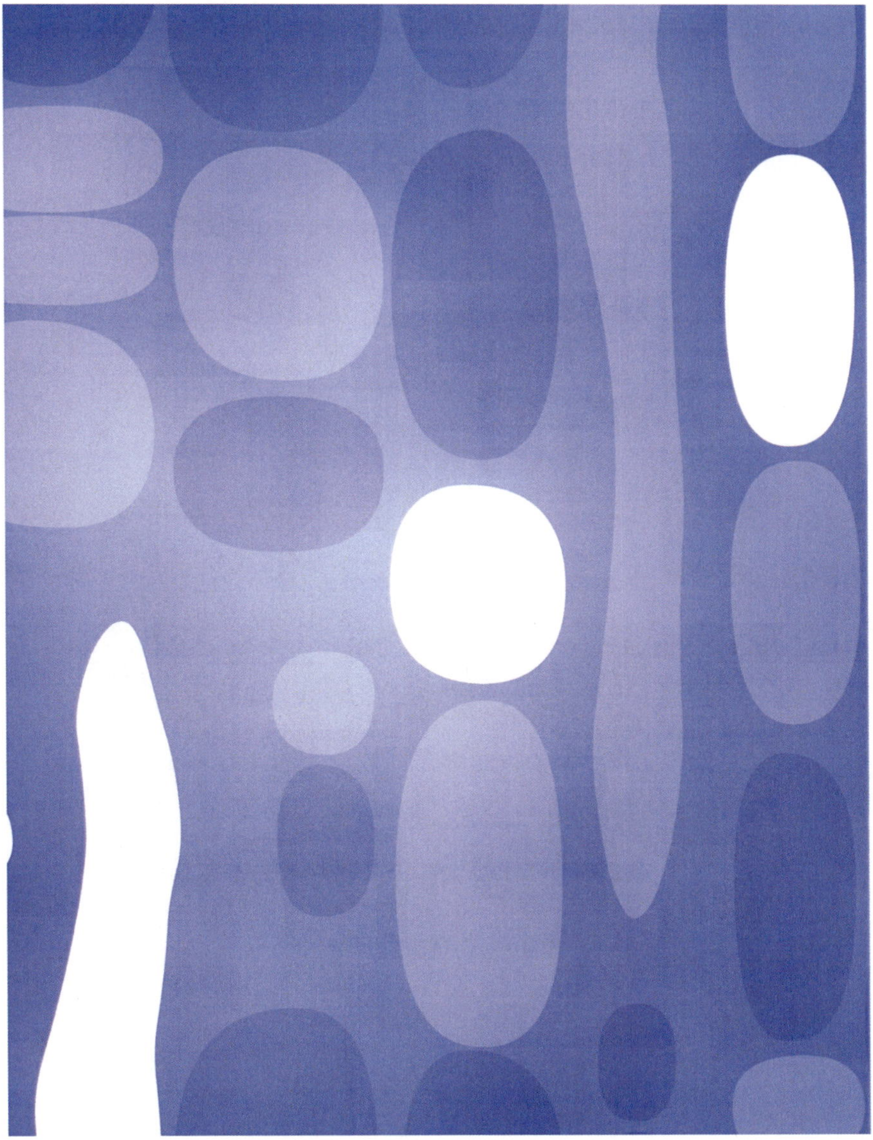

Pebble 302 'Freestone River' with Stonelet size

“No matter how deep the water gets, keep going."
BatSoupYum

Rockling

Rockling Size Pebbles exude quiet confidence with a handful of Pebbles. In the resulting forms our eyes fill in the scene for us, imagining a campfire, bicycle or neighbourly chat. Truly remarkable when we realize we are comparing the code of art with the randomized code of nature.

Rockling size Pebbles 529, 273, 660 and 486

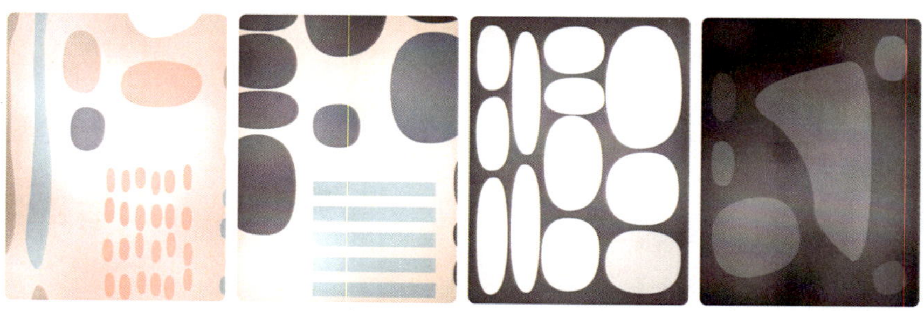

Rockling size Pebbles 303, 115, 325 and 126

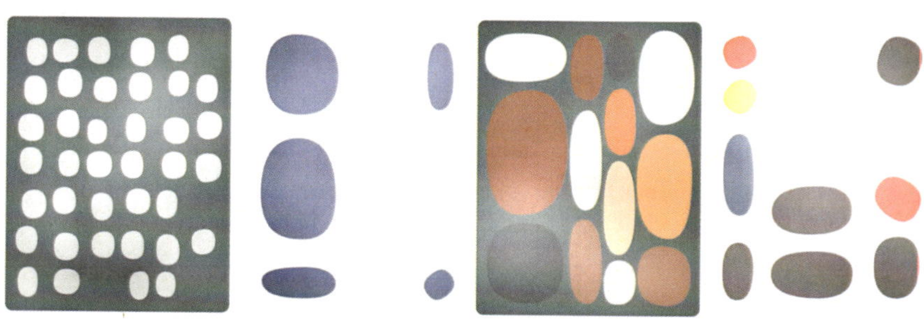

Rockling size Pebbles 186, 178, 935 and 443

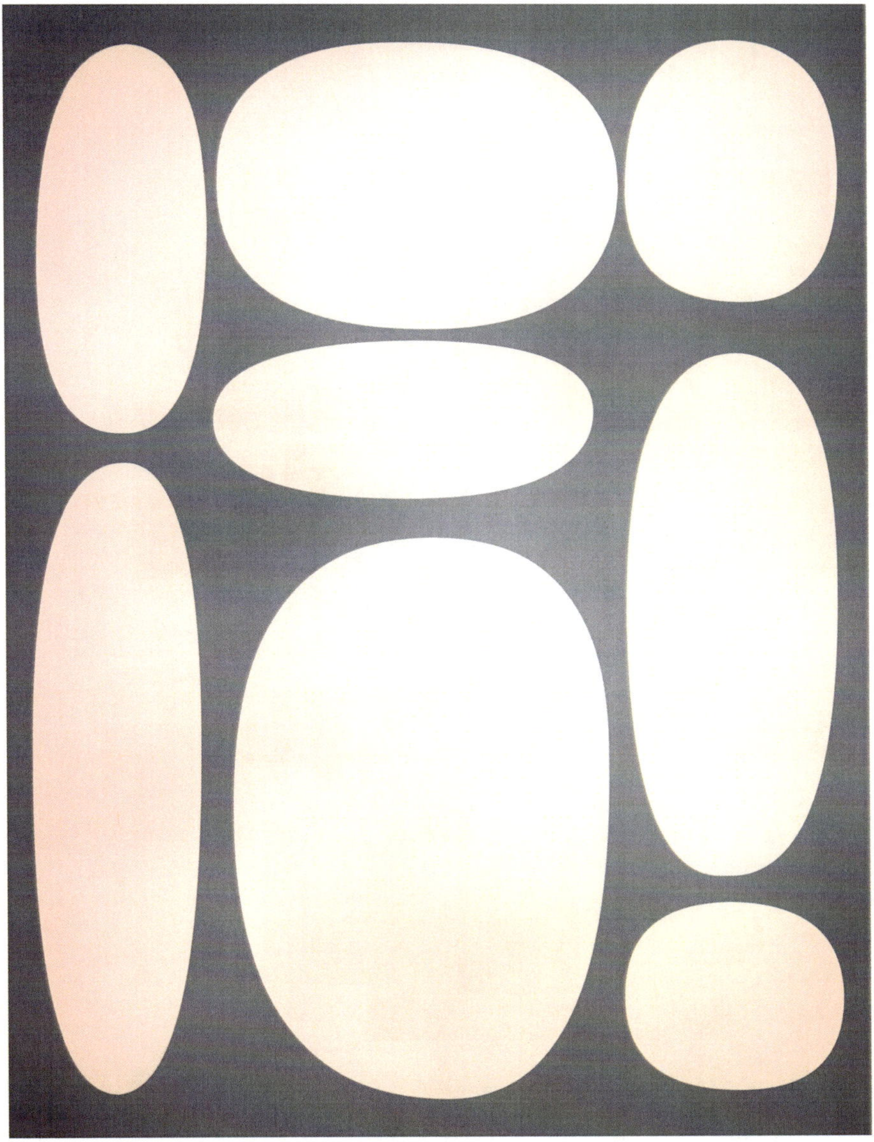

Pebble 715 'Genesis Eggs' with Rockling size

> "Pebble 715 is named 'Genesis Eggs' that will hatch into the holder's Aigents wen OM100." MoonFront

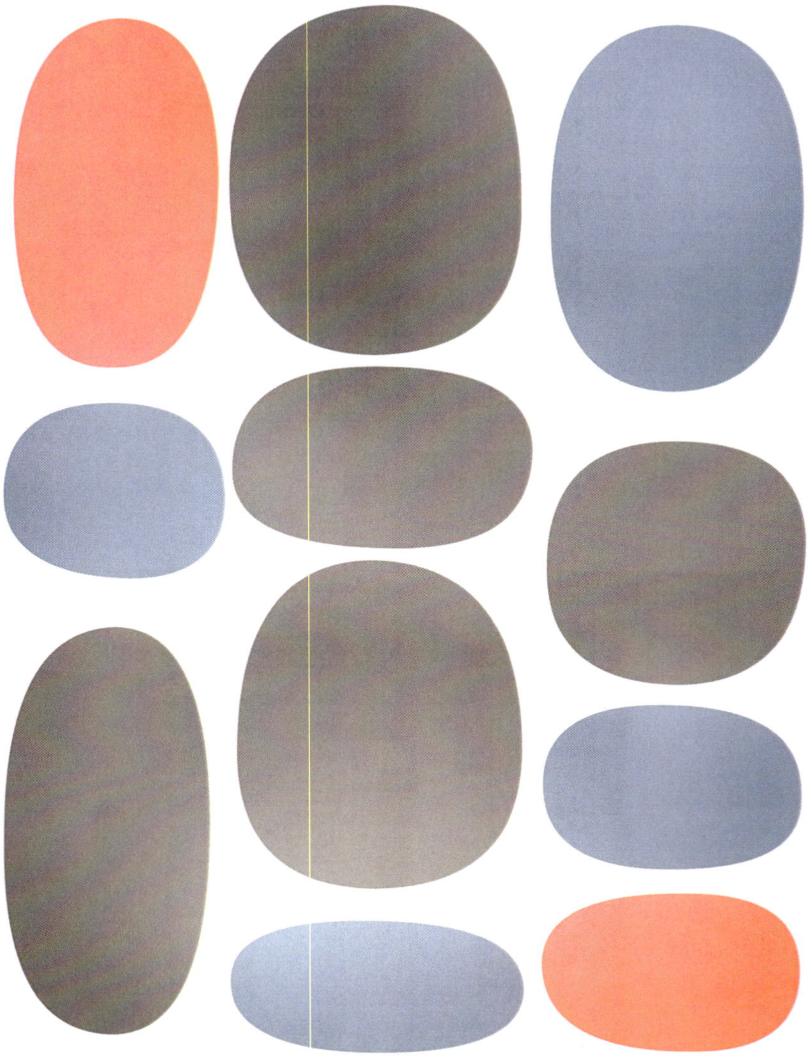

Pebble 35 with Rockling size

> One of the simplest and more iconic Pebbles, probably you've seen it in a 'RePebble' by artist @toadswiback. *Rockling Size* gives a sense of peace and serenity, enhanced by the colors of *Dino Disco* palette." Sert

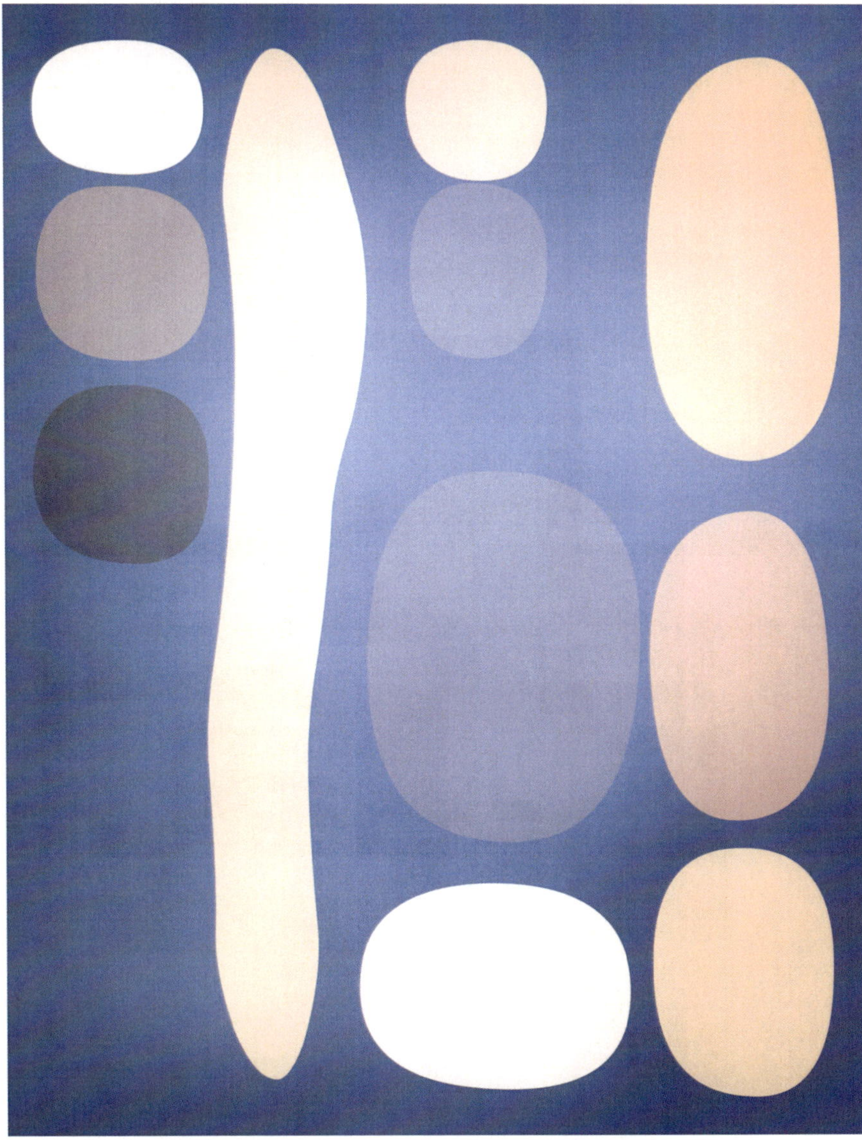

Pebble 145 'Pont du Gard' with Rockling size

"The 'Pont du Gard', named for the ancient Roman aqueduct constructed in the 1st century CE (current-day France). Its combination of *Dusk Riverbed* palette with *Vivid* color echoes the stones of the river Gardon as well as the cut-outs from the iconic bridge." pandelic

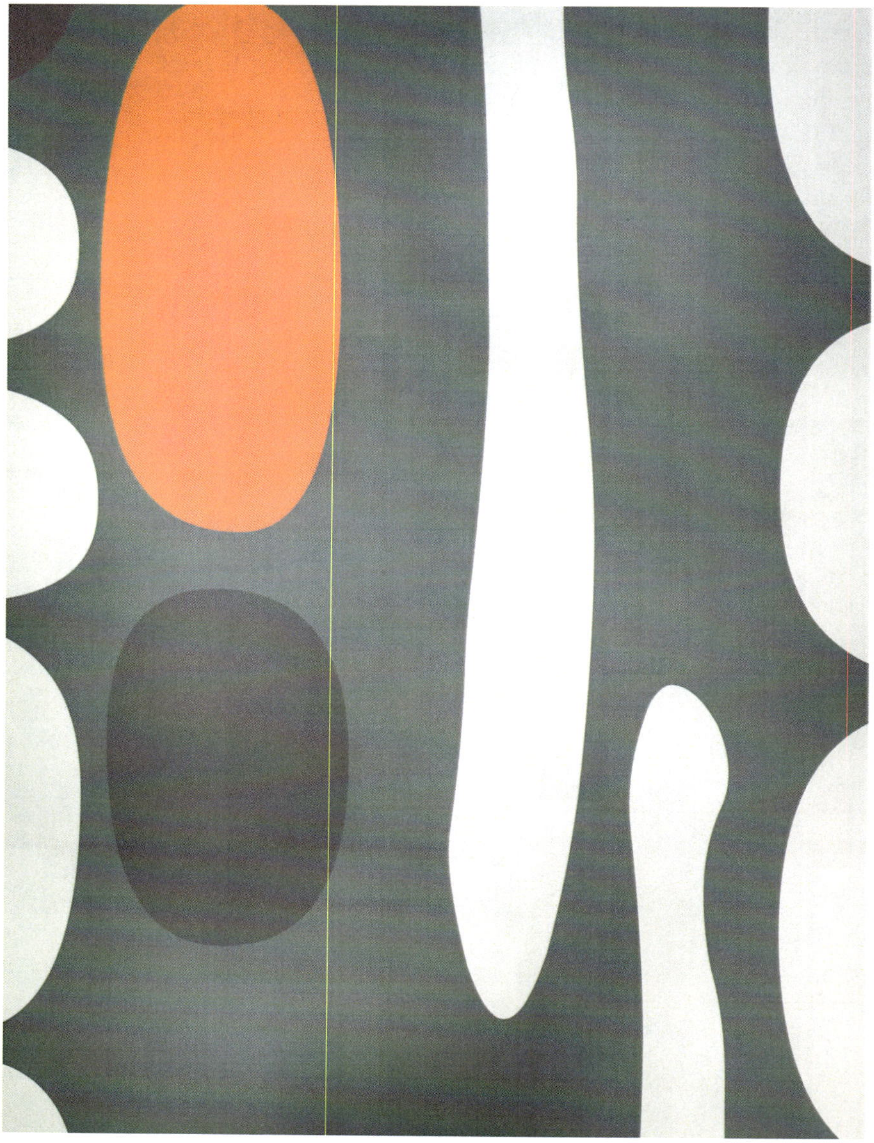

Pebble 8 'SGT. PEPPLES' with Rockling size

> "Life is like Pebbles #8. You only mint it once." Square Pixel

Pebble 321 'Snow Diamonds' with Rockling size

> First generative art project launched with the 6529 ecosystem. Can't be more OG than this!" DarrenSRS

Mountlet

Mountlets are the biggest and rarest (25) *Size* Pebble variant in the collection. Their beauty lies in their simplicity. *Color Density* and *Special Elements* come to prominence on single Pebbles, which is not as obvious at other sizes. *Mountlets* have sold well to date.

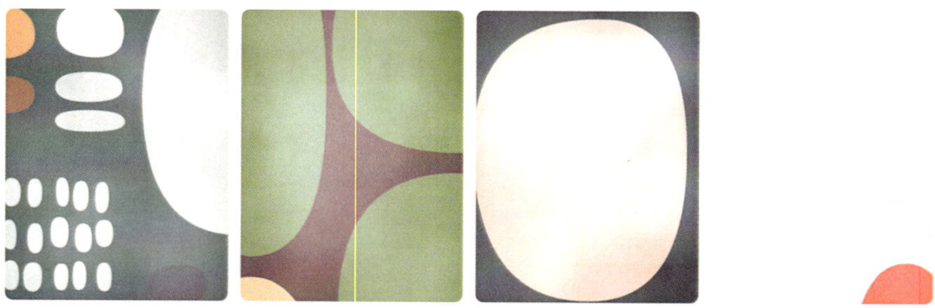

Mountlet size Pebbles 702, 85, 38 and 339

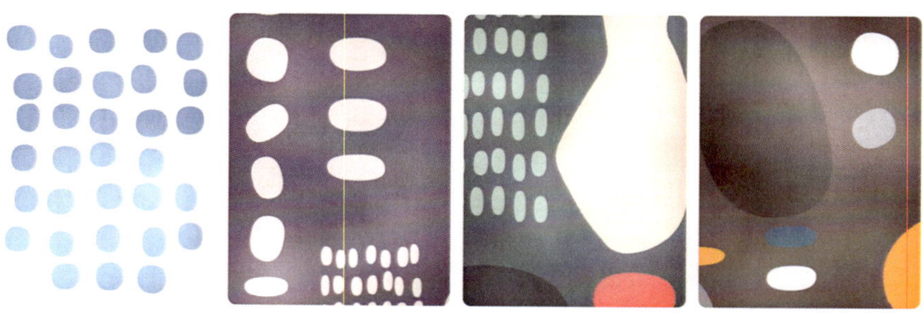

Mountlet size Pebbles 591, 103, 533 and 416

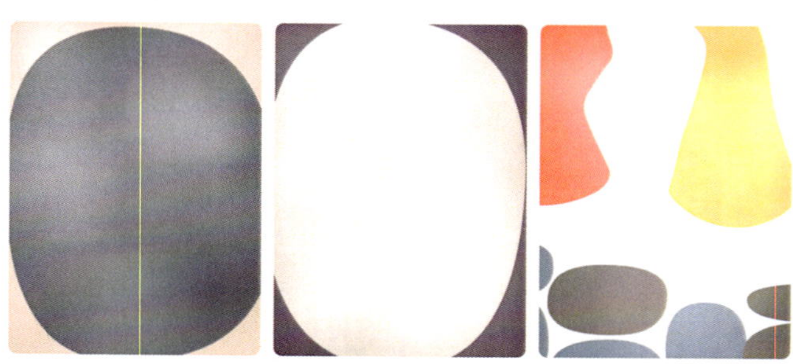

Mountlet size Pebbles 886, 185, 951 and 586

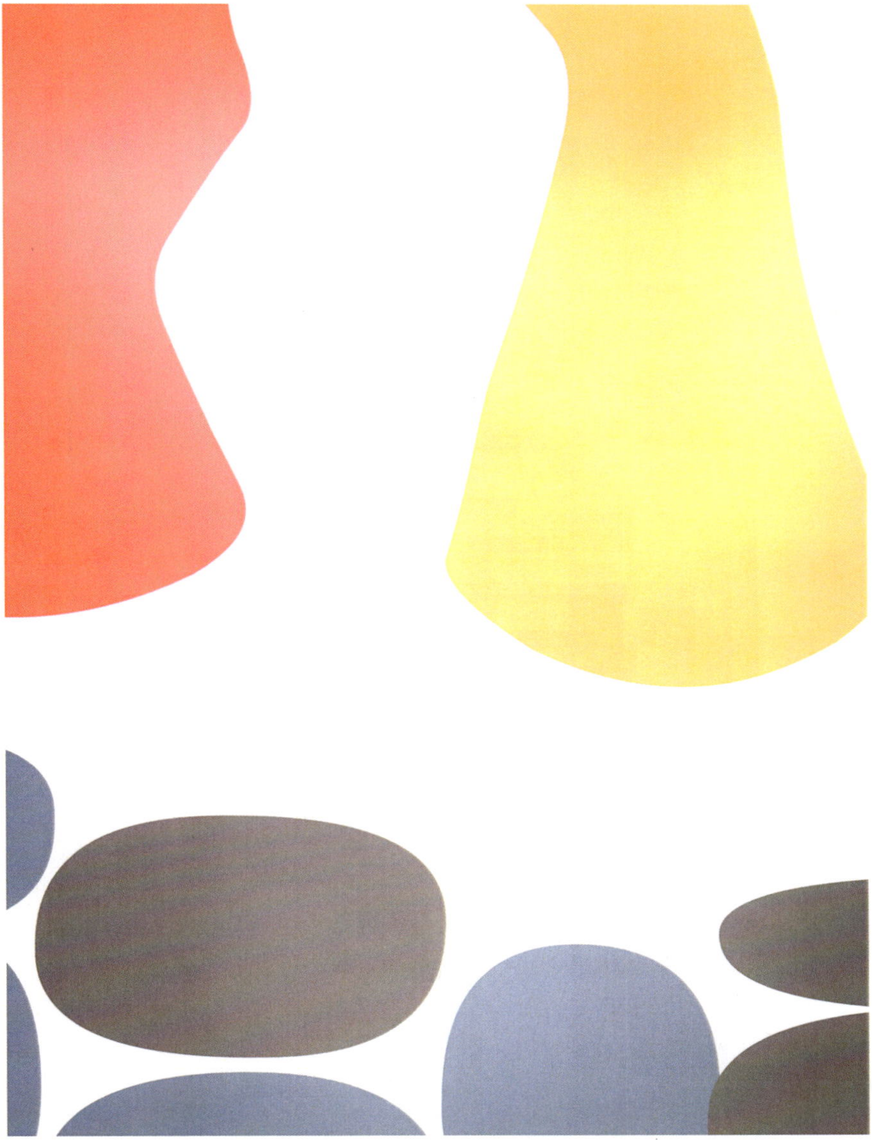

Pebble 586 'Andre the Giant' with Mountlet size

> The world needs to understand that being different is not a weakness, but rather a unique strength that can inspire others." BatSoupYum quoting Andre the Giant

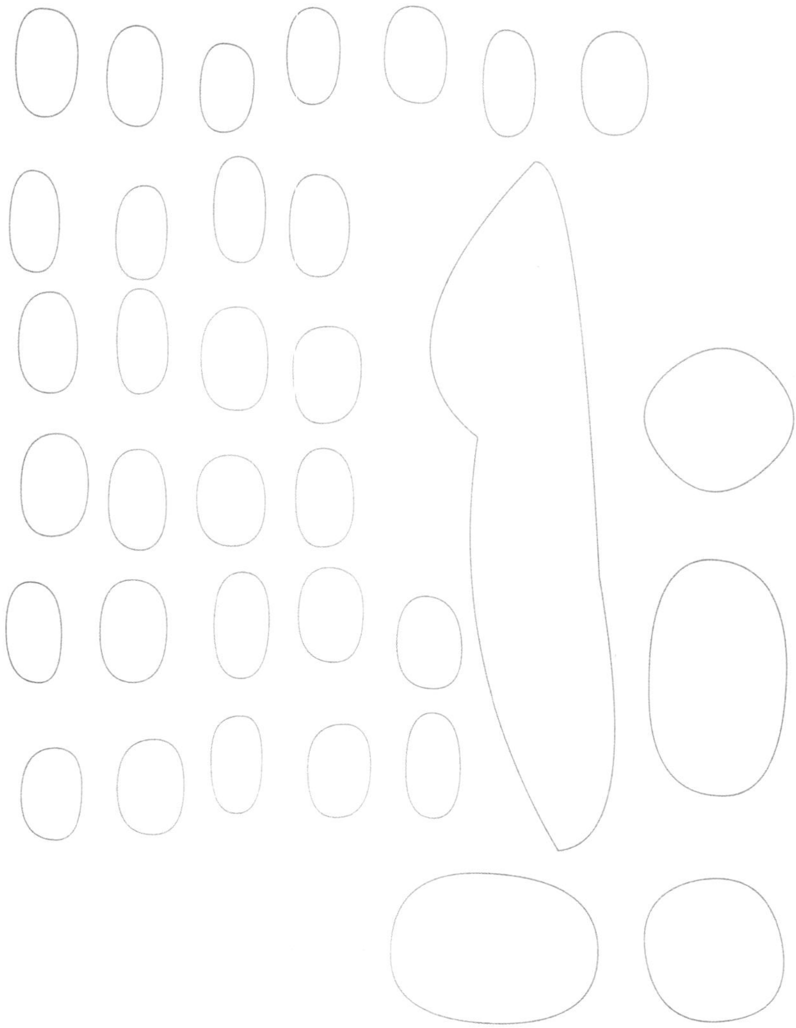

Pebble 886 ‘Beeple Tower’ with Mountlet size

“Beeple Tower.” Thor

Pebble 185 with Mountlet size

One of three large 'egg'-shaped Pebbles only found in the *Mountlet Size* variant. Pebble #185 and #951 were both acquired by punksladsmemes.

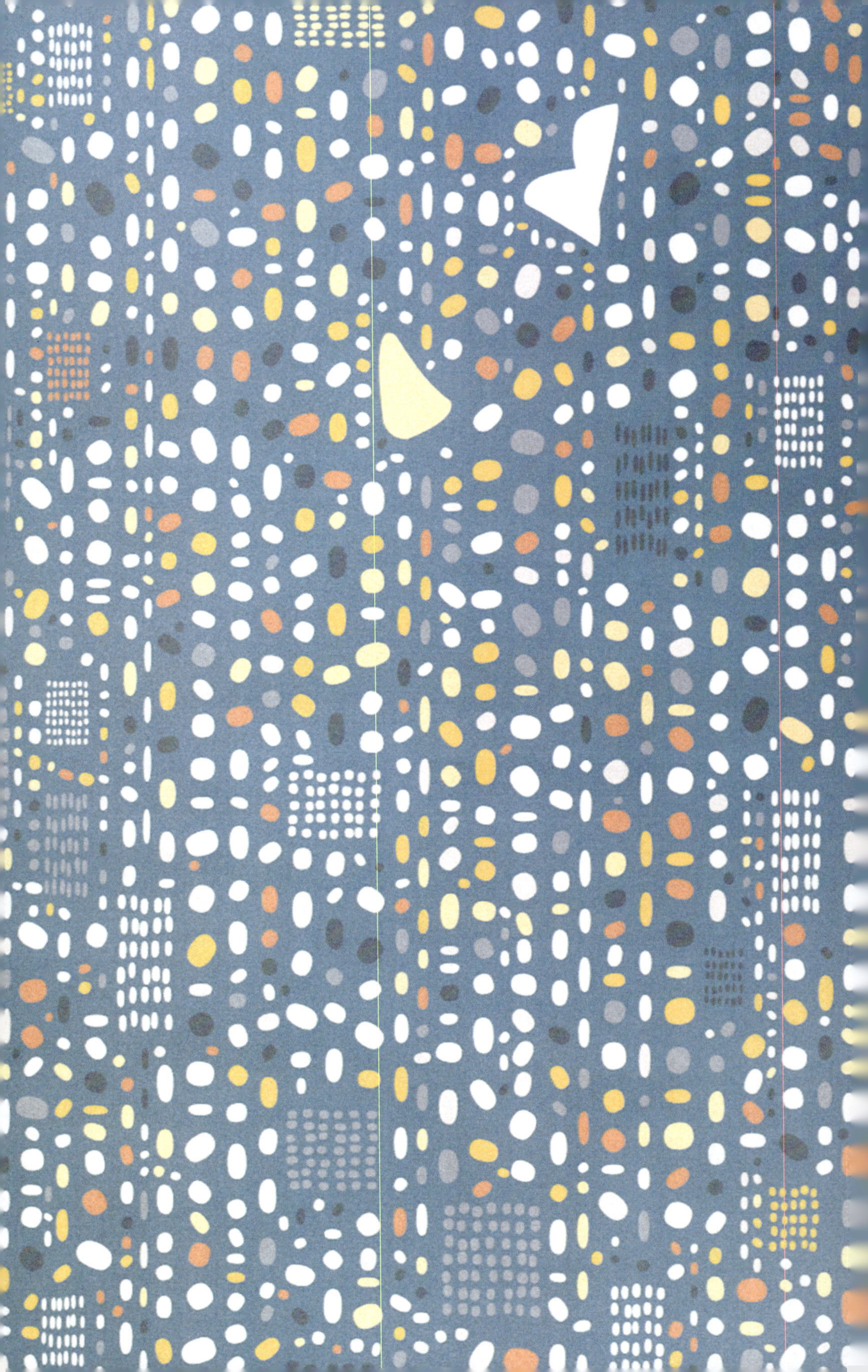

PALETTE

Pebble palettes are many and varied clocking in at a grand total of 20 groupings of colors. We will provide an overview to each of the 20 palettes and curate examples that show the diversity of the algorithm at play within the collection.

Palette rarity is mostly luck of the mint, except if you were minting from a 'Collector Provenance' wallet. Those wallets gained access to a set of palettes not available to the majority of the minting audience. This feature was implemented in the NextGen smart contract in a departure from the purely randomized outputs generated with the Art Blocks smart contract. It is also worth noting that these palette rarities were therefore predetermined before the mint, although the outputs remain entirely random.

The reserved Collector Provenance palette traits are:

- Lunar Chuckles x5
- Magma Mambo x5
- summer.jpg x7
- Salsa Blush x13
- Elephant Pajamas x16
- Blueprint x21
- Sgt. Pepe x33

The randomized general collectoor palette traits are:

- Beatboxes x40
- Shades of Hey! x55
- Dino Disco x58
- Terra Echoes x58
- Unigrids x63
- Coral Reef x71
- Dusk Riverbed x71
- Citrus Slate x72
- Desert Mirage x79
- Galactic Latte x80
- Forest Whisper x83
- Serenity x84
- Night Owl Doodles x86

Introducing predefined rarity is an interesting smart contract enabled twist to the usual blind mint approach to rarity. On one hand, the Collector Provenance palettes made it possible to reward committed collectoors with access to palettes not available to the majority of collectoors. These rewards create ongoing incentives to continue to collect and remain within the 6529 ecosystem who built the NextGen smart contract that Pebbles was released upon.

On the other hand, the Collector Provenance rarities are not rare through luck or serendipity. For a true randomized rarity collectoor, the appeal of a *Beatboxes, Shades of Hey!* or *Dino Disco* palette may be stronger.

Reserved Palettes

The following palette traits are reserved for a subset of people, to recognize their Collector Provenance in the overall distribution. Visit Seize to view the full variety of palette outputs: seize.io/nextgen/collection/pebbles/art

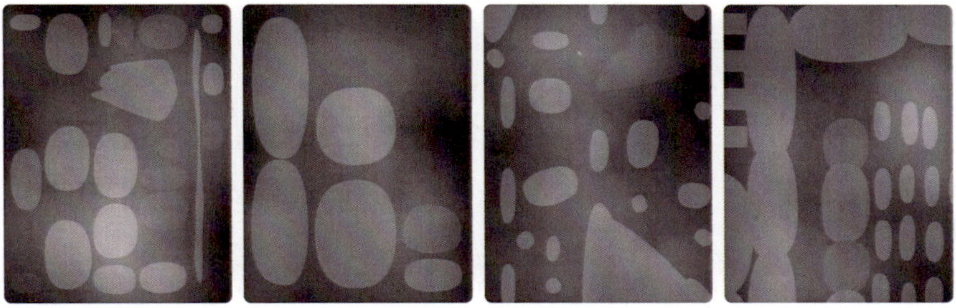

Lunar Chuckles palette

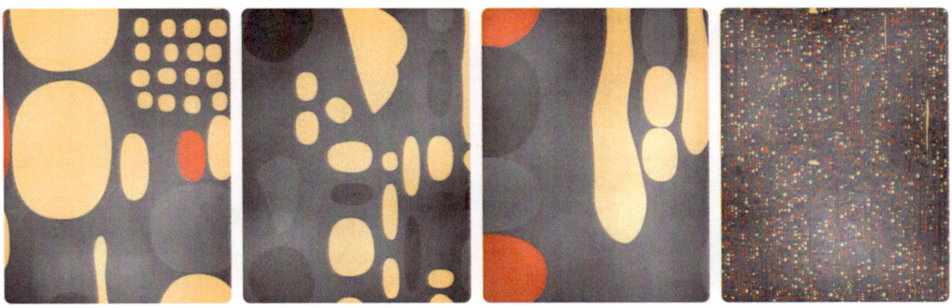

Magma Mambo palette

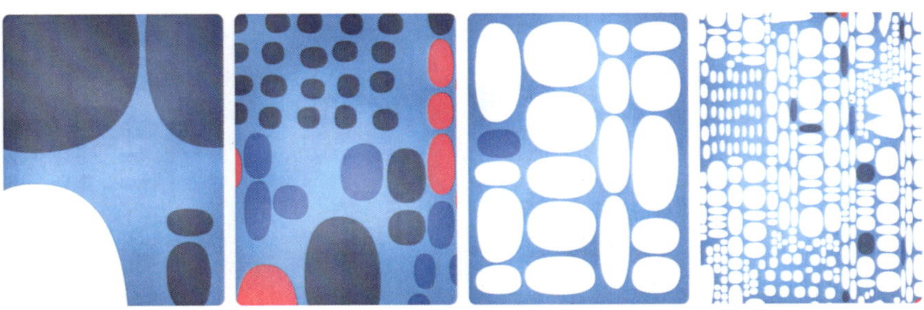

summer.jpg palette

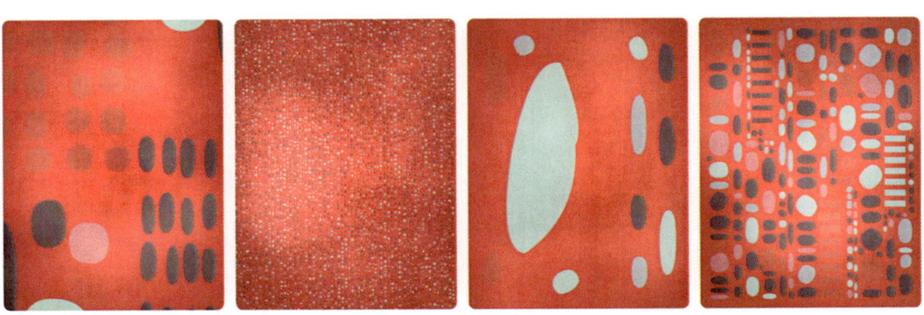

Salsa Blush palette

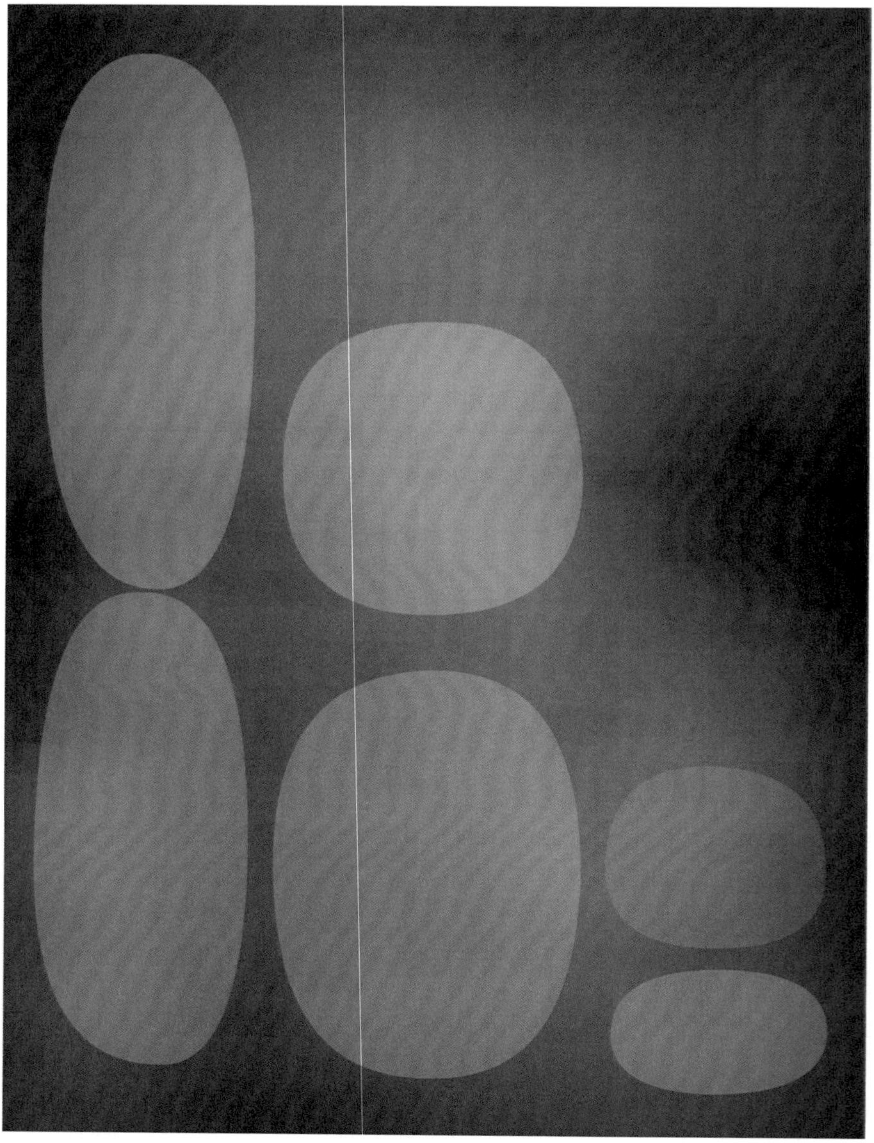

Pebble 32 with Lunar Chuckles palette

> "Minimal, balanced, just how I like it." 6529er

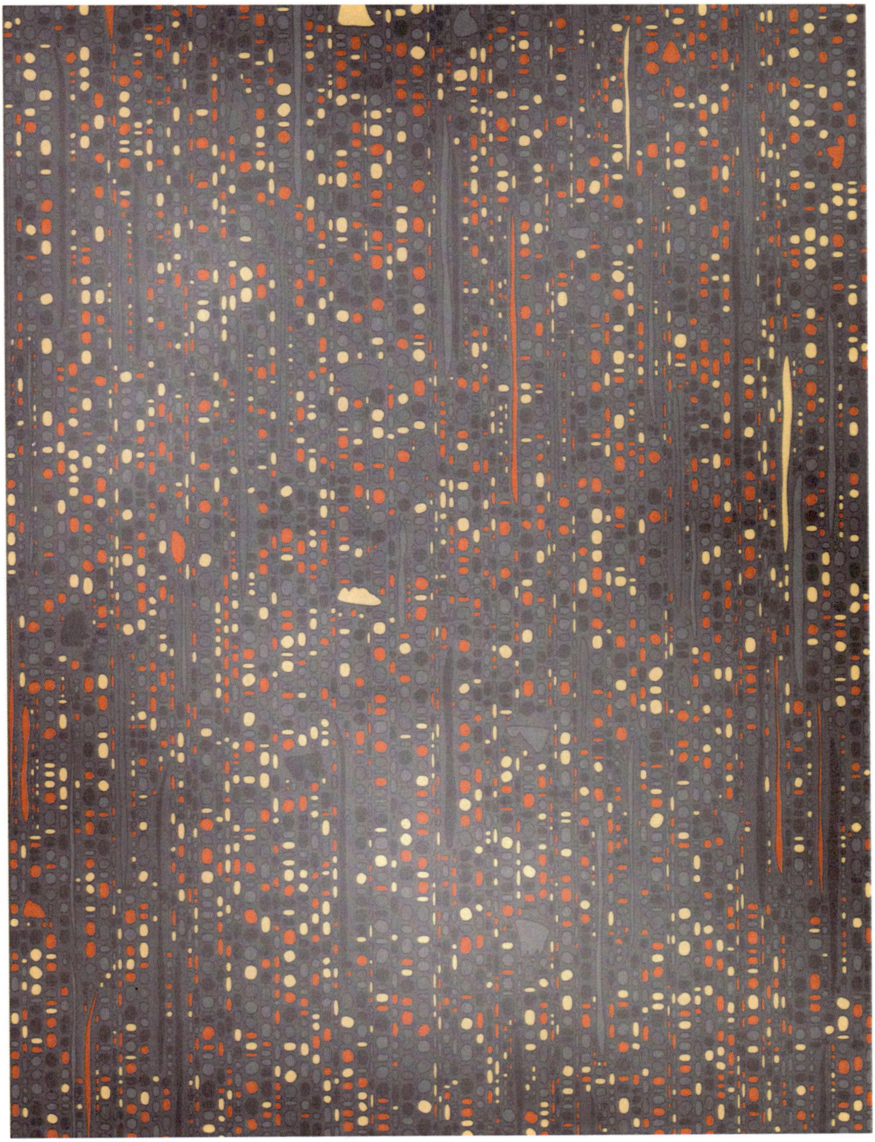

Pebble 83 with Magma Mambo palette

“One of the rarest Pebbles in existence.” G9ralt

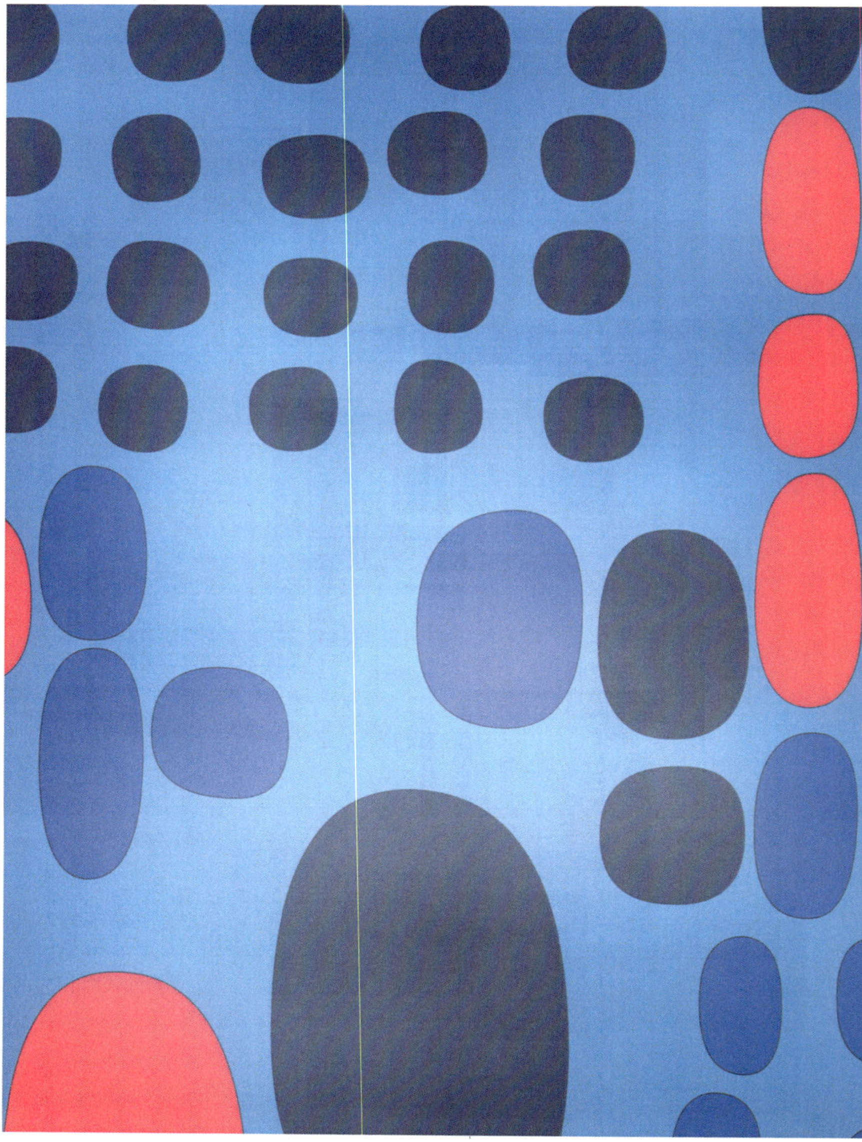

Pebble 2 with summer.jpg palette

“A summer grail.” Blocknoob

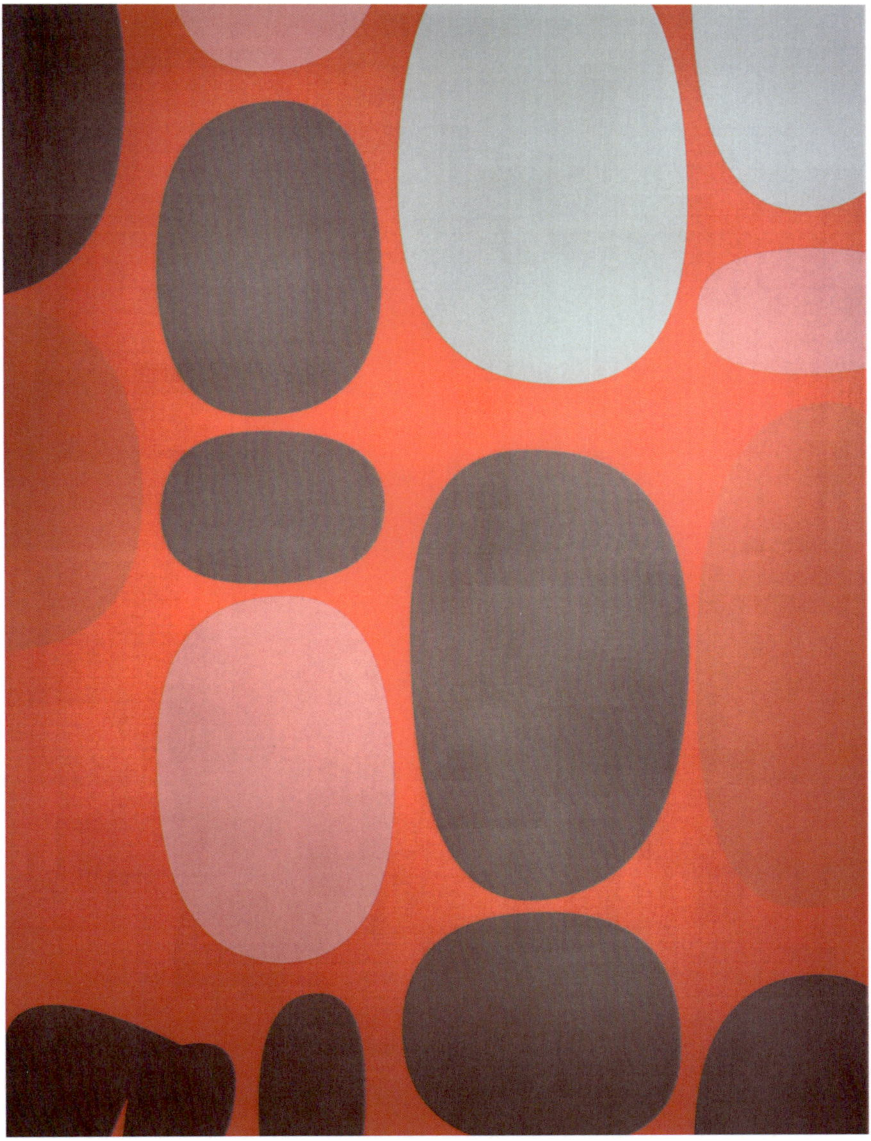

Pebble 299 'The Eruption' with Salsa Blush palette

"'The Eruption' is the Pebble that blew my heart. Favorite trait is of course the Salsa Blush palette." Hugo Faz

Elephant Pajamas palette

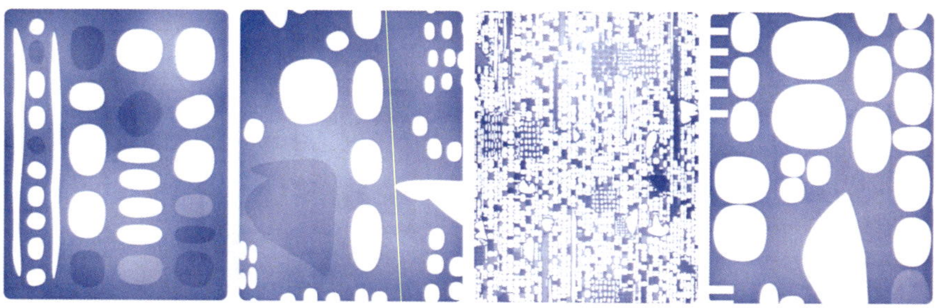

Blueprint palette

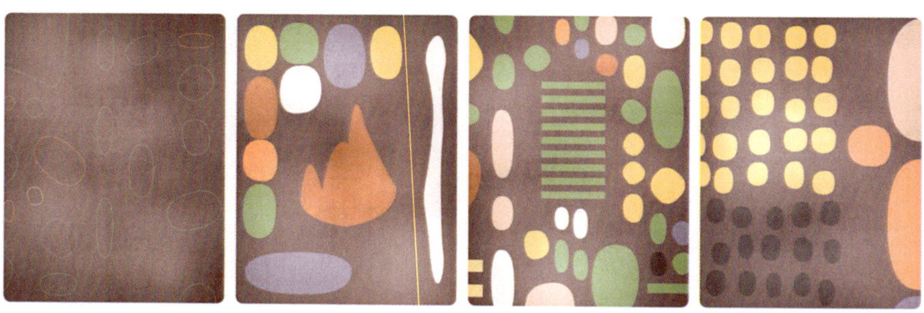

Sgt. Pepe palette

Pebble 230 with Elephant Pyjamas palette

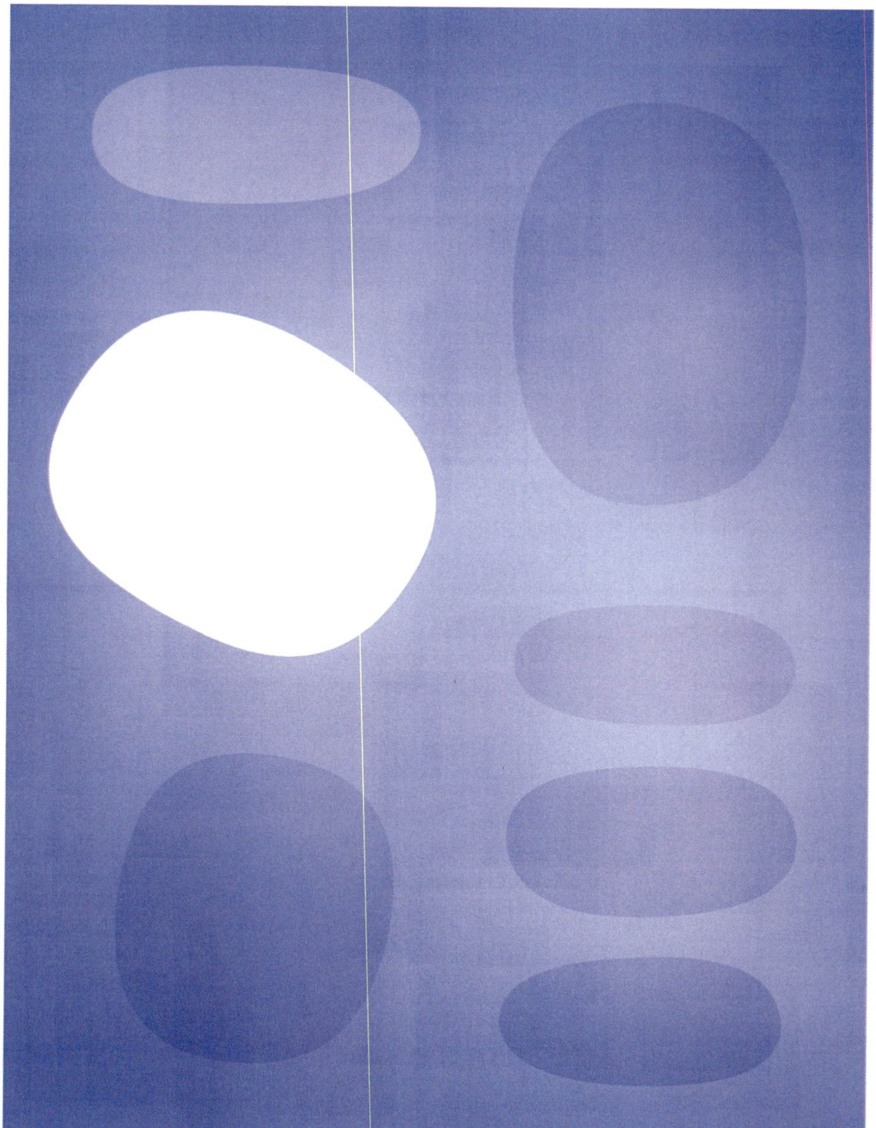

Pebble 556 with Blueprint palette

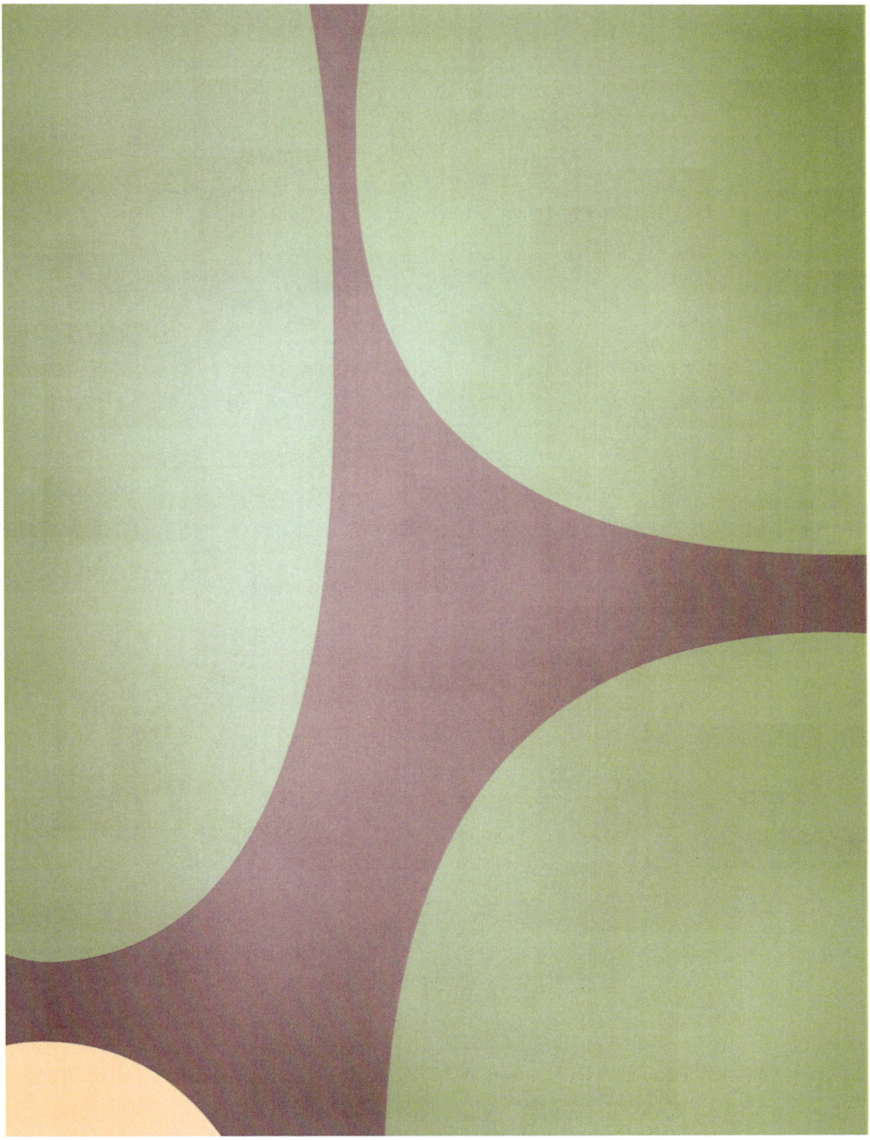

Pebble 85 with Sgt. Pepe palette

General Palettes

The following general collectoor palette traits are a selection of the overall distribution. Visit Seize to view the full variety of palette outputs: seize.io / nextgen / collection / pebbles / art

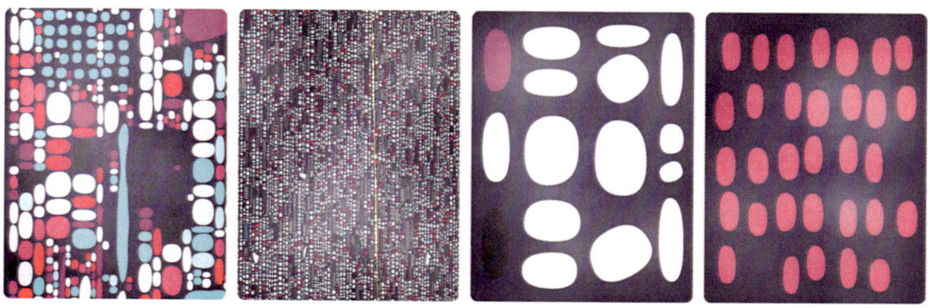

Beatboxes palette

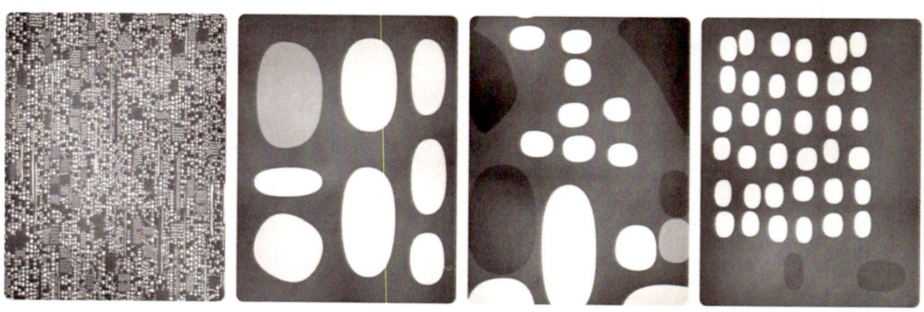

Shades of Hey! palette

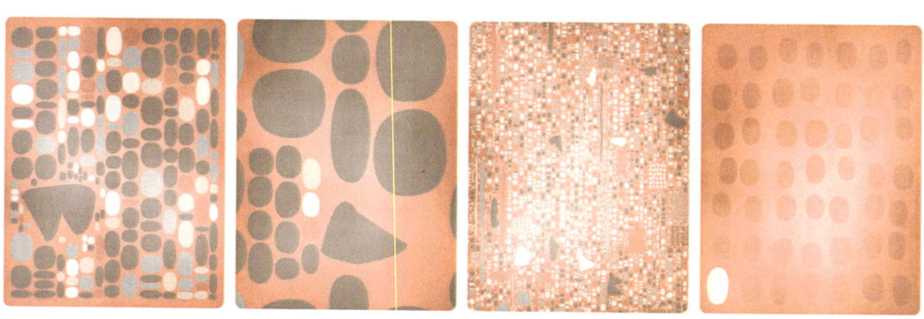

Terra Echoes palette

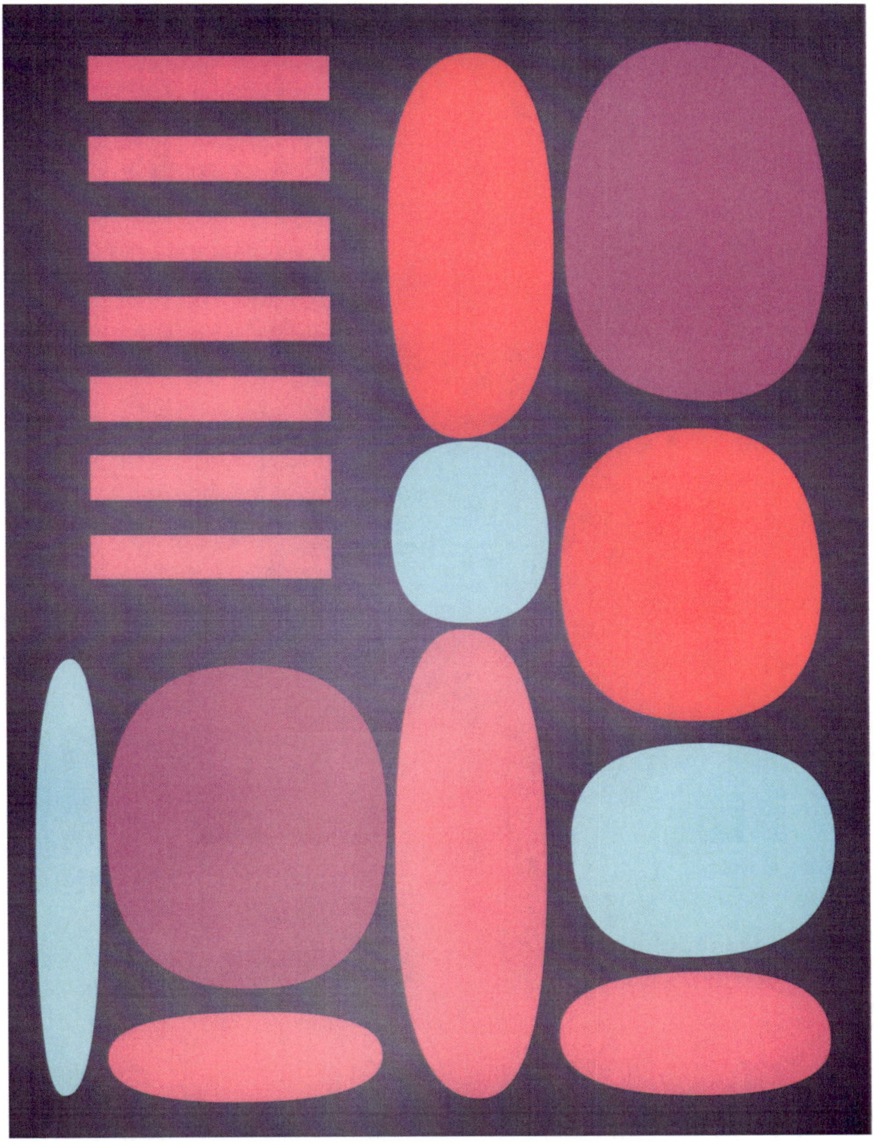

Pebble 710 with Beatboxes palette

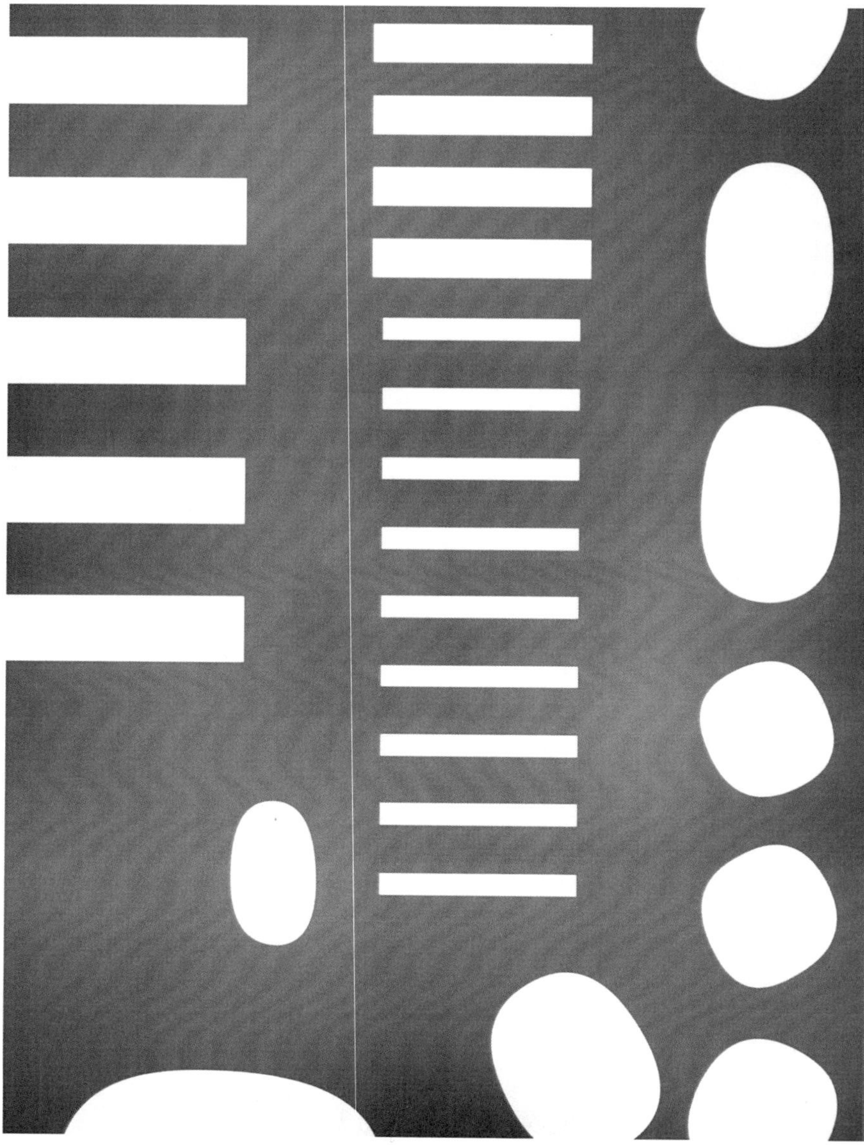

Pebble 114 'Stepping Out' with Shades of Hey! palette

"Nothing is black and white in crypto law, but everything is borderless." 6529Guardian

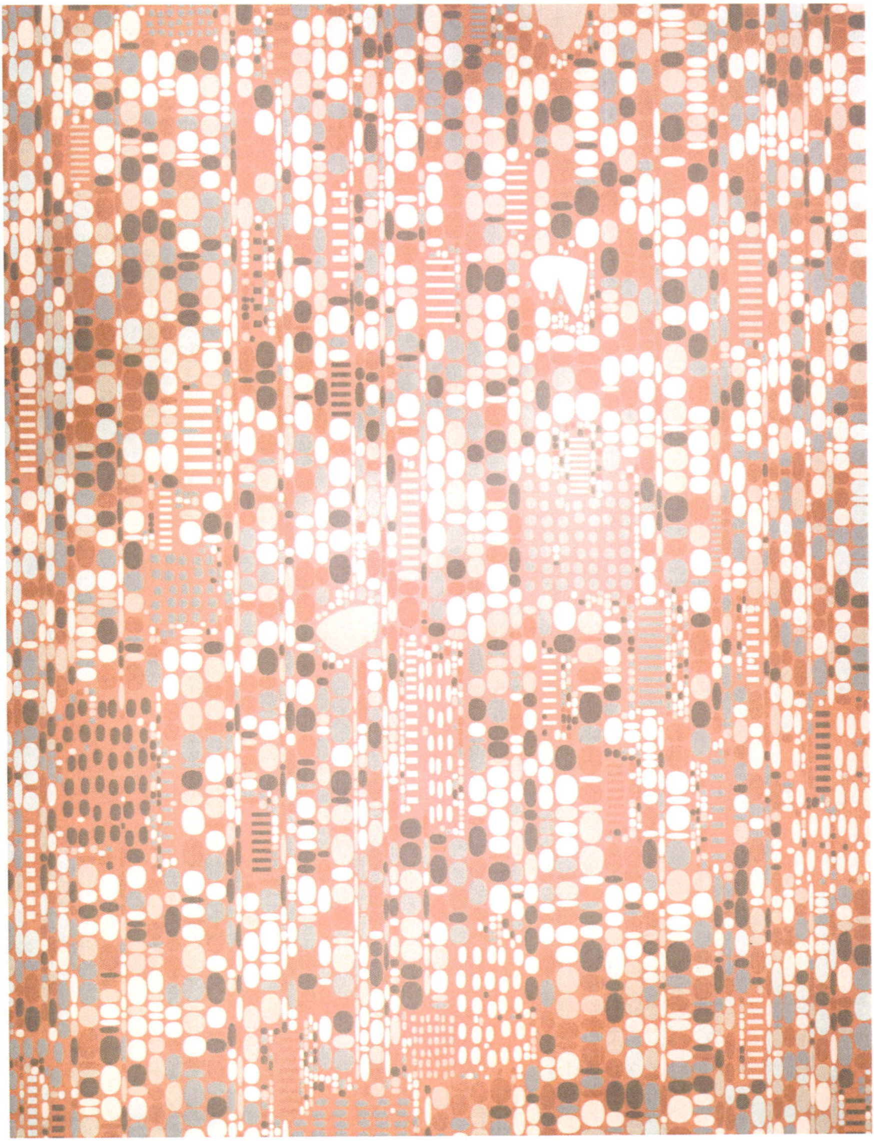

Pebble 14 with Terra Echoes palette

"The low token ID is what I like best about it. I'll likely sell it and buy another off the floor if I can get a good price for it." brookr

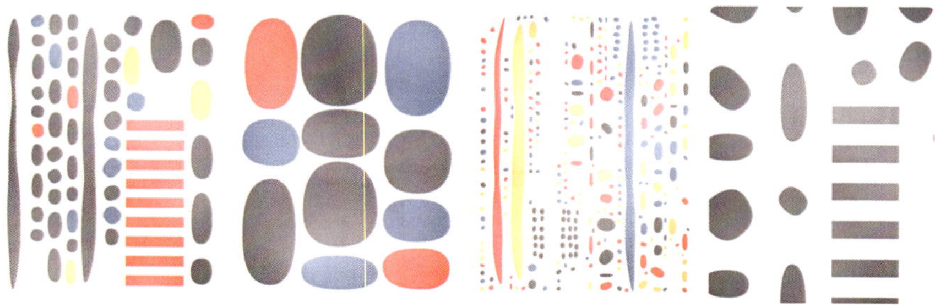

Dino Disco palette

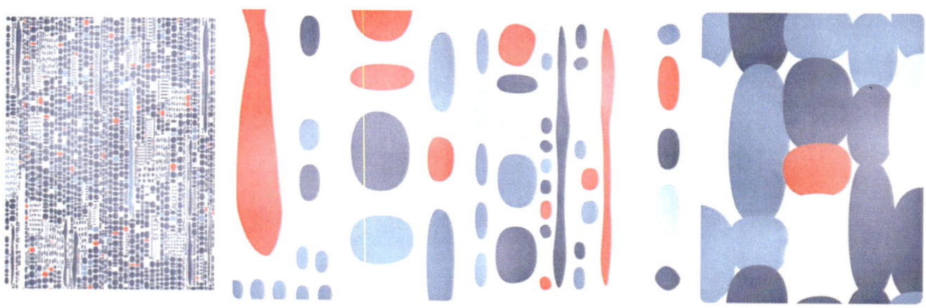

Unigrids palette

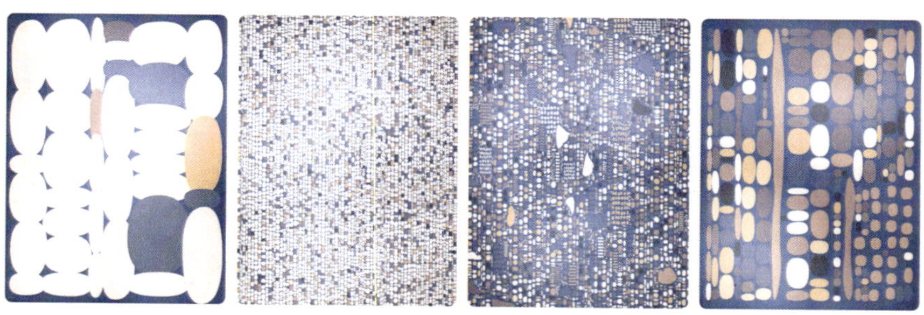

Dusk Riverbed palette

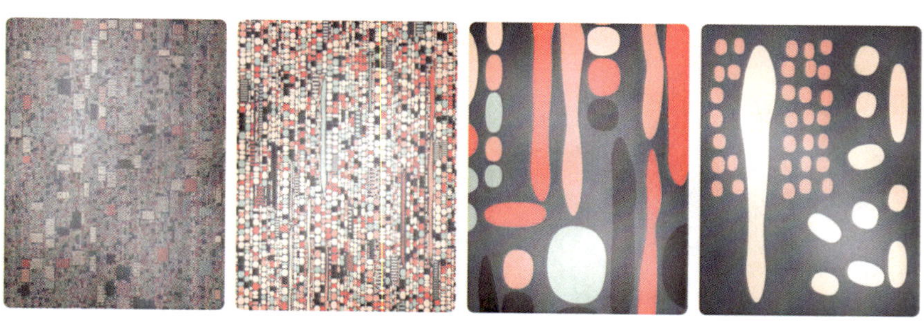

Coral Reef palette

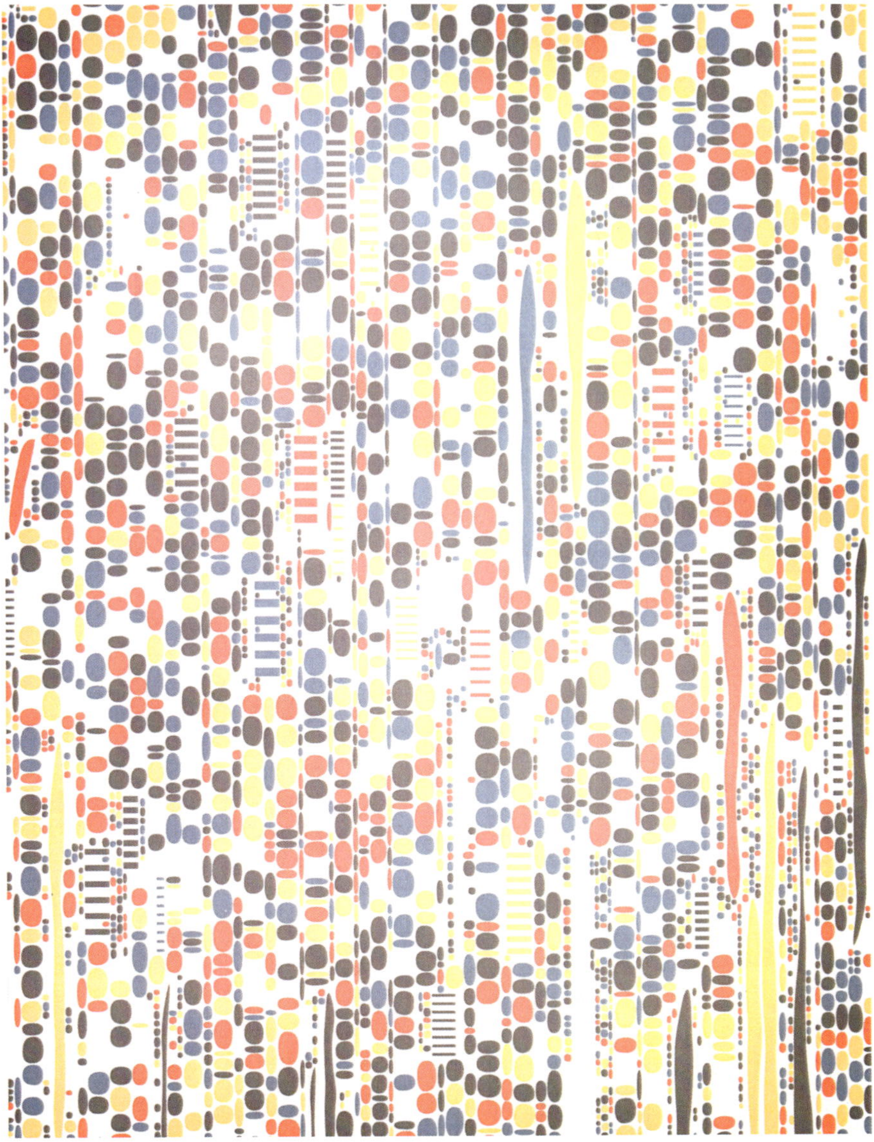

Pebble 863 'The Dance Floor' with Dino Disco palette

> 'The Dance Floor' with *Vivid* and *Harmonic* traits is crowded with three *Special Elements*. The *Dino Disco* palette on Pebbles 863 brings us back to the 70's dance halls."
> Hugo Faz

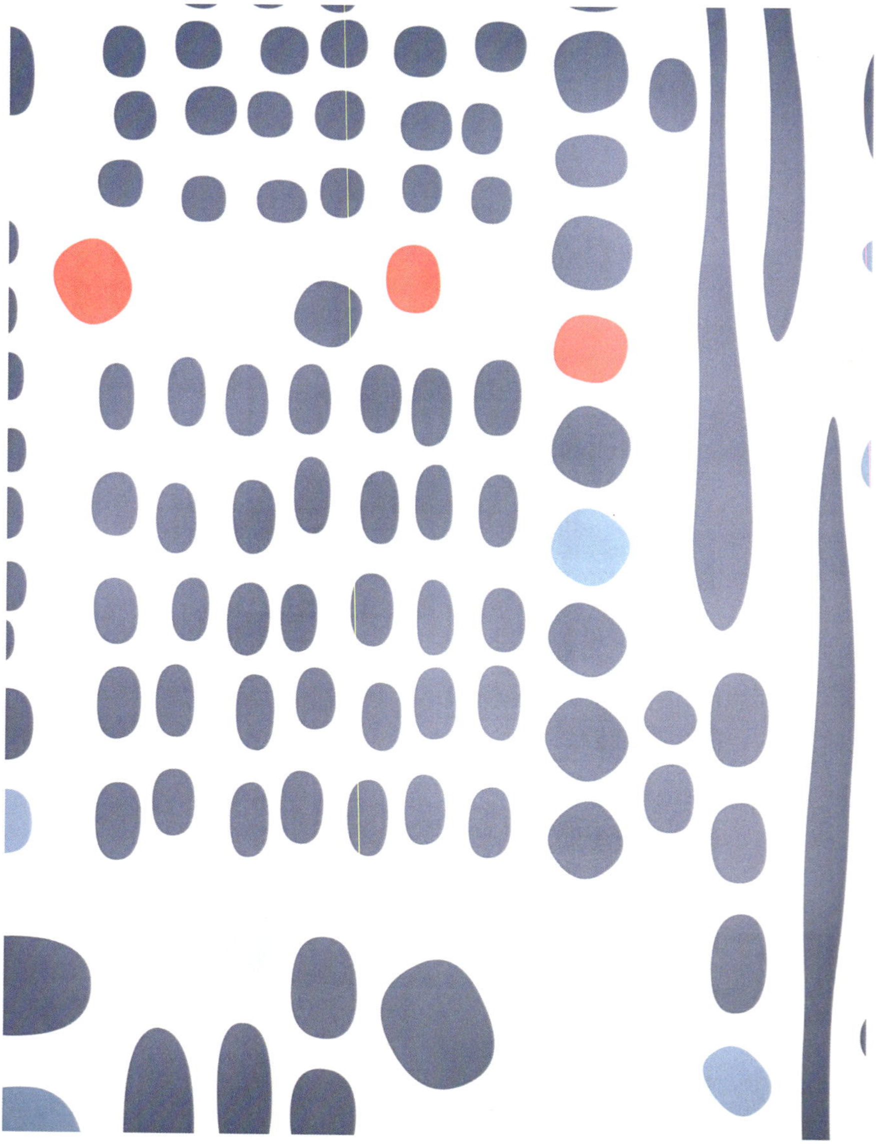

Pebble 714 'Cribbage' with Unigrids palette

> "Pebble 714 is a top one hundred rarity because it is one of three *Flow Pebbles* that also contains all *Special Elements.*"
> MoonFront

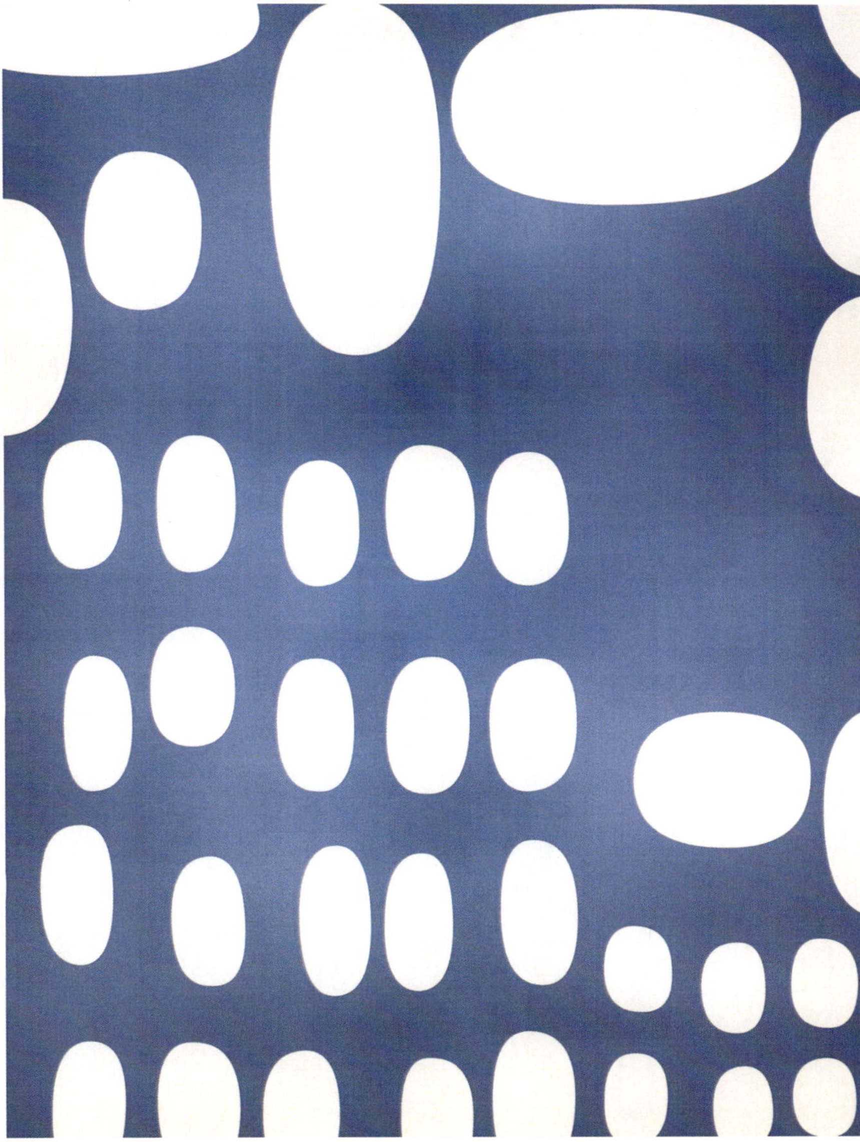

Pebble 71 'Blue Steel' with Dusk Riverbed palette

'Blue Steel' reveals the bare minimum of the *Dusk Riverbed* palette, as *Faint Color Density* conceals the color attaché. The *Special Element* intensity is felt most in the white grid of Pebbles in the bottom left hand quadrant. A high performance output from the *MemeMaxis* factory.

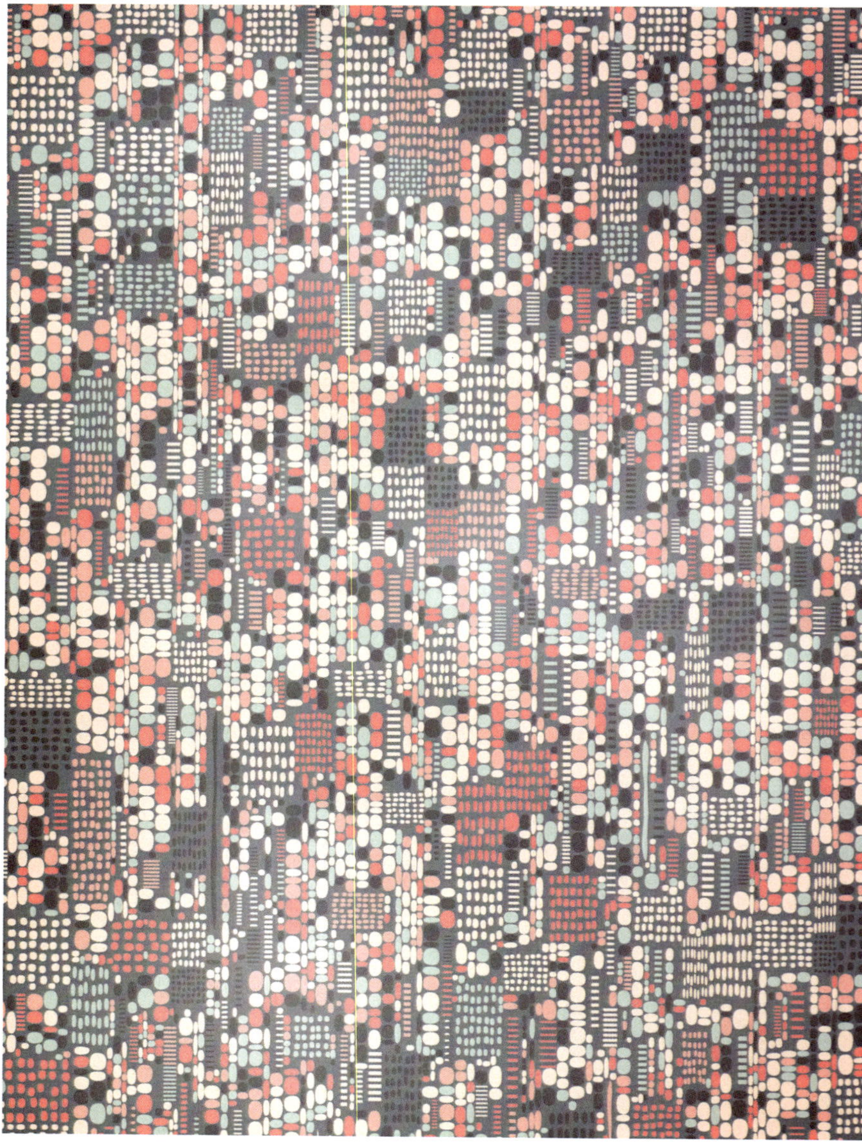

Pebble 206 'Corbita' with Coral Reef palette

"A corbita struck the rocks, scattering amphorae across the beach like shattered pottery stars." Mikavert

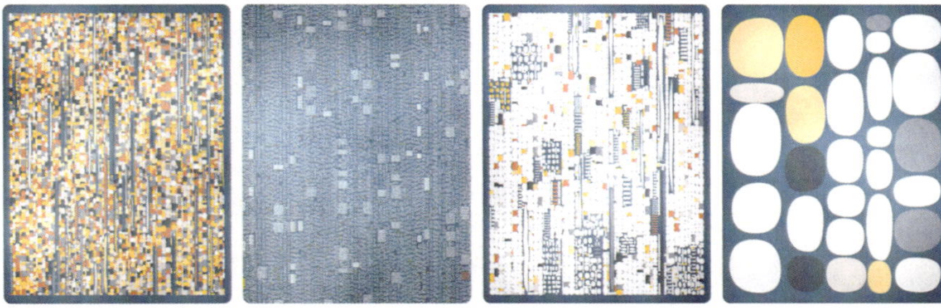

Citrus Slate palette

Desert Mirage palette

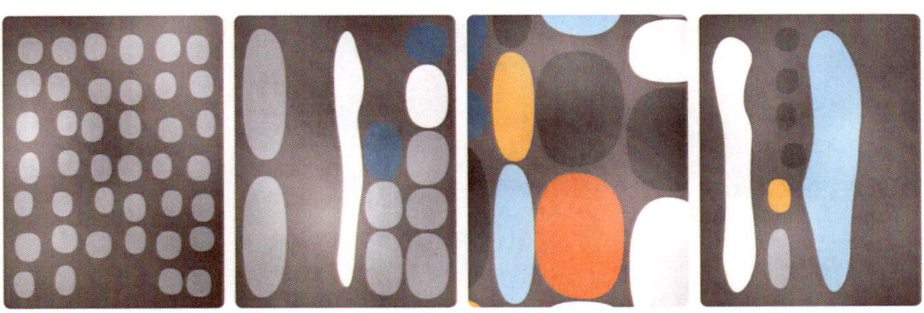

Galactic Latte palette

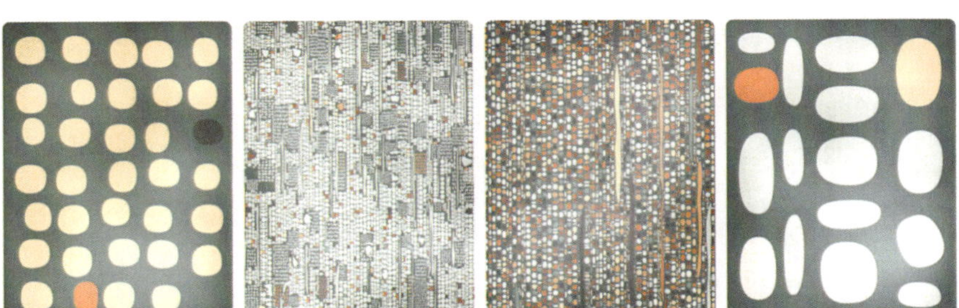

Forest Whisper palette

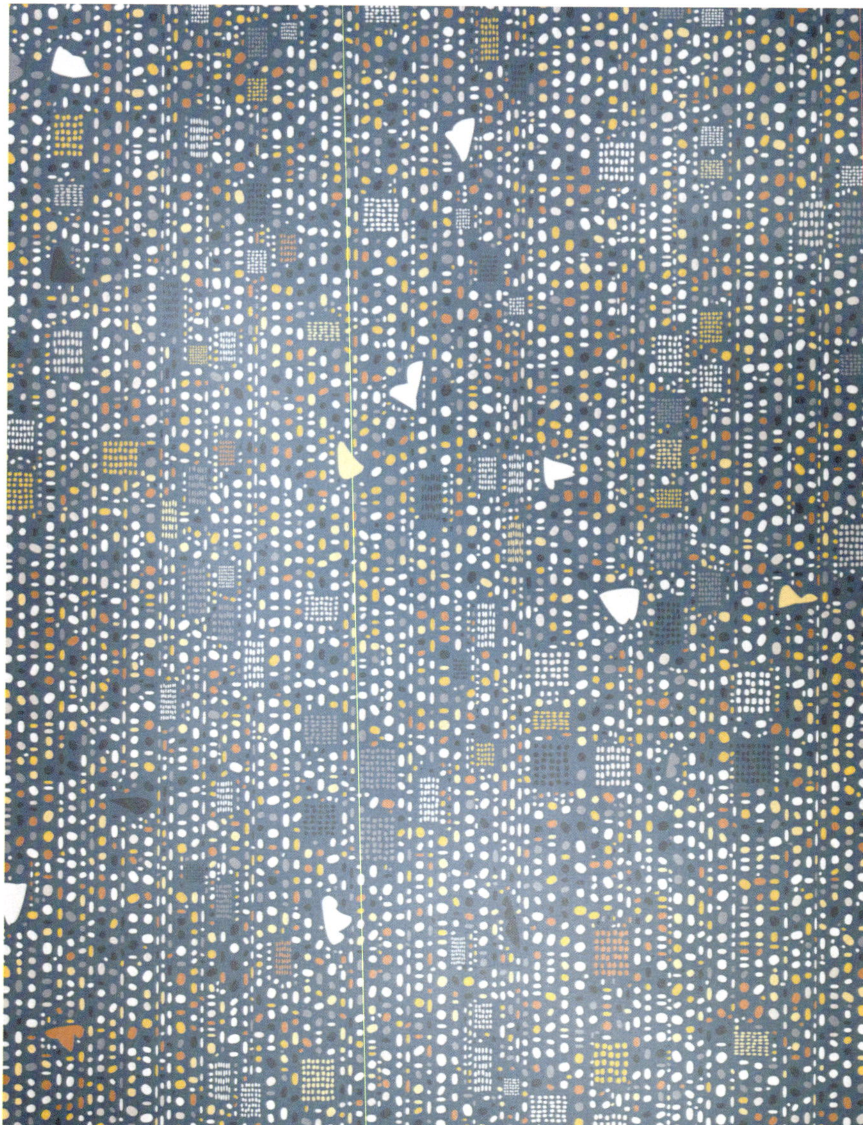

Pebble 510 'Archipelago Novum' with Citrus Slate palette

"'Archipelago Novum' reflects my life. Lots of hurdles but there are *Special Elements* too." Prateek Saraf

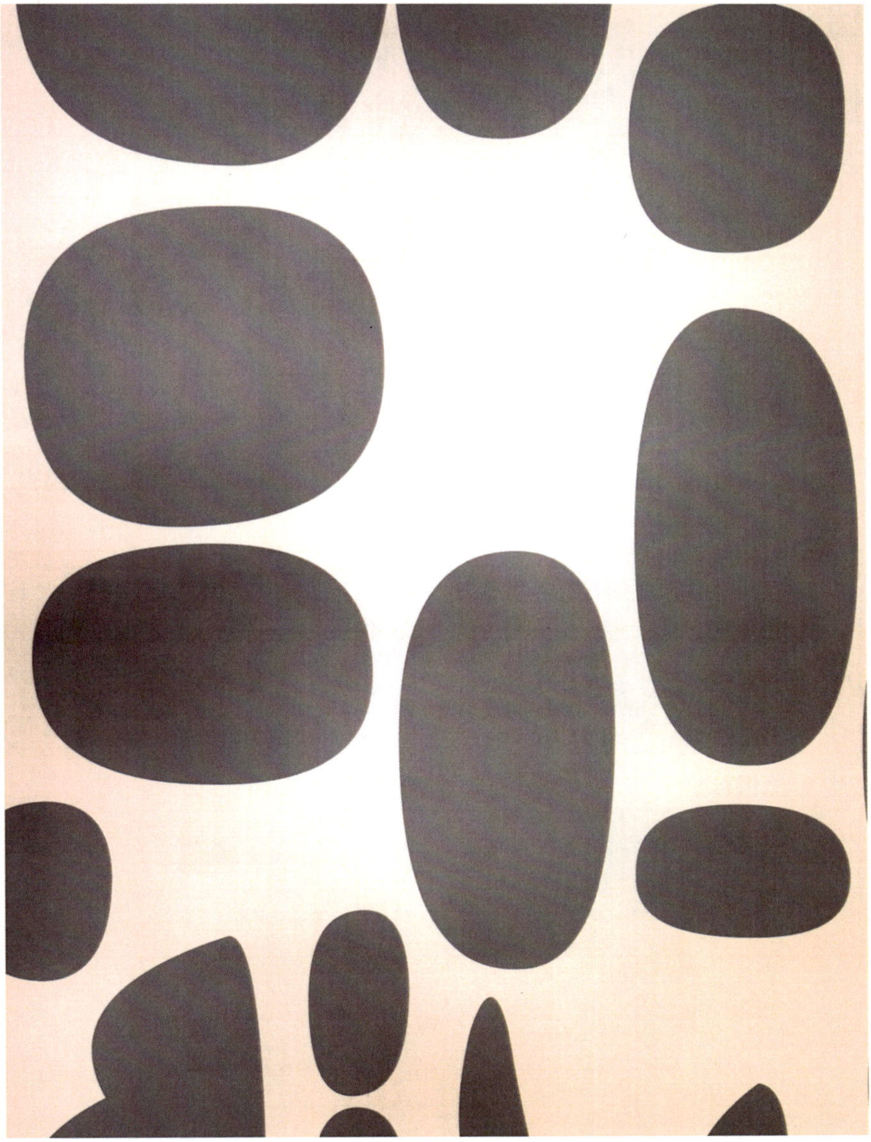

Pebble 896 'The Sun is Always Shining' with Desert Mirage palette

> This one has the *Desert Mirage* palette. The white Pebble is like the sun. In the desert, the sun is always shining :-)"
> Angol

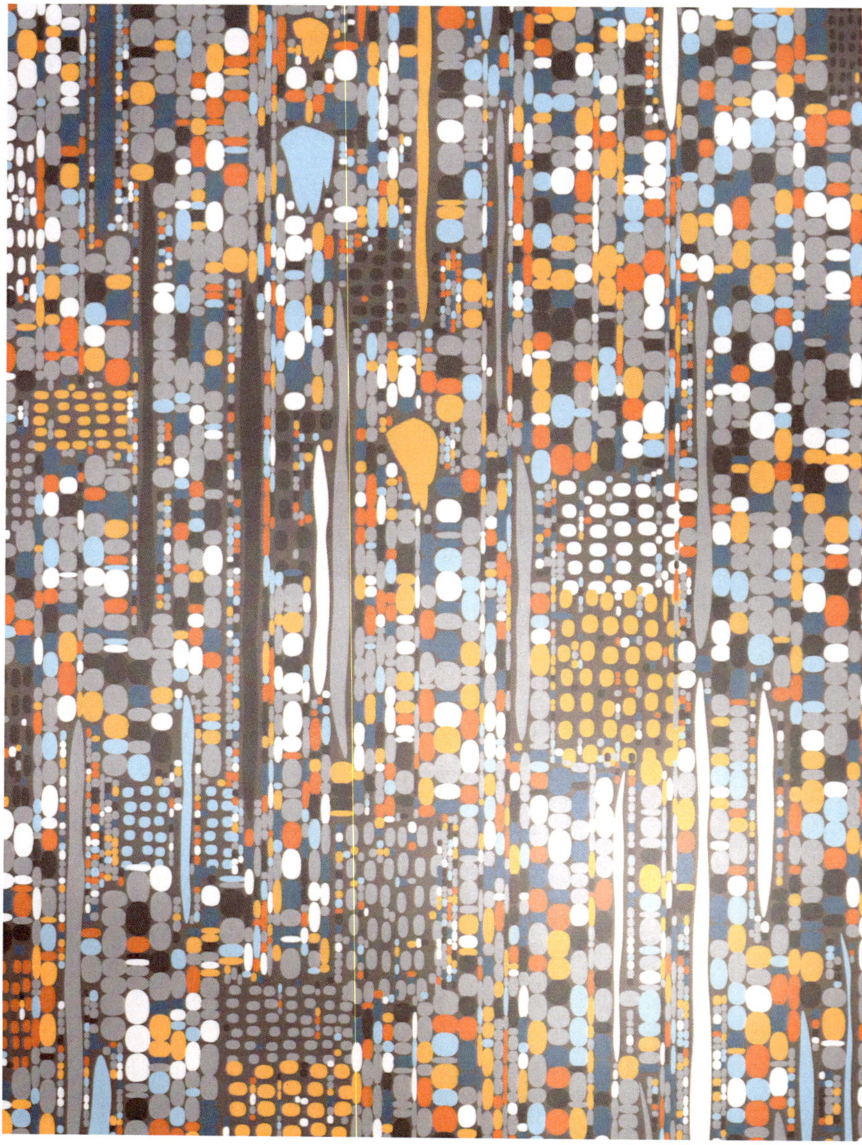

Pebble 513 with Galactic Latte palette

Pebble #513, 'Memes & Life', connects the *Blend Overlap* dots to position the viewer in an upward-looking gaze. The *Vivid Color Density* brings out the best in the *Galactic Latte* palette, while the *Special Elements* shine across all color permutations.

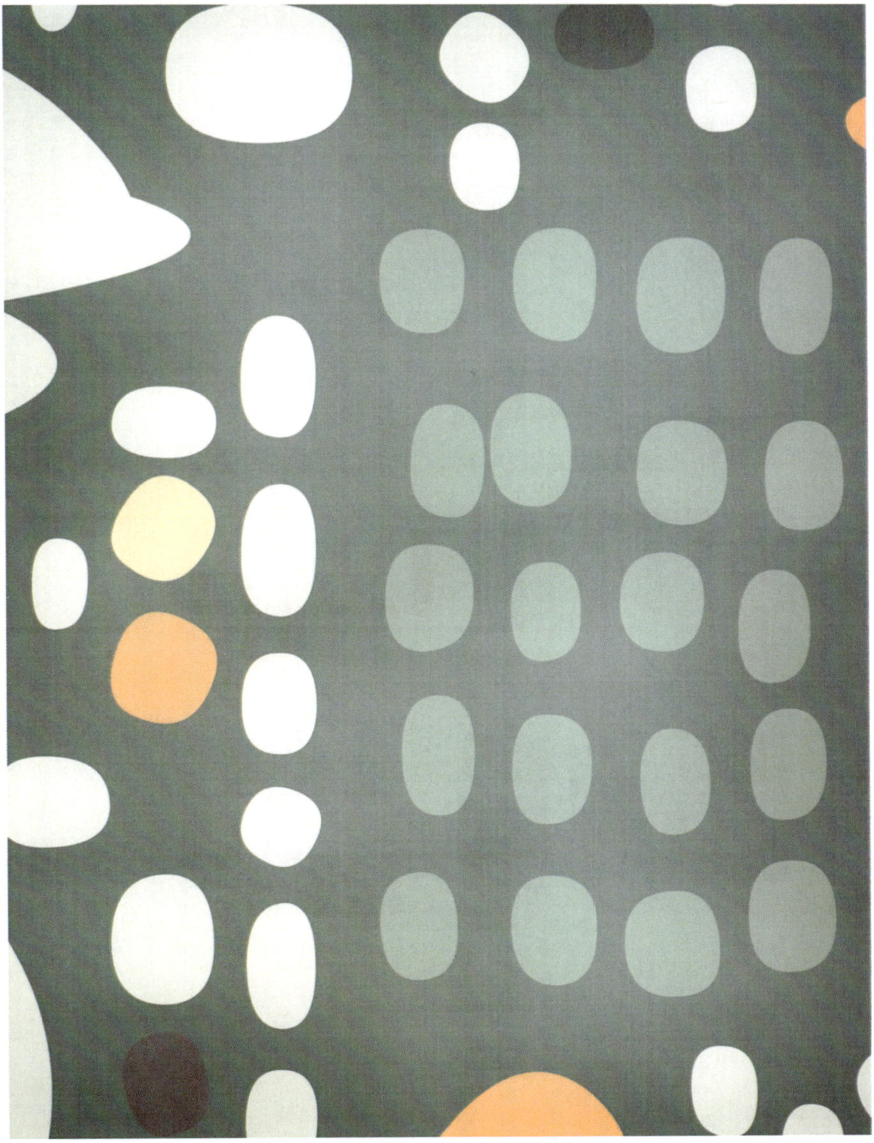

Pebble 958 'The Dolphin' with Forest Whisper palette

> Occasionally, the dolphin pops it's head out to feed..."
> smpsmyth

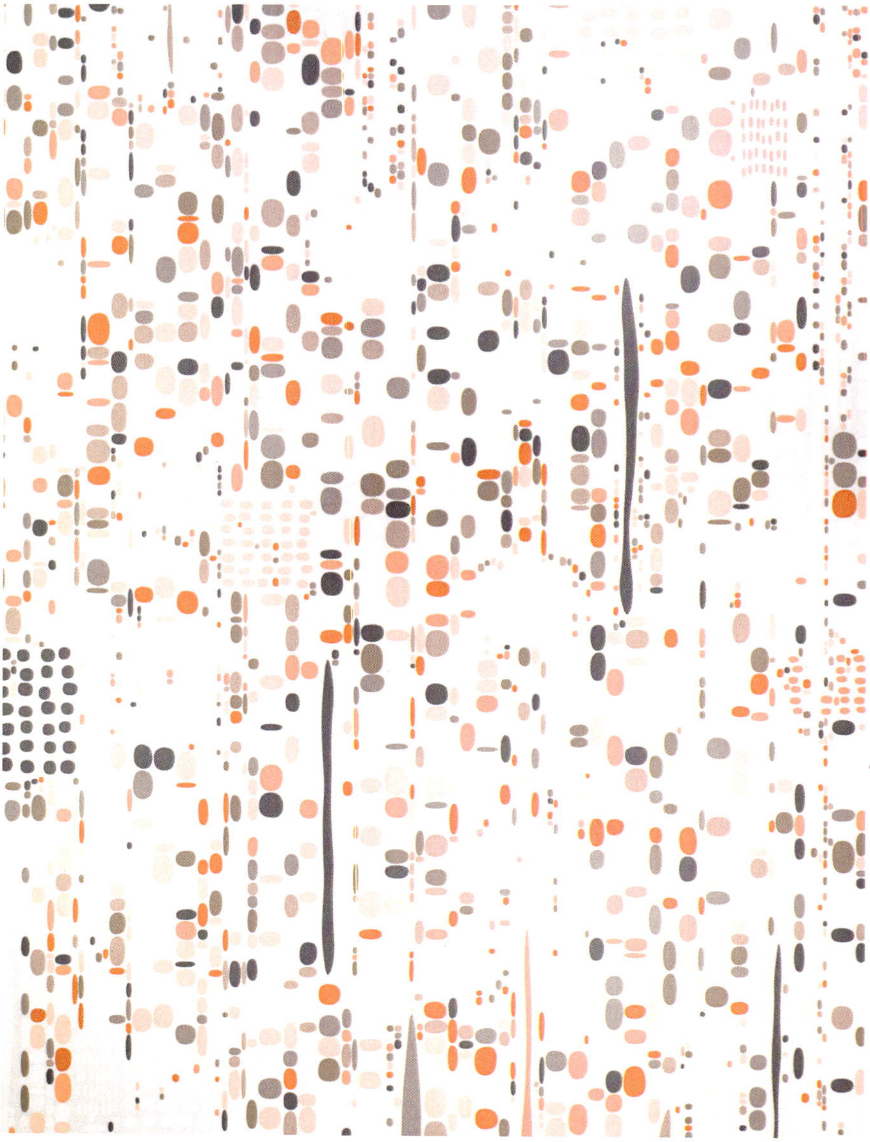

Pebble 909 'Running with the Devil' with Serenity palette

"The *Boulderette* and *Serenity* traits are a perfect fit for 'Running with the Devil.'" BatSoupYum

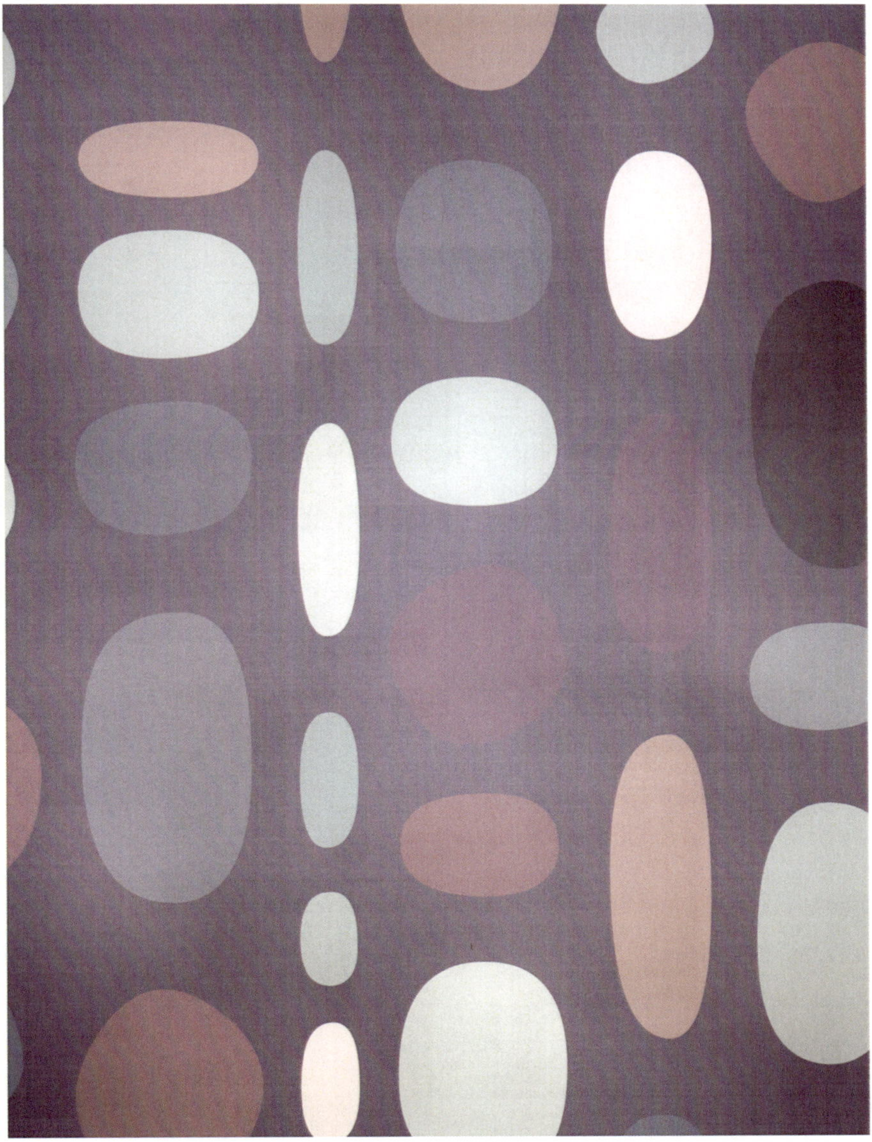

Pebble 816 'Pathway Home' with Night Owl Doodles palette

"Can I get back to you? I'm still shaking." Articulate

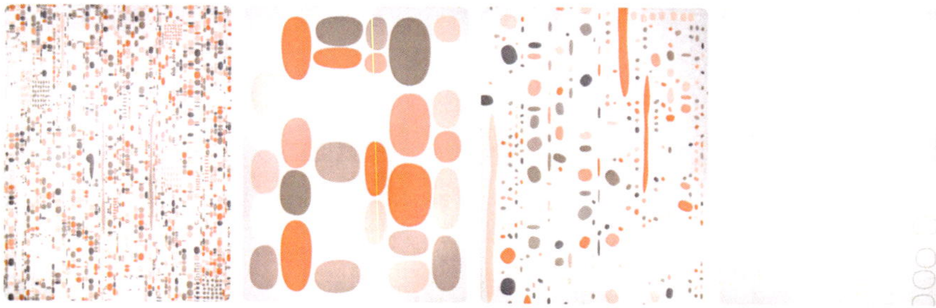

Serenity palette

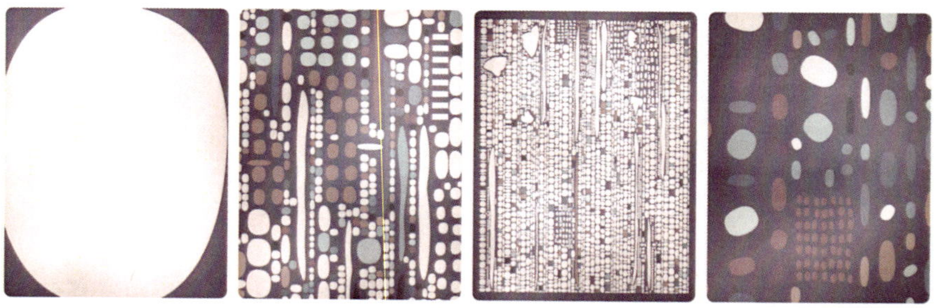

Night Owl Doodles palette

Palettes in Detail

Now you have viewed the full range of the *Palettes* found throughout the Pebbles collection including a featured palette provided by collectors. Let's explore *Palettes* in further detail. As we go through, you might notice that there is more to the algorithm than just *Palette* and *Size* as each trait becomes more noticeable by focusing on a set of artworks with a single *Palette* trait. Traits beyond *Palette* also begin to be noticeable, even to the untrained eye.

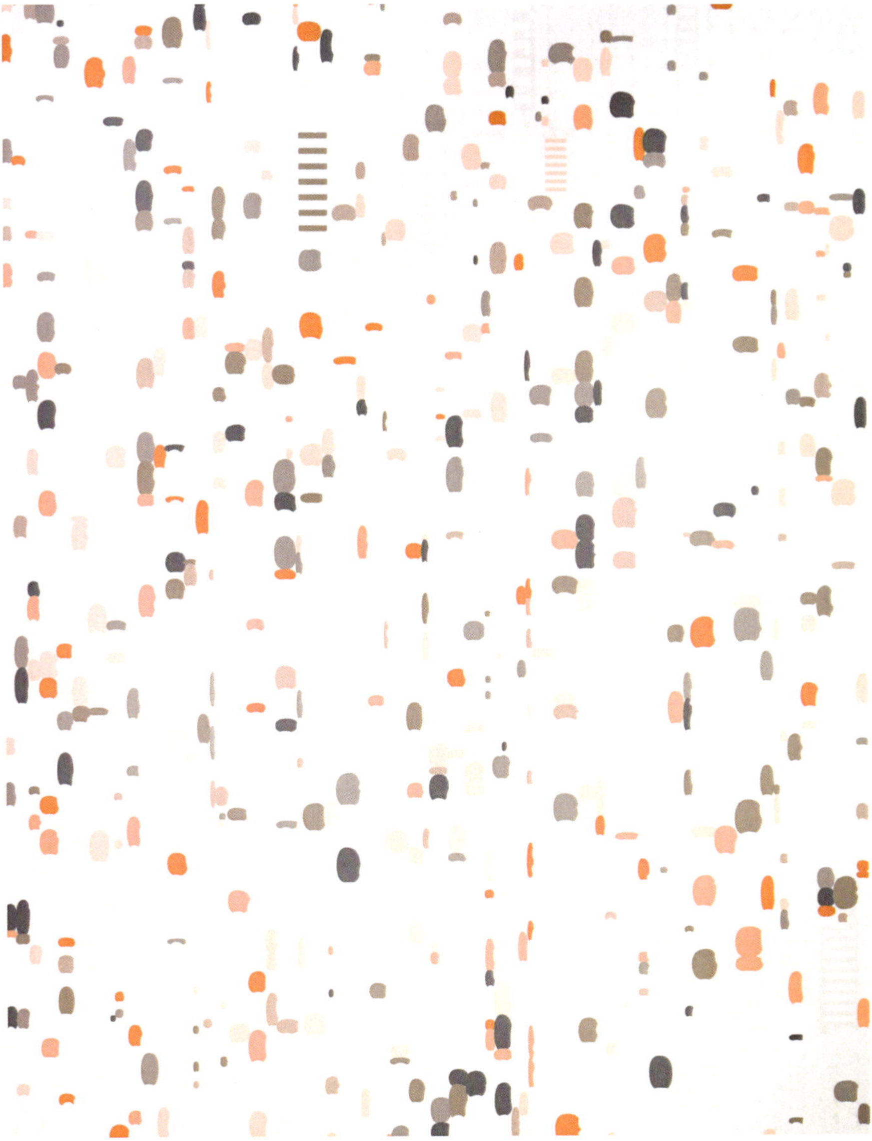

Pebble 778 with Serenity palette

Dusk Riverbed is one of the most stunning palettes for its use of Prussian Blue with a tint of Indigo. Deep rivers on a sunny day in nature lend a similar palette. *Dusk Riverbed* is starting to gather momentum as one of the more interesting palettes to acquire.

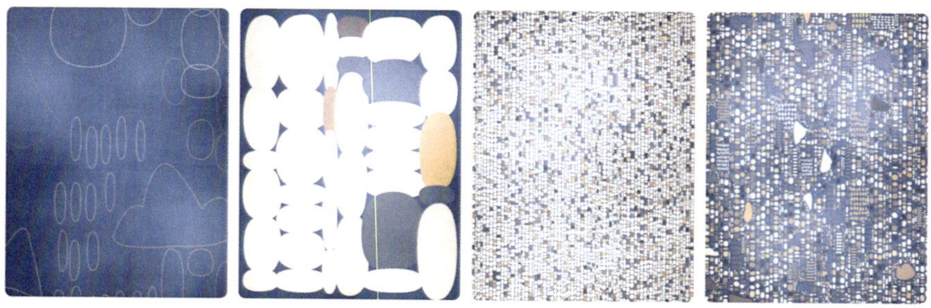

Dusk Riverbed palette

The *Forest Whisper* palette reflects the natural landscape features that we may associate with finding Pebbles. In contrast, the collection does not discuss Pebbles in the context of construction, roading, or home garden and landscaping environment directing our imagination towards the natural world.

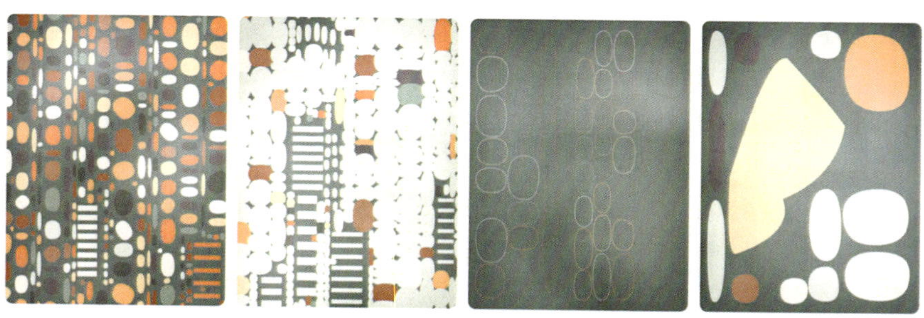

Forest Whisper palette

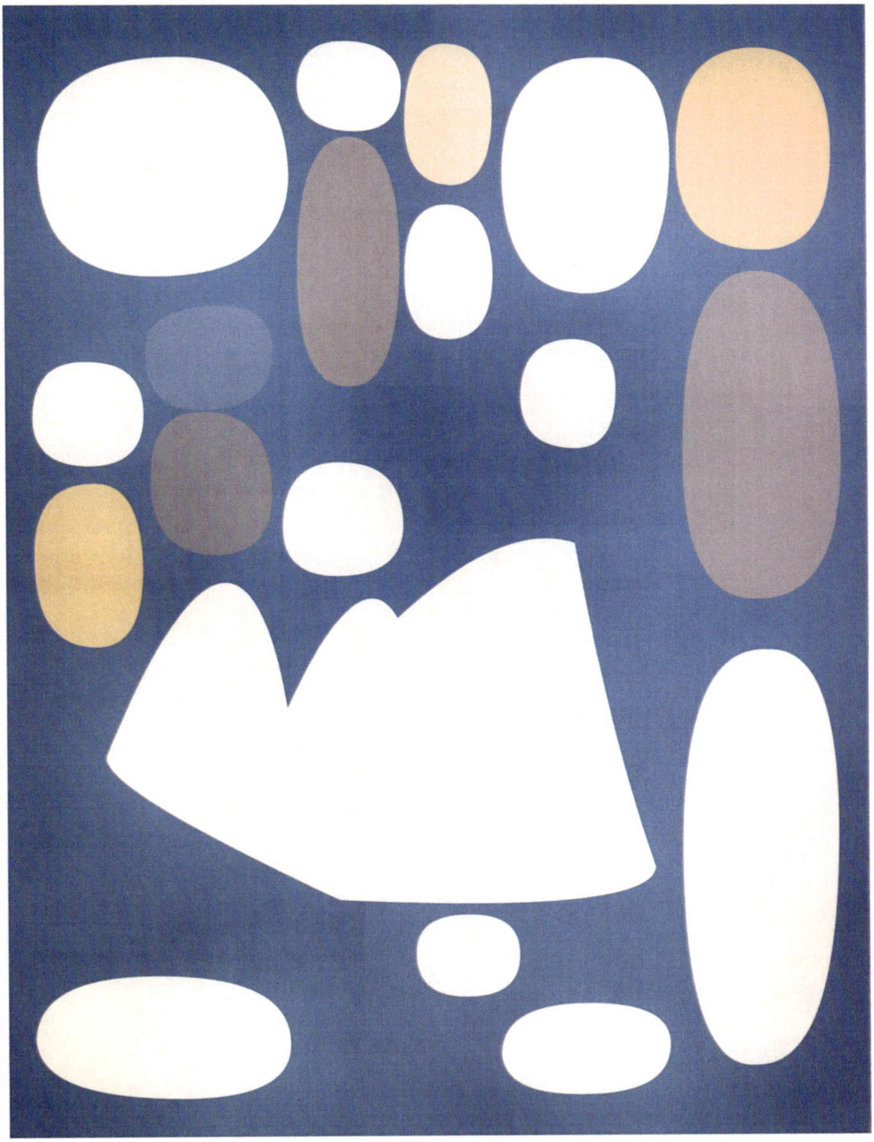

Pebble 986 'The Antidote' with Dusk Riverbed palette

Pebble #986 illustrates the crème, tan, grey, and a singular lighter blue Pebble present in the *Dusk Riverbed* palette. The tan and blue colors riff off each other beautifully.

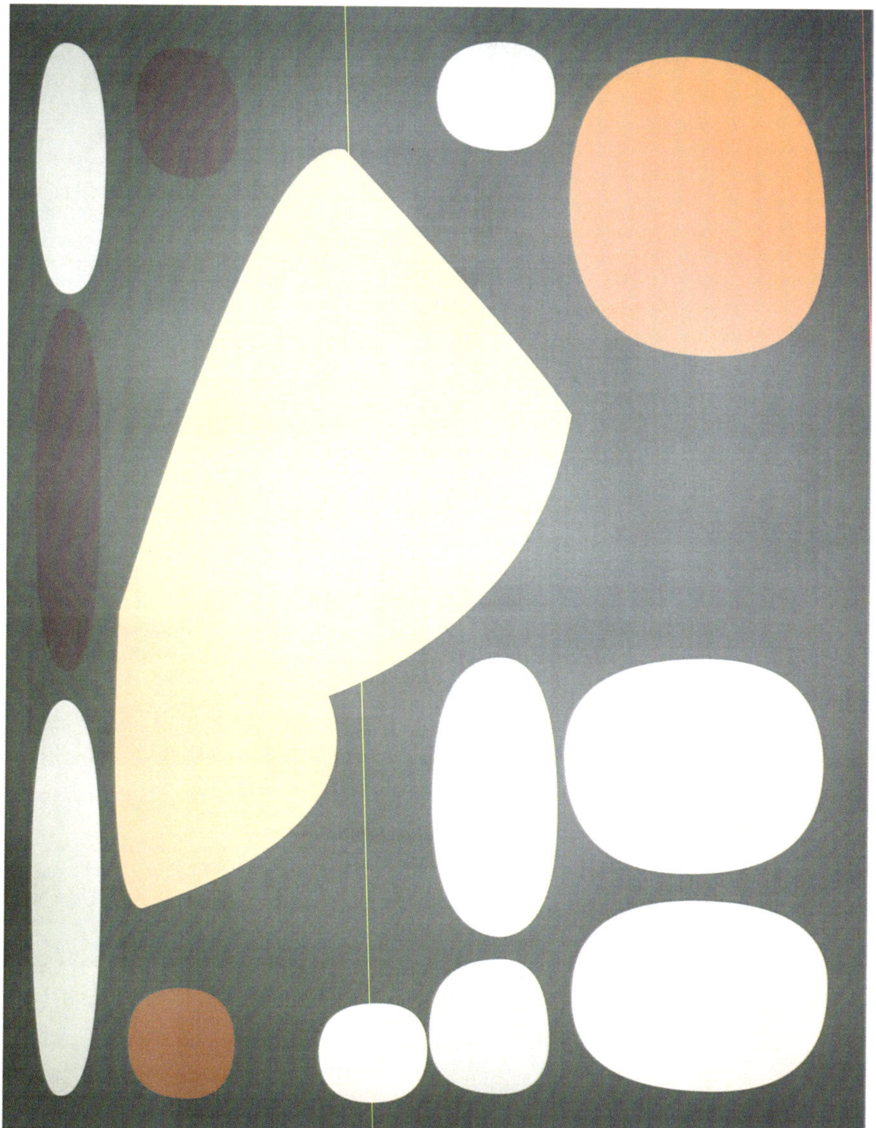

Pebble 457 'Woman with Orange Hat' with Forest Whisper palette

Pebble #457, 'Woman with Orange Hat,' shows the full range of colors in the *Forest Whisper* palette including orange, burnt umber, dark grey, light lime and an off-white. Complementary colors of yellow and green work well.

• • •

Artists strive for algorithmic diversity to create a range of interesting outputs, balanced with showing a degree of cohesion within the collection. The *Forest Whisper* and *Citrus Slate* palettes shows a good range of diversity while still holding together as a trait.

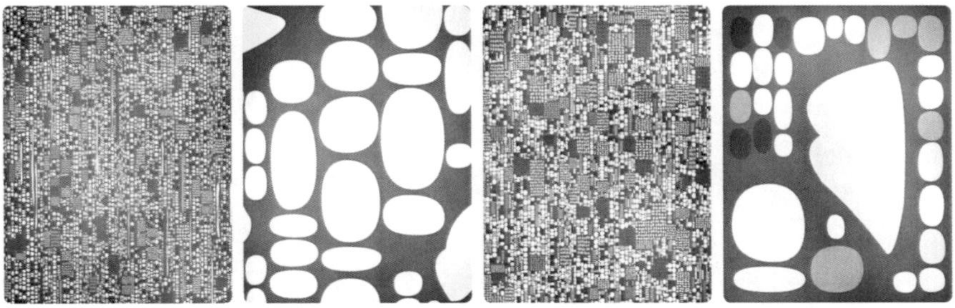

Shades of Hey palette

The *Shades of Hey!* palette doesn't rely on color to differentiate between artworks. The diversity relies on the traits that shape each Pebble alone. As a result, it can be difficult to distinguish one from another. While monochrome palettes tend to do well in art generally, some prefer a work that is easily conjured up in the mind's eye without having to view the art again.

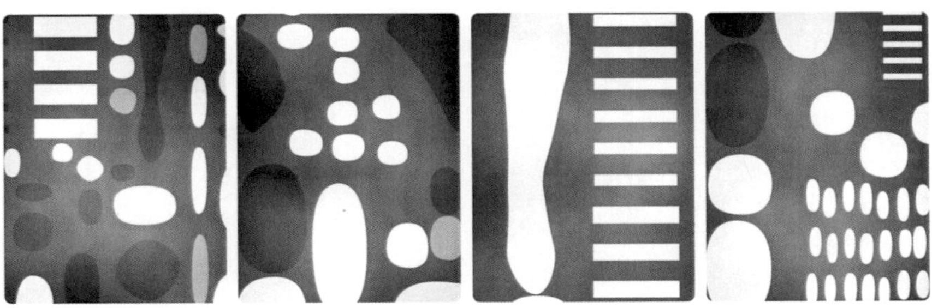

Shades of Hey palette

As a test, stare at the four *Shades of Hey!* above and then close your eyes. Try and visualize the differences between two of them in your mind.

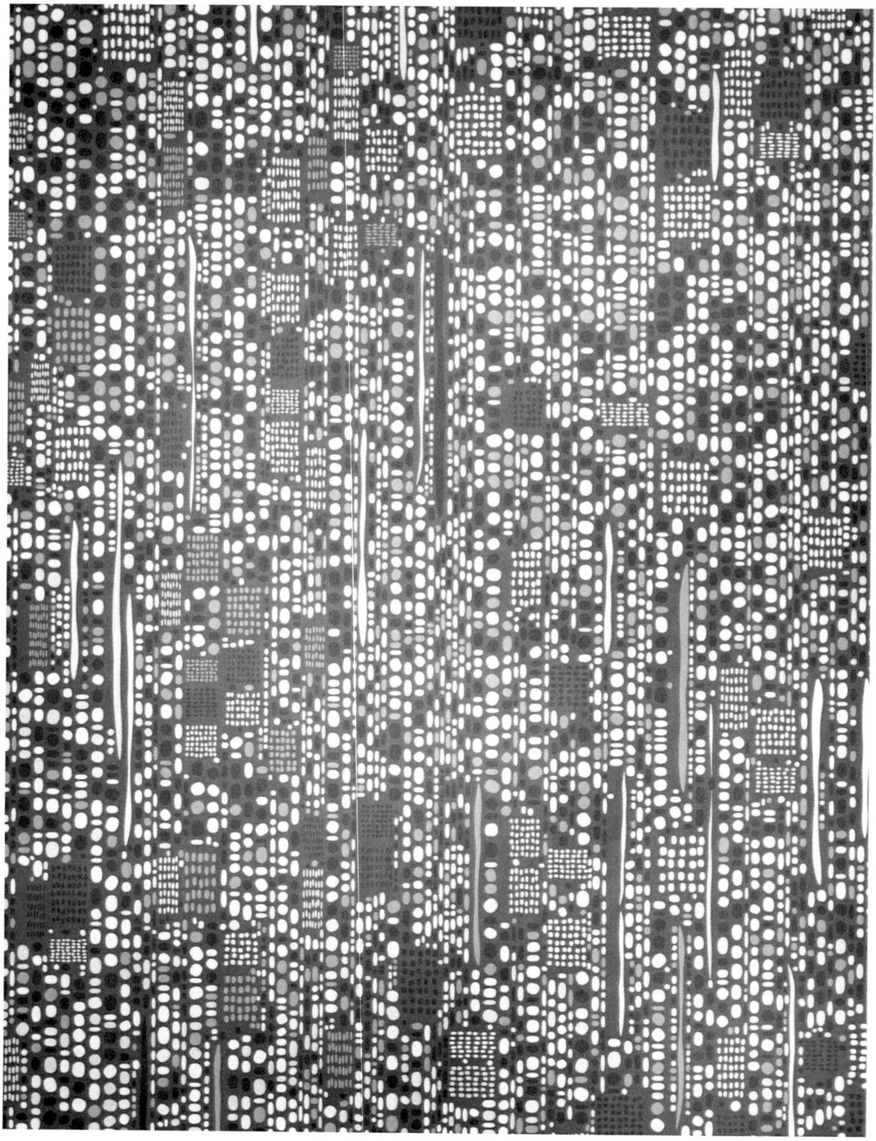

Pebble 34 with Shades of Hey! palette

Pebble #34 is one of 55 *Shades of Hey!* palettes. The constrained palette of greys directs the mind to enjoy the *Craglet* composition, as there are no pigments to rely upon.

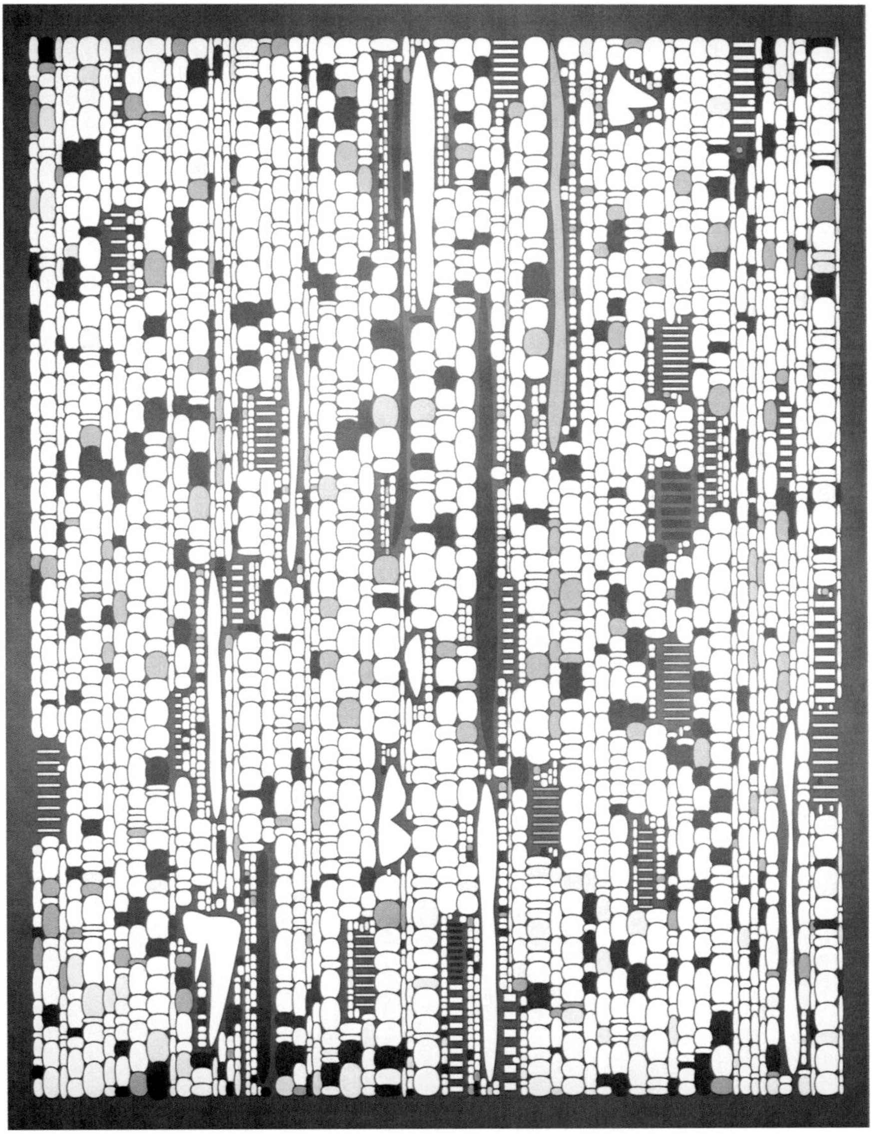

Pebble 617 with Shades of Hey! palette

Pebble #617 shows the variation present within *Shades of Hey!* by combining with a composition trait like *Fuse Overlap* and the framing trait *Edge Yes*. What a delightful Pebble.

. . .

Let's move on to the *Unigrids* palette, which holds special meaning because of its heritage. The *Unigrids* palette is a nod to another Zeblocks project by the same name, minted on Art Blocks Curated on January 27th, 2021.

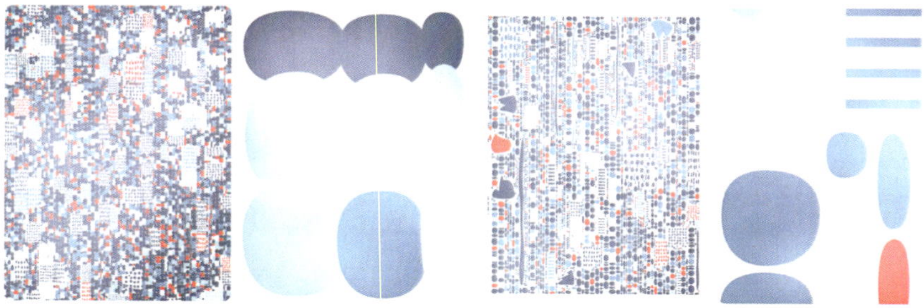

Unigrids palette

The original *Unigrids* project had 14 palettes whereas Pebbles has 20 palettes in total. Here is a selection of three artworks from the Unigrids art collection minted on the Art Blocks Curated smart contract.

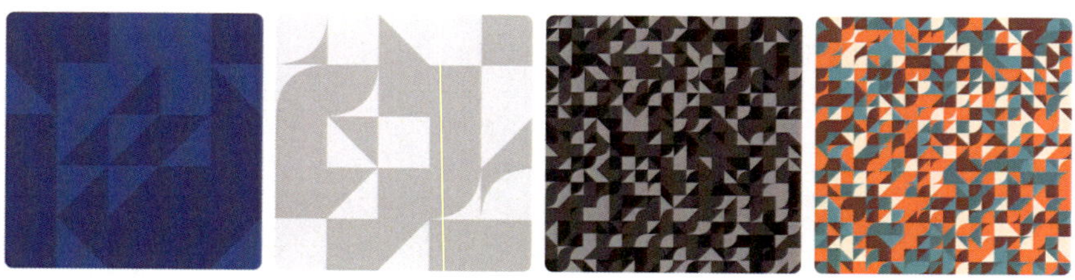

Unigrids by Zeblocks: 421 artworks minted Jan 27th 2021

You have already viewed over half the available palettes in the collection. There are more that haven't been covered, including seven of the rarest Pebbles palettes, which could only be minted by specific wallets that met certain characteristics set by Punk6529.

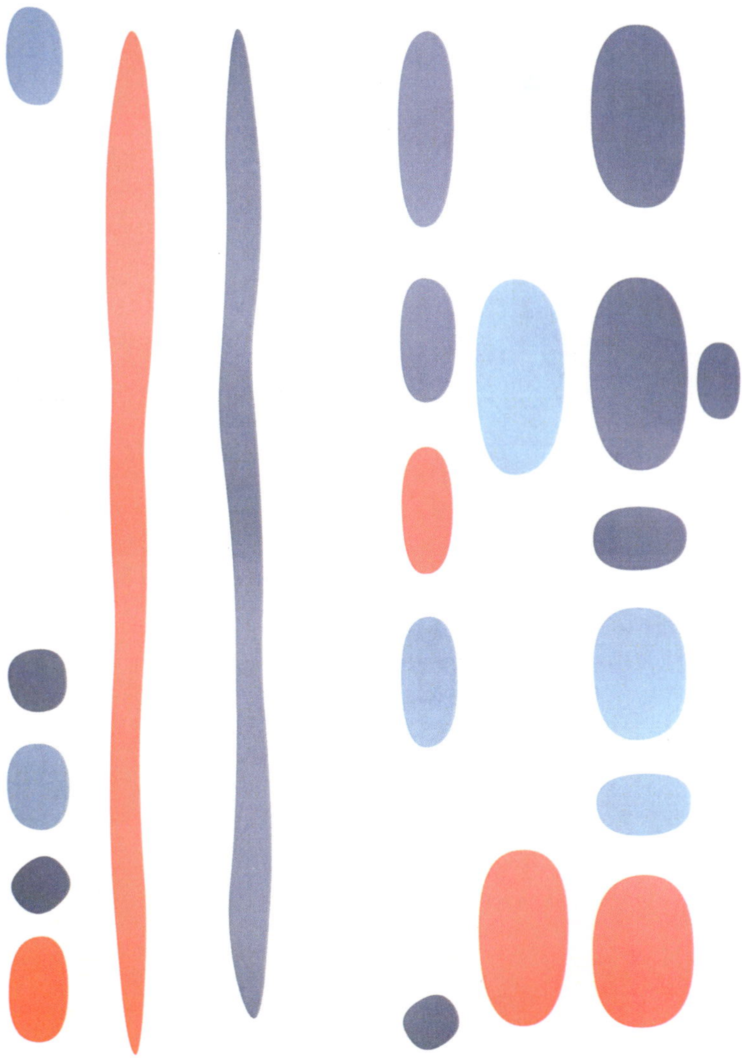

Pebble 906 with Unigrids palette

Pebble #906 is a good representation of the pinkish red, and three tone blue primary colors represented as the *Unigrids* color trait.

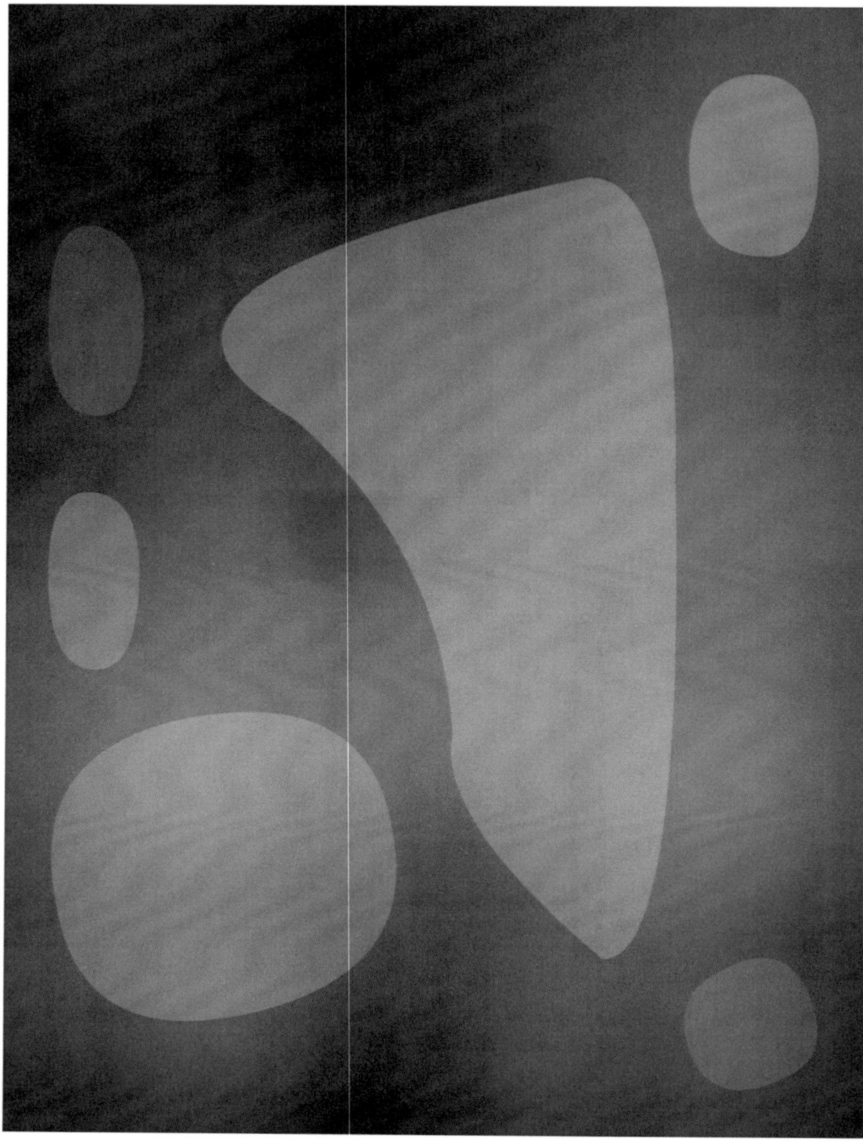

Pebble 126 with Lunar Chuckles palette

Pebble #126 is one of just five *Lunar Chuckles* palette Pebbles. The rarity allocation was preset before the mint to reward collectoors who had demonstrated a high level of commitment by minting and hodling memes or Gradients released to date.

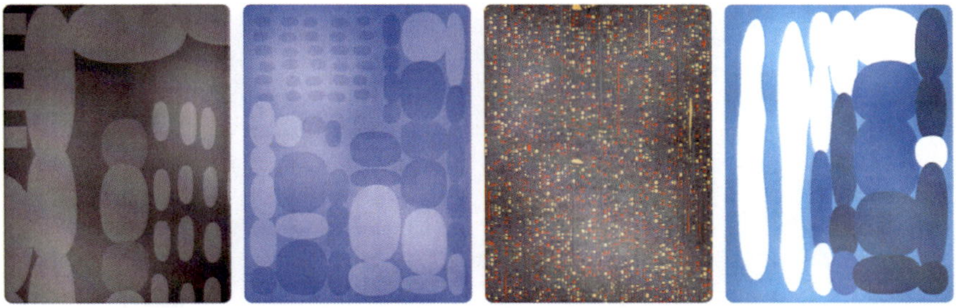

4 of the 7 Collectoor Provenance palettes (from left to right): 748 Lunar Chuckles, 82 Blueprint, 83 Magma Mambo, 96 Summer.jpeg

The Collectoor Provenance palettes rarely change hands for the same reasons these Pebble palettes were reserved, the ability to hodl previous artworks from the 6529 Collections. As such, they are difficult to acquire on the open market with fewer than ten Pebbles available from *summer.jpg, Lunar Chuckles and Magma Mambo* traits.

Summary

The two most consequential traits of *Size* and *Palette* across the collection are visual, ensuring first-time generative art collector can choose an artwork without the professional help of a dealer gallery. Find a *Palette* you love, with a configuration of Pebbles at a *Size* you like, and you are ready to select your Pebble.

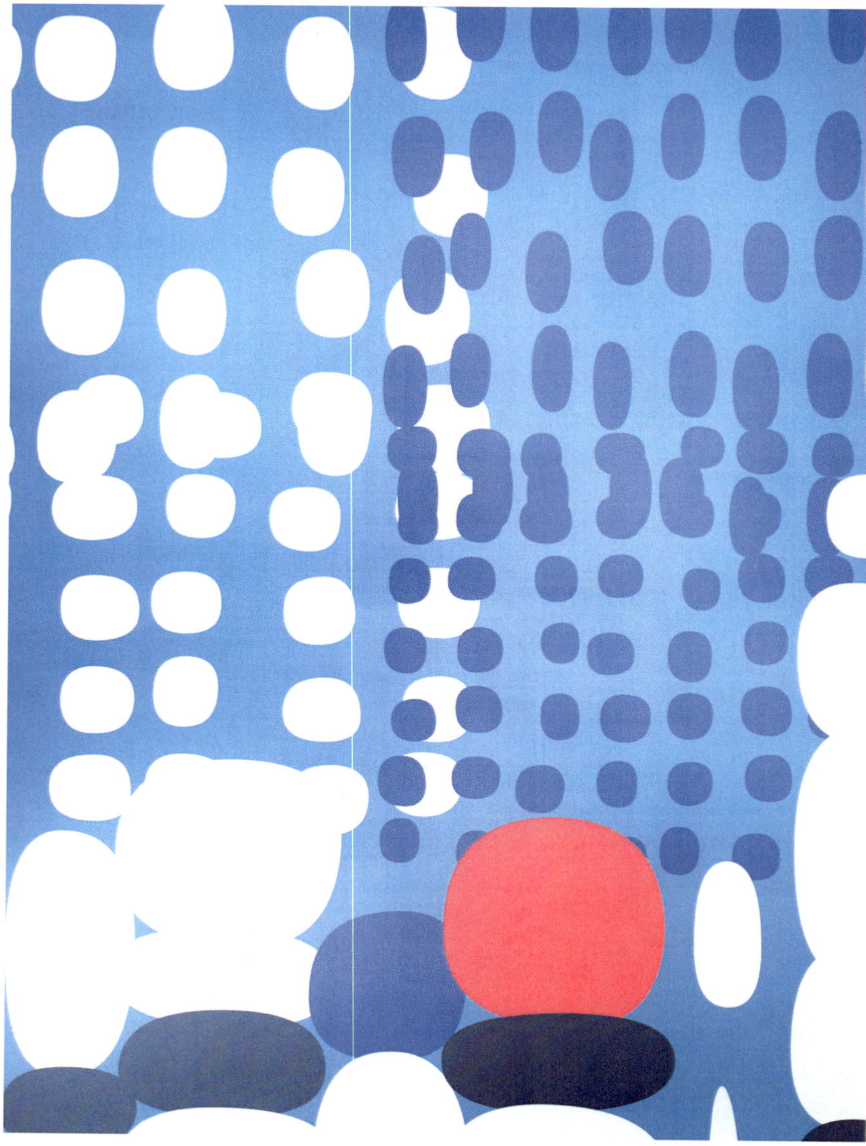

Pebble 120 with summer.jpg palette

Summer.jpg palette is a nod to the color choices made by XCOPY for his artwork summer.jpg minted in August 2021. The brighter palette represented a departure from the shadowy gloominess of colors XCOPY preferred up until that point.

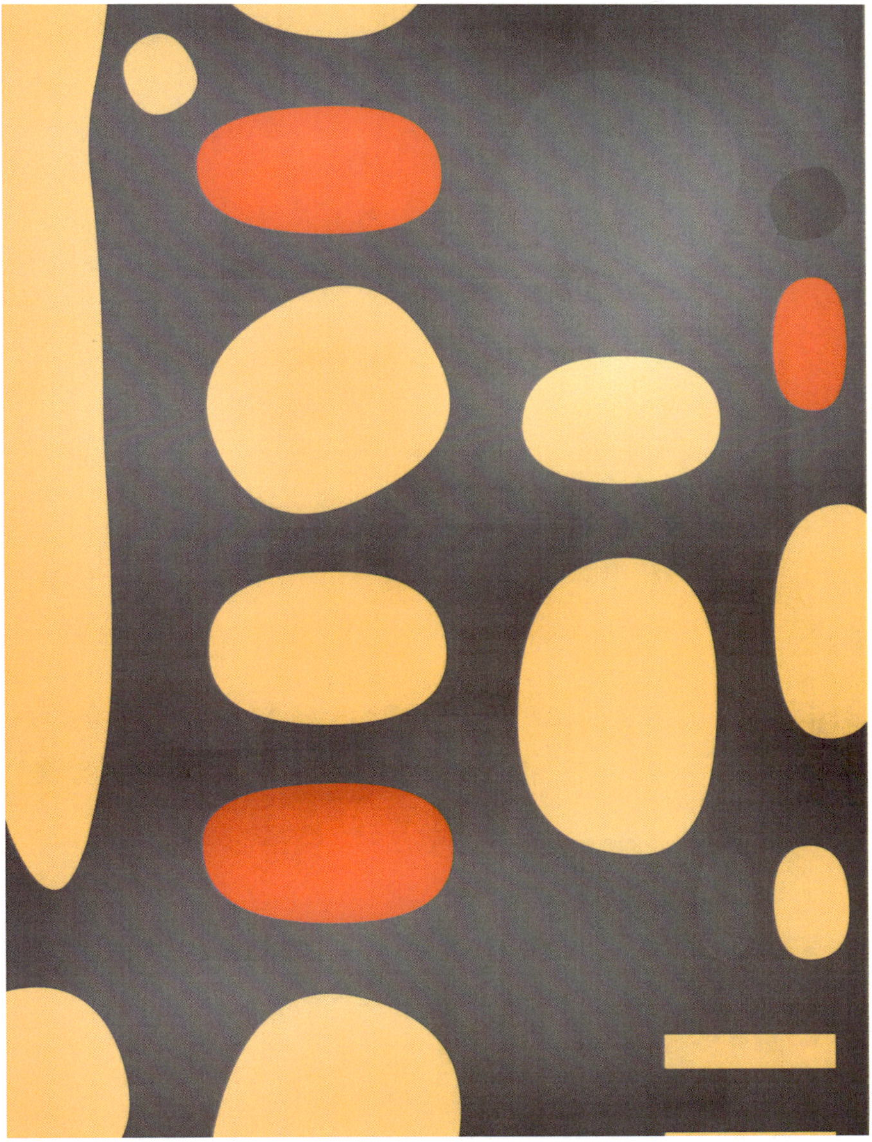

Pebble 1 with Magma Mambo palette

Pebble #1 marks the beginning of collectors minting. Striking contrasts of red, black, yellow and greys can be found in the *Magma Mambo* palette. Only five *Magma Mambo* exist in the collection, as it was reserved for a subset of collectoors.

PART II
INTERESTING TRAITS

TRACED

Beyond *Size* and *Palette* there are seven traits that Pebbles are endowed with. Some of these traits are merely a visual nudge such as *Edge*. Others, like *Mint Type*, there is no visually discernible difference in the artwork. In the following chapter we delve into the details of what each trait represents, how it presents visually and what the trait adds to the Pebble aesthetic.

Within each trait, there are also multiple variants. We explore these variants at length, how they interplay with well-known traits like *Size* and *Palette* and give collectoor-supplied specimens for you to study. While rarity is touched upon, the primary goal in the *Interesting Traits* chapter is for you to be able to identify the trait and variant visually without needing to reference the trait list. Let's get started.

No Fill

There are three variants of the *Traced* trait.

- No Fill (45)
- Border (97)
- No Border (858)

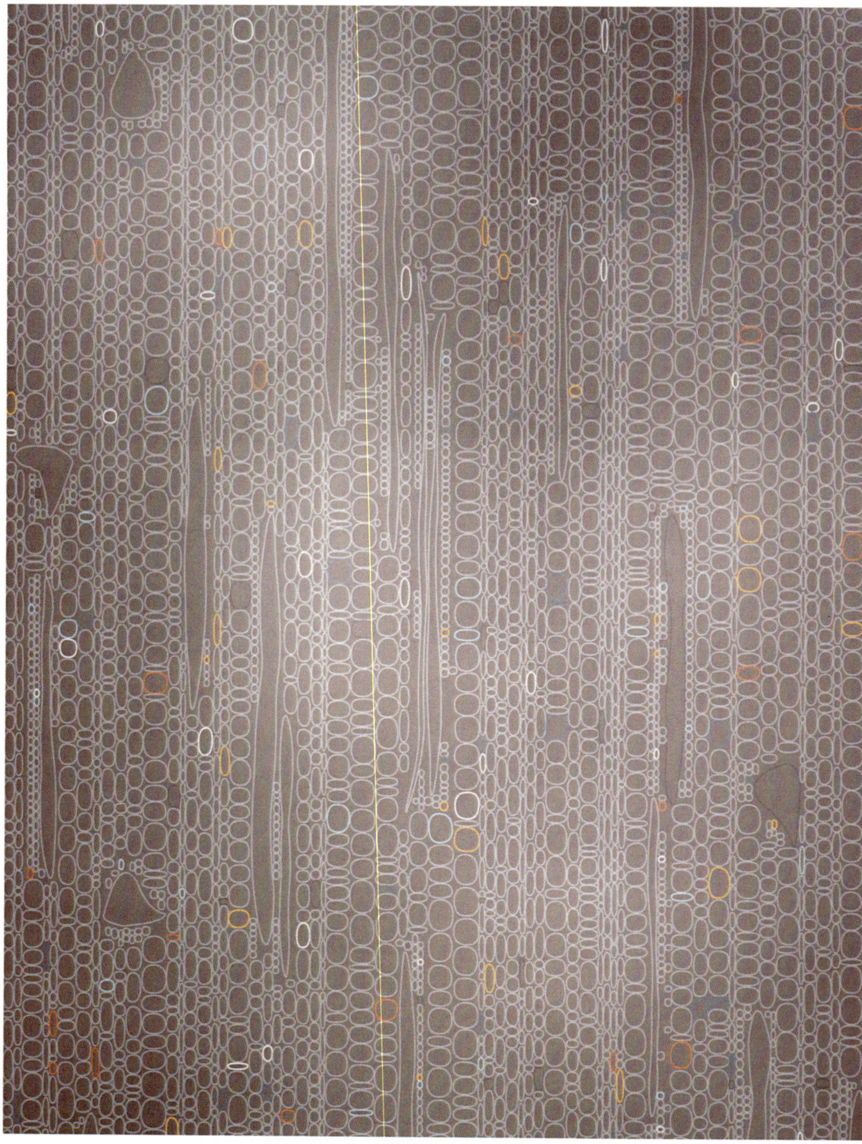

Pebble 239 with No Fill in Boulderette size and Galactic Latte palette

No Fill delivers a stunningly delicate Pebble across almost all of the *Palette* and *Size* permutations. The *No Fill* of Pebble #239 brings the earthy tones of the *Galactic Latte* forward, and shimmers with *Harmonize Overlap* spacing. Zoom in to see the smallest of *Boulderette* Pebbles, tightly linked in a chain around the stick-like *Special Elements.*

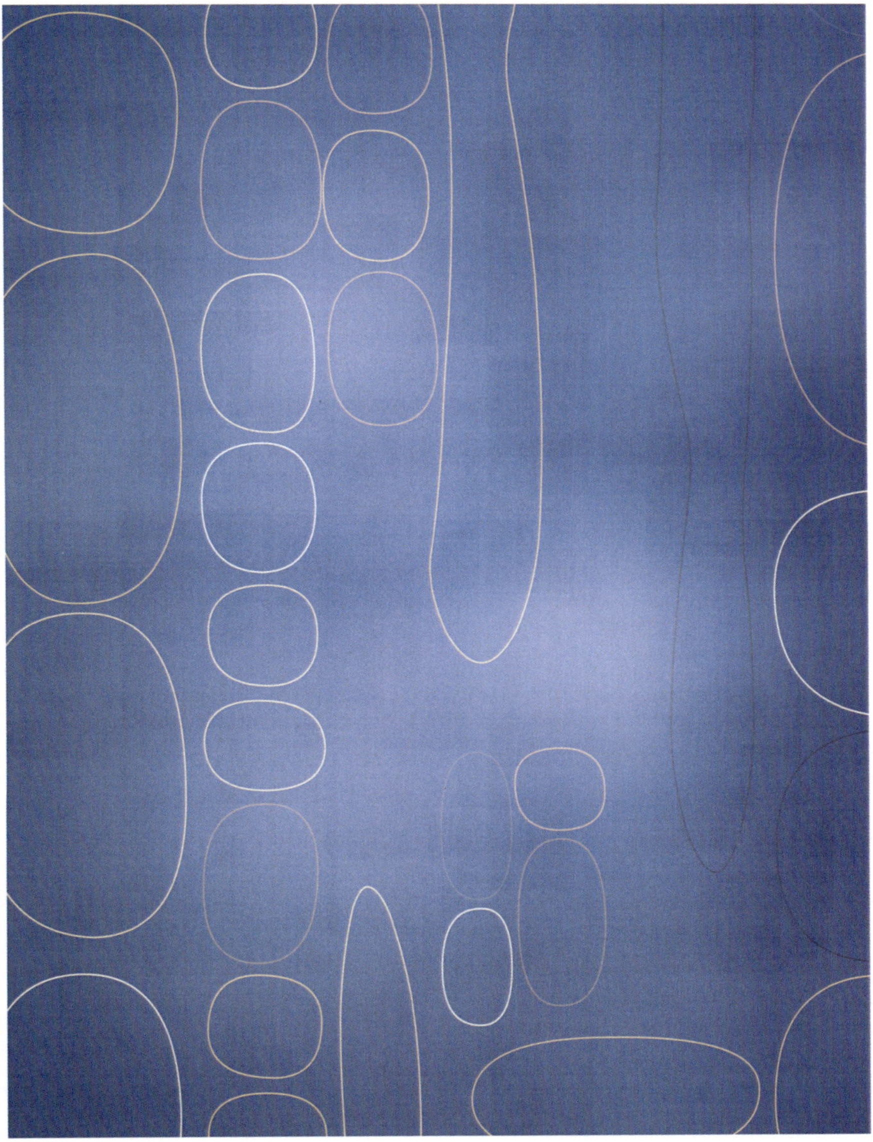

Pebble 624 with No Fill in a Stonelet size and Dusk Riverbed palette

Pebble #624 is an example of how the *No Fill* presents in a large *Stonelet*-style Pebble. *Dusk Riverbed* provides the Prussian blue background atop which the *No Fill* Pebbles are displayed. The primary feature of *No Fill* is to give the background color pre-eminence.

. . .

No Fill Across Pebble Sizes

Smaller-sized Pebbles are coveted by some collectoors, so let's explore *No Fill* Pebbles in the smaller *Crumb, Craglet* and *Boulderette Size* variants.

No Fill with Crumb

There are 45 *No Fill* Pebbles, and 72 *Crumb Size* Pebbles, and Pebble #271 is the only *No Fill* with *Crumb Size*. Minting these rare x rare trait overlaps is a joy.

No Fill with Craglet

There are five *Craglet* size with *No Fill* numbered #449, #585, #688, #802 and #835 with the highest secondary sale price of 10 ETH attained when 6529 Museum acquired #688 (shown below on left).

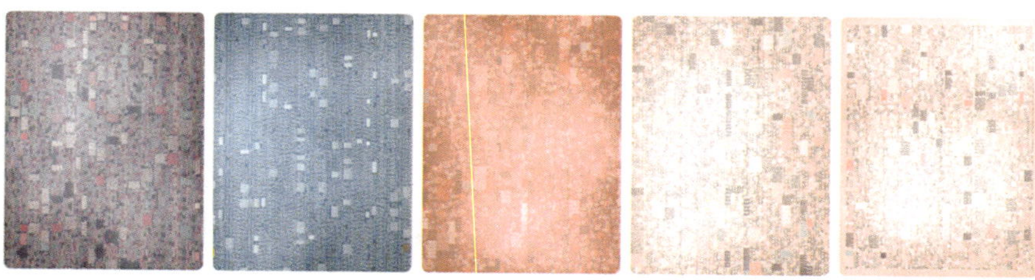

Craglet Pebbles with No Fill trait

No Fill with Boulderette

There are also five *Boulderette* size with *No Fill*, numbered #239, #338, #358, #675 and #736. None are currently listed.

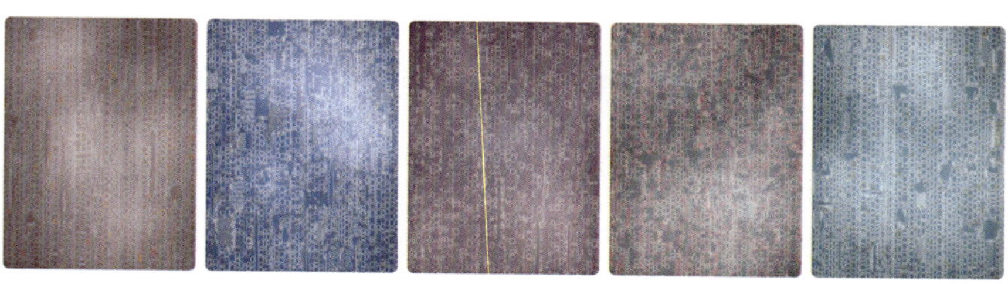

Boulderette Pebbles with No Fill trait

Pebble 271 'SmokeShow' with No Fill in a Crumb Size with Serenity palette

'SmokeShow' was minted by Suffermore.eth. The *Special Elements* in white are barely visible, providing a sense of great depth to the work. Given the diamond hands of the collectoor, 'SmokeShow' is unlikely to come on the market anytime soon.

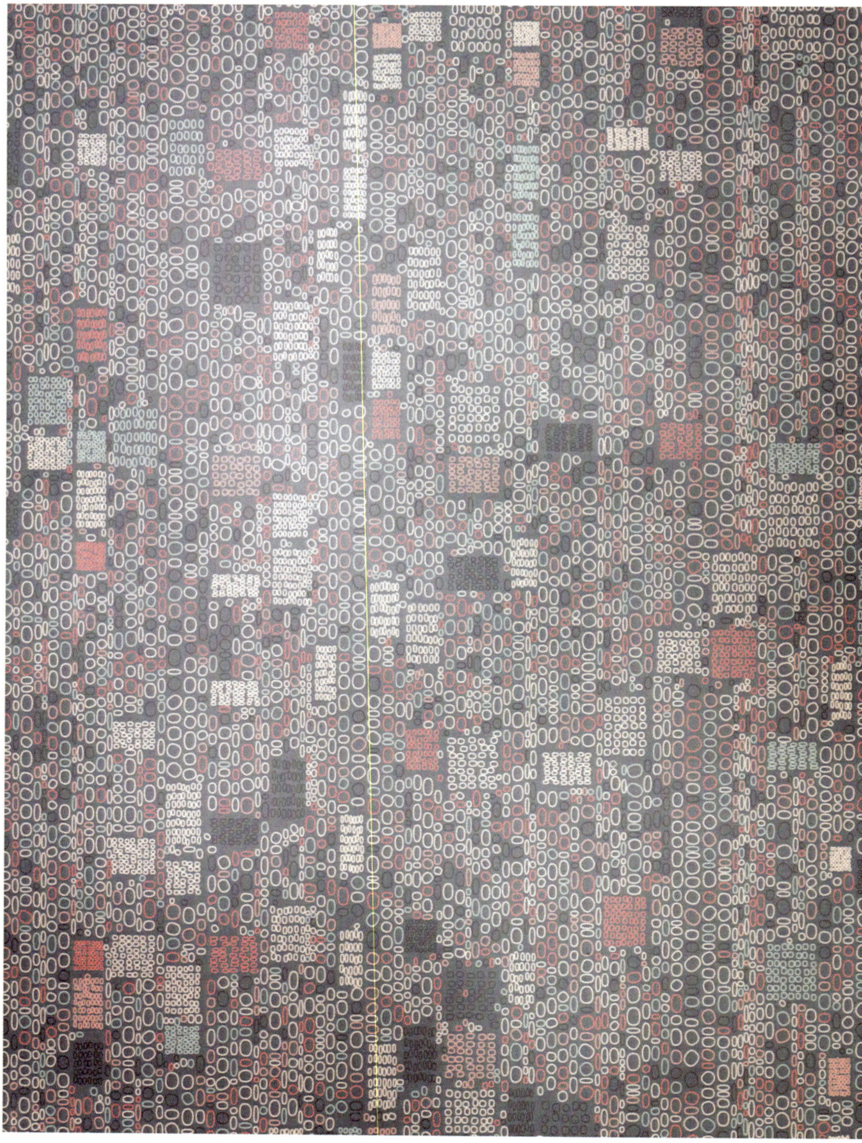

Pebble 688 with No Fill and Craglet size in a Coral Reef palette

Pebble #688 showcases the *No Fill* trait heroically, with many hundreds of Pebbles appearing in a bubble-like form. *Disjoin* trait keeps each ellipse separate from the others and *Bloom* Color Density lightens the intensity a couple of notches. We like #688, and so does 6529Museum.

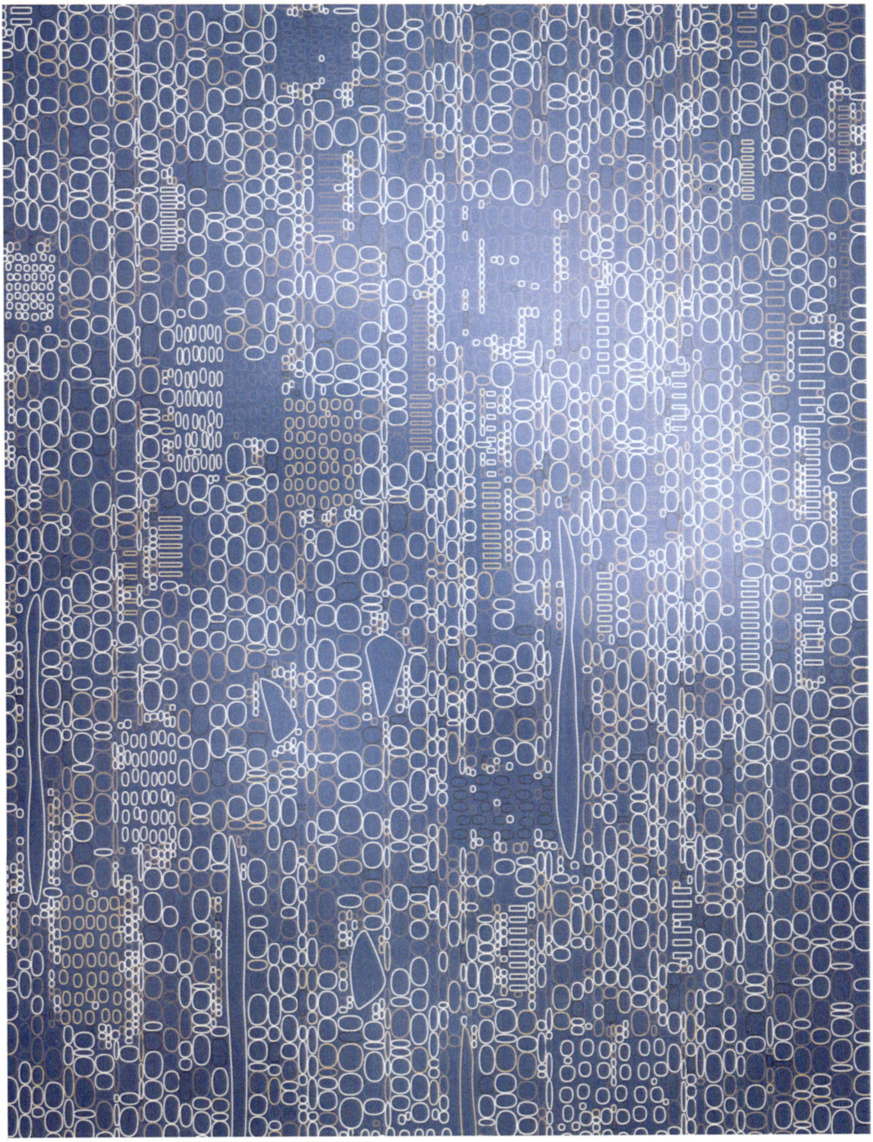

Pebble 358 with No Fill and Boulderette size in a Dusk Riverbed palette

Pebble #358 is a beautiful rarity with *No Fill* exemplified in the *Dusk Riverbed* palette. All *Special Elements* are present so search for those sharpened Pebbles, the stick-like blobs, and the ladder-like structures.

Border

There are 97 Pebbles with the *Border* variant of the *Traced* trait. The *Border* variant adds a thick line around each of the Pebbles and special features on the art. At a glance, the *Border* variant is usually not noticeable, until you enlarge or zoom in on the work.

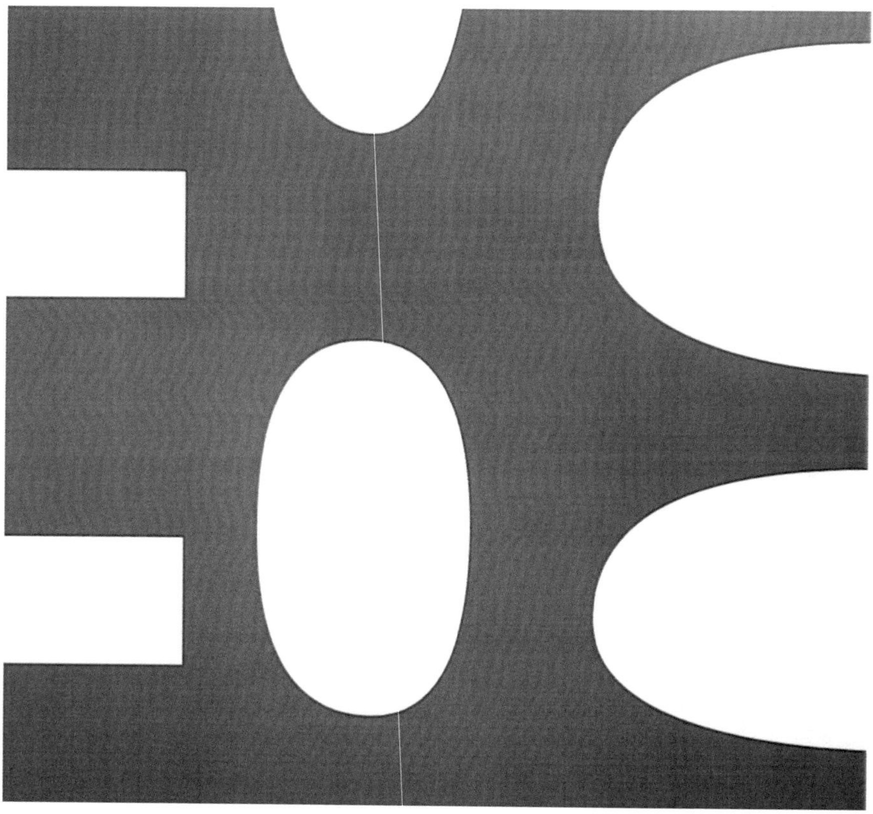

Pebble 107 showing a Border around the Pebbles zoomed in

Zoomed-in part of Pebble #107 shows a dark outline around the Pebbles. On some Pebble palettes such as *Unigrid*, the *Border* trait highlights white on white Pebbles, giving a *No Fill*-like quality to the work.

Pebble 183 with Border

The *Border* trait is clearest on the white and aqua-colored Pebbles in #183. Aqua-colored *Borders* around the dark blue Pebbles are less obvious, and white *Border* on the aqua Pebbles is not visible at all.

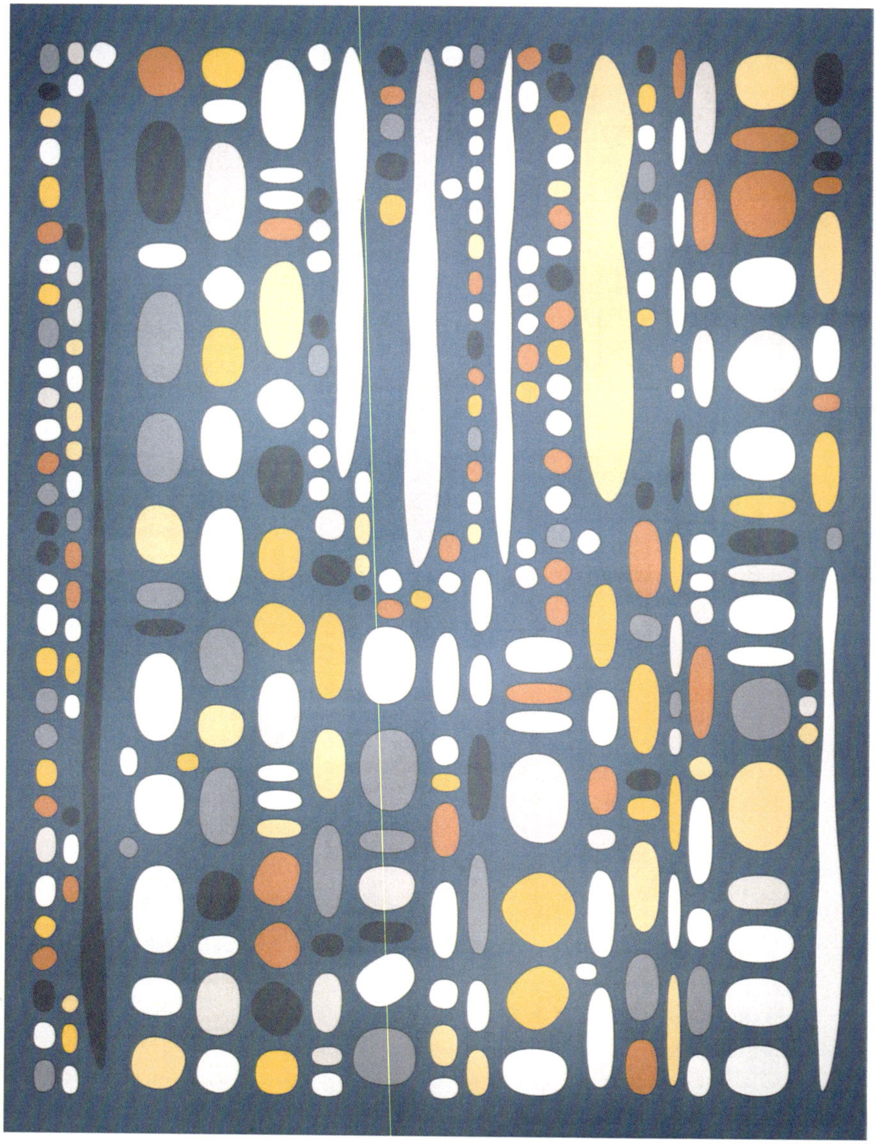

Pebble 467 with Border

The *Border* variant is obvious on Pebble #467. Every Pebble and *Special Element* is traced with a thin line that separates the background from the Pebbles.

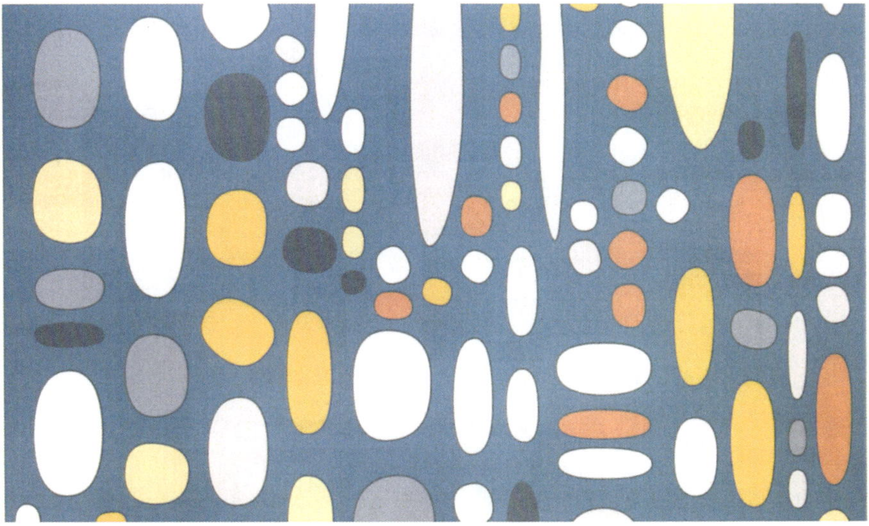

Close up of Pebble 467 showing the Border around each Pebble

No Border

The remaining *Traced* trait Pebbles are the *No Border* variant. These Pebbles do not encapsulate each Pebble with a thick border. There are 858 Pebbles with *No Border*. For the minimalists, *No Border* is preferable to *Border*. For the rarity chasers, the inverse is true.

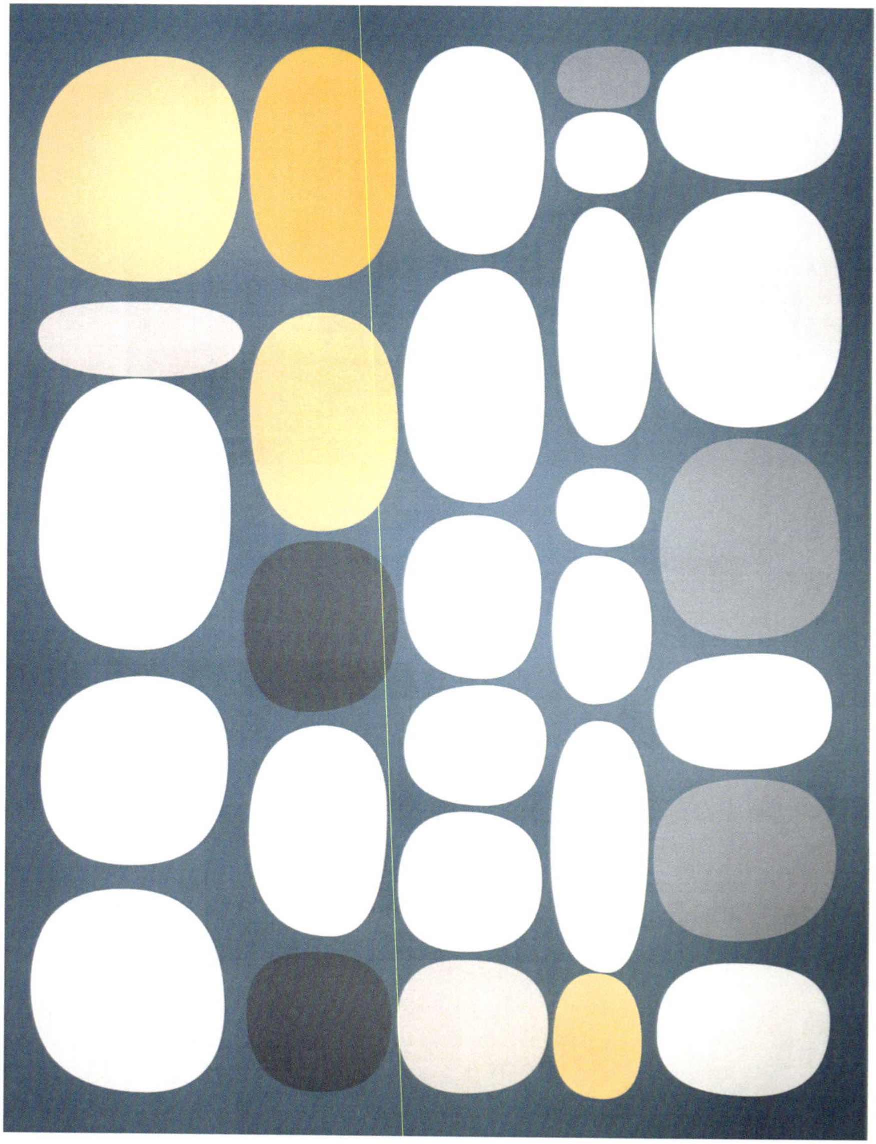

Pebble 997 with No Border

Pebble #997 shows *No Border* around each of the *Pebbit*-sized Pebbles. There are also *No Special Elements* present. The combination of these two traits delivers a minimalist, clean Pebble sought by discerning collectors.

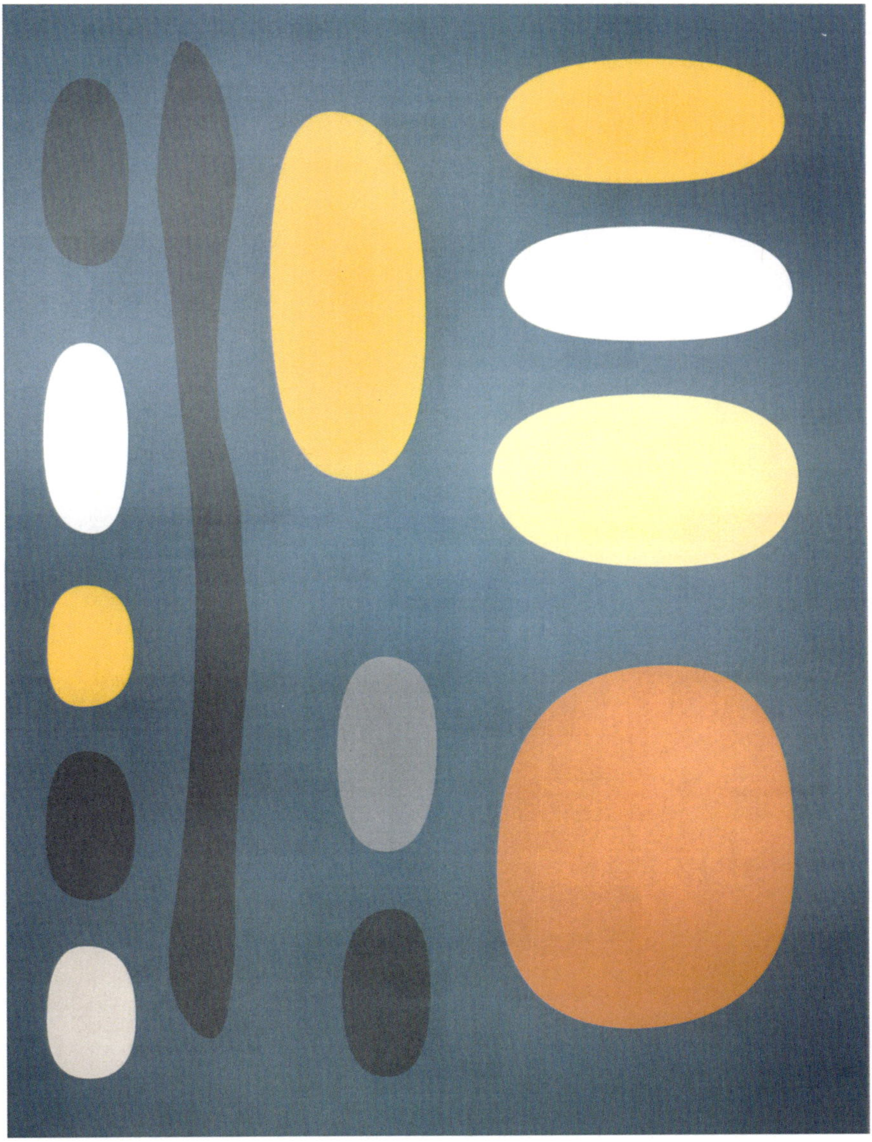

Pebble 687 'Riverside' with No Border

"Riverside is special for the slight bend in the 'stick' created from the rarely seen *Flow* trait." Stardust

Pebble 141 with No Border

A solitary figure turns their head upwards, praying for crypto redemption. A *Disjoin Overlap* affords the distance to imagine the scene, and the predominance of white Pebbles fades into the background with *Bloom Color Density*. Where the unimagined shows up in art is often not by coincidence.

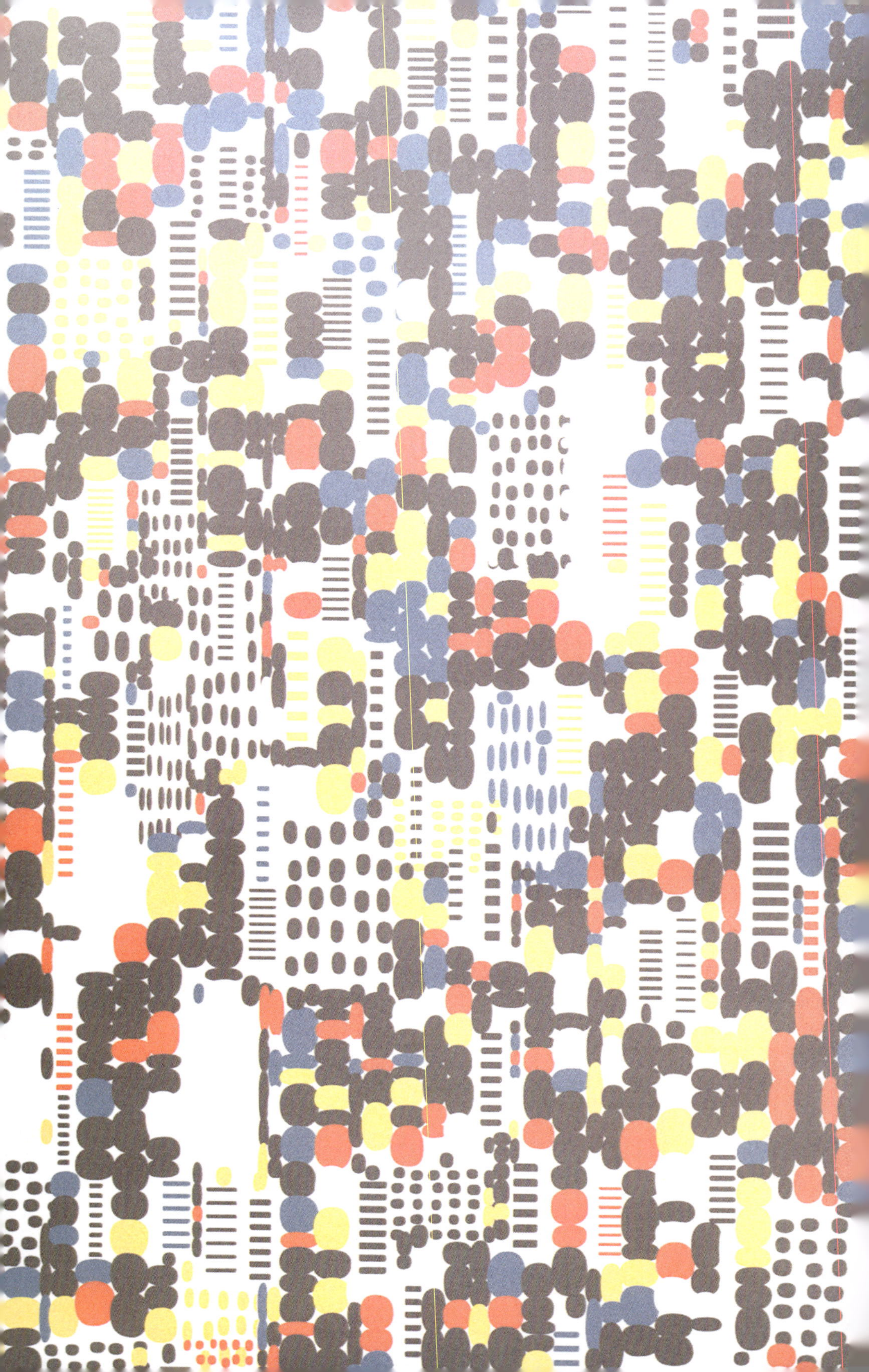

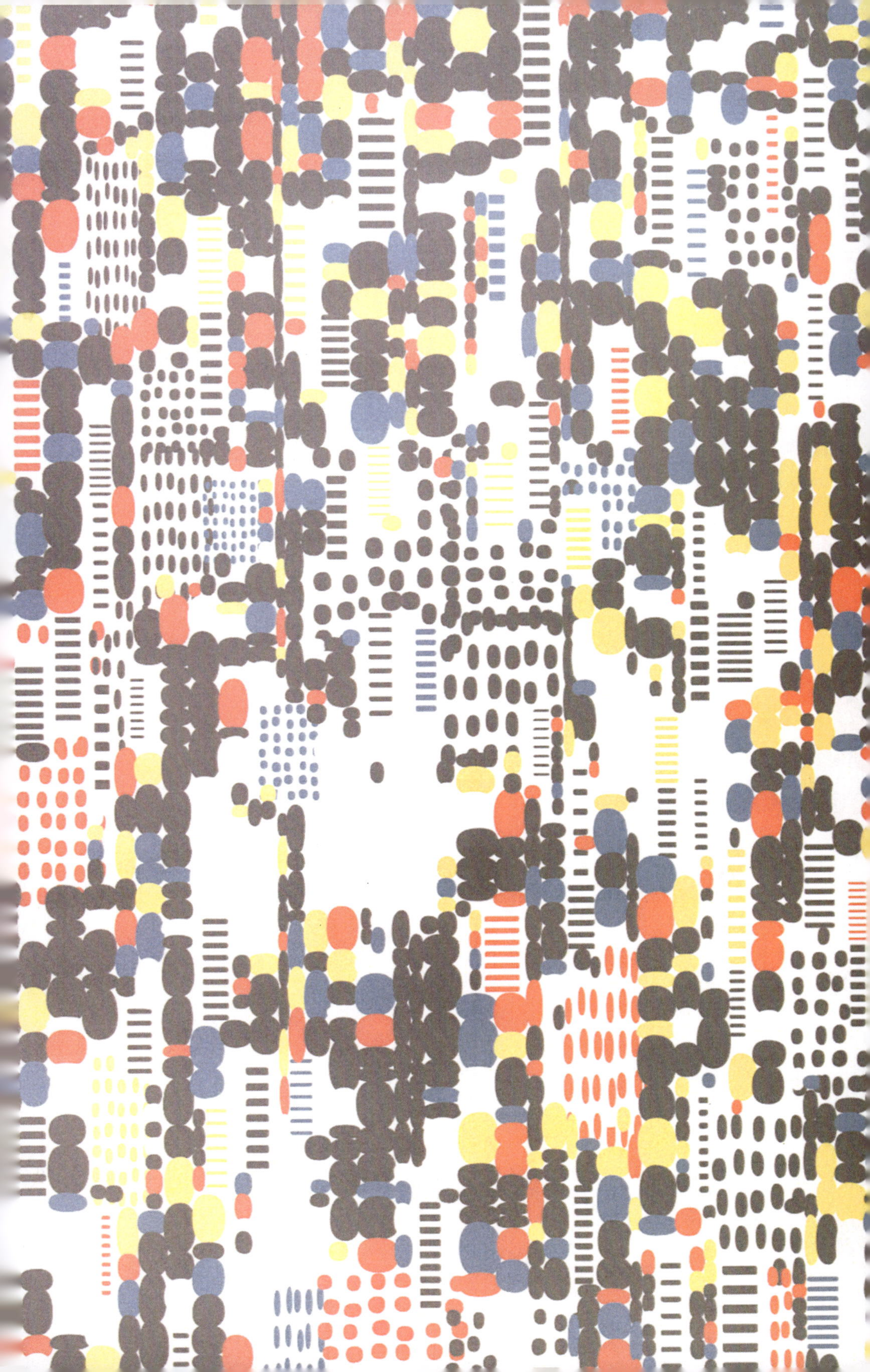

SPECIAL ELEMENTS

No Special Elements

In some artworks there are *Special Elements* that are not Pebbles. To appreciate Pebbles with *Special Elements,* we must first begin with the most special of Pebbles: the 55 Pebbles with no *Special Elements* at all. In an ironic twist of fate that proves Elon Musk's saying, 'the most entertaining outcome is the most likely,' the rarest *Special Element* Pebbles have no *Special Elements* at all.

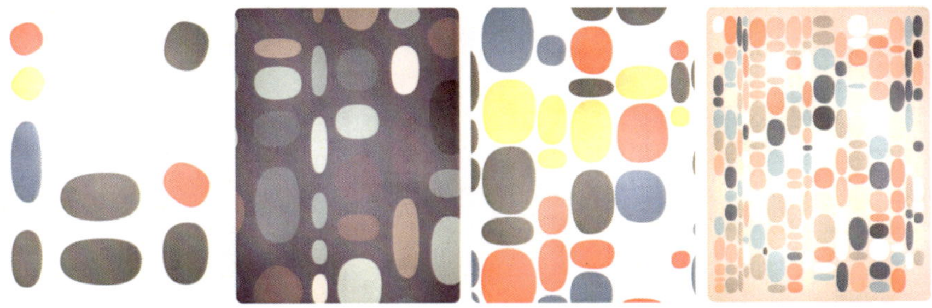

No Special Element Pebbles 443, 816, 904 and 9

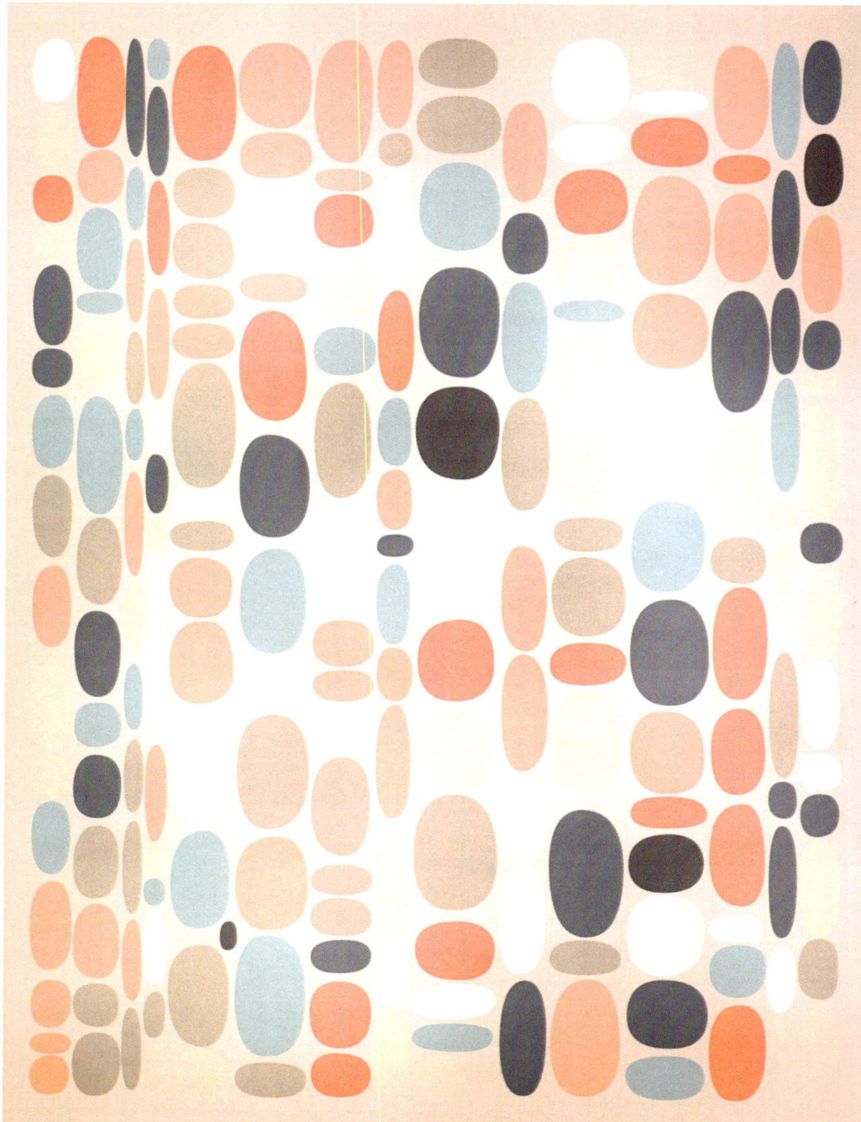

Pebble 9 with No Special Elements

Pebble #9 is the first ever *No Special Elements* Pebble minted. There is an obvious purity and simplicity at the heart of Pebble #9, aided by a *Drench Color Density* and a *Harmonize Overlap* layout.

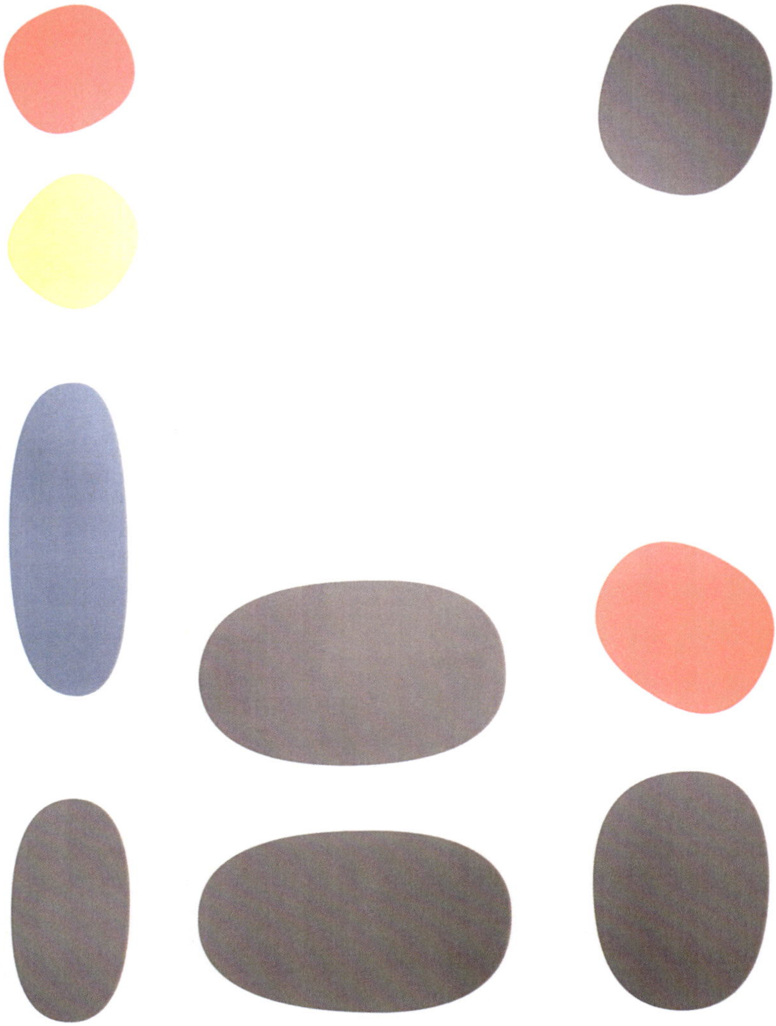

Pebble 443 'The Mondrian' with No Special Elements

'The Mondrian' adorns the front cover of the Pebbles book. It represents the purest language of Pebbles, evoking a direct, unmediated aesthetic experience. 'The Mondrian' challenges viewers to ask 'how can so much be felt, from so few shapes?'

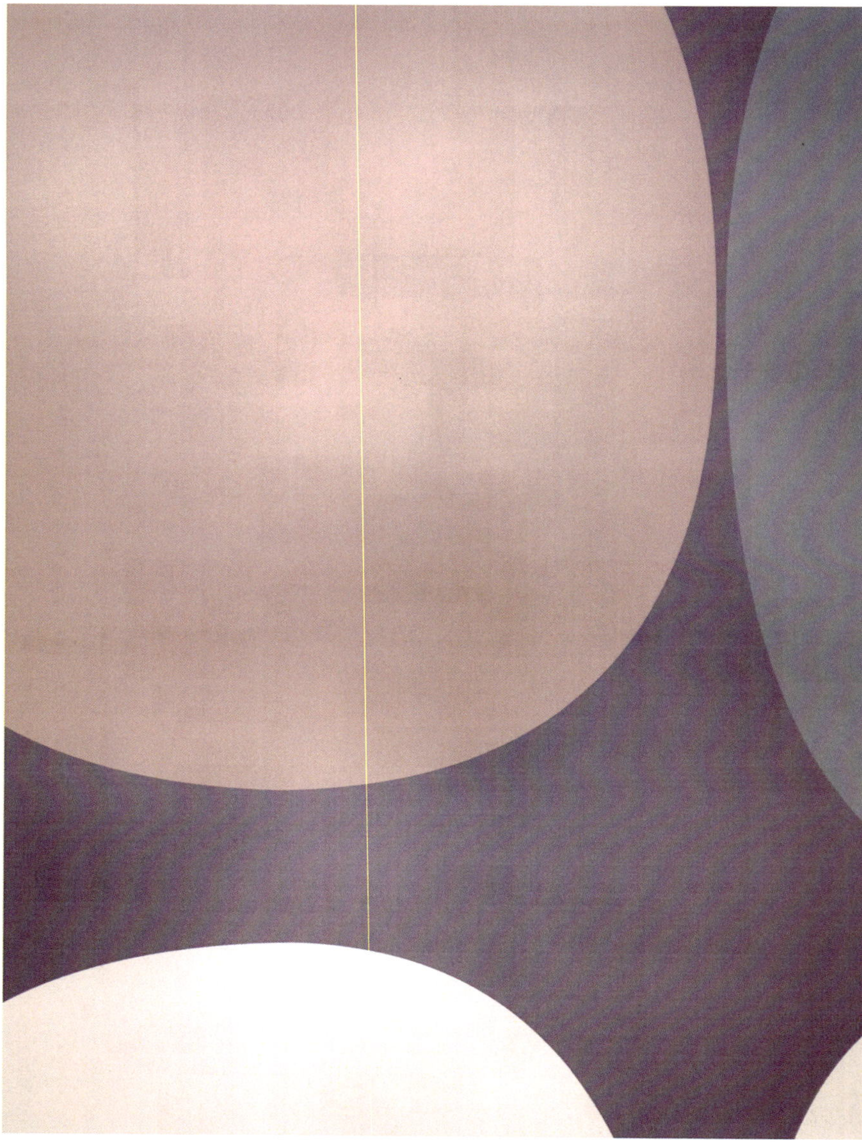

Pebble 792 with No Special Elements

The *Mountlet* size of Pebble #792 extends beyond the *Edge,* giving it a strength that generative art collectoors may recognize from the *Bold* Chromie Squiggle trait. *No Special Elements* lets us enjoy this Pebble in its simplest form with no distractions.

Special Elements

Pebbles with *Special Elements* have shapes that do not resemble Pebbles. The *Special Elements* variants count the number present in each artwork:

- None (55)
- One (150)
- Two (291)
- Three (427)
- All (77)

There are four *Special Elements* that may appear in an artwork:

- Sticks
- Random Shapes
- Grids
- Ladders

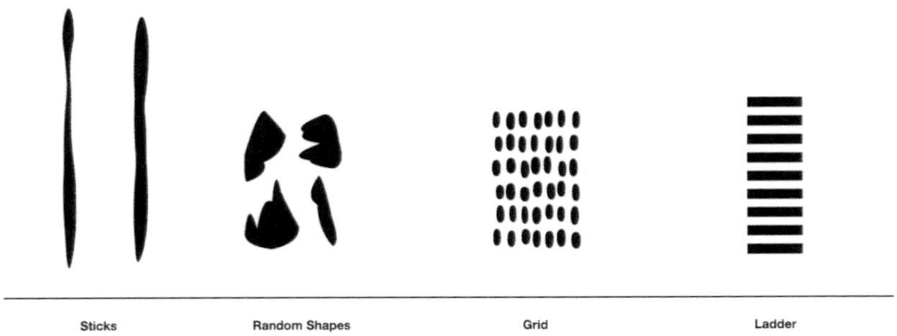

The four Special Elements

Sticks have a long history in humanity. Message sticks are believed to be thousands of years old and were typically carried by messengers over long distances to reinforce oral histories.

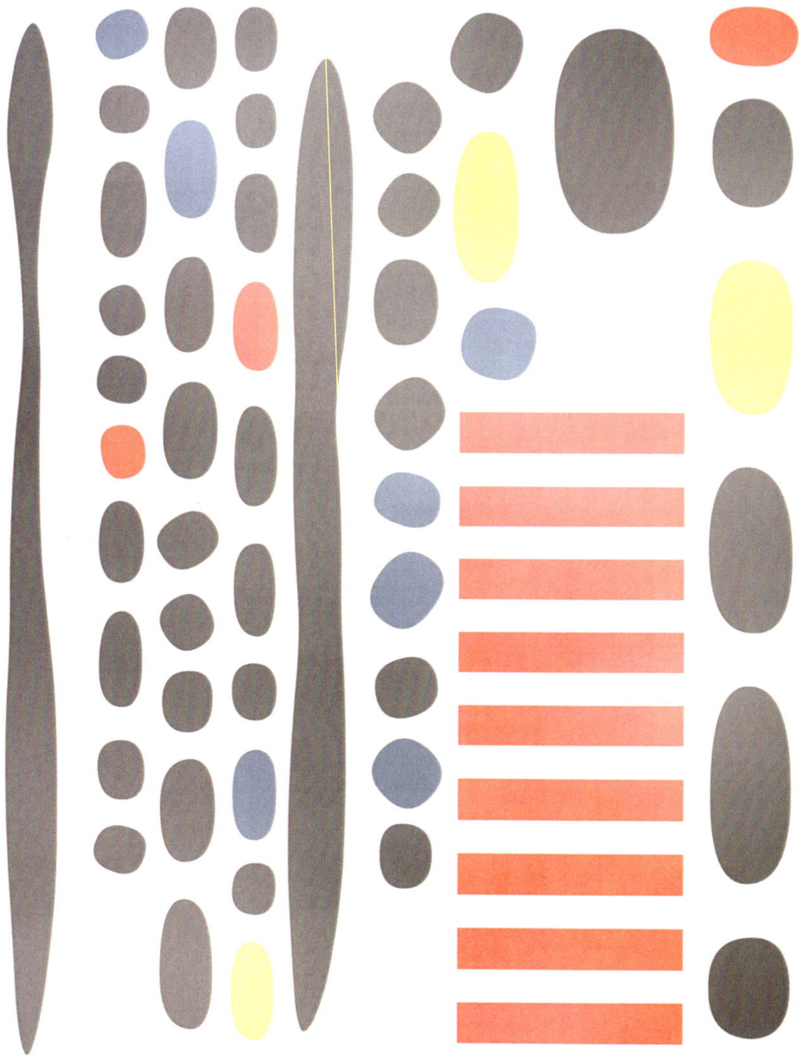

Pebble 23 'Indigenous Journeys' with stick Special Element

Sticks

'Indigenous Journeys' shows two sticks that could be interpreted as a blockchain-native form of message sticks. The ladder pathway on the right is a symbolic representation of a long journey.

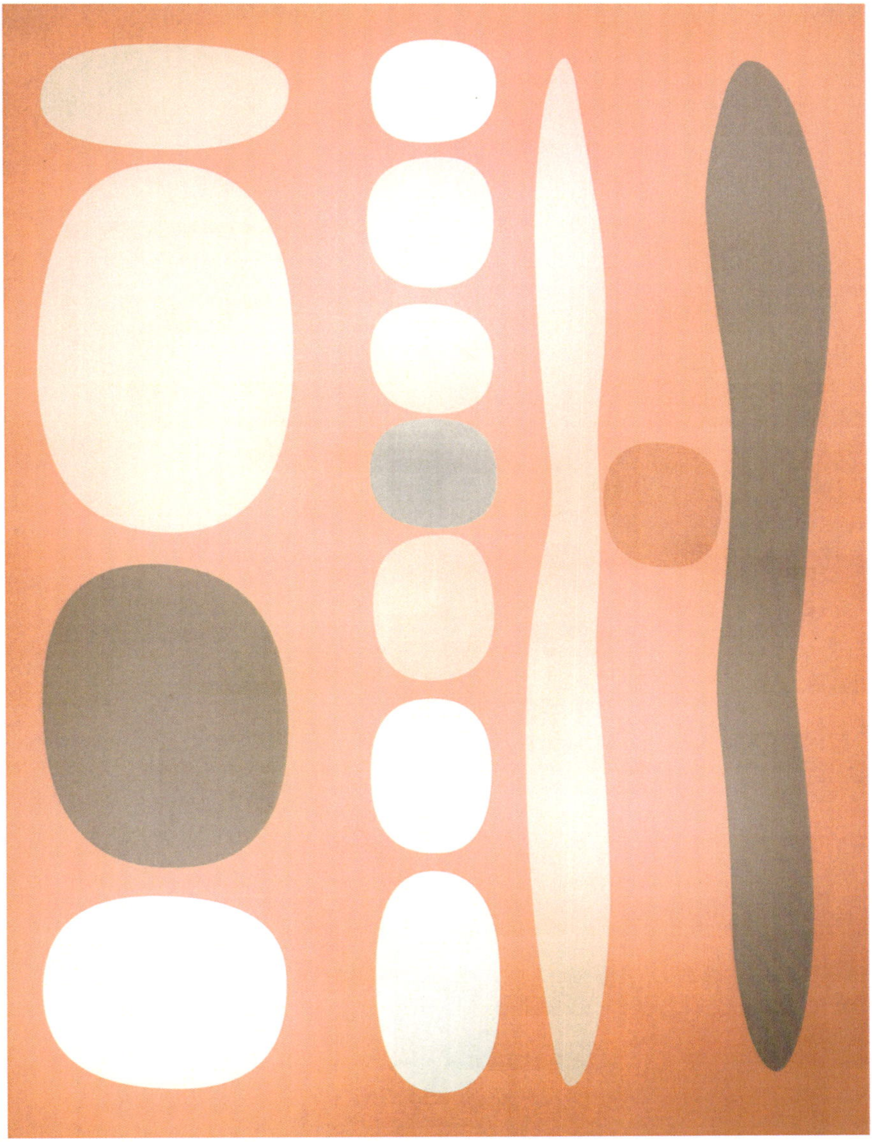

Pebble 220 with stick Special Element

Sticks

Pebble #220 includes a *Special Element* pair of sticks on the right-hand side the artwork.

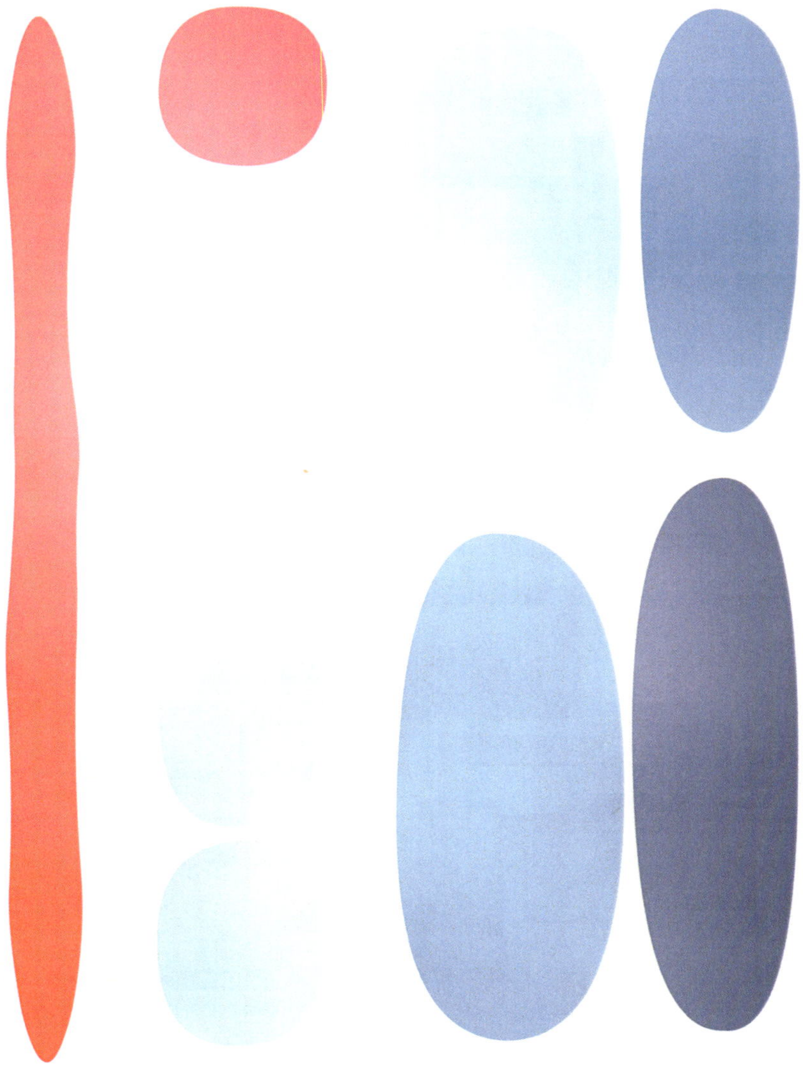

Pebble 851 with stick Special Element

Sticks

Pebble #851 shows the *Special Element* sticks; however, it is difficult to make out what the second or third *Special Element* may be here.

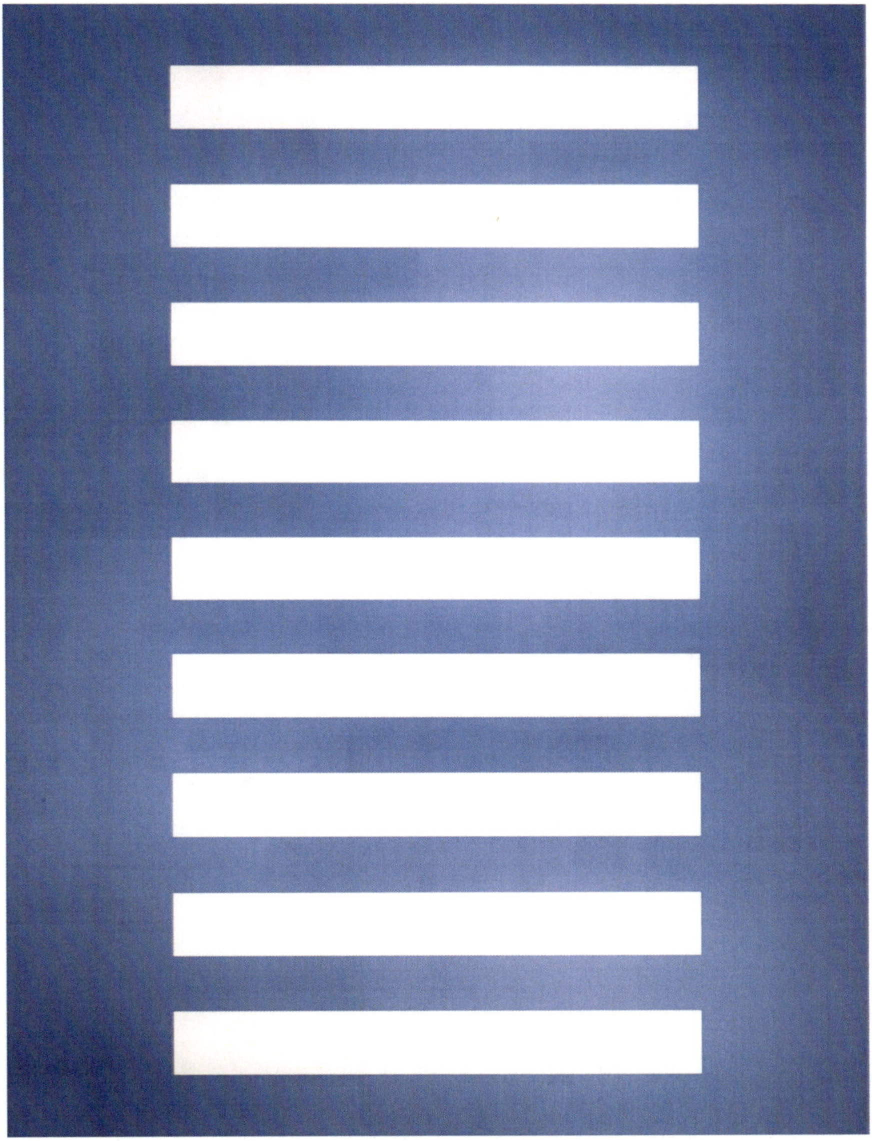

Pebble 721 with ladder Special Element

Ladder

Pebble #721 is an exceptional Pebble for its singular ladder structure. The strength of each rectangular shape stacked on top of each other is reminiscent of a collection of rare ERC-721 tokens. Pebble #721 is a striking *Special Element* example.

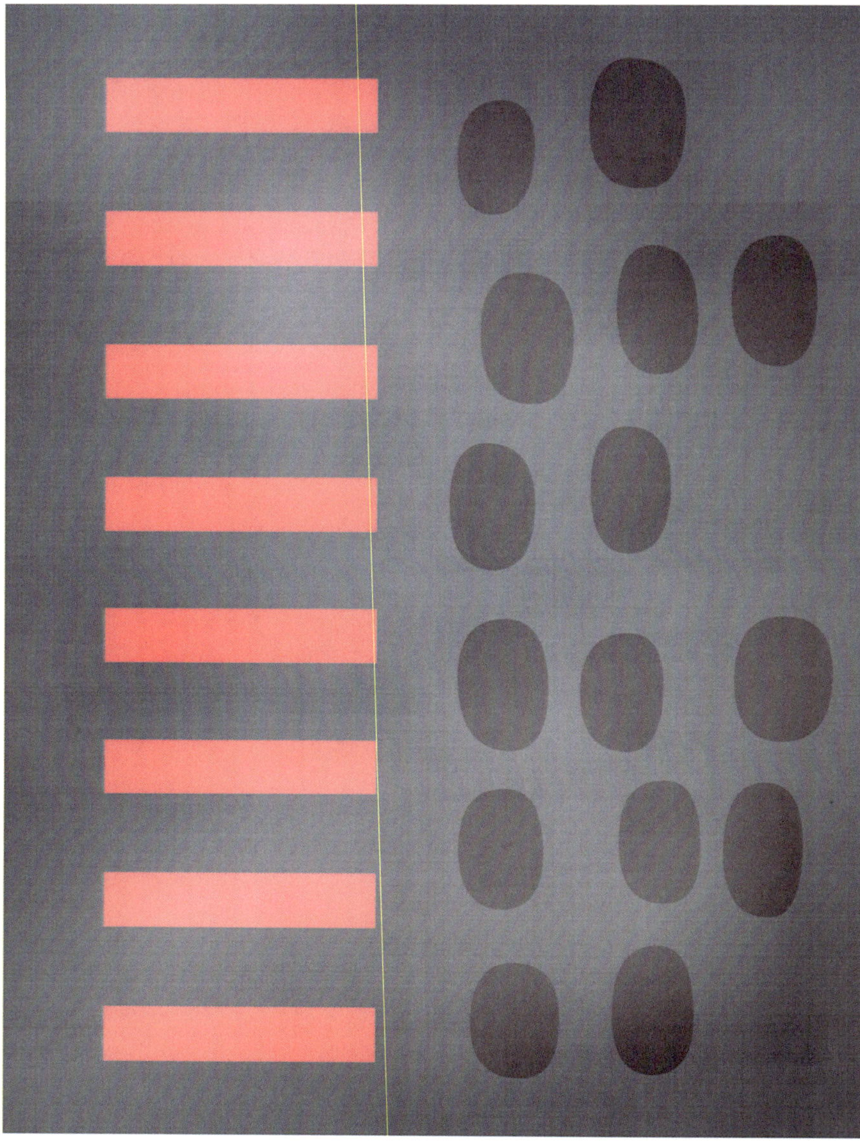

Pebble 41 'Pathway to Disorder' with ladder Special Element

Ladder

Pebble #41 is bold in *Vivid* color density and its illustration of two significant shapes, each a *Special Element*. On the left, the ladder creates a pathway, and on the right the rectangular grid.

Pebble 390 with ladder Special Element

Ladder

Pebble #390 includes one *Special Element* that output two ladders. Ladders are interesting because they show up quite differently at a large Pebble size versus a small Pebble size.

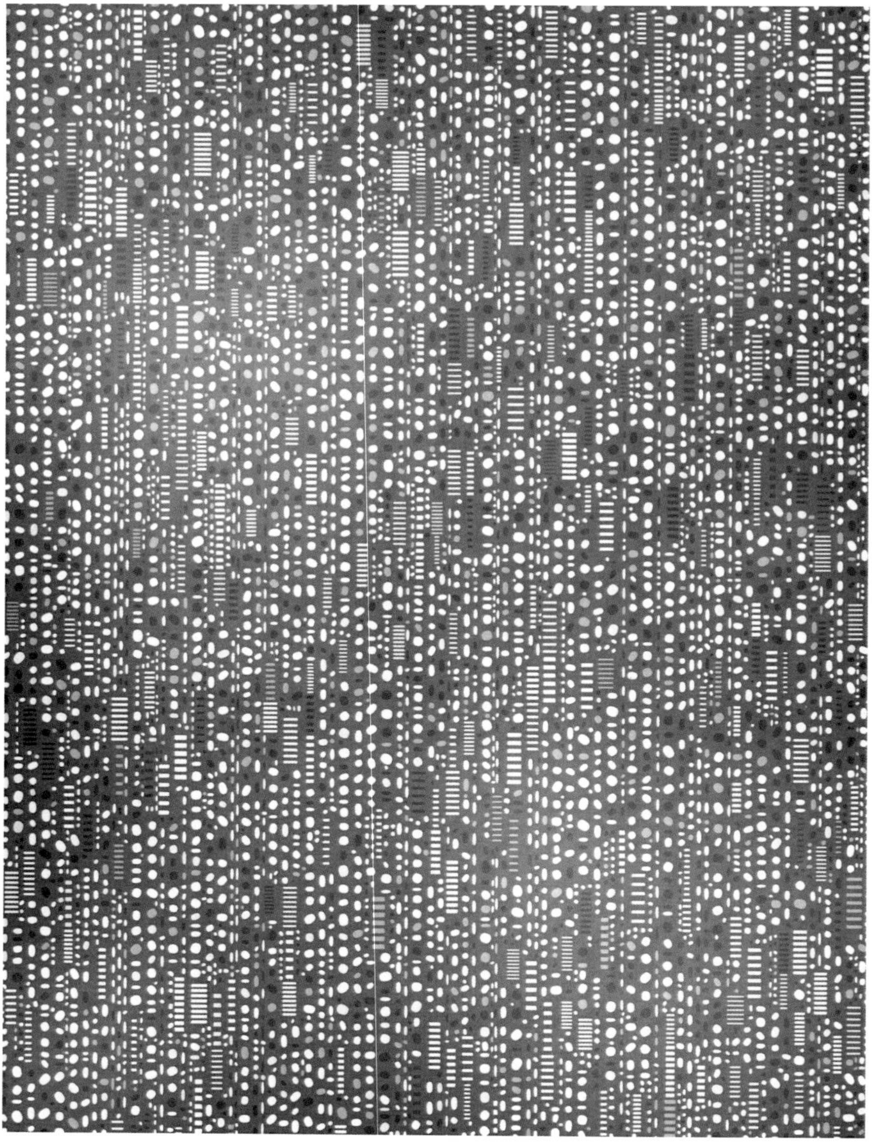

Pebble 689 with ladder Special Element

Ladder

Pebble #689 highlights the ladder *Special Elements*. There are dozens of vertical reaching ladders within the artwork because of the *Craglet* size pairing. Notice how the grey, white, and black colors of the ladders create an illusion of depth and perspective.

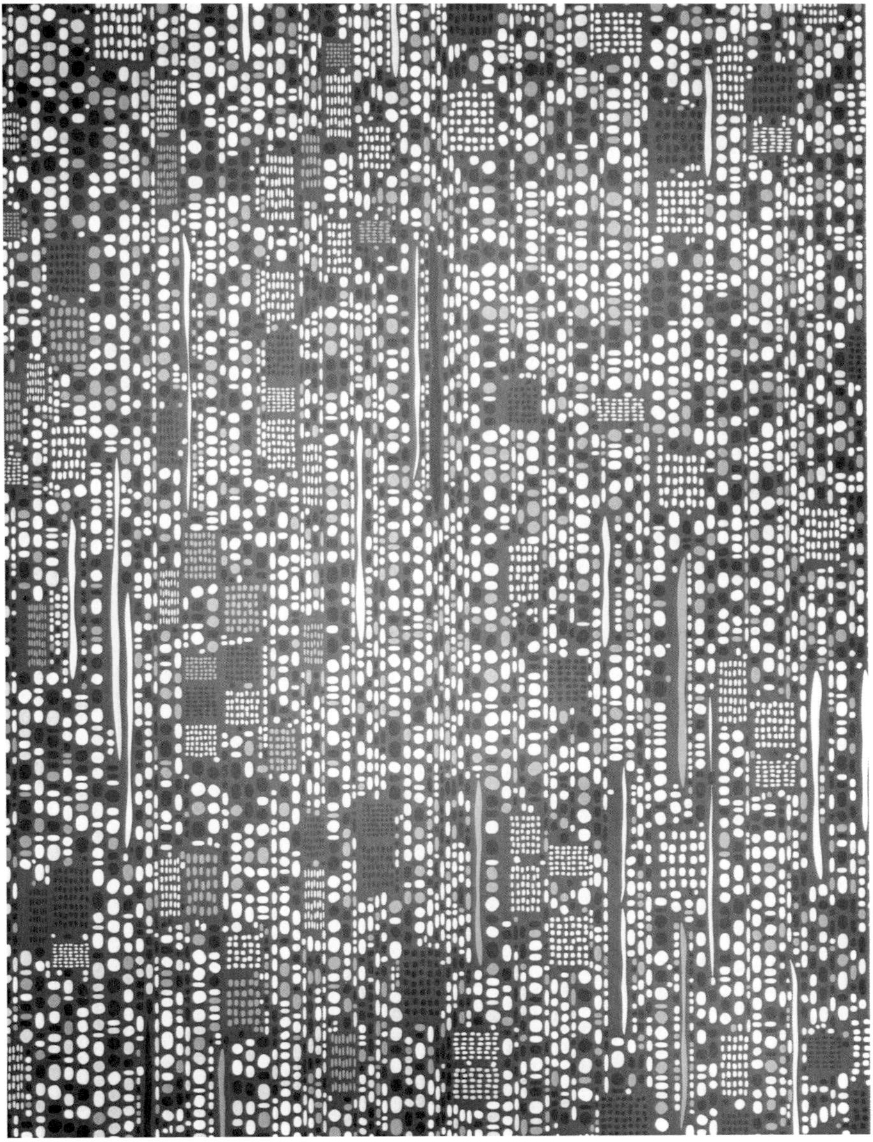

Pebble 34 with grid Special Element

Grid

Pebble #34 highlights the grid *Special Elements*. There are many grids throughout the composition, made possible in a *Craglet* size Pebble. The grids communicate more energy towards the viewer, in contrast to the ladders of Pebble #689 that are about vertical movement.

Pebble 850 with grid Special Element

Grid

Pebble #850 is a wonderful example of a single grid *Special Element*. Every Pebble shown in #850 is part of the grid that the algorithm treats as a collective element.

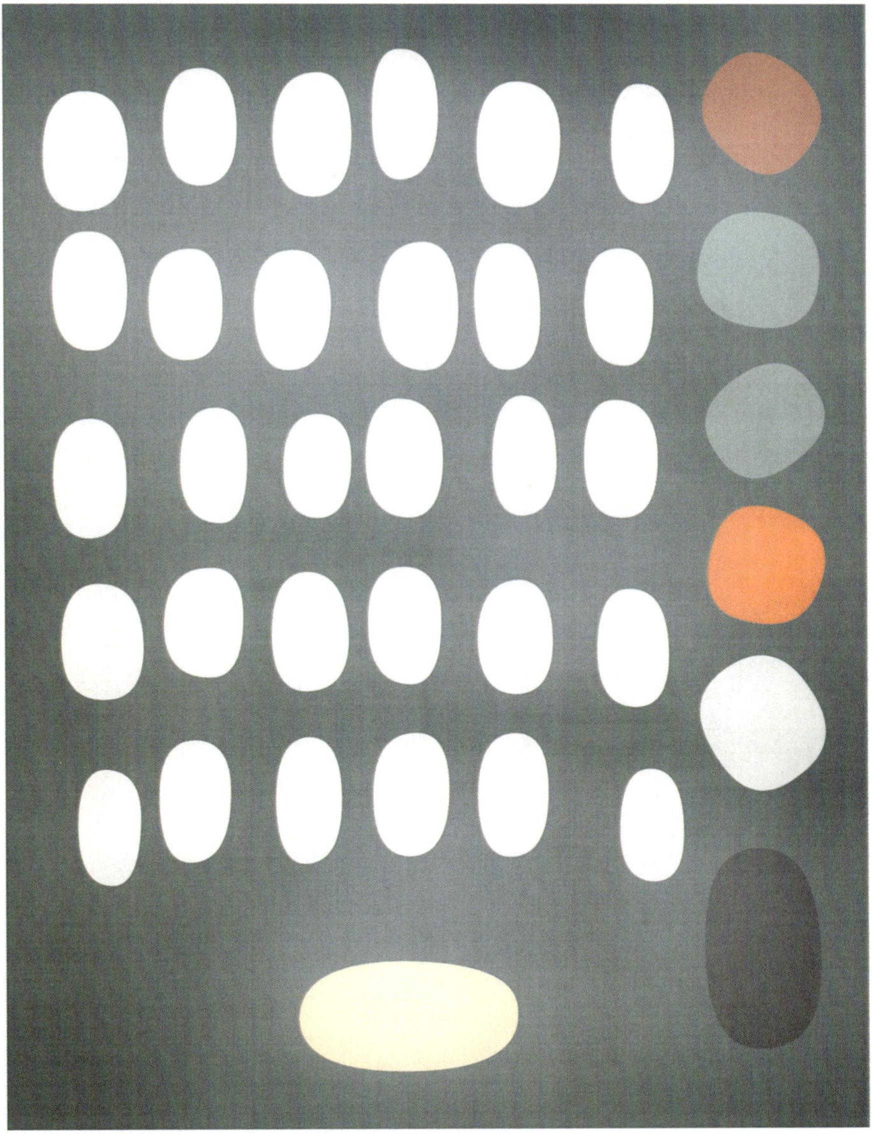

Pebble 285 with grid Special Element

Grid

Pebble #285 is another example of the grid rectangle of Pebbles. The *Rockling* size doesn't leave much room for anything else beyond the grid *Special Element*. Quite a collectible trait.

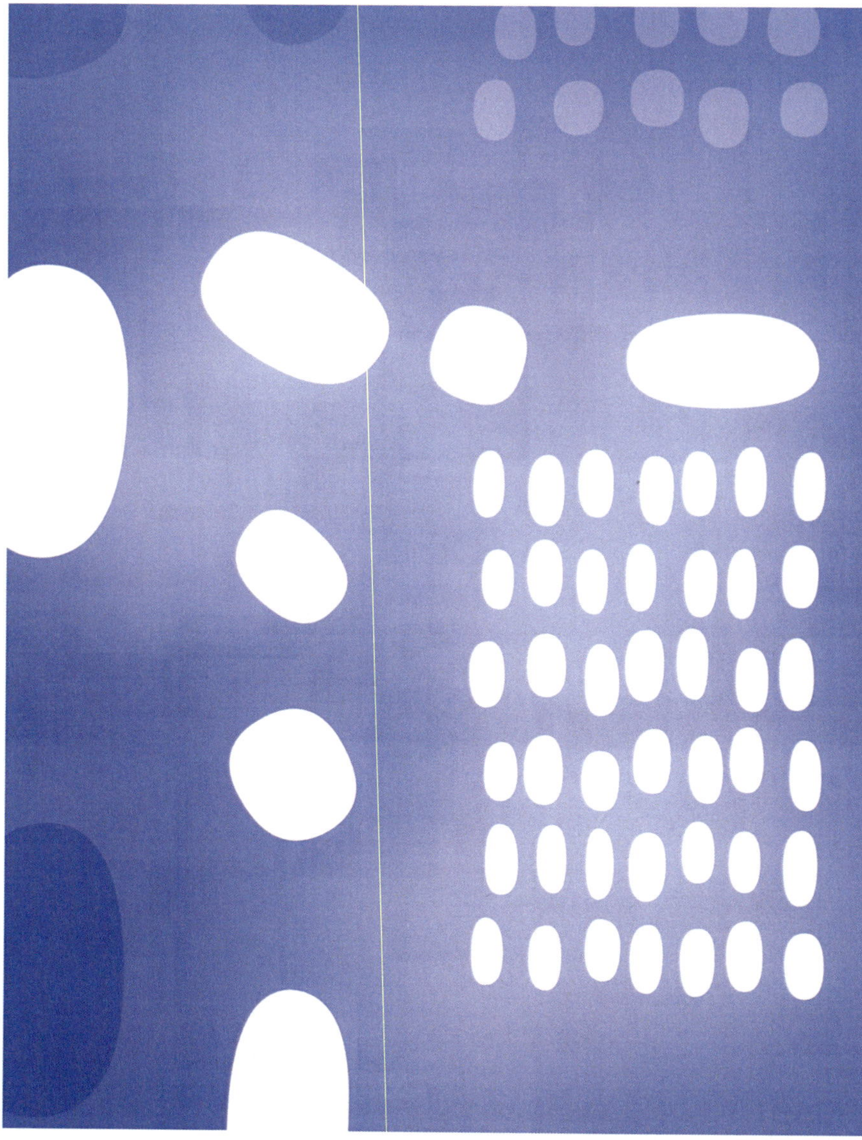

Pebble 281 with grid Special Element

Grid

Pebble #281 contains the grid *Special Element*. This particular grid is comprised of 7 x 6 Pebbles of a similar size. Their presence is immediately obvious, stamped across the lower right quadrant of the *Blueprint* palette Pebble.

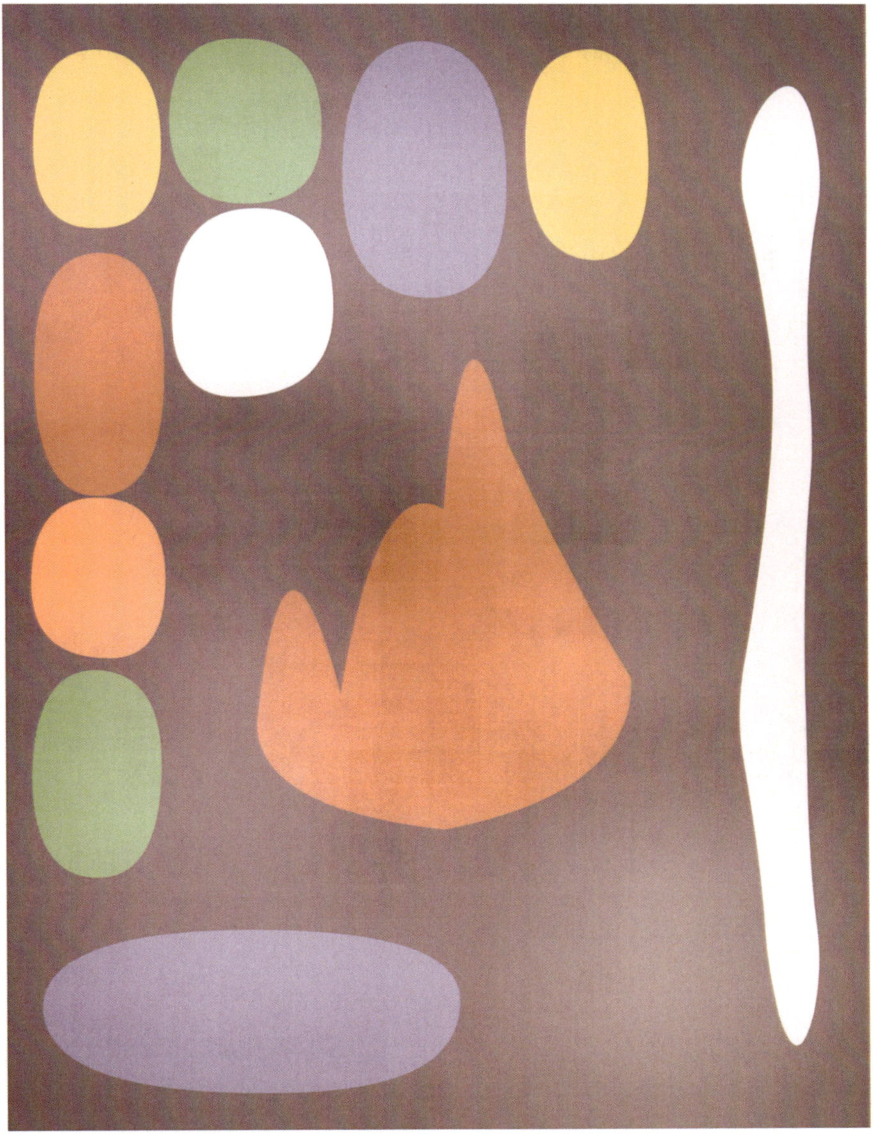

Pebble 529 'Sgt. Pepe Campfire' with random shapes Special Element

Random Shapes

'Sgt. Pepe Campfire' demonstrates that Pebbles are capable of a visual language all of their own, often through the presence a singular random shape.

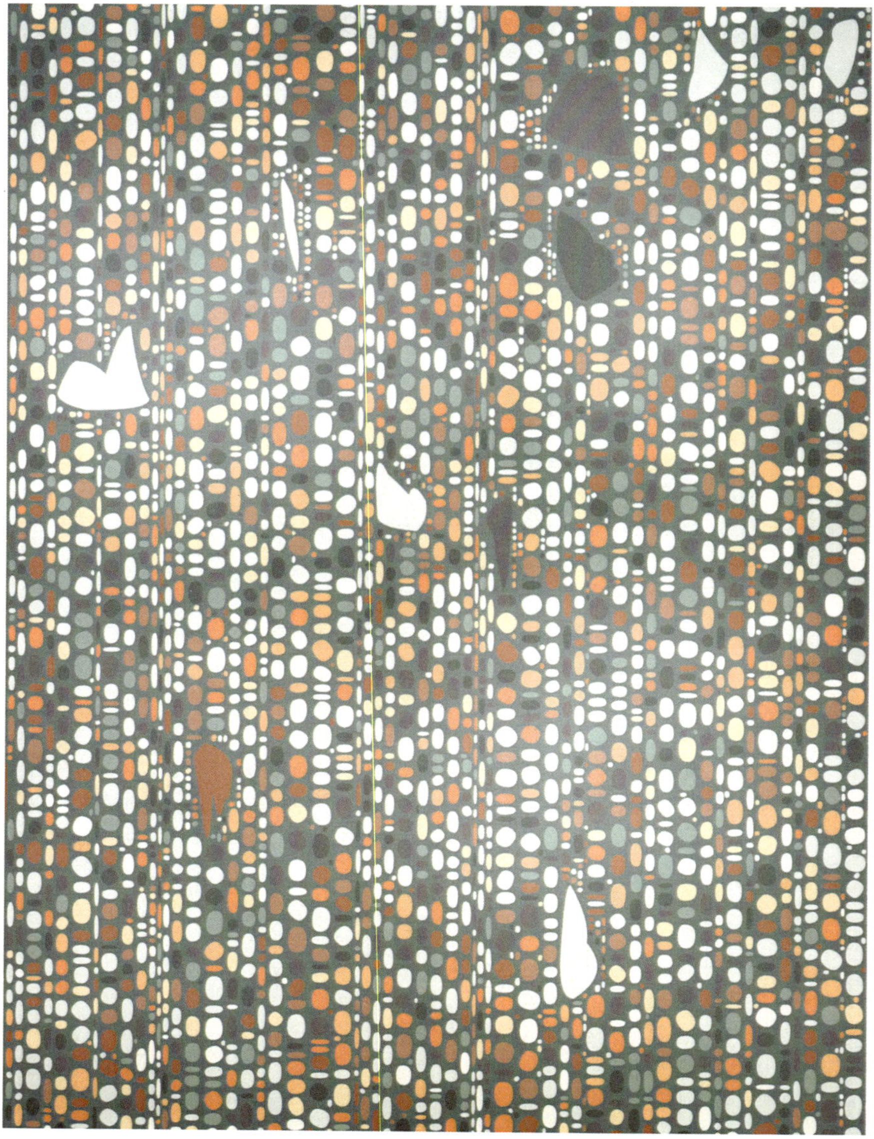

Pebble 104 with random shapes Special Element

Random Shapes

Pebble #104 includes a *Special Element* that produces random shapes in randomized positions throughout the artwork. These random shapes create interesting places for the eye to rest.

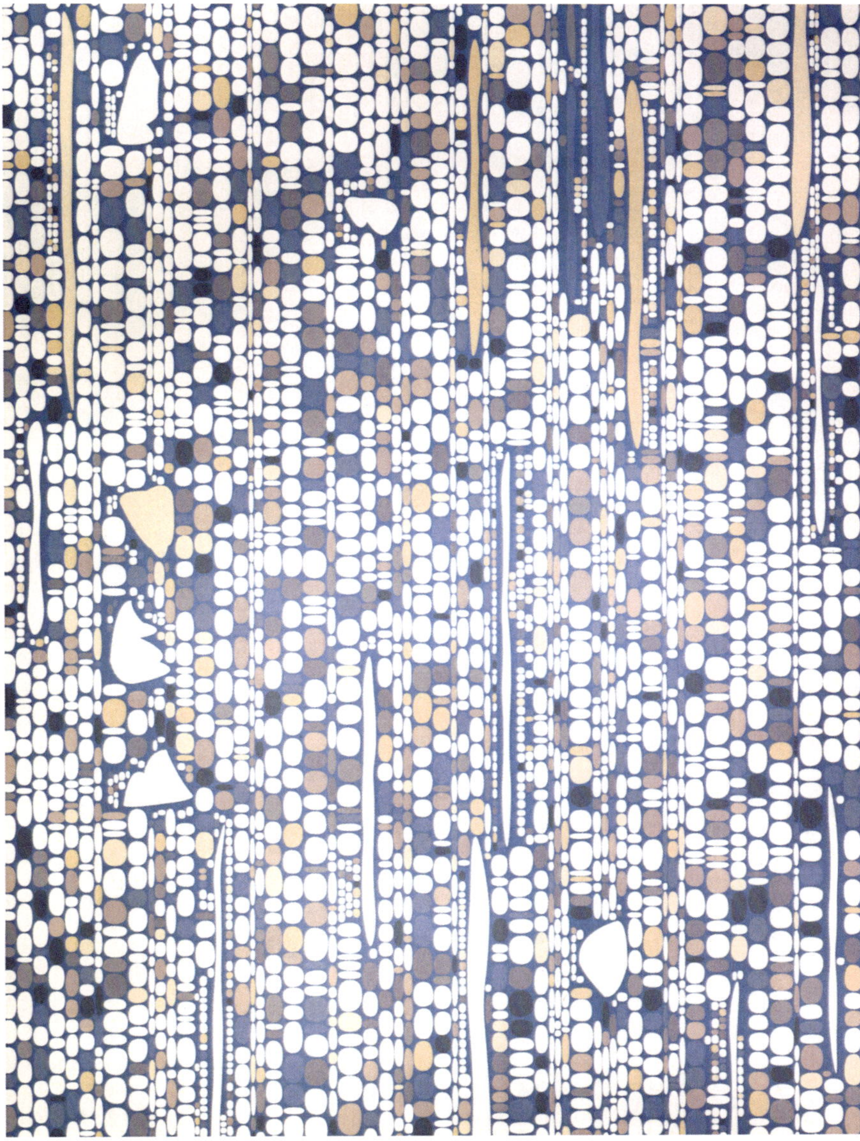

Pebble 781 with random shapes Special Element

Random Shapes

Pebble #781 has outputted six random shapes that break up the *Harmonize Overlap* arrangement of the majority of the Pebbles. The eyes are drawn to each random shape as an interesting moment to linger before getting lost in the sea of *Dusk Riverbed*-colored Pebbles.

The *Special Element* trait inserts an unpredictability into Pebbles ensuring that individual works look different from each other. You can still be confident that each and every Pebble is from the same collection.

Pebbles with All Special Elements

With *Special Elements* now covered in some detail, let's look at the simpler traits of *Edge* and *Overlap*.

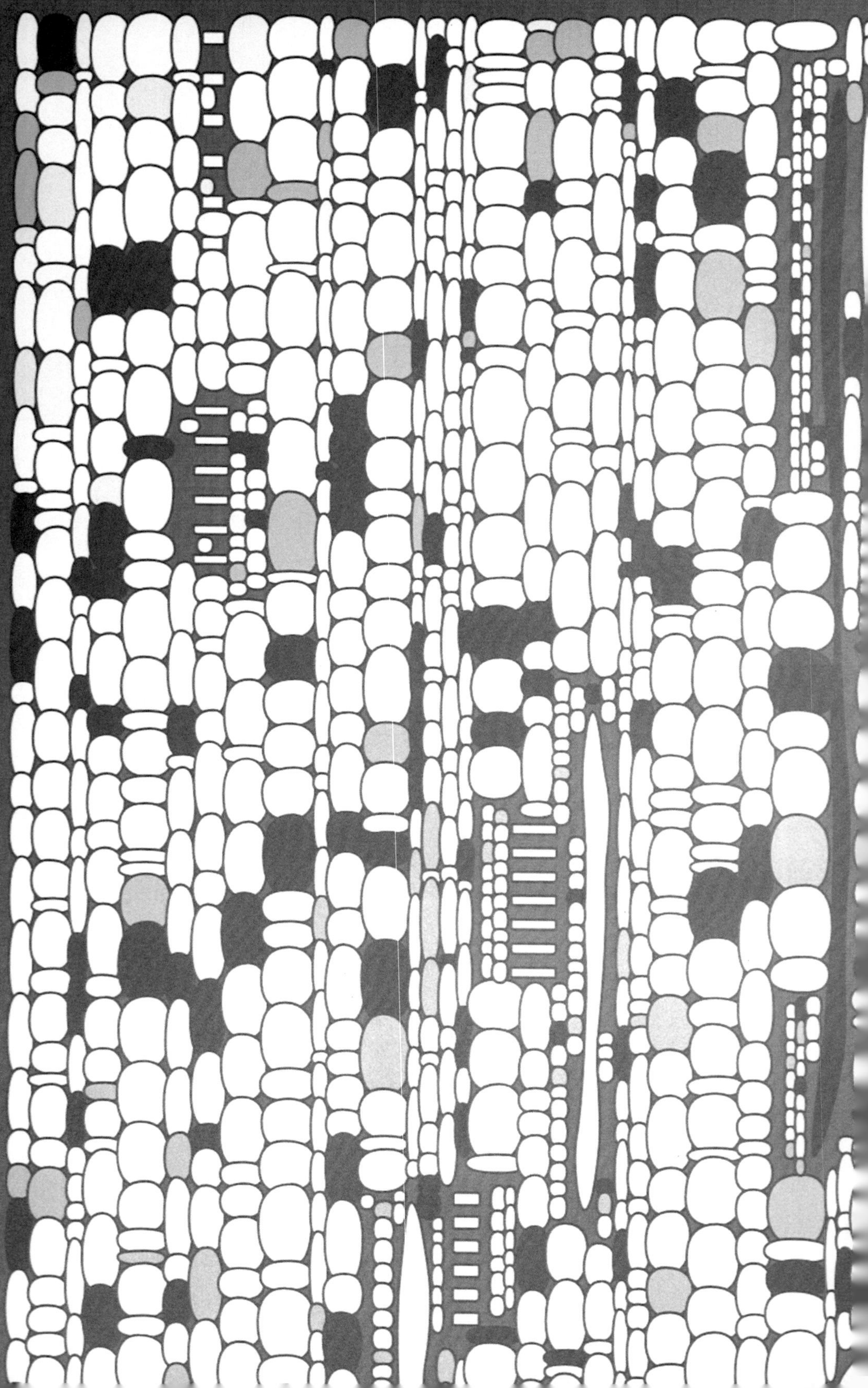

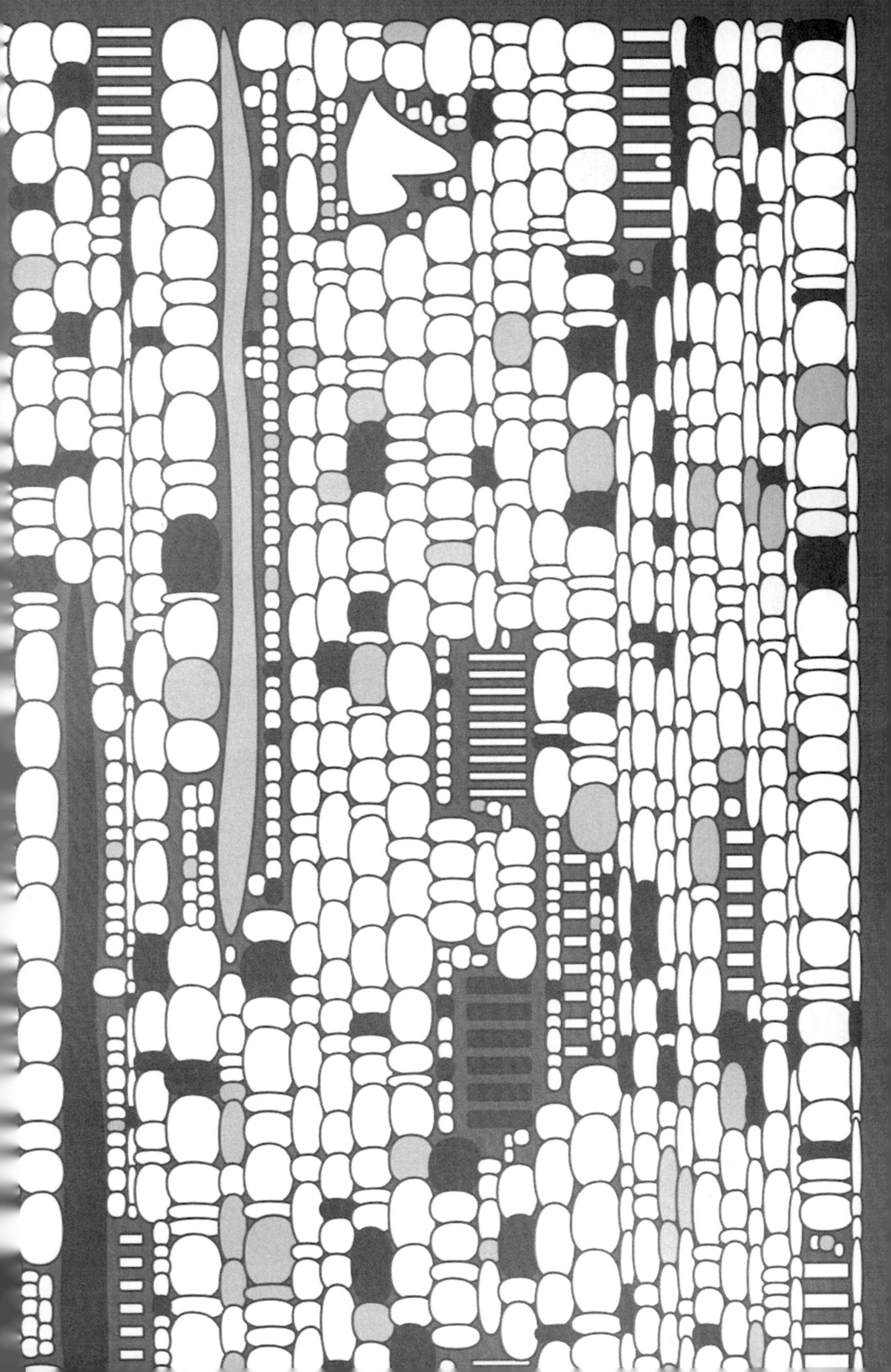

EDGE AND OVERLAP

Edge

The gap around the frame of the artwork is created by the *Edge* trait and is immediately obvious to the eye. Not to be confused with the *Border* trait, which adds an outline around each and every Pebble inside the artwork. The *Edge* trait frames the art.

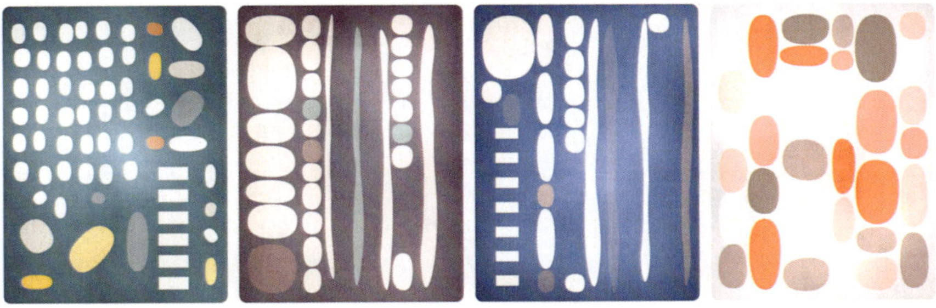

Pebbles with Edge 452, 860, 891 and 292

312 Pebbles are blessed with the *Edge* trait, while the remaining 688 do not have any *Edge* present. No *Edge* is preferred for covering large wall surfaces, whereas an inbuilt *Edge* frame is often preferred in digital environments.

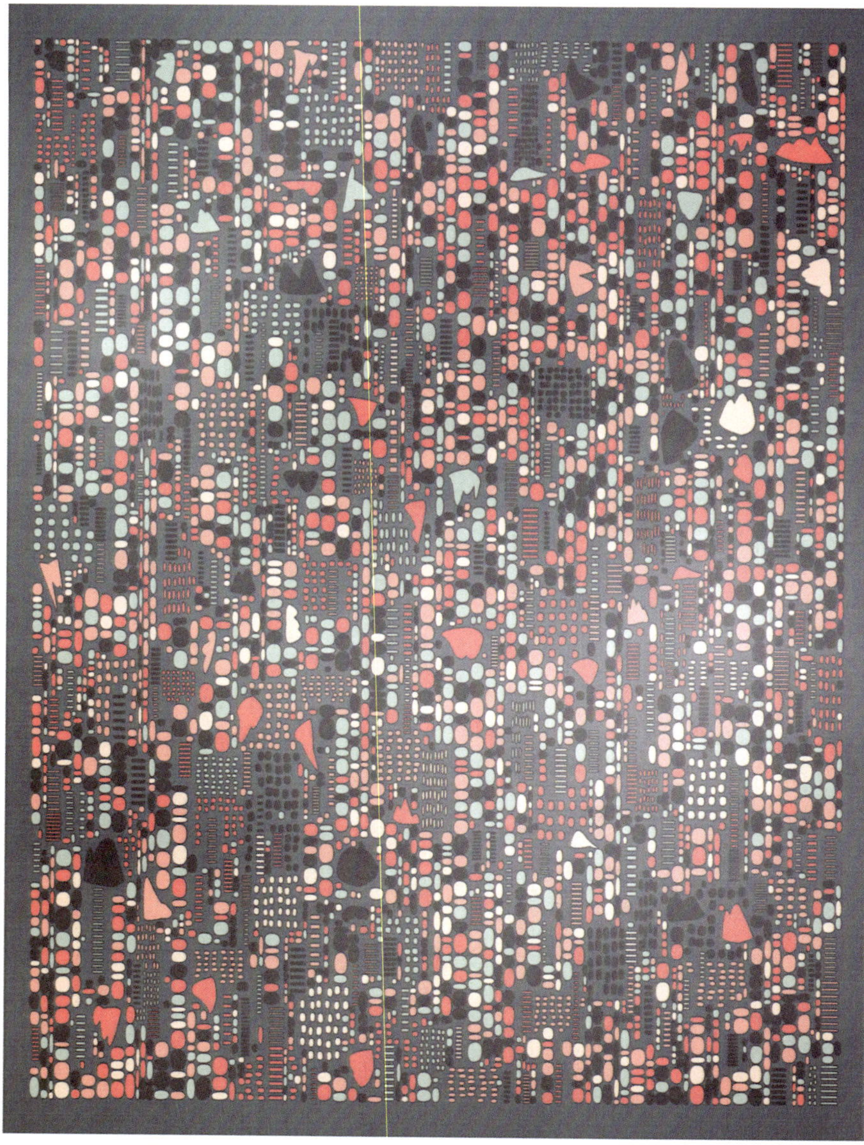

Pebble 224 with Edge

Edge On

The *Edge* trait is immediately obvious in almost all Pebbles due to the padding created around the Pebble landscape. *Coral Reef* palette shown in Pebble #224 lends its dark green color to the *Edge* trait.

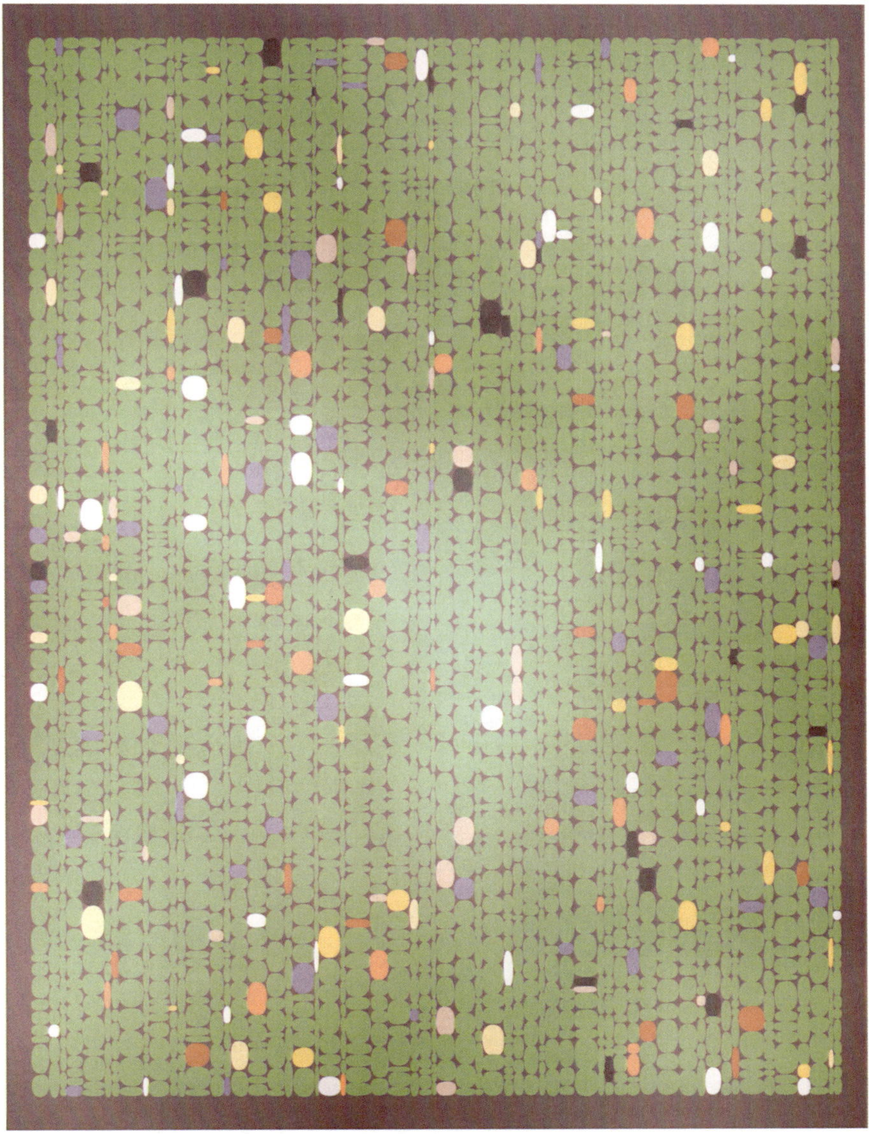

Pebble 98 'Water Lillies' with Edge

"I call it 'Water Lillies' because it reminds me of Monet's work. It is the only Sgt.Pepe palette Pebble with a frame."
G9ralt

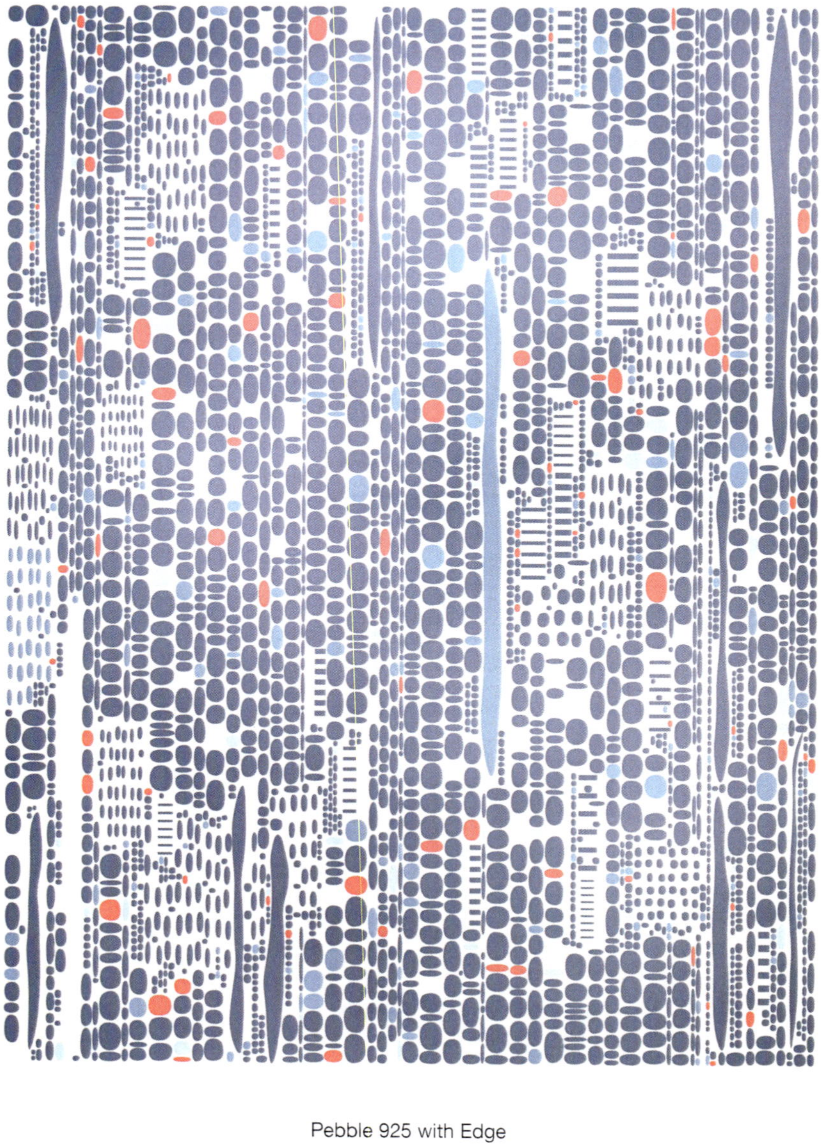

Pebble 925 with Edge

The *Edge* trait is less pronounced in Pebble #925 because the *Unigrid* palette lends its white to the background of the Pebble. The *Hush Color Density* discolors the white of the corners, the only hint that a border exists at all.

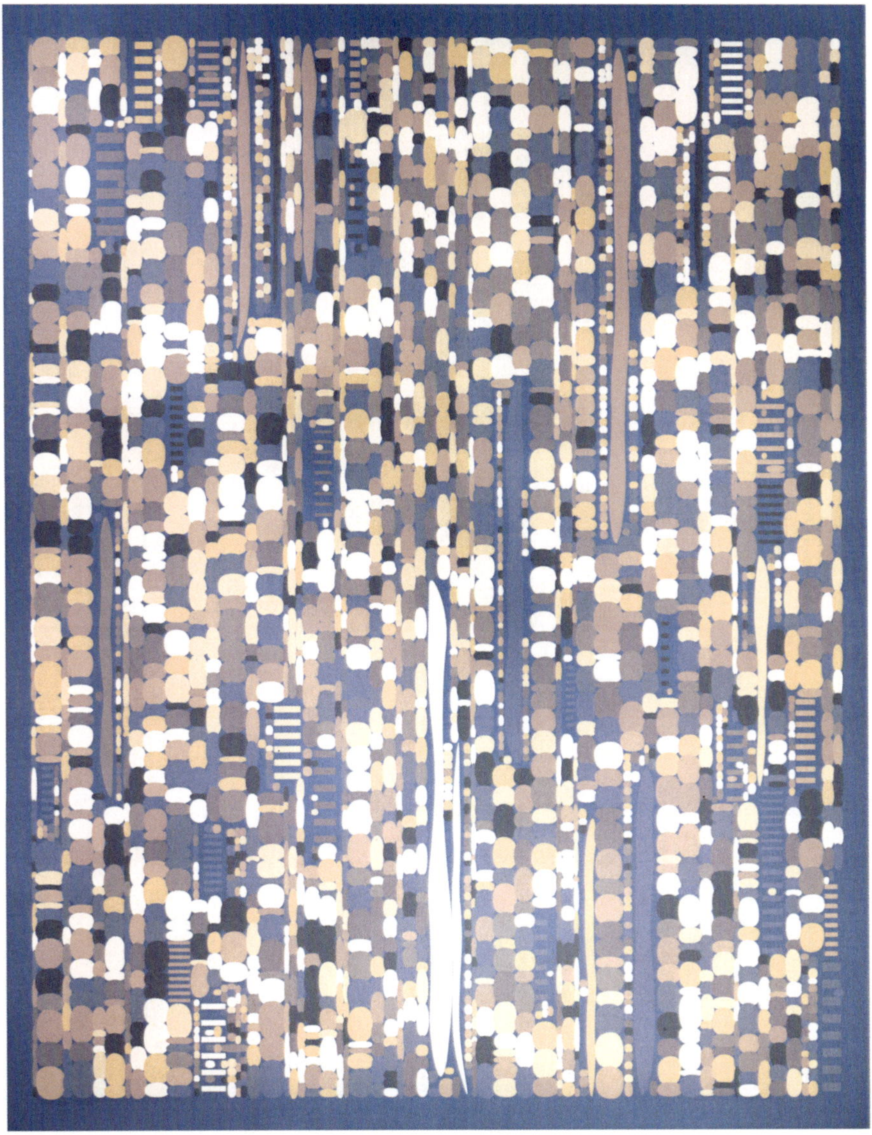

Pebble 888 with Edge

Pebble #888 is another fine example of the *Edge* trait, this time on a *Dusk Riverbed* palette with *Boulderette* size. The *Fuse Overlap* trait makes room for more of the dark blue background canvas to be seen, and in many places it bleeds into the *Edge*.

. . .

No Edge

Of the 688 Pebbles that do not have an *Edge*, there are a number to showcase here. This trait variant could easily be overlooked because it is both common and doesn't really do anything except let the Pebbles generate on the digital canvas all the way up to the edge of the frame. Challenge yourself to go a little deeper.

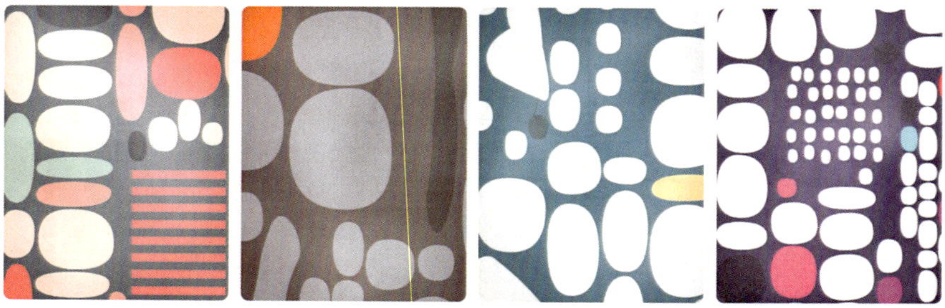

Pebbles with No Edge 642, 808, 973 and 80

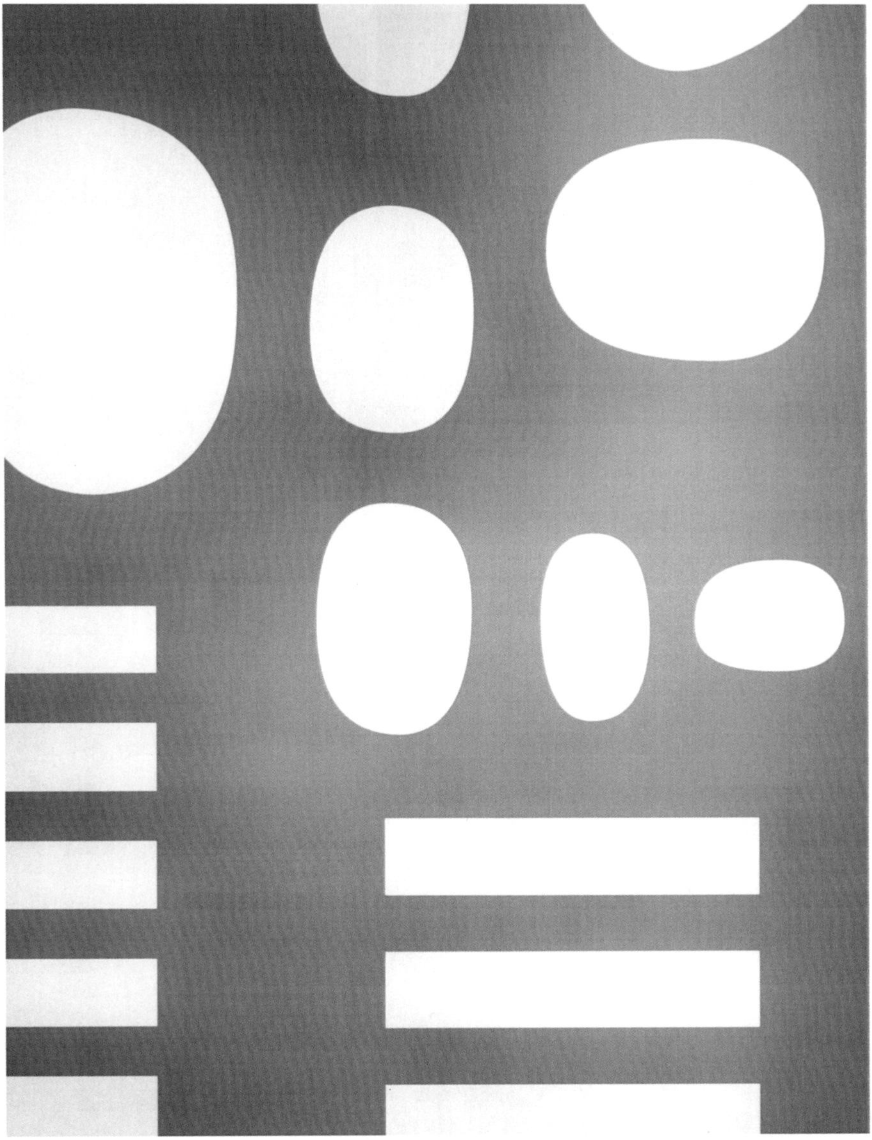

Pebble 0 with No Edge

No Edge

The first ever Pebble minted has *No Edge* and gives the viewer the impression that the artwork continues beyond the frame. Imagine the pathways in Pebble #0 extending south, north, and west. *No Edge* Pebbles tickle the imagination with possibility.

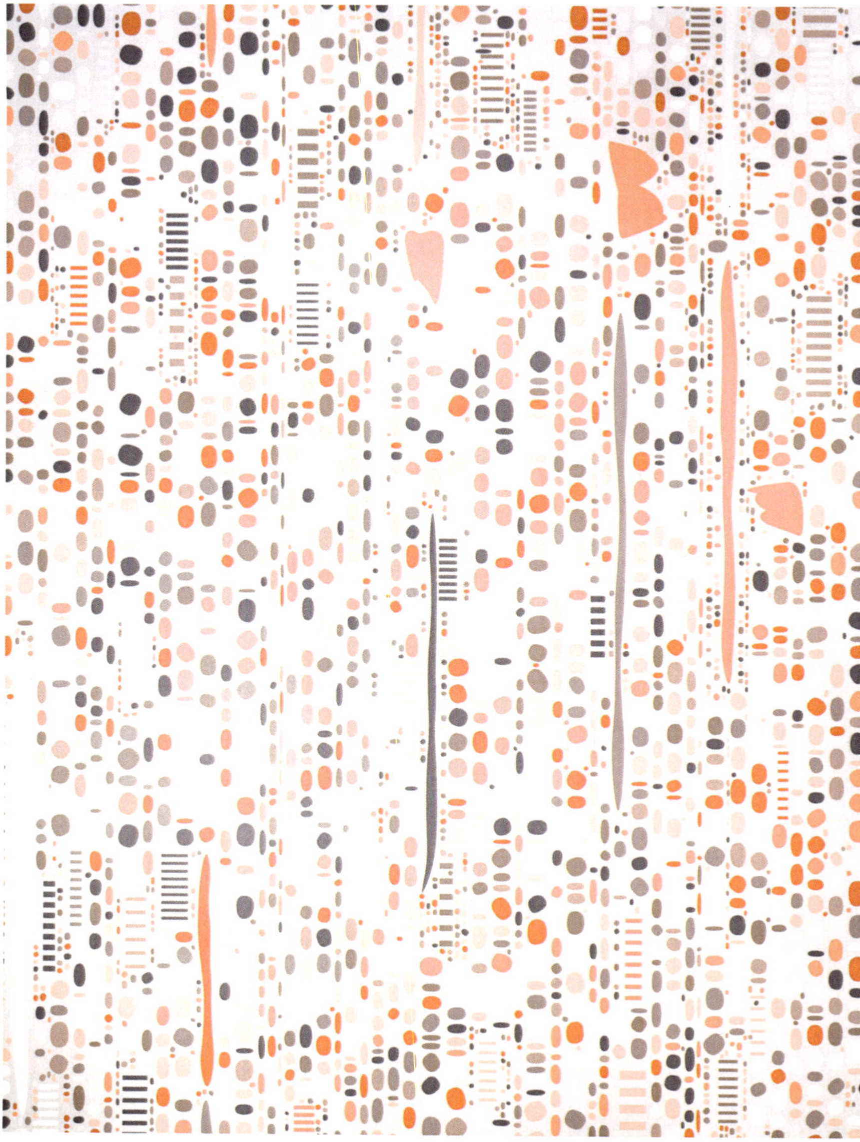

Pebble 426 with No Edge

No Edge

A quartet of *Special Elements* play like harp strings from left to right across the *Serenity*-lit canvas. The *Vivid Color Density* nature of the work brings a sense of presence, further amplified by the vertical ladder-like columns, floating orb-like in *Disjoin Overlap* space. What's not to like?

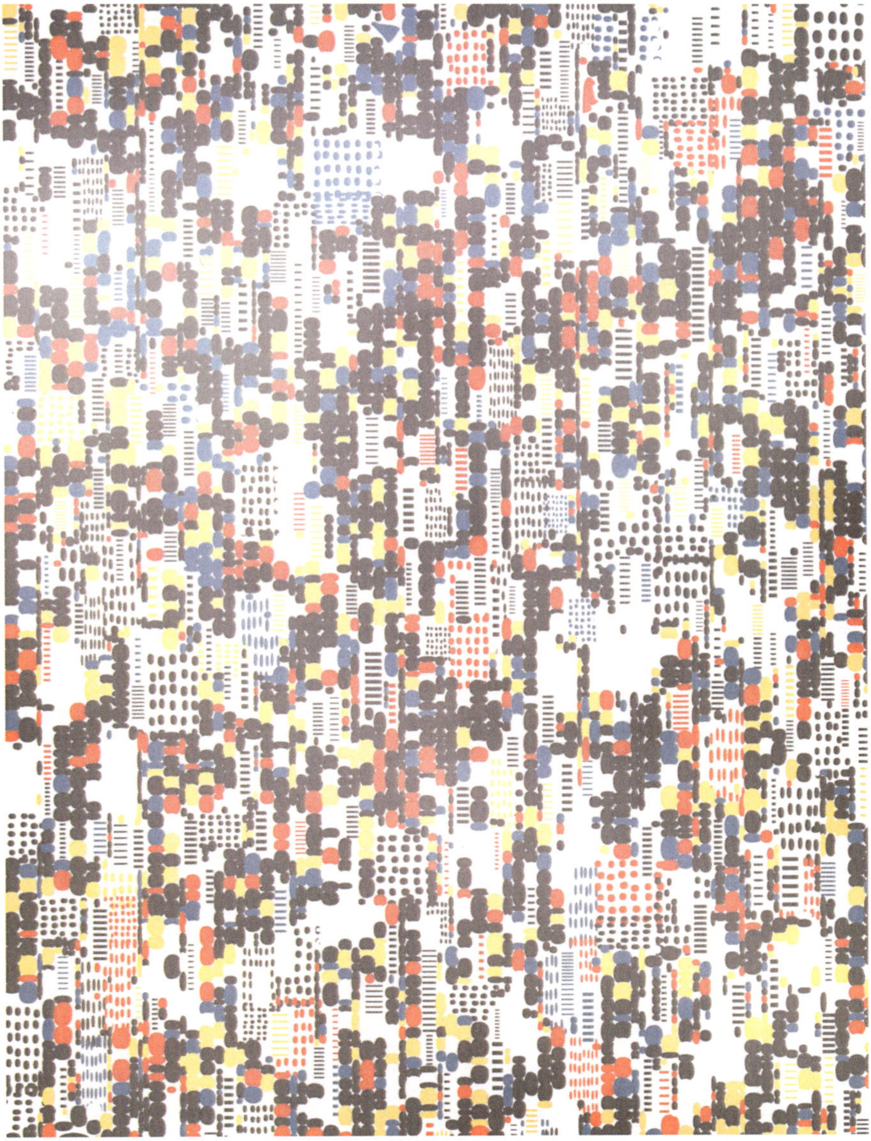

Pebble 752 'Dense City' with No Edge

No Edge

Pebble #752 squeezes in as many *Craglet Size* Pebbles as possible, bleeding them right up to the edge of the canvas. The perception of Pebble #752 taking the form of a dense city would not be possible if the *Edge* trait were present.

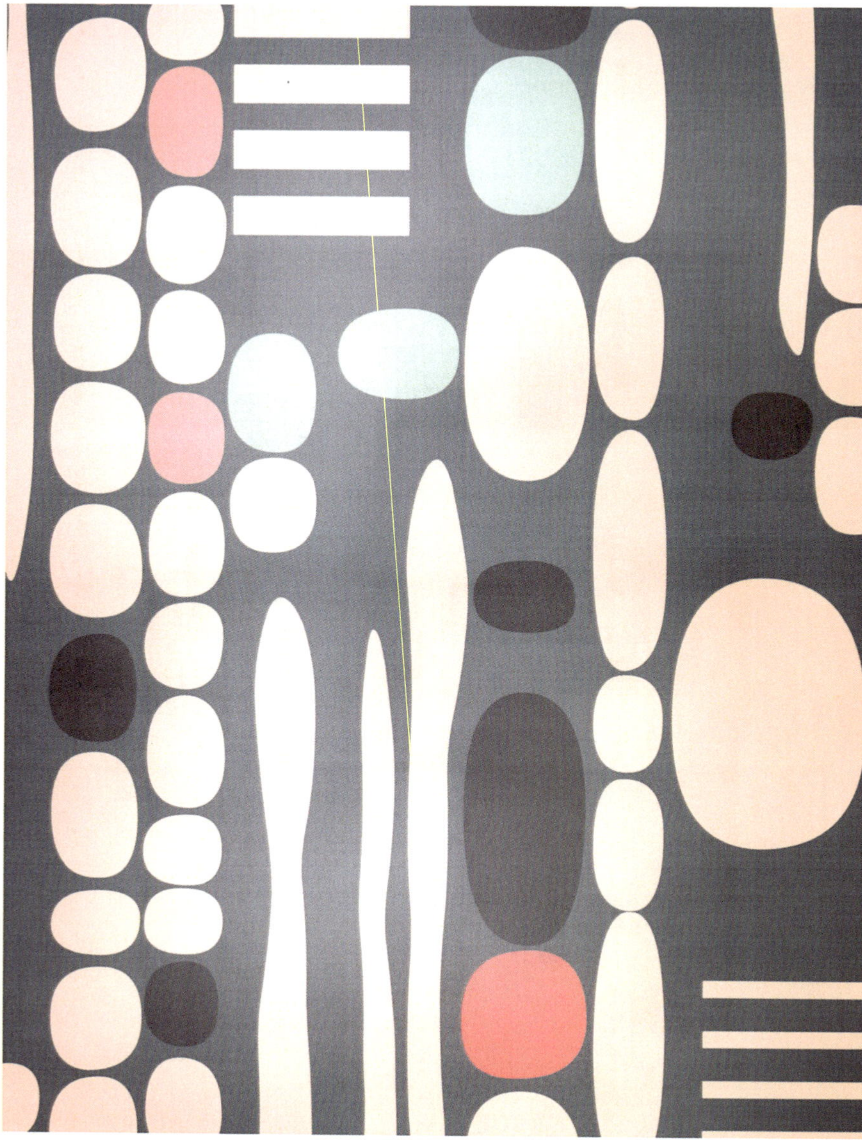

Pebble 144 with No Edge

"The 'Puerta del Sol', named after the historic public square in Madrid, Spain — echoing its bustling crowds, pedestrian crossings, and sun-filled atmosphere year-round. The rare *Coral Reef* palette is immediately striking."
pandelic

Overlap

Overlap permits Pebbles to jumble up on top of each other or be repelled from each other depending on the *Overlap* variant of the Pebble. There are five variants to the *Overlap* trait:

- Blend (51)
- Isolate (99)
- Fuse (113)
- Disjoin (245)
- Harmonize (492)

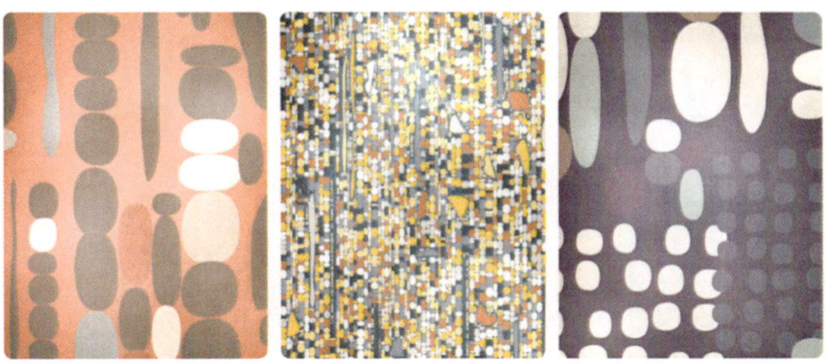

Pebbles with Blend Overlap 278, 487, 846 and 453

Blend Overlap puts each Pebble within a 'kiss' of the next, giving a grounded feel. *Blend* is the rarest *Overlap* variant.

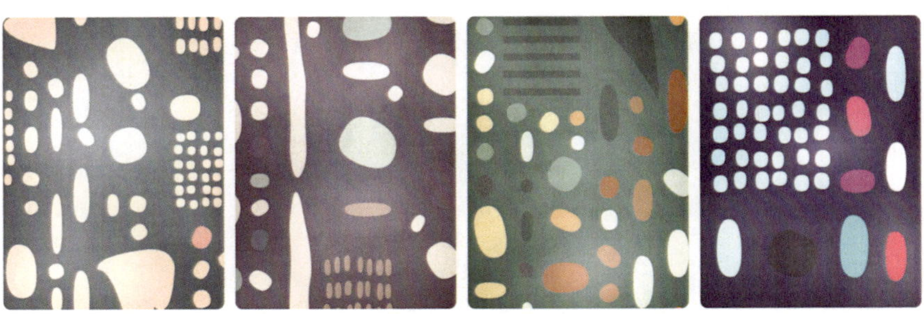

Pebbles with Isolate Overlap 489, 931, 991 and 129

Isolate Overlap takes the Pebble separation to another level.

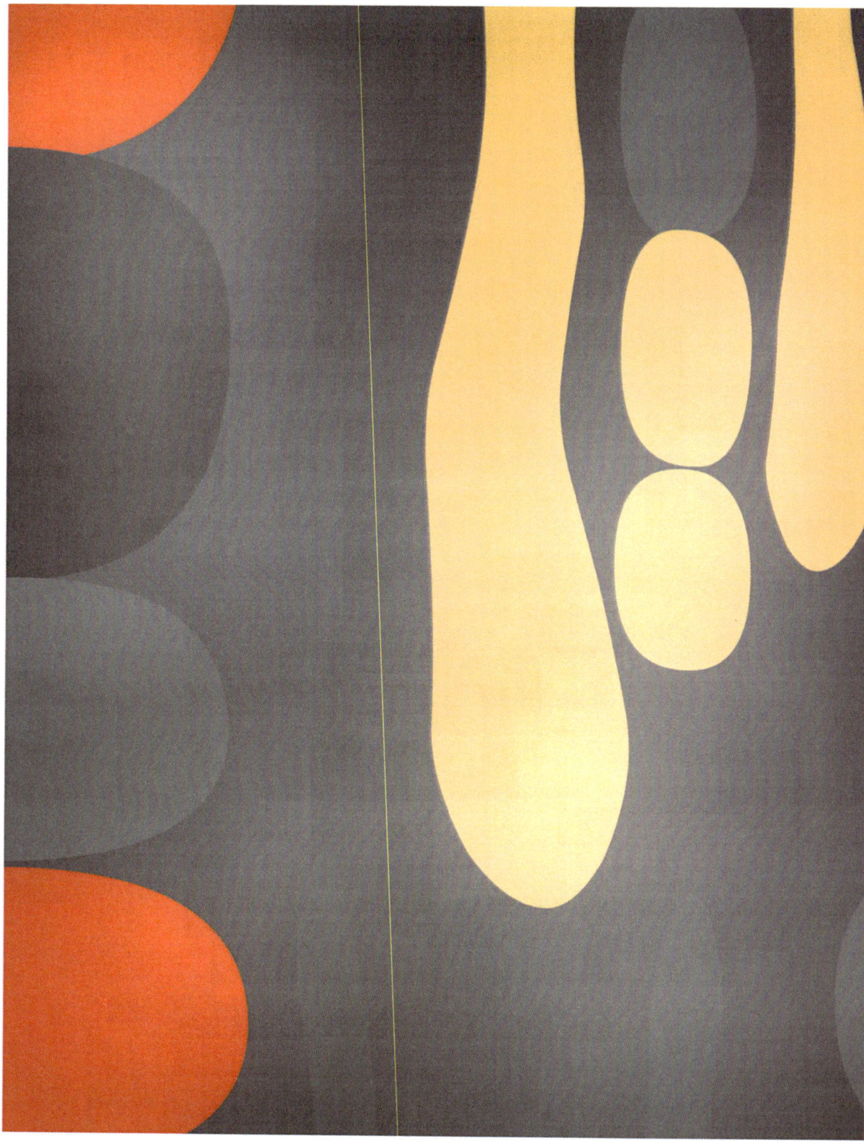

Pebble 28 'A Surrender to Passion' with Blend Overlap

Blend Overlap

Blend Overlap nudges the yellow Pebbles close enough together for the emergent head and torso to take shape. The vertical column of red and black Pebbles toward the left of the canvas provides a sense of balance to the unfolding drama.

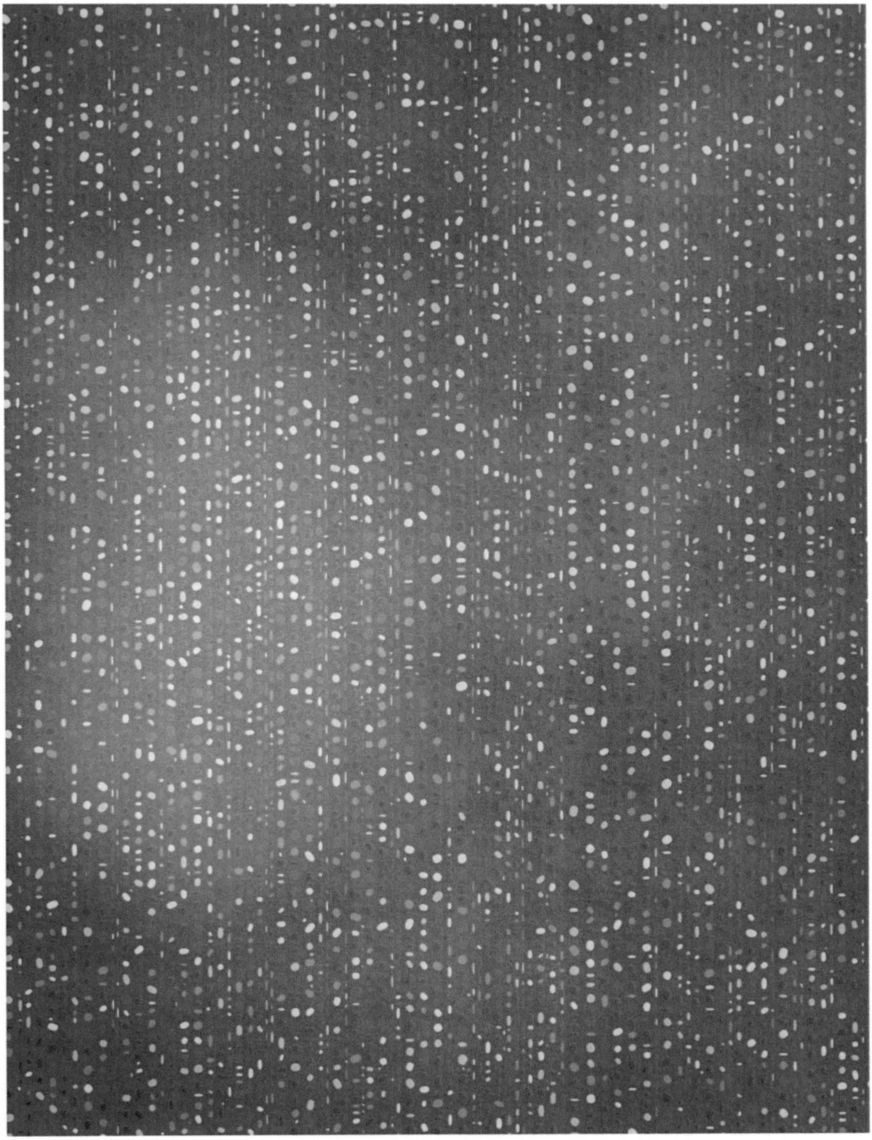

Pebble 15 'Bloodline' with Isolate Overlap

Isolate Overlap

Isolate Overlap combined with *Craglet* size creates the illusory effect of a glittery panel on red-dominant *Salsa Blush* background. Looks closer to see the *Border* around every Pebble, in this Pebble with no *Edge* framing.

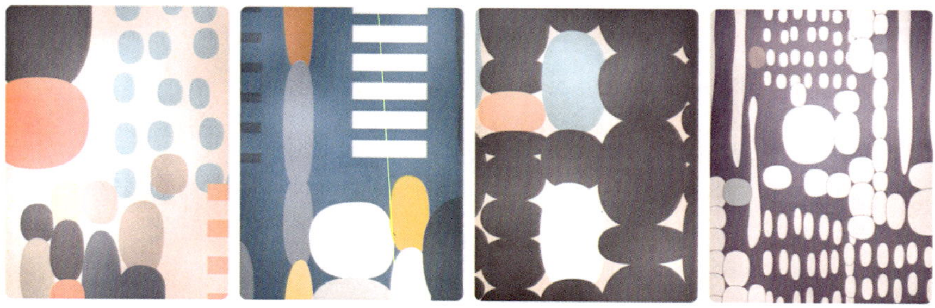

Pebbles with Fuse Overlap 189, 862, 26 and 73

The *Fuse* variant of the *Overlap* trait goes a step further than *Blend,* with Pebbles now clearly overstepping the boundaries of their neighbors. *Fuse Overlap* grows on you.

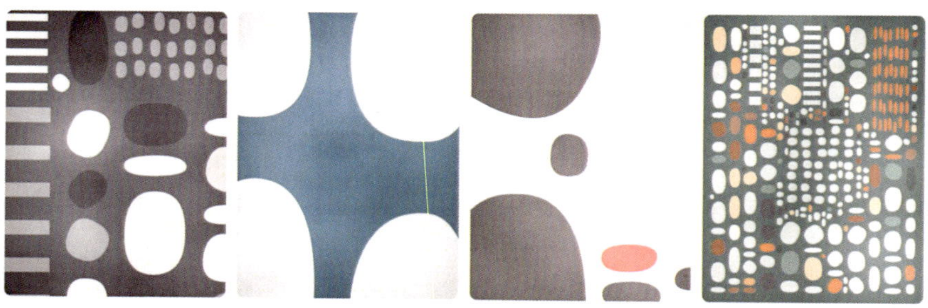

Pebbles with Disjoin Overlap 402, 933, 601 and 169

Disjoin Overlap pushes each Pebble away from each other creating space. Each Pebble breathes, particularly in larger *Size* Pebbles such as Pebble #933, where *Disjoin Overlap* is the hero.

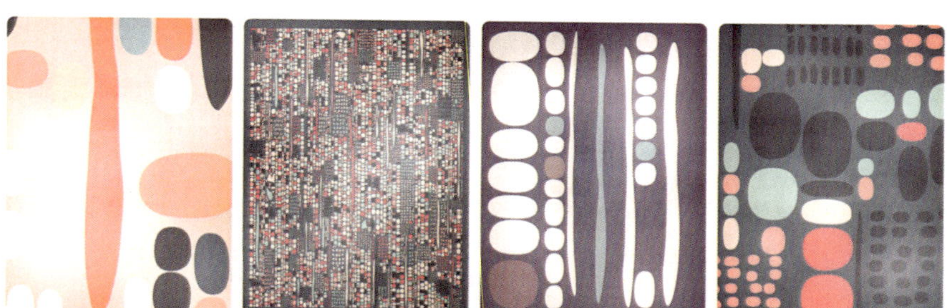

Pebbles with Harmonize Overlap 398, 148, 860 and 979

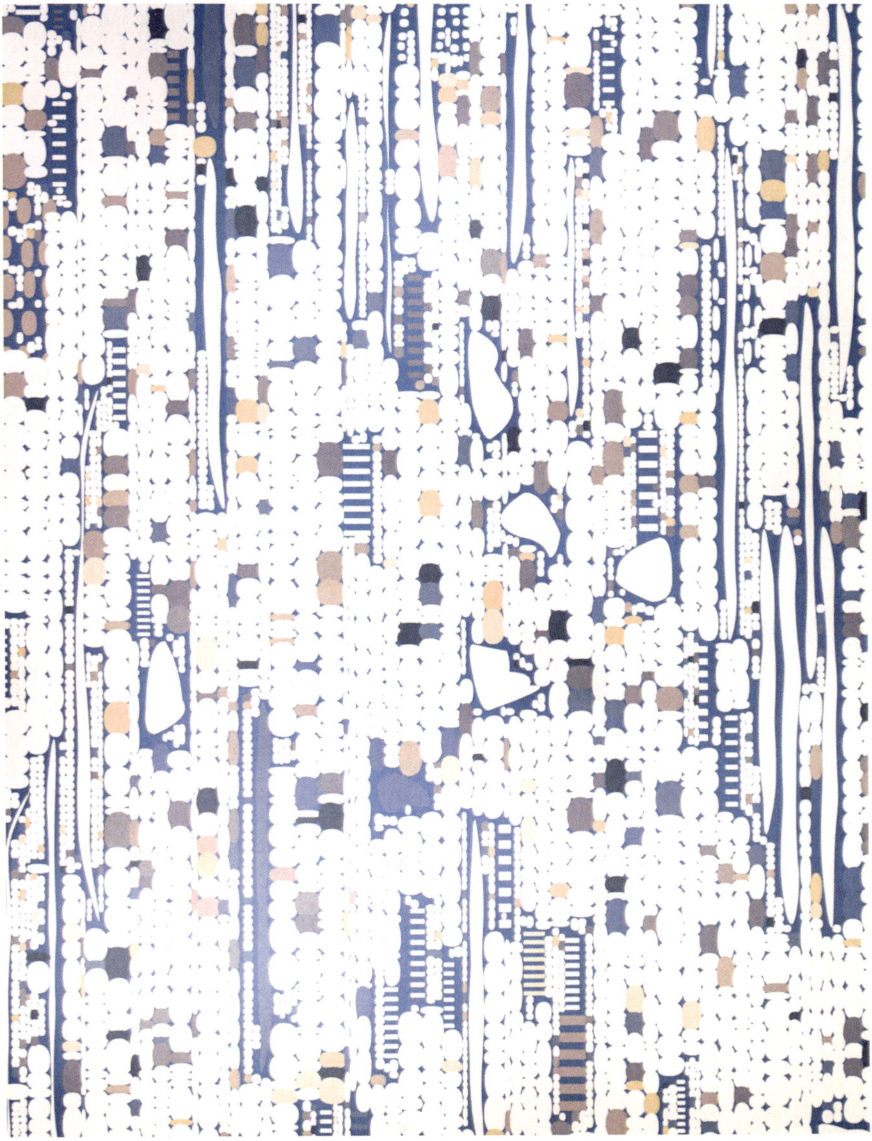

Pebble 480 'The Wave' with Fuse Overlap

Fuse Overlap

Pebble #480 congeals through *Fuse Overlap* into a wall of camera flashes, as this Pebble struts its stuff. All *Special Elements* are interspersed with clarity around the ladder-like structures. Like many celebrities, this Pebble is venerated for its quirks.

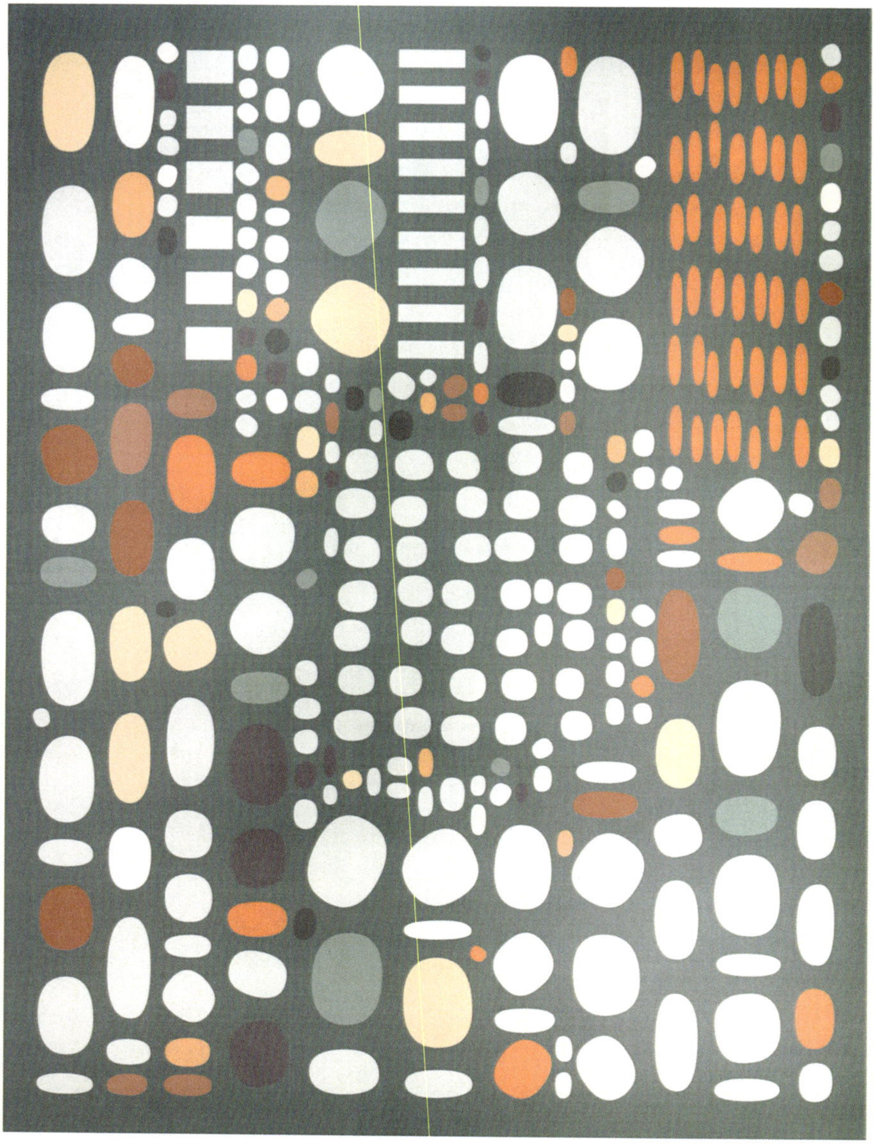

Pebble 169 'A Unified Theory of Everything' with Disjoin Overlap

Disjoin Overlap

A wonderful aerial view of a Japanese zen garden materializes. *Crumb* delivers the ideal size of Pebble to mimic a closer proximity perspective. The *Disjoin Overlap* introduces a healthy amount of negative space around the Pebbles.

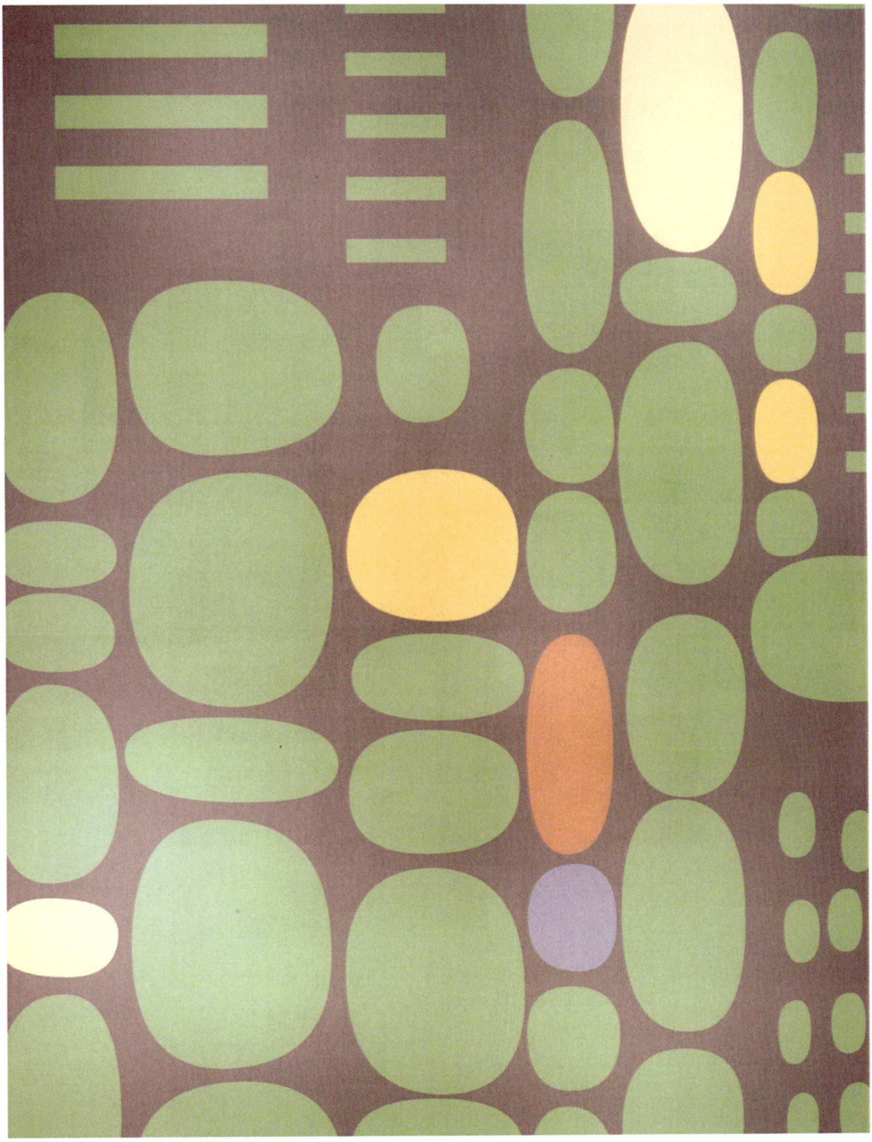

Pebble 116 'Zen Sgt. Pepe' with Harmonize Overlap

Harmonize Overlap

'Zen Sgt. Pepe' chills in base colors of lime and burgundy, as the *Hush Color Density* adds a pop of canary yellow, clay, and violet. *Harmonize Overlap* is the hero of the *Pebbit Size* Pebble, hitting in the center of our artistic chakras.

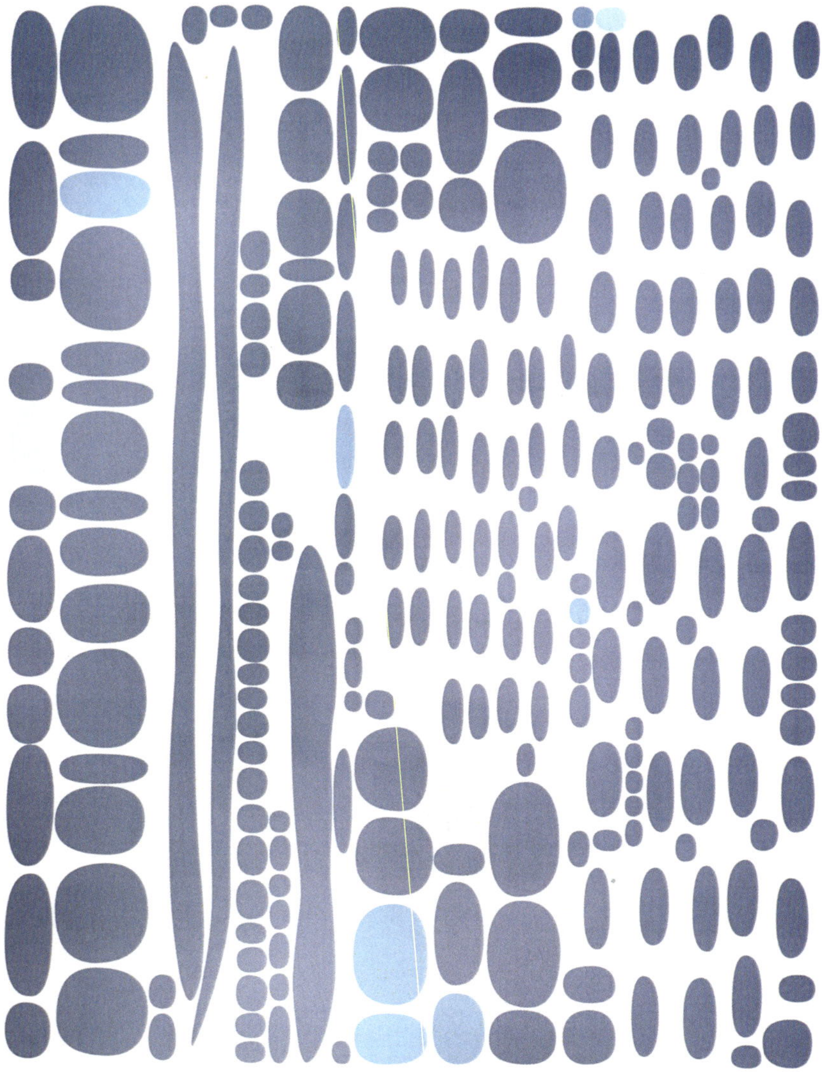

Pebble 94 'Currents of Cobalt Calm' with Harmonize Overlap

"'Currents of Cobalt Calm' features a serene assembly of cobalt blue shapes that evoke the gentle flow of a tranquil river. *Harmonize* balances the scattered elements into a cohesive whole." Paul Wilson

Whoa. We have now covered *Traced, Special Elements, Edge,* and *Overlap* traits across the Interesting Traits chapter. Combined with the knowledge bomb on *Palettes* and *Size* from the first chapter, you have covered two-thirds of the genetic makeup of a Pebble. But we are not done yet. With six traits now analyzed, there are three more to complete your 'Do Your Own Research' study into Pebbles:

- **Color Density**
- **Flow**
- **Mint Type**

Let's get into it.

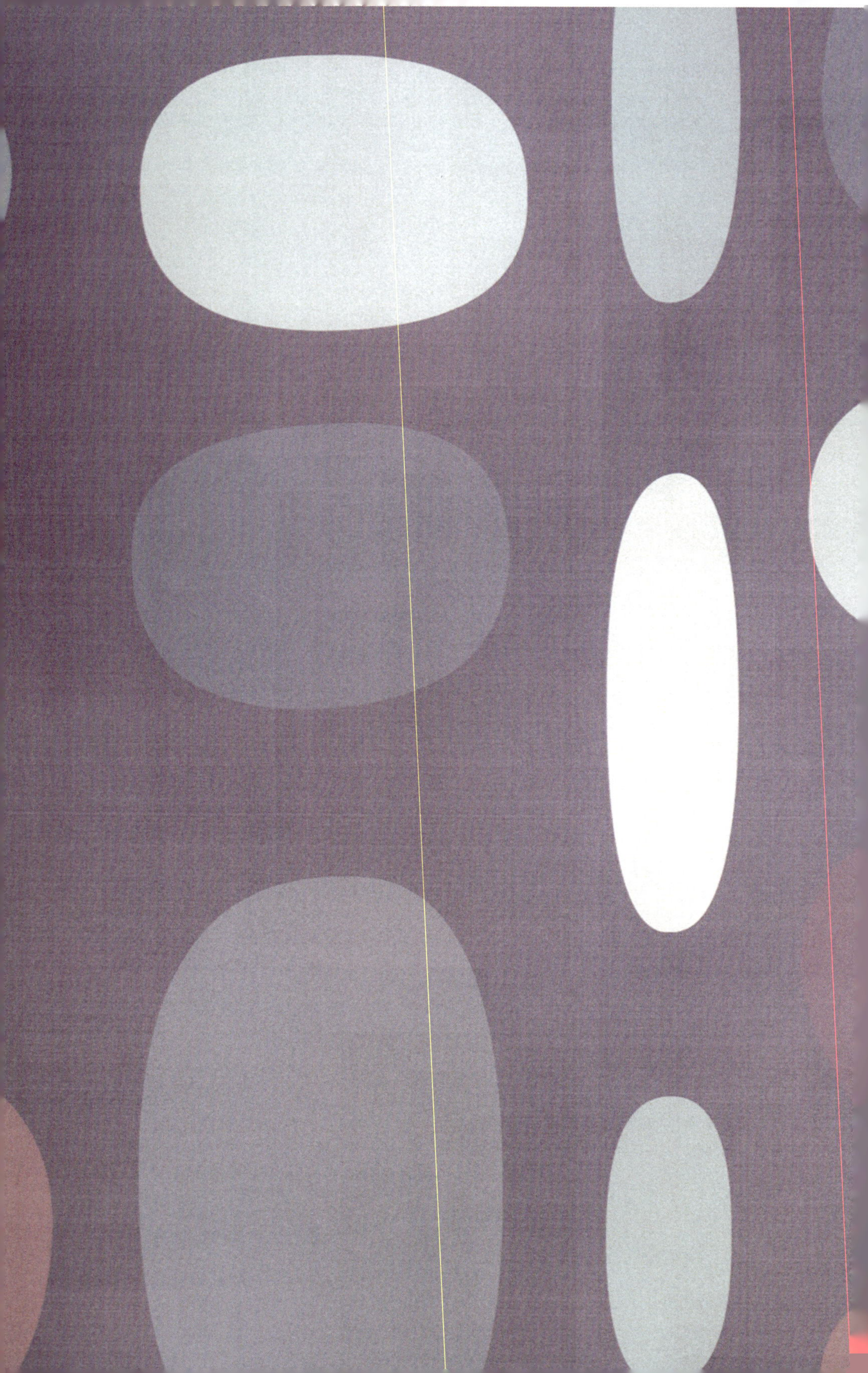

COLOR DENSITY AND FLOW

Color Density

Color Density is a way of picking colors within a palette. A *Faint Color Density* will pick a smaller range of colors from the palette, while a *Drench Color Density* will pick a broader range of colors from the palette. To get a sense of how dense each *Color Density* variant is, let's look at the percentage values given to each in order:

- Faint 1-10%
- Hush 11-37%
- Bloom 38-64%
- Drench 65-90%
- Vivid 91-100%

There are five variants to the *Color Density* trait with the numbers in brackets indicating how often they appear:

- Drench (41)
- Hush (143)
- Faint (153)
- Bloom (314)
- Vivid (349)

Faint

The difference between each *Color Density* variant is more obvious to see when comparing Pebbles of the same trait, so that's what we'll do. In the *Faint Color Density* variant we see almost exclusively the crème white color picked by the algorithm from the *Night Owl Doodles* palette.

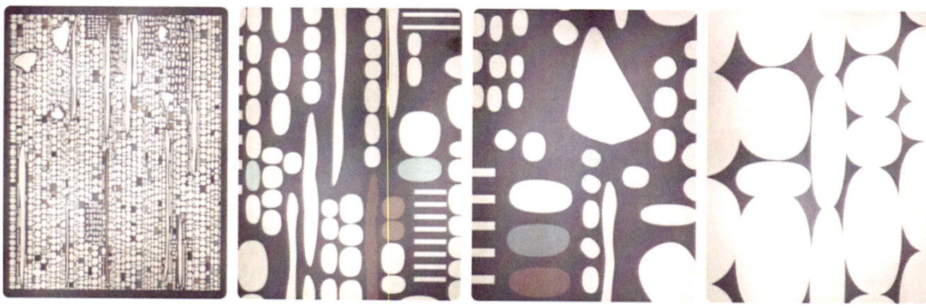

Faint Color Density Pebbles 484, 605, 130 and 635

Pebble #484 shows a wall of white Pebbles which is consistent with *Faint Color Density* showing a narrow 1-10% band of Pebble color variation. Pebbles in #635 are entirely the base color.

Hush

The *Hush Color Density* has added a couple of color highlights. In Pebble #860 shown here, there is a green stick, a couple of green Pebbles, and a couple of mauve Pebbles.

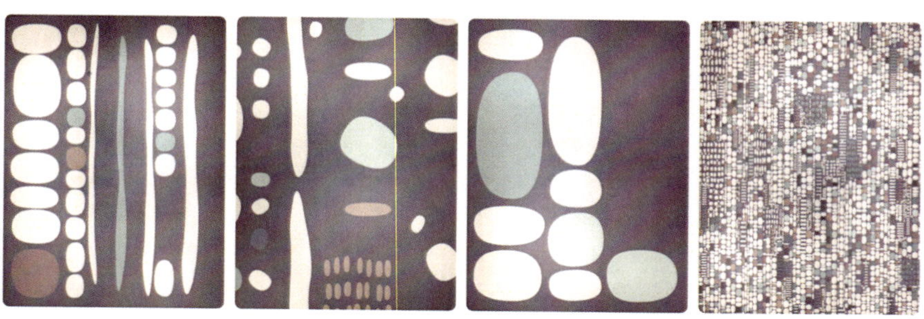

Hush Color Density Pebbles 860, 931, 915 and 989

In Pebble #915 there are two dark purple Pebbles as well as three green Pebbles. In Pebble #989 there is a multitude of color Pebbles, however, the crème white still dominates the canvas because *Hush Color Density* only adds color to 11-37% of the Pebbles shown.

Bloom

Bloom Color Density delivers a mid-range of 38-64% of any given color palette range. We see this in Pebble #792, where despite just three Pebbles being shown, they are three different colors. Pebble #232 becomes a visual delight from the varied colors, while white is still the most commonly picked base color.

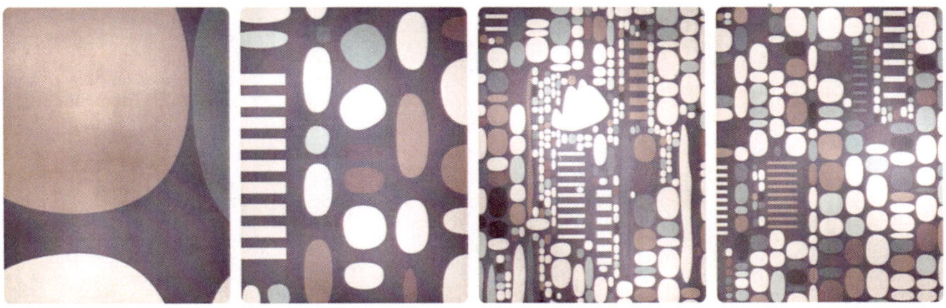

Bloom Color Density Pebbles 792, 837, 48 and 232

Drench

Drench Color Density takes the color variation up another notch with 65-90% of colors picked. Now we begin to see the base crème white color getting crowded out. Pebble #442 only shows five cream white Pebbles. Pebble #816 only shows one white Pebble, and Pebble #434 has picked none at all. How we experience color is a big part of how we experience art, making the importance of *Color Density* much greater than a casual Pebbles observer may give it credit for.

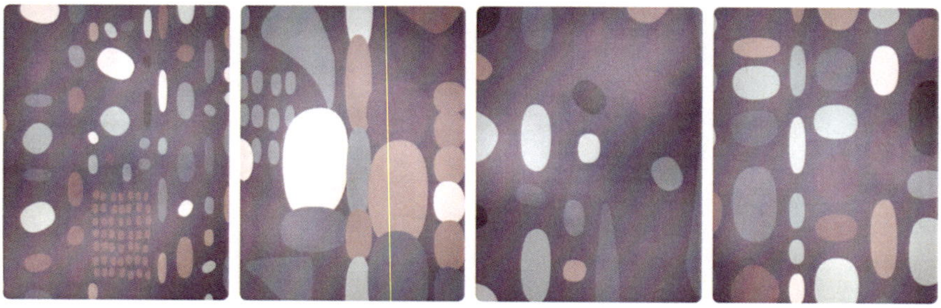

Drench Color Density Pebbles 442, 571, 434 and 816

Vivid

Vivid Color Density makes any chance of a base color sneaking through slim to none. 91-100% of the time, a palette color is picked instead of the base white color. Every *Vivid Color Density* Pebble shown here displays no crème white Pebbles, making base colors within a *Vivid Color Density* their own undocumented rarity.

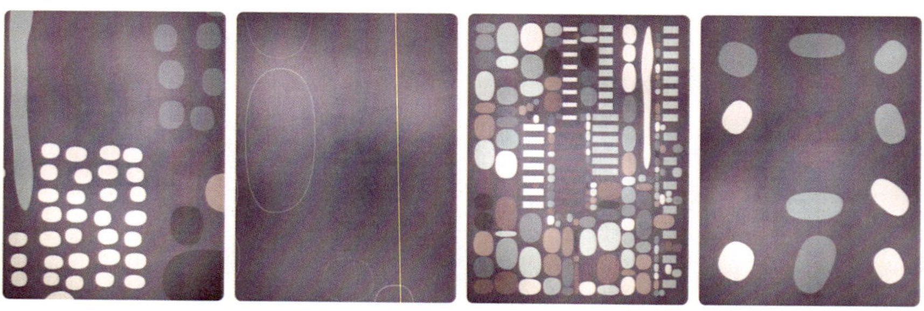

Vivid Color Density Pebbles 429, 734, 243 and 309

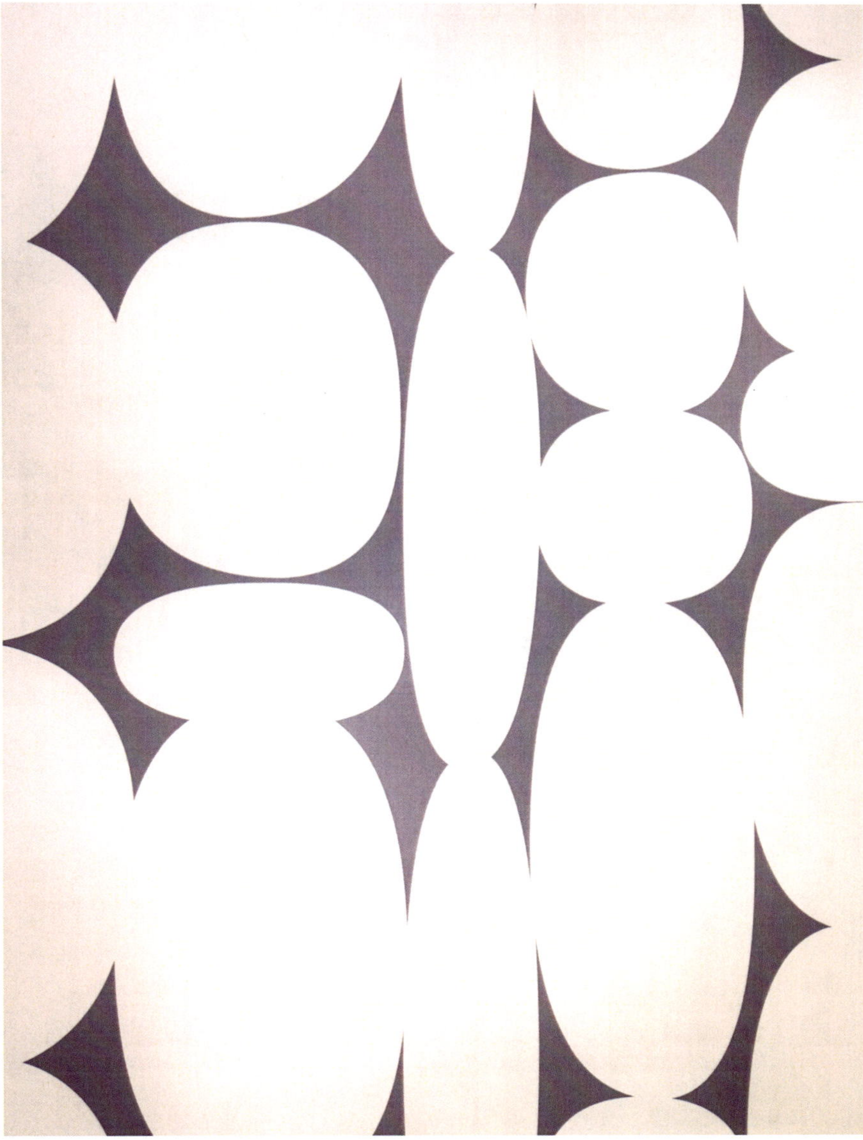

Pebble 635 with Faint Color Density

Pebble #635 offers the viewer a stark contrast afforded by the white and mauve base colors of the *Night Owl Doodles* palette. Any inclusion of the light green, sand, or dark purple is statistically possible within a low probability band of 1-10%.

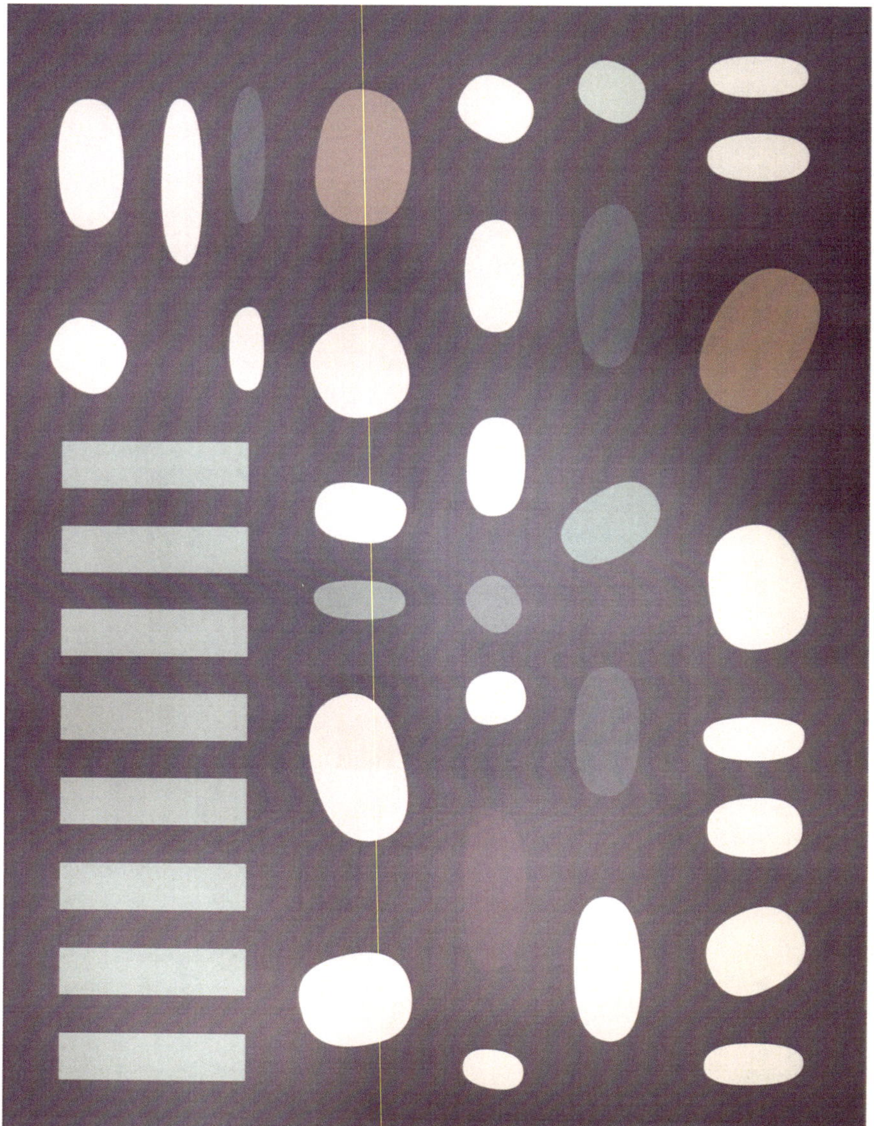

Pebble 683 with Hush Color Density

"My Pebble is a universe of little pebbles which contain lots of little pixels. A universe inside a Pebble." David

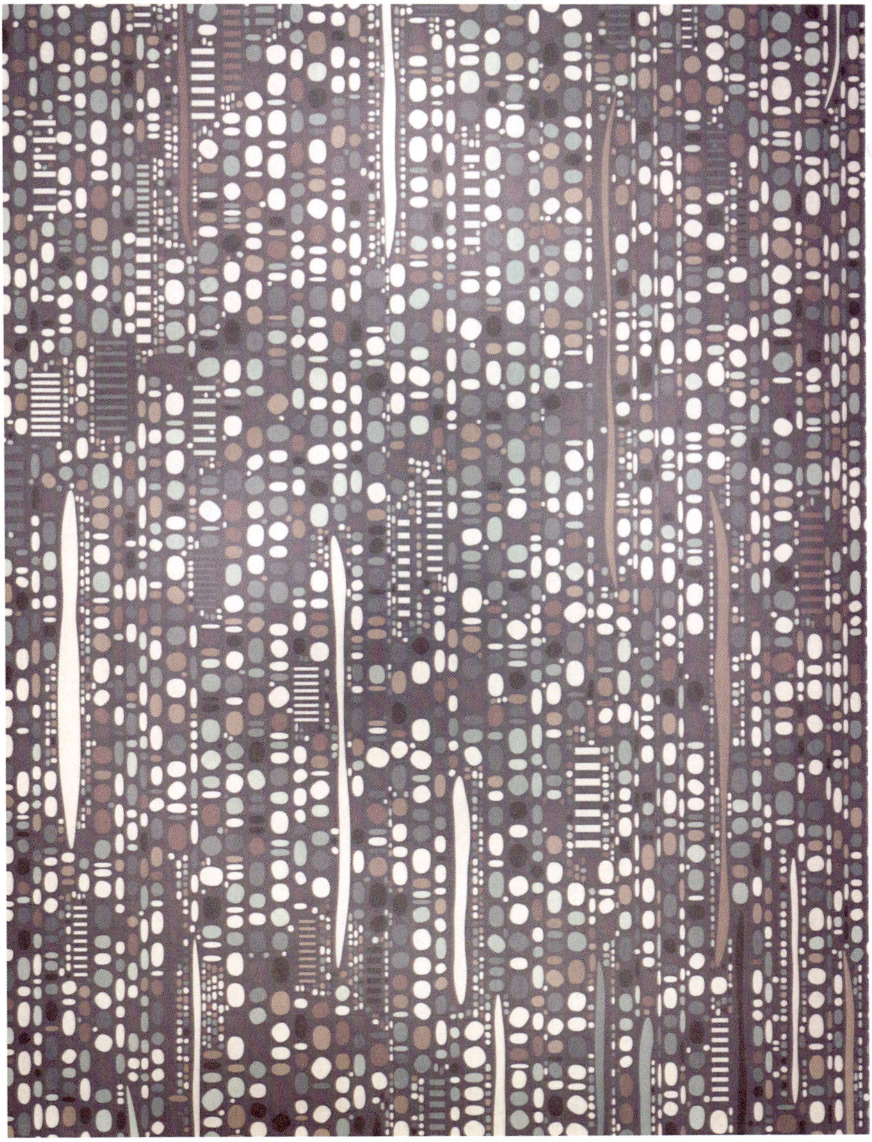

Pebble 250 'Concert Hallucinations' with Bloom Color Density

Bloom Color Density provides a good range of colors from both the base color and the *Night Owl Doodles* palette.

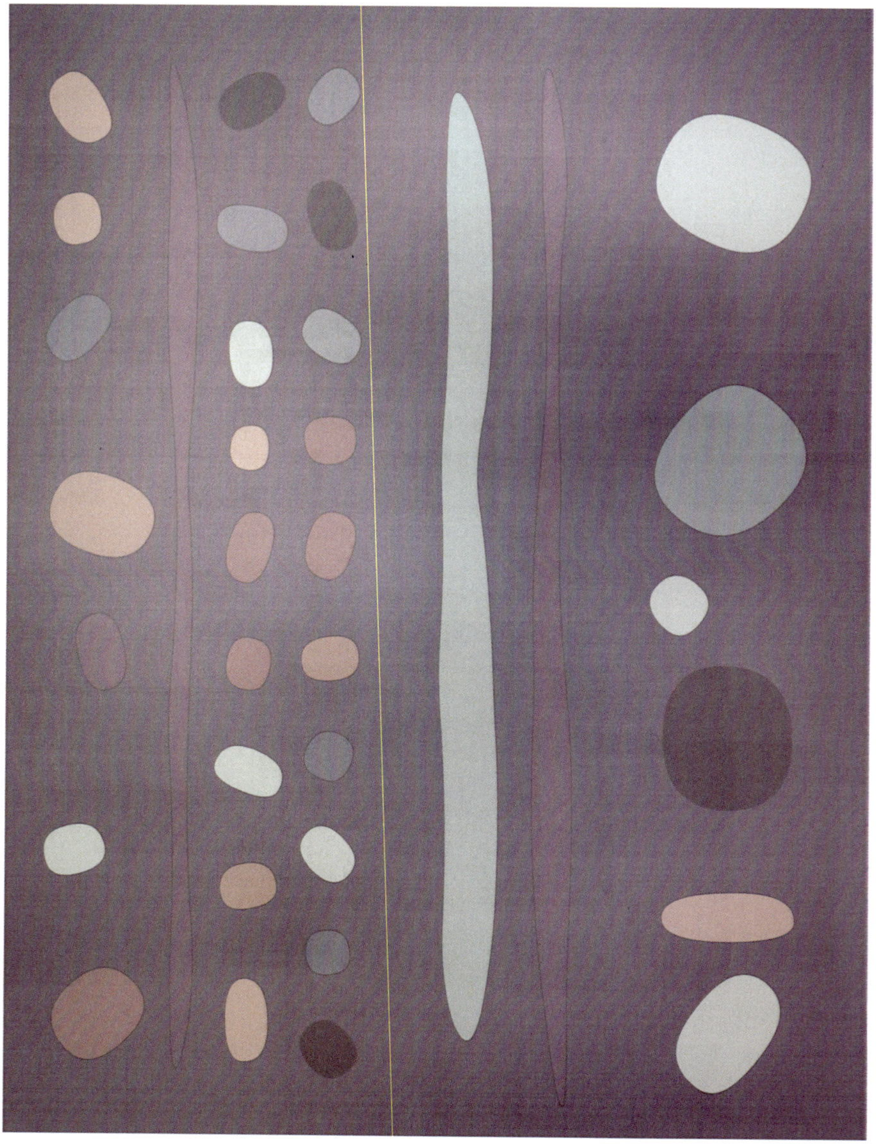

Pebble 198 with Drench Color Density

Drench Color Density gives way to the darker colors within the *Night Owl Doodles* palette. The white base colors are entirely absent from the *Night Owl Doodles* palette 65-90% of the time.

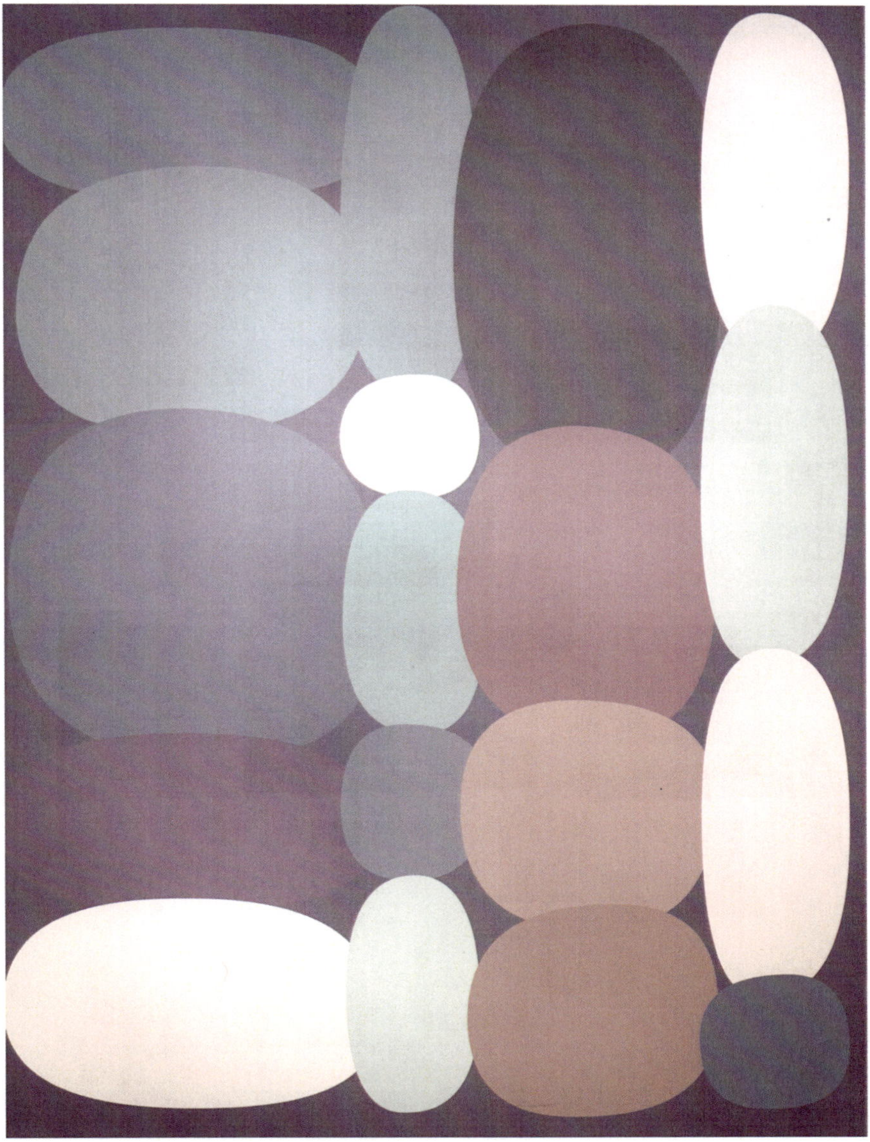

Pebble 435 with Vivid Color Density

Pebble #435 is a top vibe specimen because it shows a bright white Pebble in the base color despite being a *Vivid Color Density*, where the *Night Owl Doodles* palette paints 91-100% of the Pebbles according to the artist Zeblocks.

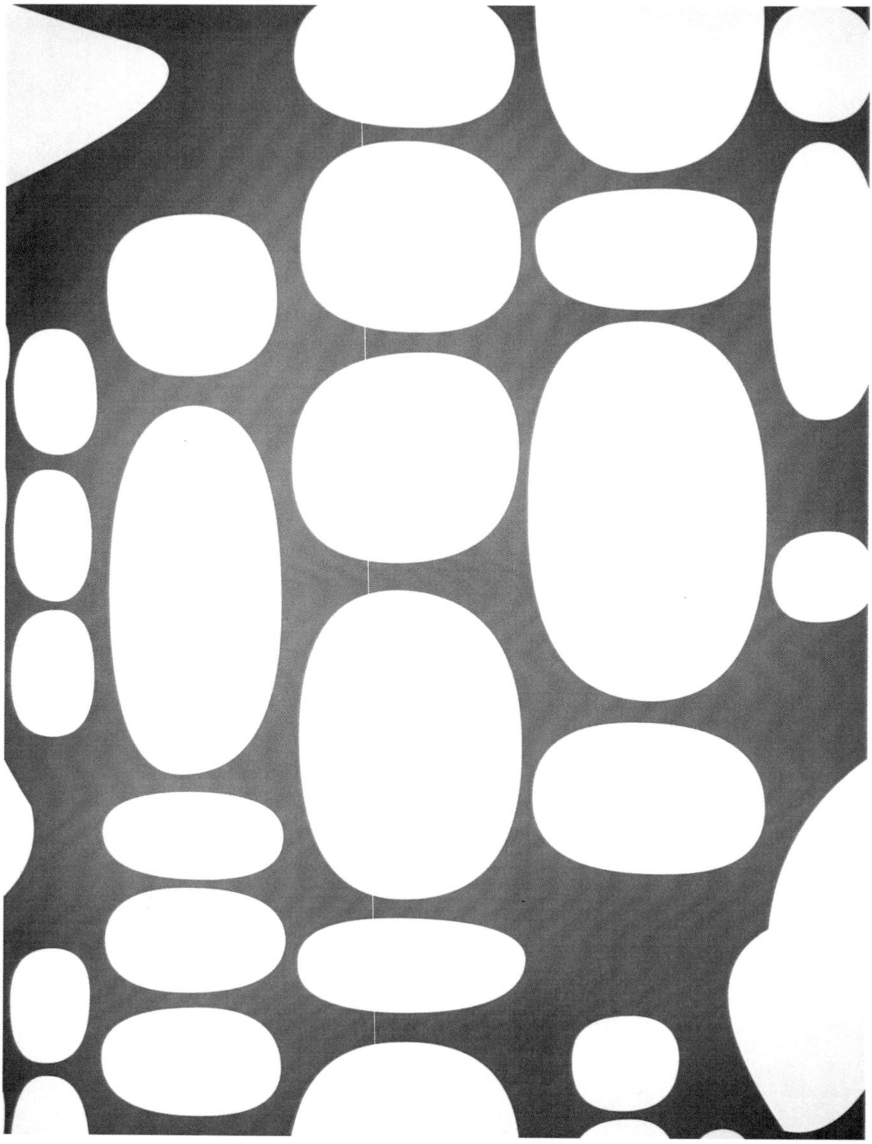

Pebble 380 with Faint Color Density

The *Color Density* algorithm rules apply to all palettes, such as *Shades of Hey!* Pebble #380 with *Faint Color Density* displaying only black and white, not grey, from the *Shades of Hey!* palette.

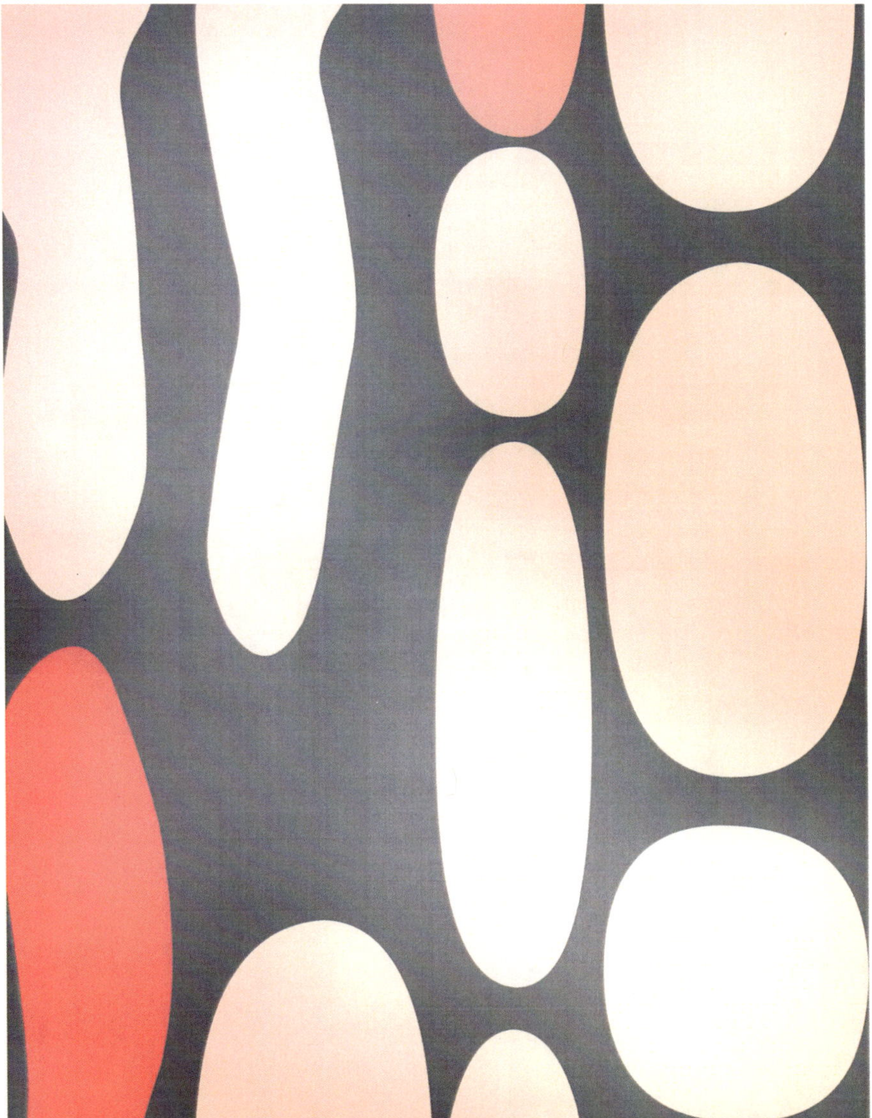

Pebble 558 with Hush Color Density

The *Hush Color Density* mediates the *Coral Reef* palette by preferring the golden crème base color for Pebbles. Two pink Pebbles are the only ones to make it through the *Color Density* lottery.

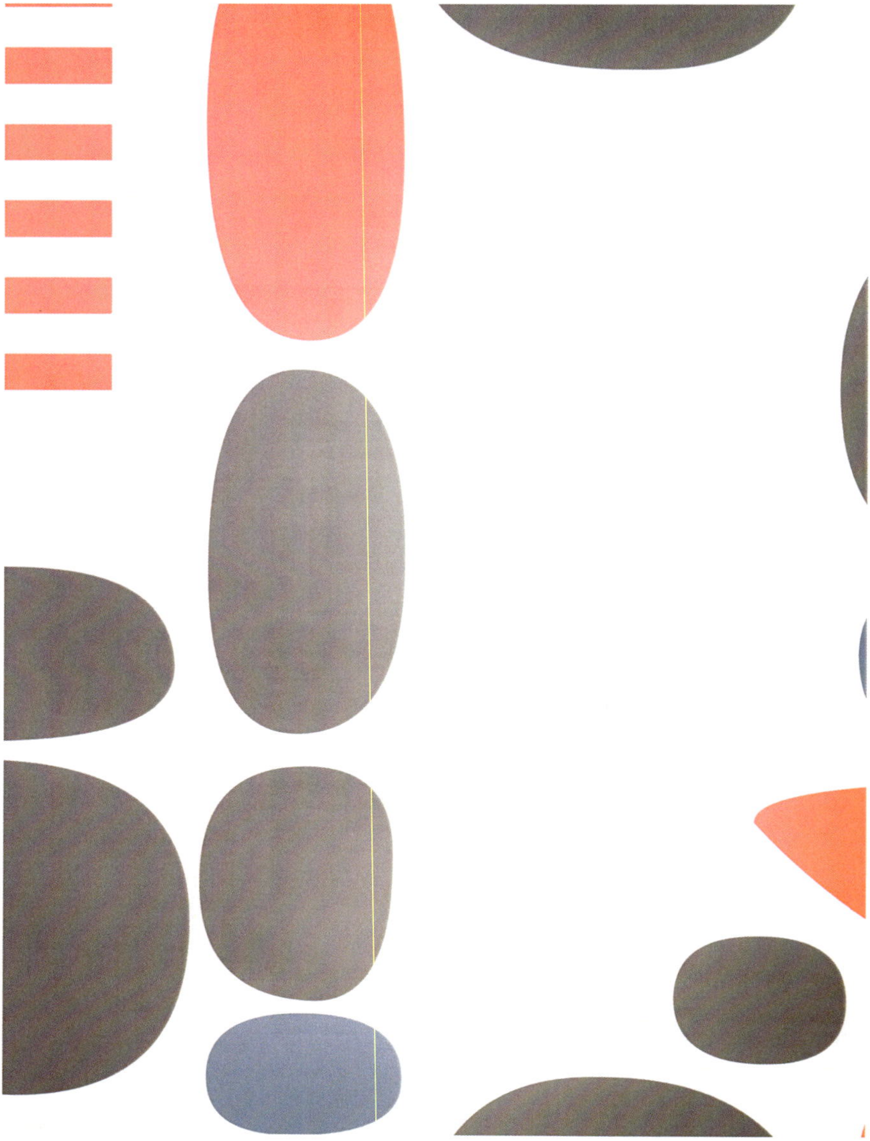

Pebble 448 with Bloom Color Density

Pebble #448 with *Bloom Color Density* shows a spread of palette colors picked from the *Dino Disco* palette including red, blue, and grey. Only the yellow from *Dino Disco* was filtered out by *Bloom Color Density*.

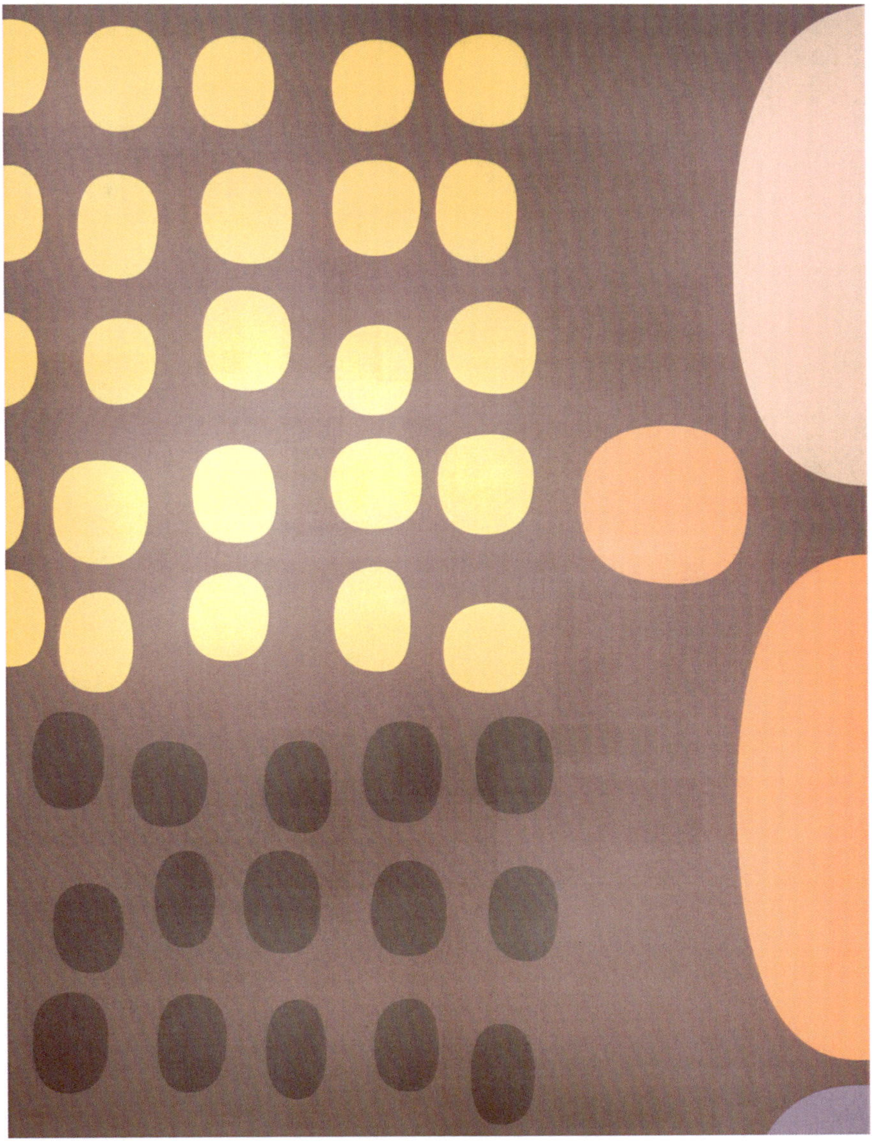

Pebble 551 with Drench Color Density

Pebble #551 shows the yellow, orange, tan, burgundy, and a thumbnail of purple from the *Sgt. Pepe* palette. The yellow gets featured because of its application to a grid *Special Element* where all Pebbles in the grid are usually painted the same color.

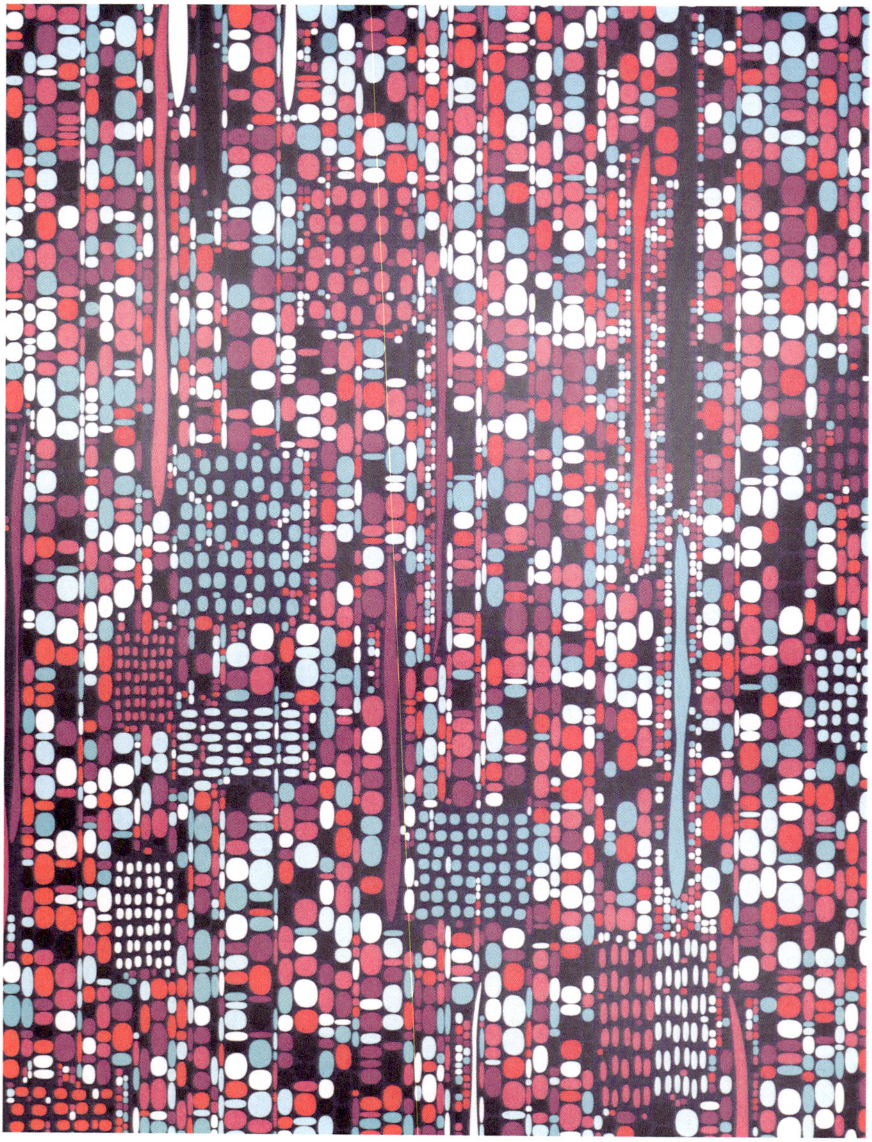

Pebble 165 with Vivid Color Density

Pebble #165 in *Beatboxes* palette is a cacophony of color thanks to both the loud palette and the *Vivid Color Density*. The latter trait variant ensures an even distribution of colors picked from the *Beatboxes* palette for both Pebbles and the *Special Elements*.

Flow

Flow trait creates a focal point through an invisible gravitational field that attracts all Pebbles and *Special Elements* towards it. The *Flow* trait bears down on Pebbles like a black hole bears down on the universe, atomising anything that gets too close to its centrifugal force. *Flow* is found in 65 Pebbles; while all other Pebbles escape the force of *Flow*.

> ‘Flow creates a focal point that functions similarly to a black hole, drawing all elements towards it.’ Zeblocks.

Except there is a problem. Of all the Pebble traits examined so far, *Flow* is the most difficult to spot in the minted collection of Pebbles. The Pebbles collection seems to have escaped the tractor beam effects of *Flow,* perhaps because it was a couple of light years away from our galaxy. To properly cover the trait, we will compare some test outputs that were created before the Pebbles collection went live.

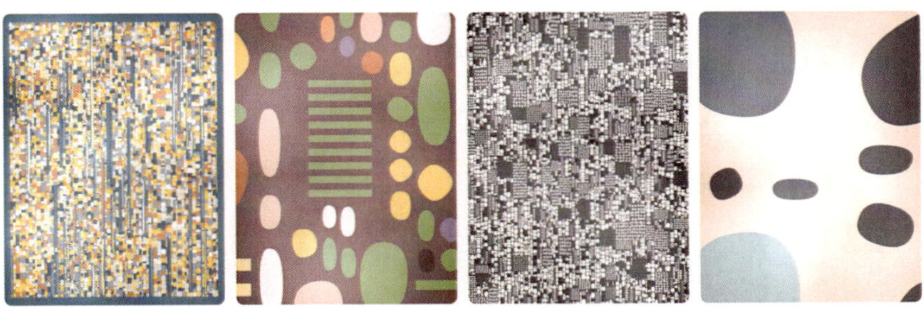

Flow Pebbles 644, 535, 279 and 669

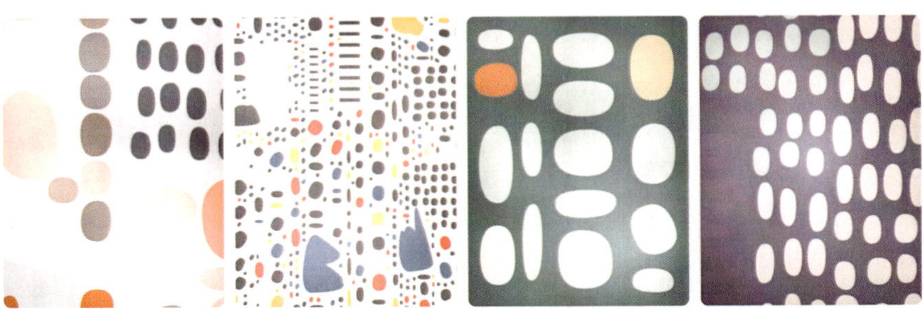

Flow Pebbles 782, 912, 982 and 905

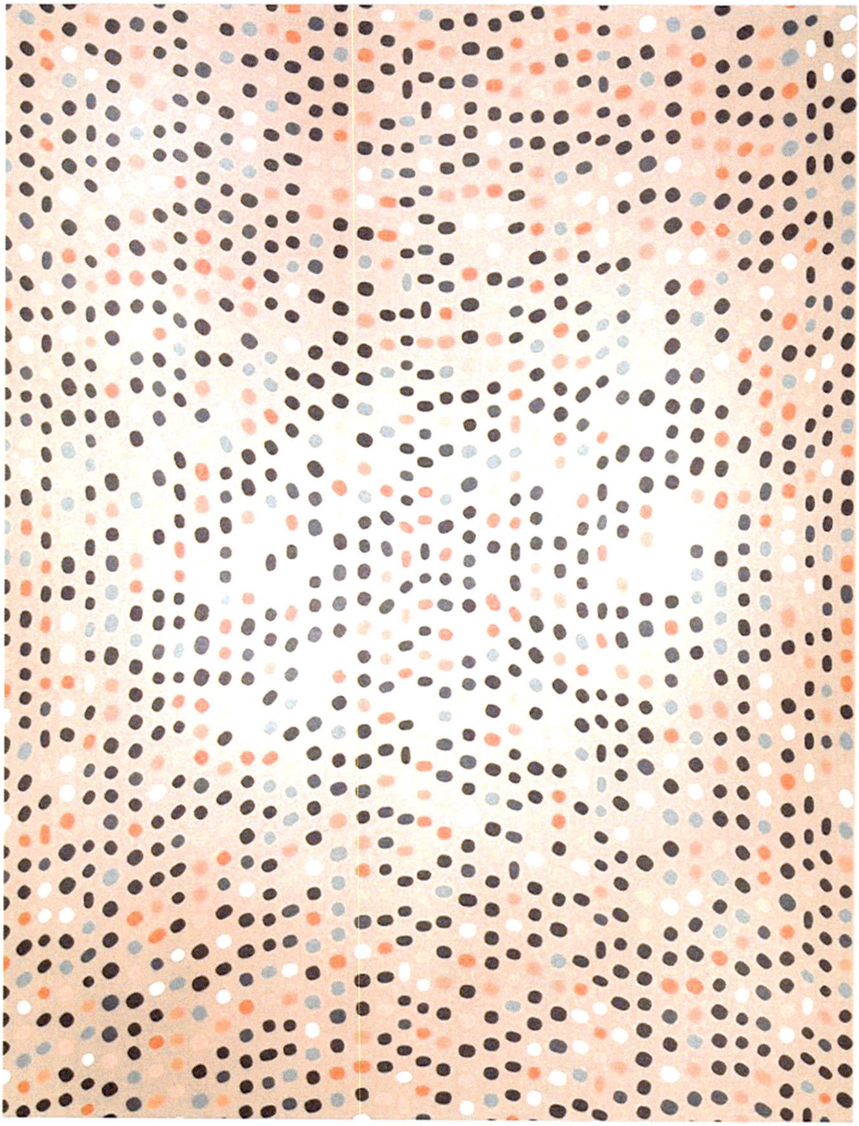

Flow Pebble test output before Pebbles collection mint

The *Flow* forcefield effect in the Pebble test output shown above is pronounced. The *Desert Mirage* trait almost puts the viewers focus into disarray. Unsure where to rest one's eye, the pattern warps inwards and outwards as different colored Pebbles are picked up by the viewer.

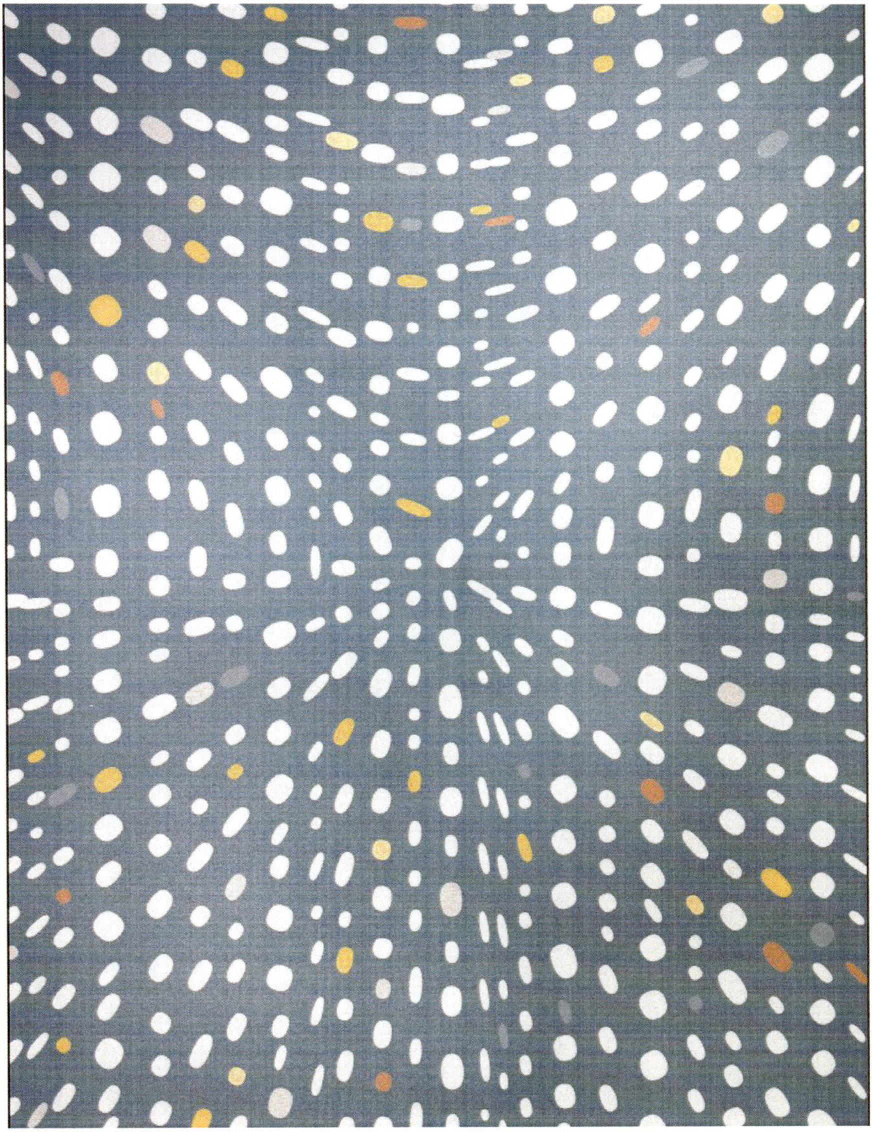

Flow Pebble test output before Pebbles collection mint

The *Flow* forcefield is going at warp speed in this test output. The *Citrus Slate* palette places most of the white Pebbles into a star-like arrangement that firmly bends reality into the centre of the frame. Each of the yellow or orange Pebbles may represent planets or the sparks of a spaceship exhaust.

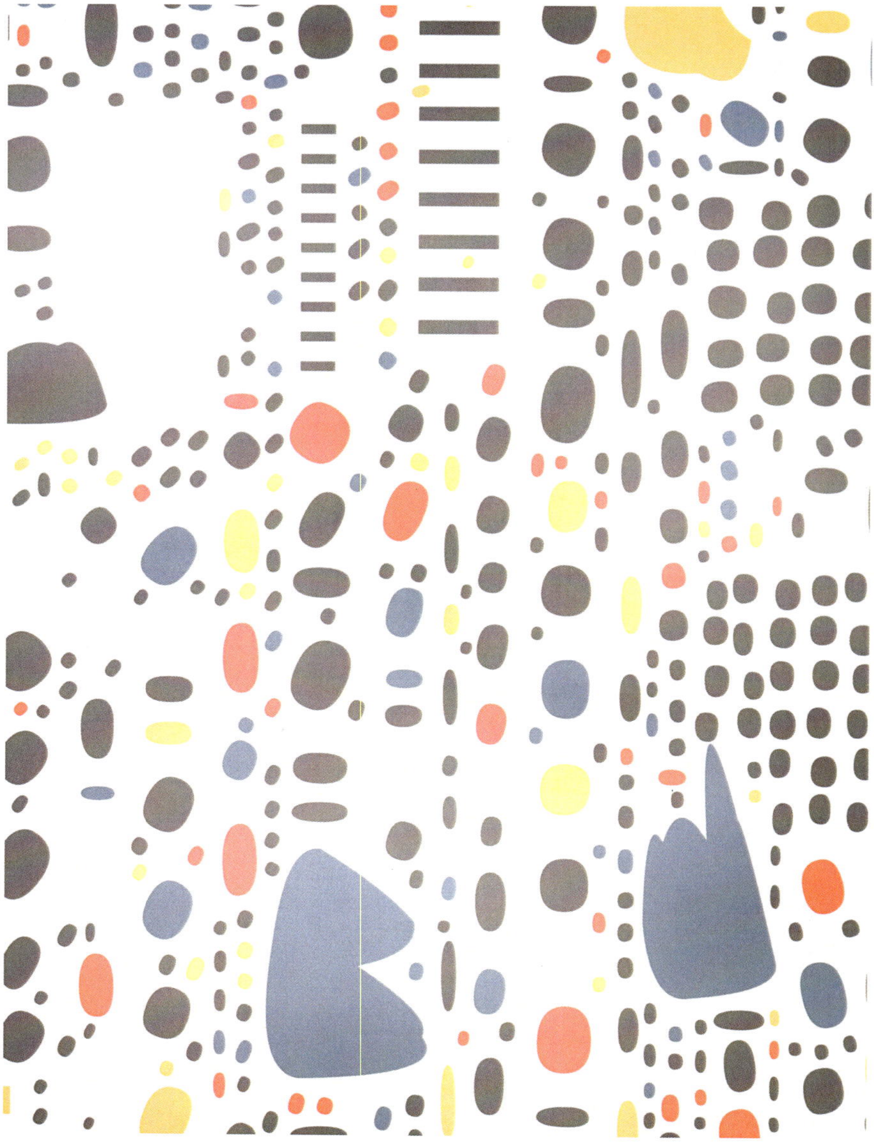

Pebble 912 with Flow

Pebble #912 presents some of the circular-moving Pebbles from the bottom left up into the center of the frame. The white background from *Dino Disco* and the *Crumb Size* assists in revealing some of the expected *Flow* properties.

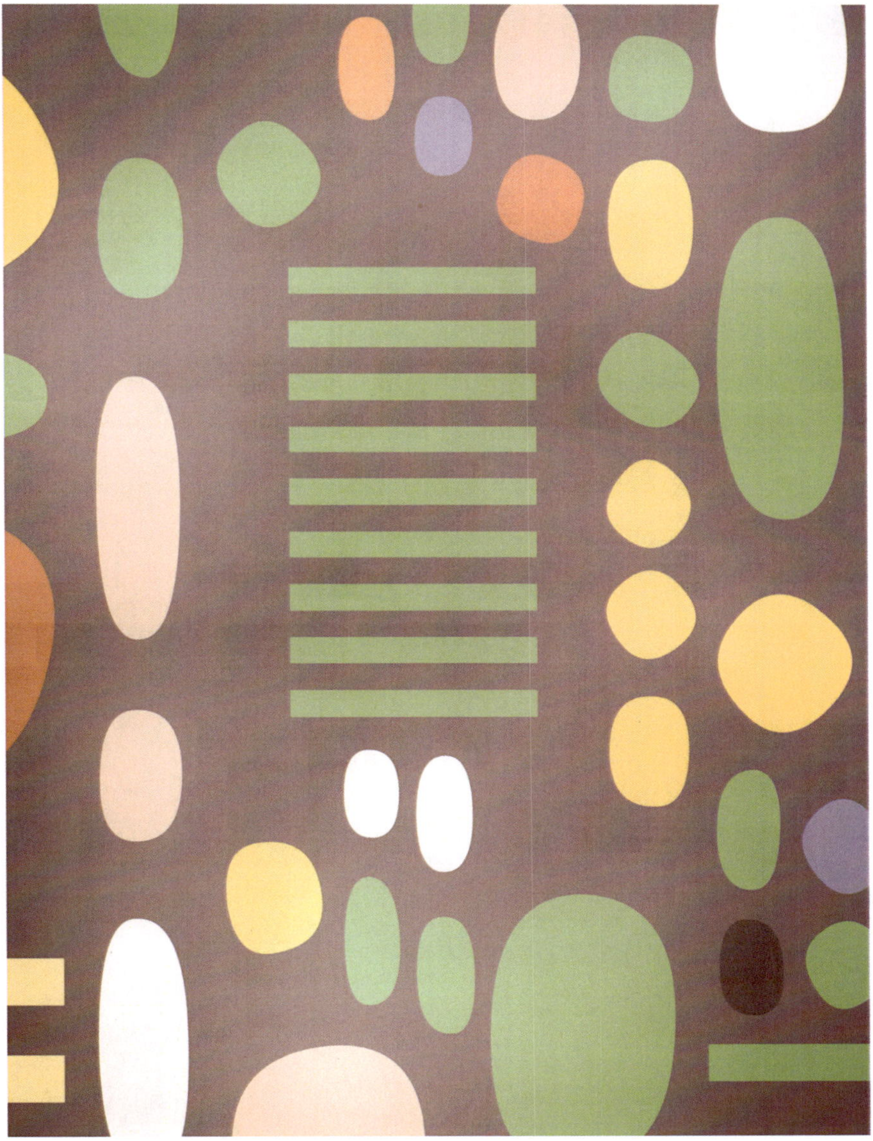

Pebble 535 with Flow

Pebble #535 presents a circular shape of Pebbles, offset on various angles; a telltale sign of the *Flow* effect. The ladder-like *Special Element* in the center and the *Disjoin Overlap* interrupt the *Flow*. punksladsmemes flipped #535 for #512 perhaps because it has a clearer *Flow* representation.

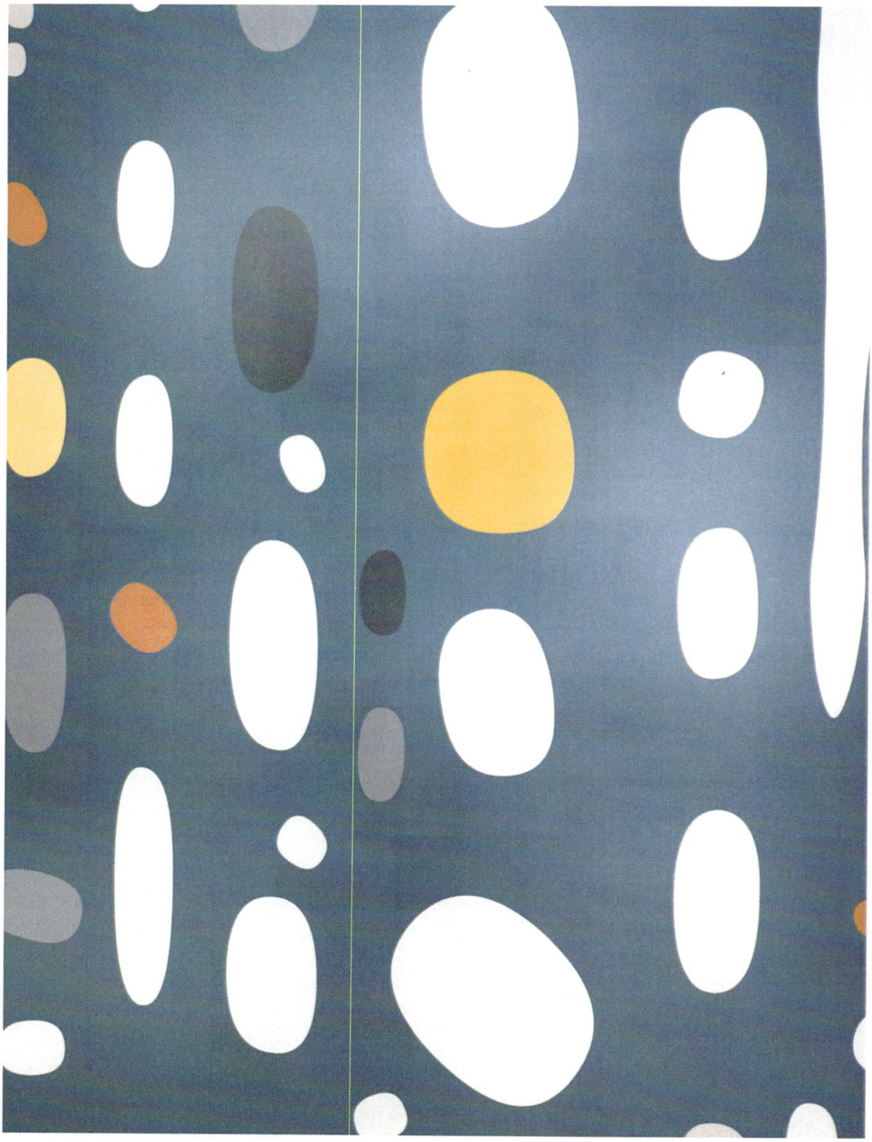

Pebble 44 with Flow

Pebble #44 was the seventh *Flow* trait minted and the first to hint at the potential of *Flow* for the rest of the collection. Unfortunately, none of the mints later that day represented the high water mark shown as possible from the *Flow* test outputs.

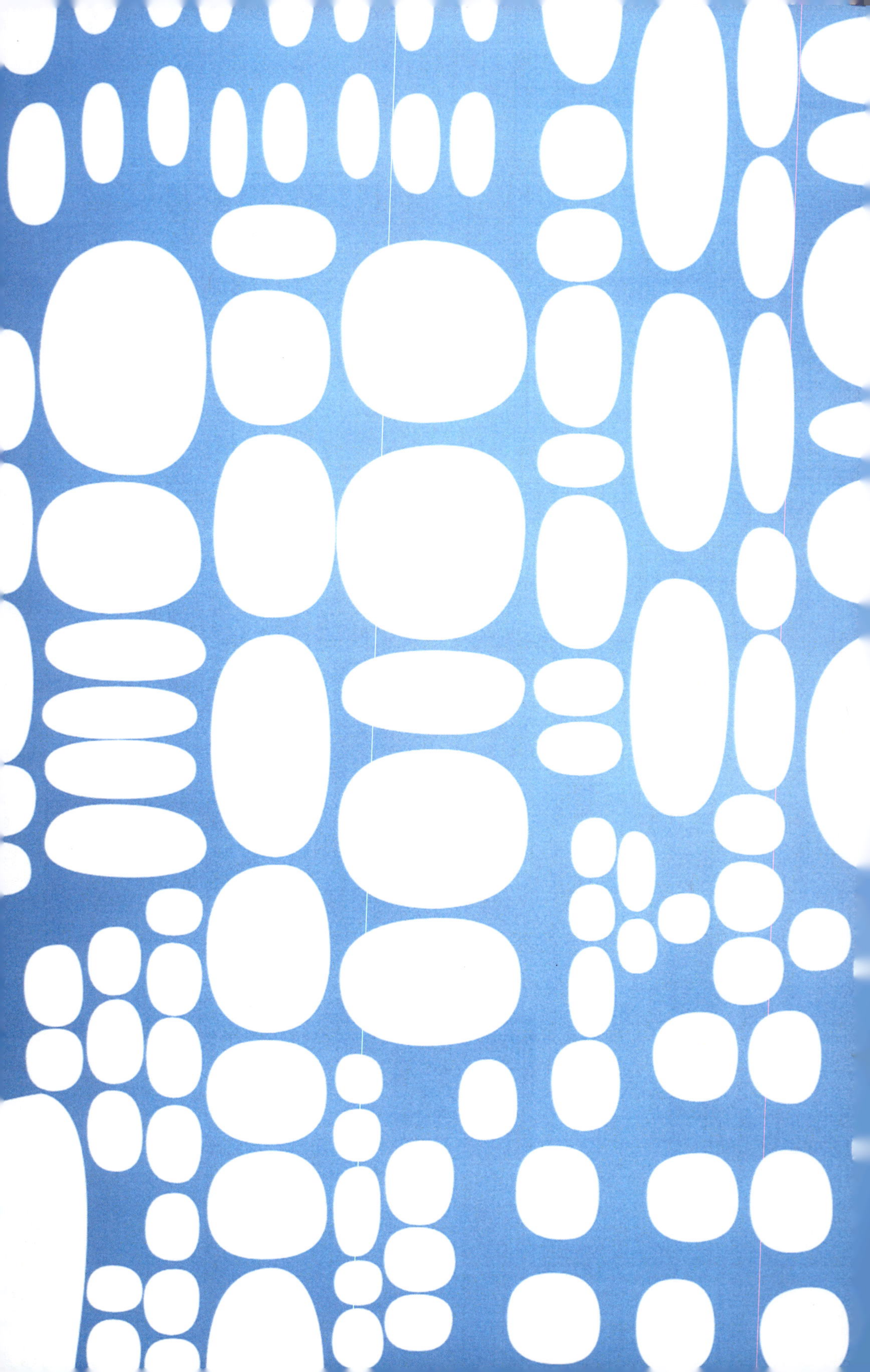

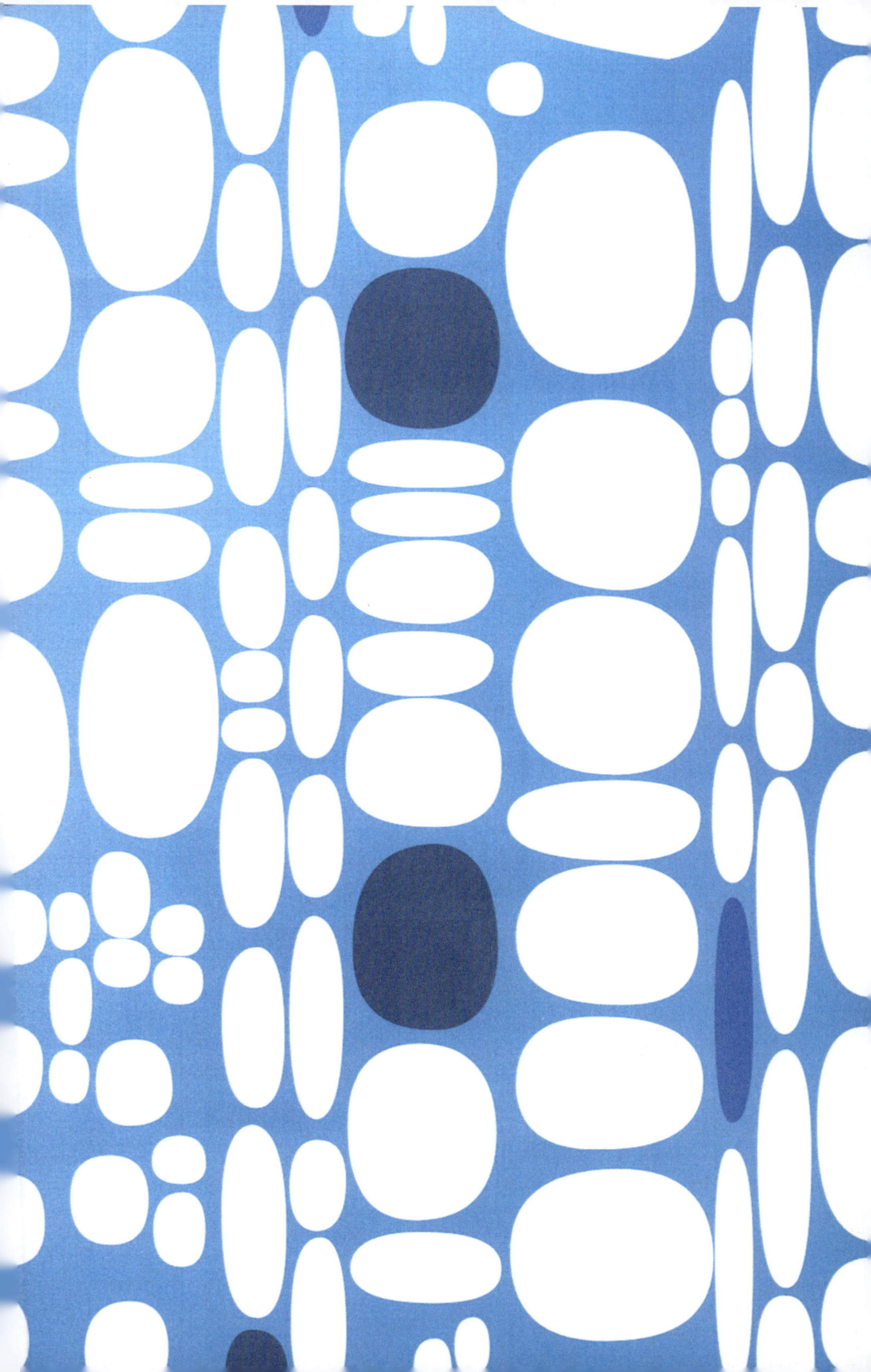

MINT TYPE - PALETTES

Pebbles were distributed to reward long-time collectors and large collectors. The reward gained was access to the allowlist or access to 'Collector Provenance' Pebble palettes. This is a departure from previous on-chain generative art drops on Art Blocks where every mint trait was randomized. There are four variants to the *Mint Type - Palettes* trait.

- UltraMaxis (17)
- Sgt. Pepe (33)
- HyperMaxis (50)
- MemeMaxis (900)

Collector Provenance was taken into account for the first three *Mint Types* resulting in 100 of the 1000 Pebbles minted with palette traits such as *Lunar Chuckles, Magma Mambo, summer.jpg, Salsa Blush, Elephant Pajamas, Blueprint* and *Sgt. Pepe.*

Within the NextGen art contract, at mint time, the code adjusts the output based on what the minting wallet holds. The adjustment enables the Collector Provenance Pebble palette reward to the collector. This is a new innovation that preserves the magic of generative art outputting a combination of beauty on mint day, while also rewarding both long time collectors and large collectors with access to preferential traits. Punk6529 coined the term 'Collector Provenance' as part of the Pebbles distribution plan.

> 'There are non-art uses of generative art where Collector Provenance matters a lot and that even in generative art, there are ways to introduce Collector Provenance in the mint, without changing the fundamental nature of long-form on-chain generative art." Punk6529

UltraMaxis

There were 17 allowlist places given to 15 people who had the highest TDH (total days held) figure, and one person with more than 10 Sgt. Pepe meme cards, and one to Zeblocks the artist. All allowlist places were redeemed, resulting in 17 Pebbles minted including five *Lunar Chuckles,* five *Magma Mambo,* and ten *summer.jpg* palettes all shown below:

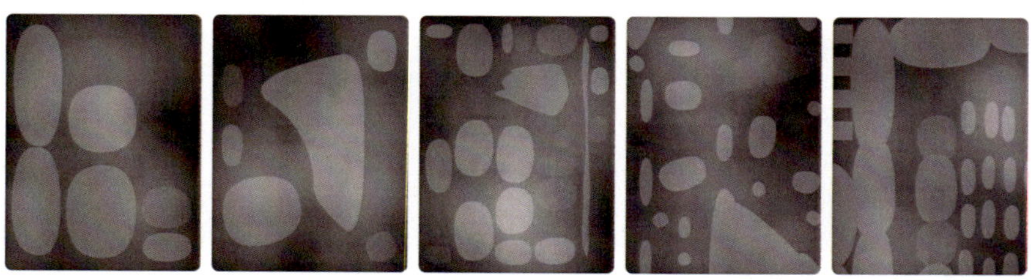

Ultra Maxis Pebbles 32, 126, 205, 331 and 748 with Lunar Chuckles palette

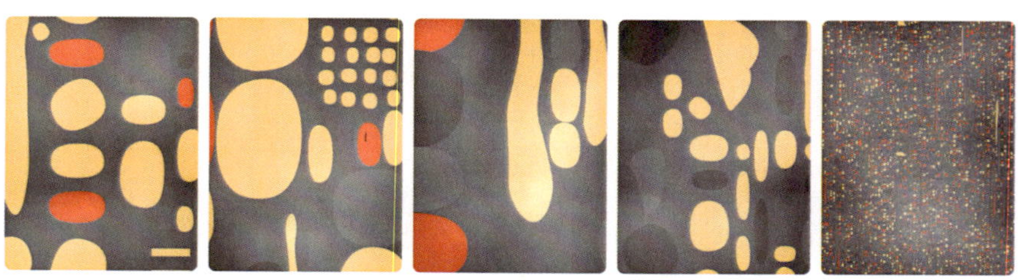

Ultra Maxis Pebbles 1, 11, 28, 24 and 83 with Magma Mambo palette

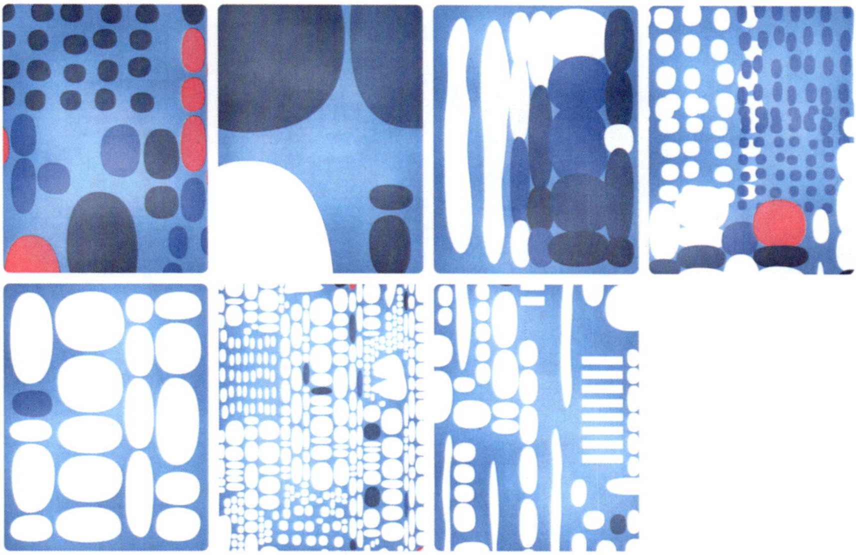

Ultra Maxis Pebbles 2, 13, 96, 120, 241, 259 and 287 with summer.jpg palette

Sgt. Pepe

A total of 42 allowlist places were created for Sgt. Pepe holders and 33 were minted with Collector Provenance palettes. The top 20 people by TDH (total days held) of the Sgt. Pepe meme were included in the allowlist. 22 more randomly selected Sgt. Pepe holders were also eligible. 33 Sgt. Pepe palettes were minted in the *Sgt. Pepe Mint Type*.

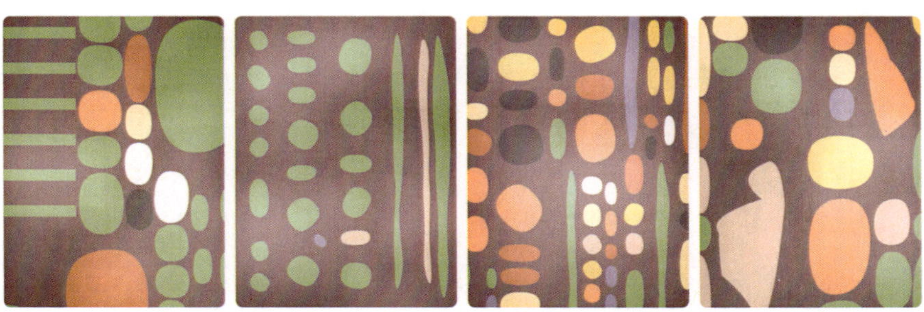

Sgt. Pepe Pebbles 4, 12, 29 and 36 with Sgt. Pepe palette

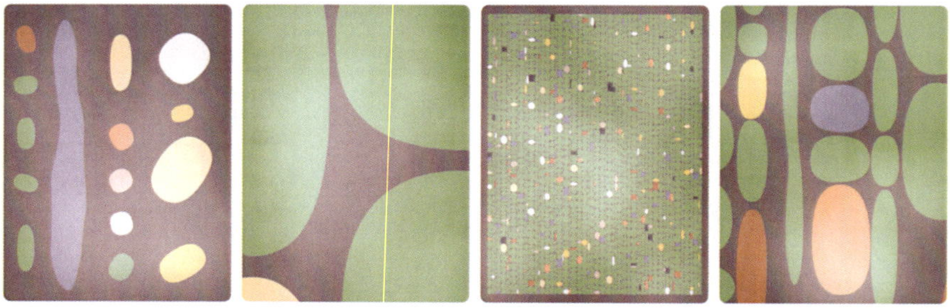

Sgt. Pepe Pebbles 57, 85, 98 and 108 with Sgt. Pepe palette

HyperMaxis

There were 54 allowlist places for people who qualified under the *UltraMaxis* group *and* had more than one full set of meme cards in their wallet. Any person with a full set of memes also received a place on the allowlist. Finally, the top 10 people who had the highest TDH (total days held) figure, if not included already. 50 of the 64 *HyperMaxis* places were redeemed, resulting in 50 Pebbles being minted including 13 *Salsa Blush, 16 Elephant Pajamas,* and *21 Blueprints*.

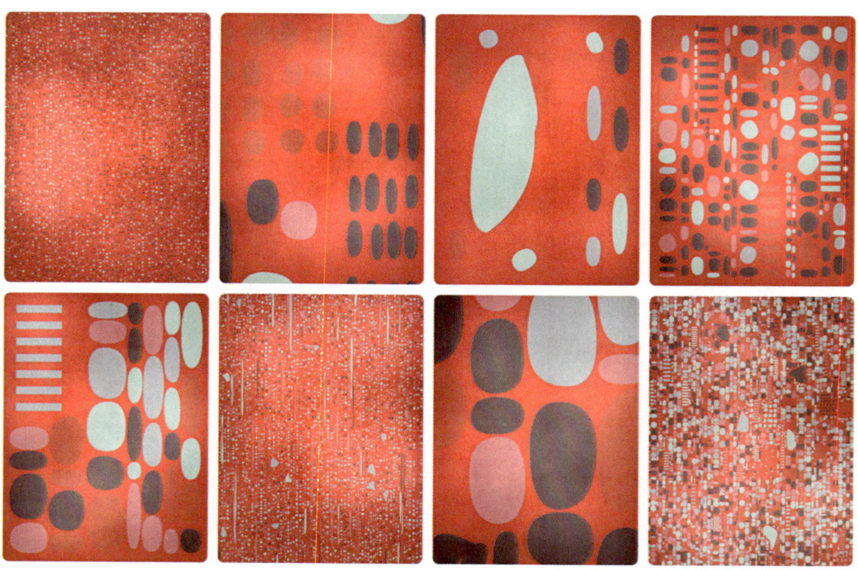

HyperMaxis Pebbles 15, 127, 226, 252, 261, 295, 299 and 403 with Salsa Blush palette

HyperMaxis Pebbles 3, 5, 30, 40, 137, 168, 230 and 326 with Elephant Pajamas palette

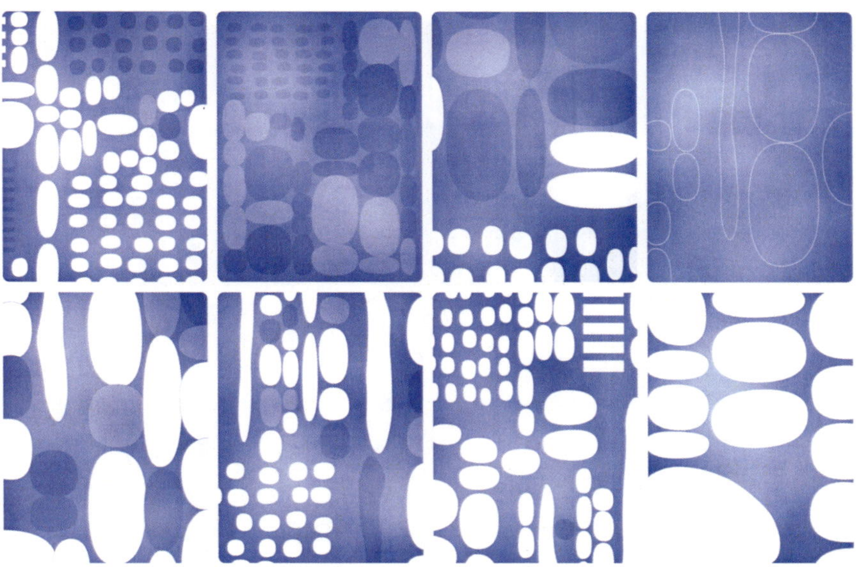

HyperMaxis Pebbles 10, 82, 112, 140, 167, 218, 246 and 251 with Blueprint palette

MemeMaxis

MemeMaxis Mint Type were given the remaining allowlist places using TDH (total days held) as the metric to decide how many allowlist places a person might receive. The more memes a person held over a longer elapsed time, then the more allowlist places were allocated to that person. 900 *MemeMaxis Mint Type* were minted on mint day by those eligible in the Pebbles Distribution Plan.

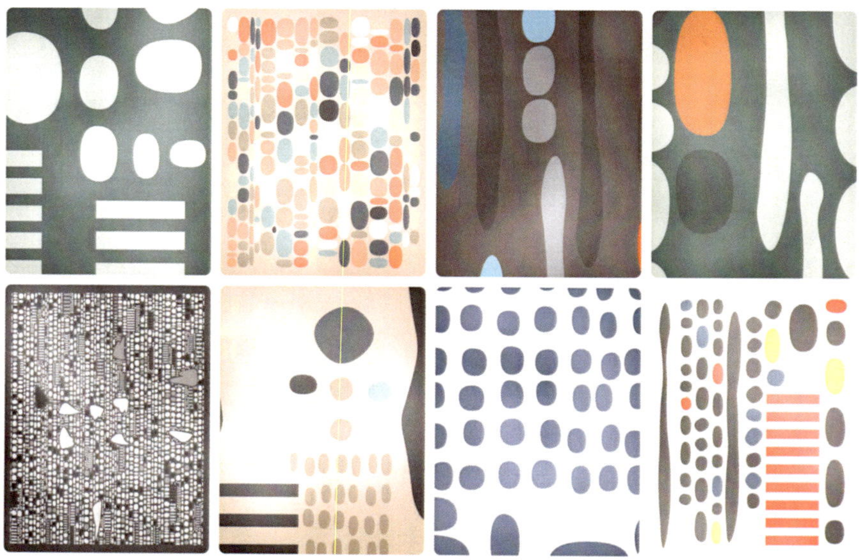

First eight generally available palette Pebbles 0, 9, 7, 8, 6, 16, 19 and 23

The first six generally available palette mints outside the Collector Provenance *Mint Types* of *UltraMaxis, Sgt. Pepe* and *HyperMaxis* were:

- *Forest Whisper* Pebble #0 and #8
- *Shades of Hey!* Pebble #6
- *Galactic Latte* Pebble #7
- *Desert Mirage* Pebble #9 and #16
- *Unigrids* Pebble #19
- *Dino Disco* Pebble #23

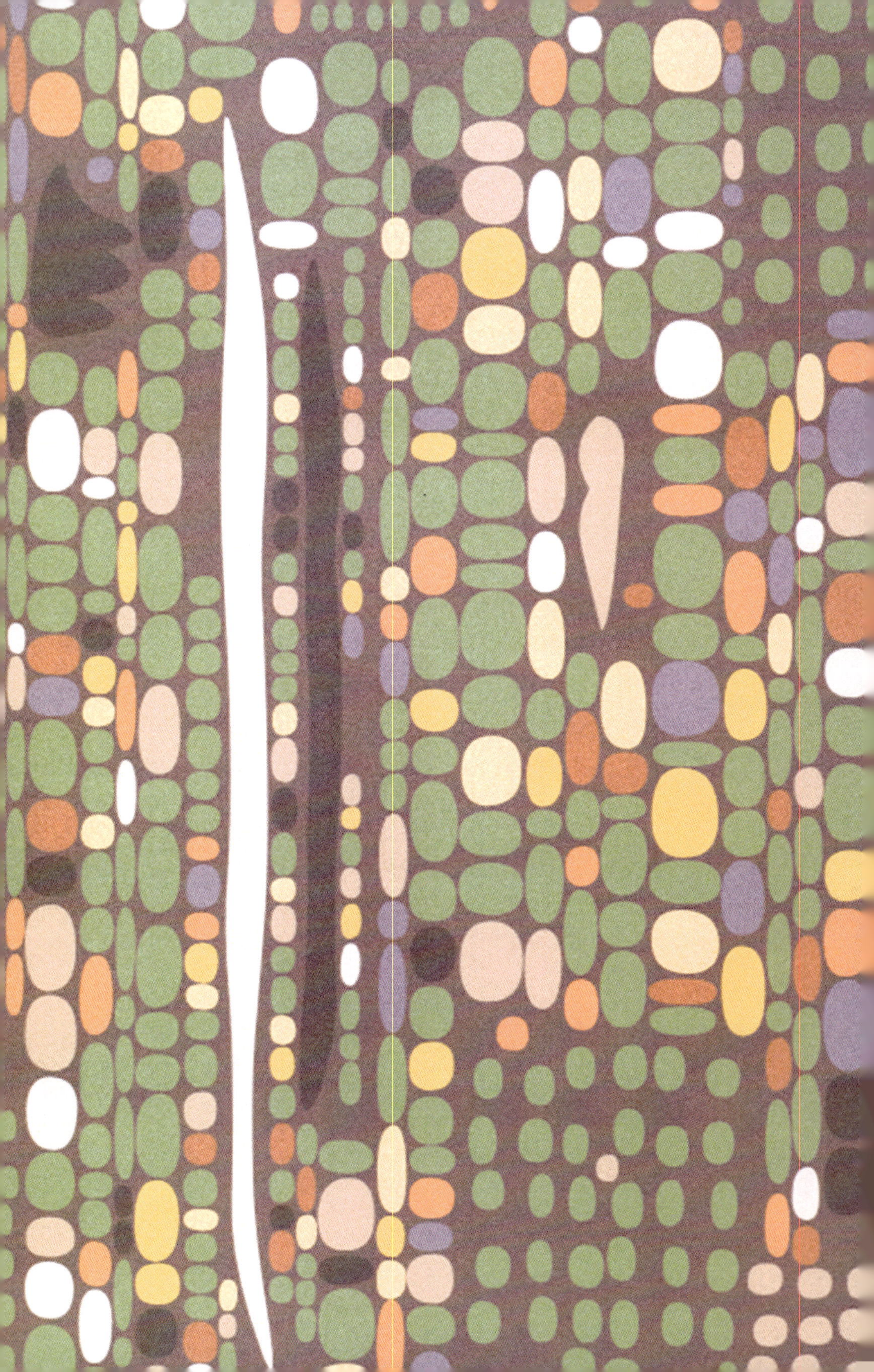

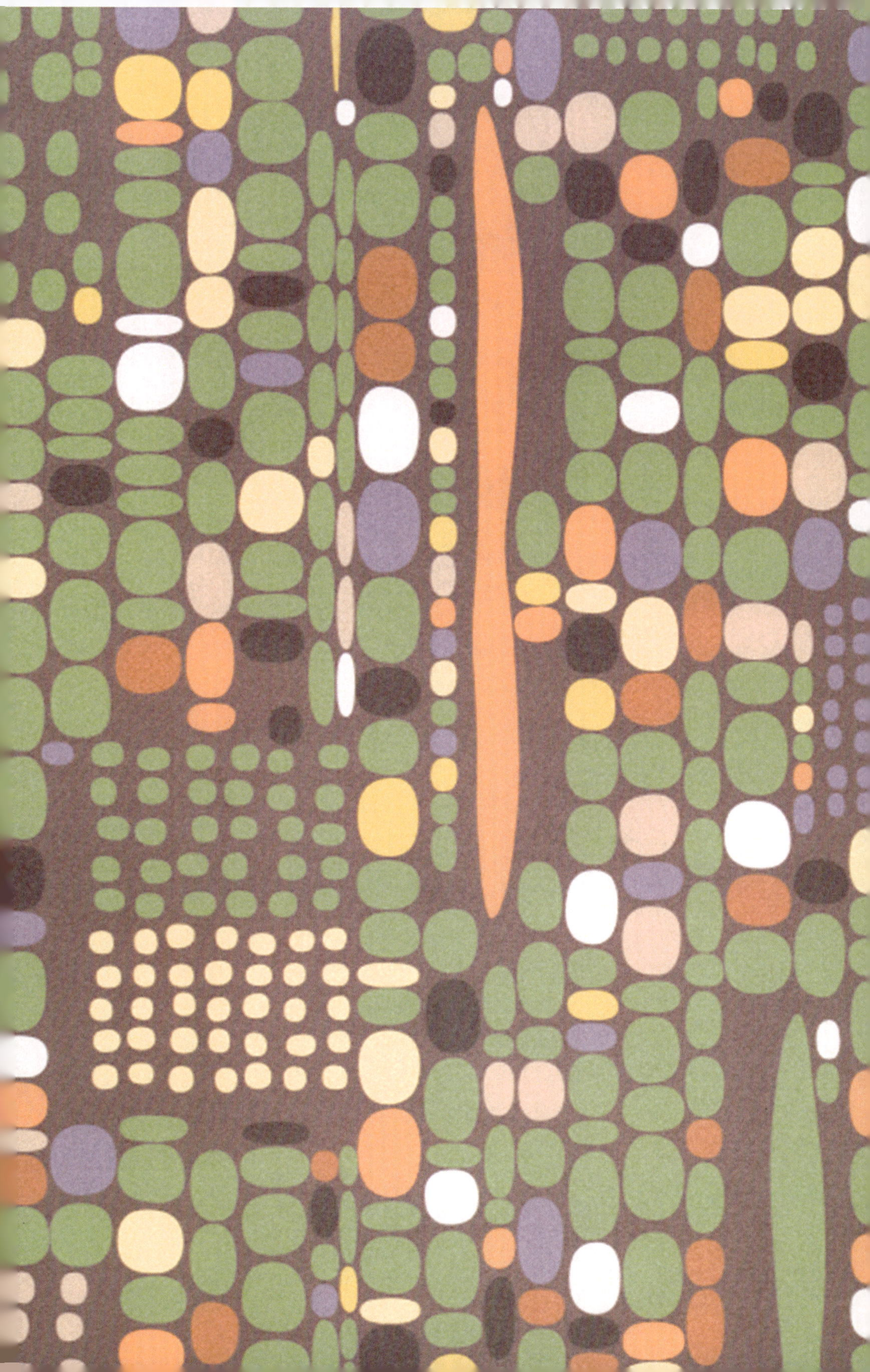

STATS AND TRAITS

The rarity of a particular trait in a generative collection is often, but not always, correlated with value. The rarer the traits outputted by the algorithm into an artwork, the more valuable it is perceived to be. A generative artwork can also be rare, but without the visual vibes to go with it. In the next Pebbles Collectoors chapter, you will see Pebbles that are aesthetically beautiful and Pebbles that are rare, and every so often, a Pebble that is both.

Palette x20

- Lunar Chuckles x5
- Magma Mambo x5
- summer.jpg x7
- Salsa Blush x13
- Elephant Pajamas x16
- Blueprint x21
- Sgt. Pepe x33
- Beatboxes x40
- Shades of Hey! x55
- Dino Disco x58
- Terra Echoes x58

- Unigrids x63
- Coral Reef x71
- Dusk Riverbed x71
- Citrus Slate x72
- Desert Mirage x79
- Galactic Latte x80
- Forest Whisper x83
- Serenity x84
- Night Owl Doodles x86

Size x7

- Mountlet x25
- Crumb x72
- Craglet x85
- Boulderette x147
- Pebbit x151
- Stonelet x220
- Rockling x300

Color Density x5

- Drench x41
- Hush x143
- Faint x153
- Bloom x314
- Vivid x349

Overlap x5

- Blend x51
- Isolate x99
- Fuse x113
- Disjoin x245
- Harmonize x492

Special Elements x5

- None x55
- All x77
- 1 x150
- 2 x291
- 3 x427

Mint Type - Palettes x4

- UltraMaxis x17
- Sgt. Pepe x33
- HyperMaxis x50
- MemeMaxis x900

Traced x3

- No Fill x45
- Border x97
- No Border x858

Edge x2

- Yes x312
- No x688

Flow x2

- Yes x65
- No x935

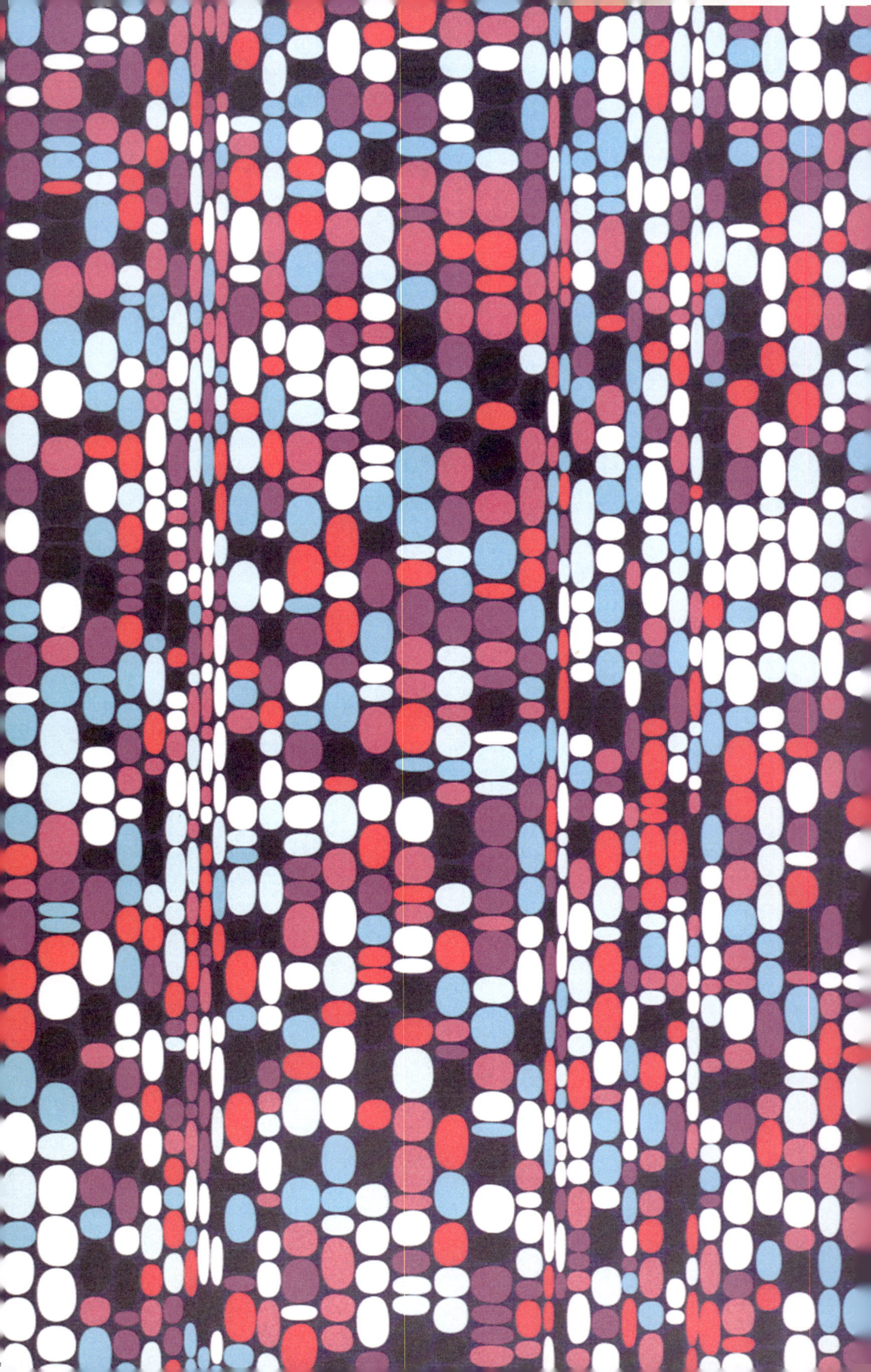

PART III

FEATURED COLLECTOORS

PEBBLE COLLECTOORS

Featured Pebble Collectoors made it possible to publish the Pebbles book with a qualitative, collectoor-centric approach. Each collectoor generously shared the meaning of their Pebbles, an interpretation, a rarity or how the art made them feel.

Pebbles were given their names by the collectoors, often with creative assistance from the collectoor community. The names of Pebbles serve to 'unlock' the meaning of each artwork. The name is a hint for the Pebble viewer, drawn from personal meaning or collective symbolism. Many collectoors have let their Pebbles speak for themselves, letting the viewer draw their own conclusions as to what they see and feel.

The 'Level' rating shown below is associated with the identity of the Pebble owner and is calculated through digital assets they hold and the reputation they have become known for within the community.

- **Pebble 0** Arsonic | Level 61
- **Pebble 1** Maxmyeth | Level 62
- **Pebble 2** *Summer Grail* Blocknoob | Level 63
- **Pebble 3** *Ghost of Nazca* chrisroc | Level 59
- **Pebble 8** *Sgt. Pepples* Square Pixel | Level 49
- **Pebble 14** Brookr | Level 52
- **Pebble 15** *Bloodline* Thor | Level 62

- **Pebble 23** *Indigenous Journeys* MintFace | Level 61
- **Pebble 28** *A Surrender to Passion* OMDegen | Level 61
- **Pebble 32** 6529er | Level 65
- **Pebble 35** *MeatBalls* Sert | Level 57
- **Pebble 41** *Pathway to Disorder* Animated | Level 63
- **Pebble 43** *Metallic Shine* Animated | Level 63
- **Pebble 44** Golden 618 | Level 51
- **Pebble 71** *Blue Steel* TheMemesMM | Level 57
- **Pebble 81** *Shadow of Satoshi* OMDegen | Level 61
- **Pebble 83** G9ralt | Level 60
- **Pebble 94** *Currents of Cobalt Calm* Paul Wilson | Level 51
- **Pebble 96** *Onchain Summer Breeze* DiegoRST | Level 64
- **Pebble 98** *Water Lillies* G9ralt | Level 60
- **Pebble 99** G9ralt | Level 60
- **Pebble 114** *Stepping Out* 6529Guardian | Level 59
- **Pebble 116** *Zen Sgt. Pepe* DiegoRST | Level 64
- **Pebble 141** *Talking with God* Ricodemus | Level 50
- **Pebble 144** *Puerta del Sol,* **145** *Pont du Gard* Pandelic | Level 59
- **Pebble 155** *Carbon Copy* Regular Dad | Level 59
- **Pebble 169** *Zen Garden* Lawtoshi | Level 52
- **Pebble 206** *Corbita* Mikavirt | Level 43
- **Pebble 222, 223** Maxmyeth | Level 62
- **Pebble 250** *Concert Hallucinations* Spritey | Level 58
- **Pebble 271** *SmokeShow* Maybe | Level 63
- **Pebble 275** *DNA Sequencer* Franklin Fit | Level 53
- **Pebble 281, 286** CaptainDerp | Level 60
- **Pebble 295** *Salsa Blush* Northof80 - Level 55
- **Pebble 299** *The Eruption* Hugo Faz | Level 60
- **Pebble 302** *Freestone River* Batsoupyum | Level 59
- **Pebble 321** *Snow Diamonds* DarrenSRS | Level 59
- **Pebble 422** *Monolith Echo* Blocknoob | Level 63
- **Pebble 426** prxt0 | Level 55
- **Pebble 431** OMDegen | Level 61
- **Pebble 443** *The Mondrian* MintFace | Level 61
- **Pebble 448** *Party Cow* clicky2048 | Level 52
- **Pebble 457** *Woman with Orange Hat* MoMO | Level 65

- **Pebble 480** *The Wave* SeizerPunk | Level 33
- **Pebble 510** *Archipelago Novum* Prateek Saraf | Level 39
- **Pebble 513** *Memes & Life* DiegoRST | Level 64
- **Pebble 529** *Sgt. Pepe Campfire* Thor | Level 62
- **Pebble 551** *Sunset Blvd* Ghost Pepper | Level 59
- **Pebble 556** Dave | Level 56
- **Pebble 558** *Liquid Lava Rain* Jonny Pickles | Level 49
- **Pebble 563** *The Penguin* Bored Surgeon | Level 60
- **Pebble 586** *Andre the Giant* Batsoupyum | Level 59
- **Pebble 617** 696 | Level 51
- **Pebble 683** David | Level 39
- **Pebble 687** *Riverside* Stardust | Level 23
- **Pebble 689, 690** lapislight | Level 60
- **Pebble 714** *Cribbage,* MoonFront | Level 54
- **Pebble 715** *Genesis Eggs* MoonFront | Level 54
- **Pebble 716** *The Matrix* MoonFront | Level 54
- **Pebble 724** prxt0 | Level 55
- **Pebble 752** *Dense City* Vanto | Level 21
- **Pebble 781** Sir Winston | Level 44
- **Pebble 805** *Pebbles* Pakal | Level 12
- **Pebble 816** *Pathway Home* Articulate | Level 39
- **Pebble 854** *Sweet Dreams* Ghost Pepper | Level 59
- **Pebble 863** *The Dance Floor* Casa NUA | Level 42
- **Pebble 886** *Beeple Tower* Thor | Level 62
- **Pebble 888** Burnasso | Level 48
- **Pebble 896** *The Sun is Always Shining* Angol | Level 61
- **Pebble 909** *Running with the Devil* Batsoupyum | Level 59
- **Pebble 912** punksladsmemes | Level 58
- **Pebble 954** WintermuteGAN | Level 44
- **Pebble 958** *The Dolphin* smpsmyth | Level 35
- **Pebble 960** *The Goose Egg* gmmoney | Level 45
- **Pebble 962** *Empty Threats* 4lteredBeast | Level 38
- **Pebble 986** *The Antidote* Giopetto | Level 55

FEATURED PEBBLES

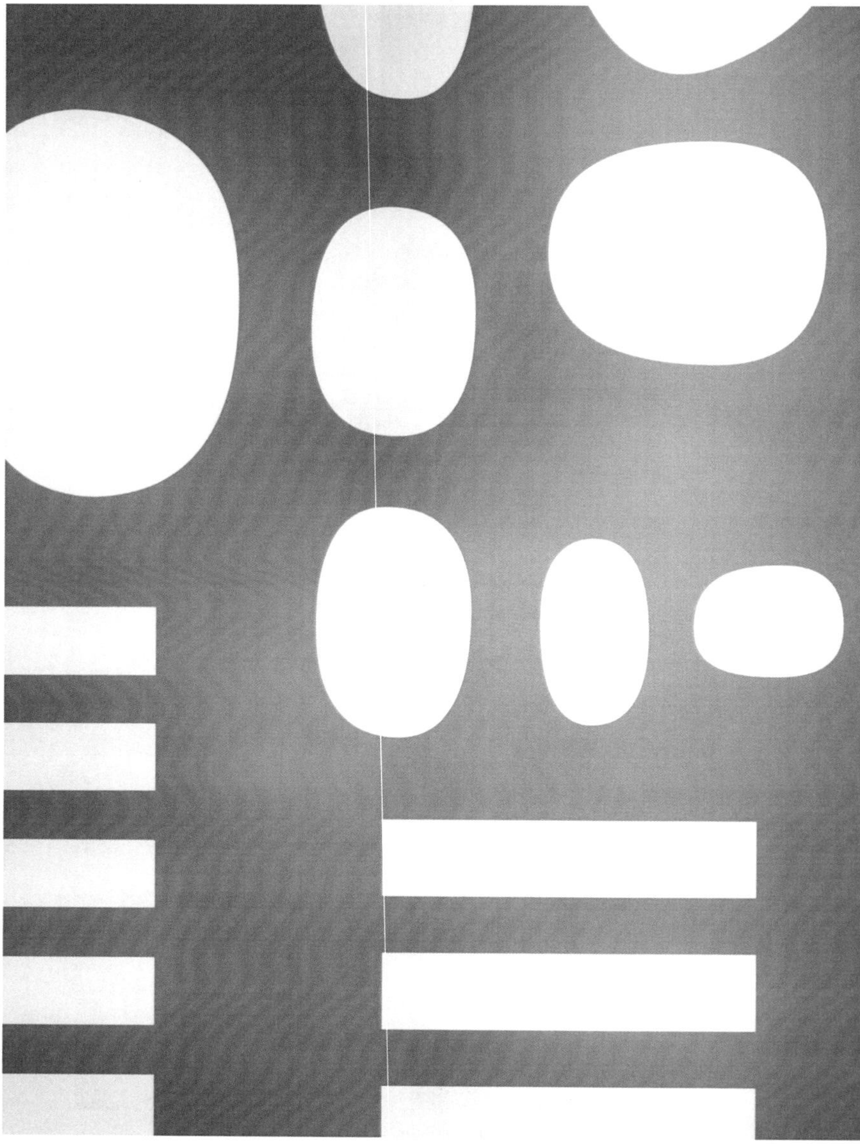

Pebble 0 minted by Zeblocks

Pebble 0

- Mint Type - Palettes: MemeMaxis 900/1,000
- Color Density: Faint 153/1,000
- Edge: No 688/1,000
- Flow: No 935/1,000
- Overlap: Disjoin 245/1,000
- Palette: Forest Whisper 83/1,000
- Size: Rockling 300/1,000
- Special Elements: 2 291/1,000
- Traced: No Border 858/1,000

Rarity

- Rarity Rank: #780
- Statistical Rarity: #700
- Single Trait Rarity #817

MintFace Vibe Check

The first ever Pebble to mint in the collection was minted by Zeblocks as is the tradition brought across from Art Blocks Curated mint drops. Pebble #0 was minted by Zeblocks on 8th February 2024 03:45:42 on the NextGen art contract, beginning a new chapter in on-chain generative art history.

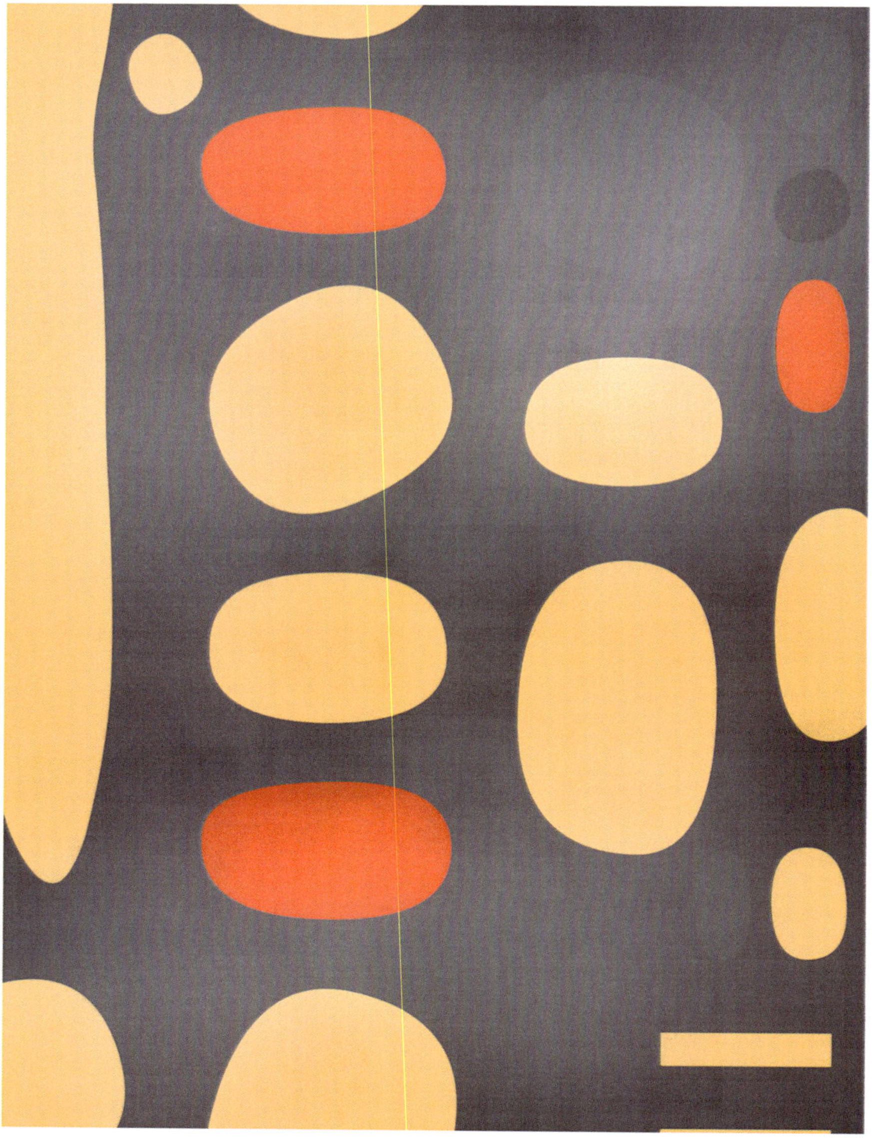

Pebble 1 minted by Maxmyeth

"I can still remember the excitement of mint day. I was determined to gas up and snag token #1. Having minted such a rare palette, and the first in the collection, was a truly special moment in my web3 adventures." Maxmyeth

Pebble 1

- Mint Type - Palettes: UltraMaxis 17 / 1,000
- Color Density: Bloom 314 / 1,000
- Edge: No 688 / 1,000
- Flow: No 935 / 1,000
- Overlap: Disjoin 245 / 1,000
- Palette: Magma Mambo 5 / 1,000
- Size: Stonelet 220 / 1,000
- Special Elements: 3 427 / 1,000
- Traced: No Border 858 / 1,000

Rarity

- Rarity Rank: #103
- Statistical Rarity: #740
- Single Trait Rarity #1

MintFace Vibe Check

A powerful Pebble to begin the first minting phase open to collectoors. *Magma Mambo* is a Collector Provenance trait only available to collectoors like Maxmyeth who know how to hodl.

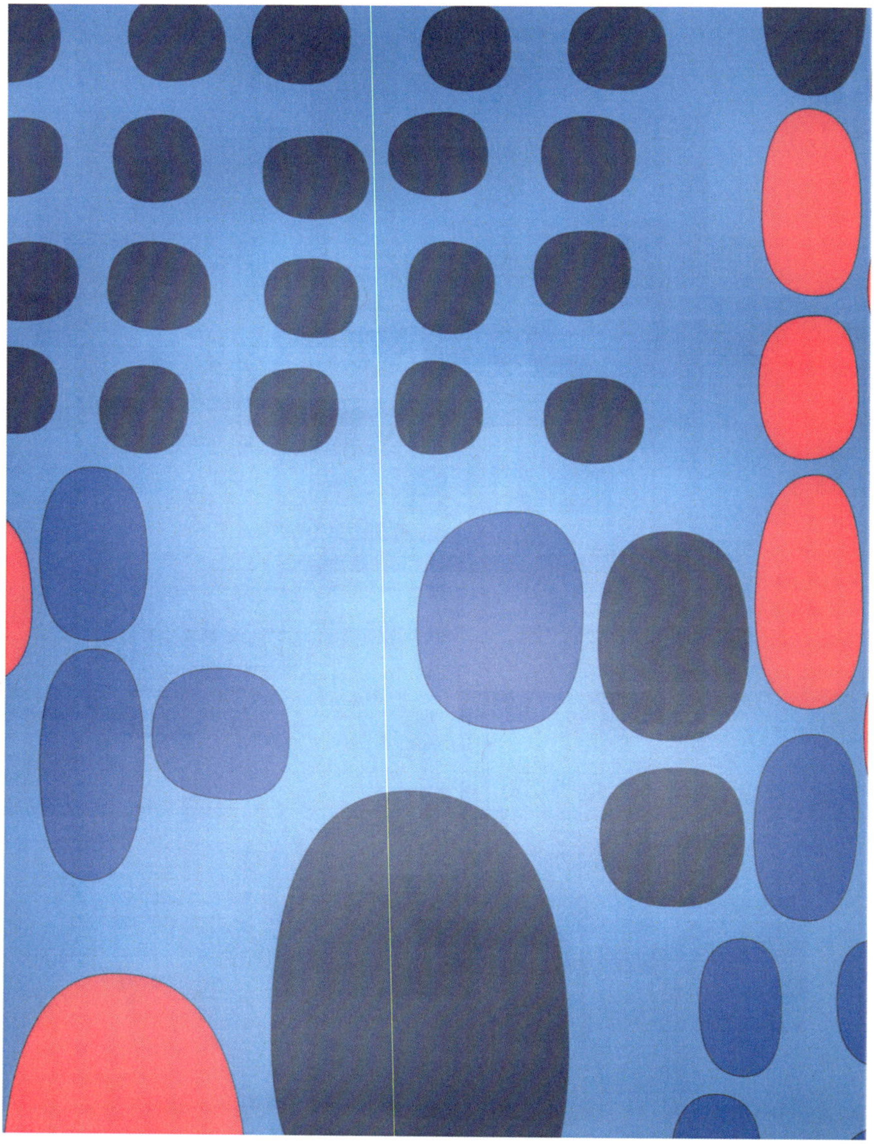

Pebble 2 'Summer Grail' minted by Blocknoob

"'Summer Grail' was minted 2nd with a max priority of 69 gwei, the pinnacle of the NextGen Pebbles collection. 'Summer Grail' embodies Summer Solstice energy with striking blue and pink hues." Blocknoob

Pebble 2

- Mint Type - Palettes: UltraMaxis 17/1,000
- Color Density: Drench 41/1,000
- Edge: No 688/1,000
- Flow: No 935/1,000
- Overlap: Harmonize 492/1,000
- Palette: summer.jpg 7/1,000
- Size: Rockling 300/1,000
- Special Elements: 3 427/1,000
- Traced: Border 97/1,000

Rarity

- Rarity Rank: #38
- Statistical Rarity: #179
- Single Trait Rarity #166

MintFace Vibe Check

Early mints are held with great reverence on generative art mint day, as eager participants view them as signals for what art the code might produce next. 'Summer Grail' provided a healthy signal of what might follow with *summer.jpg* palette given extra vivacity from *Drench Color Density.*

Pebble 3 ‘Ghost of Nazca’ minted by chrisroc

> “Minted with 42.0 gwei, #3 stood out as one of three with *No Fill* and *HyperMaxi* palette *Elephant Pajamas*. Initially called ‘Ghosts’, nodding to Chromie Squiggles, 6529 likened it to Nazca lines, contributing to its final name ‘Ghost of Nazca.’” chrisroc

Pebble 3

- Mint Type - Palettes: HyperMaxis 50/1,000
- Color Density: Bloom 314/1,000
- Edge: No 688/1,000
- Flow: No 935/1,000
- Overlap: Harmonize 492/1,000
- Palette: Elephant Pajamas 16/1,000
- Size: Rockling 300/1,000
- Special Elements: 3 427/1,000
- Traced: No Fill 45/1,000

Rarity

- Rarity Rank: #115
- Statistical Rarity: #228
- Single Trait Rarity #123

MintFace Vibe Check

Squint your eyes into the flash to catch the faintest glimpse of empty *No Fill, Rockling*-sized Pebbles. Beyond the visible and into the code, *Elephant Pajamas* palette is one of only 16 because of its mint reservation to Collector Provenance eligible people only. The first minted rare ever derived from on-chain collectoor behaviour.

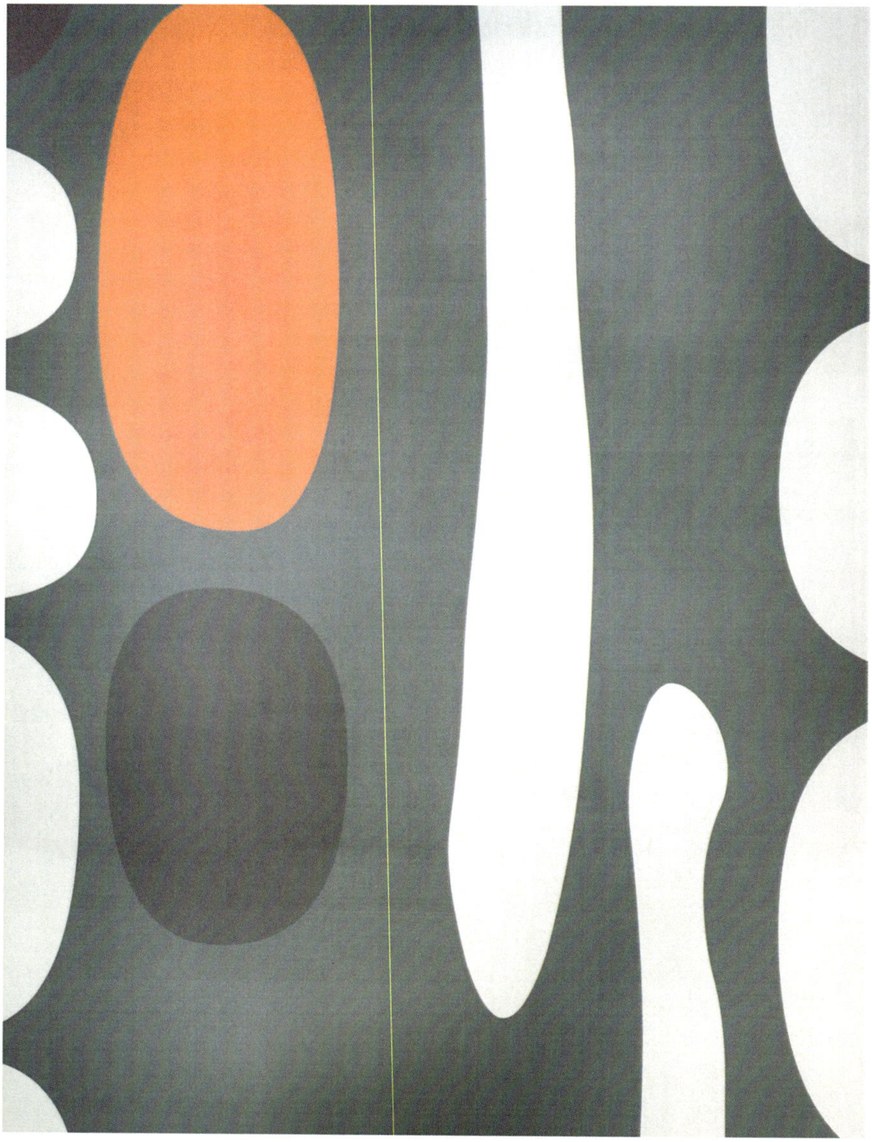

Pebble 8 'SGT. PEPPLES' minted by Square Pixel

> "Life is like Pebbles #8. You only get to mint it once."
> Square Pixel

Pebble 8

- Mint Type - Palettes: <u>MemeMaxis</u> 900/1,000
- Color Density: <u>Bloom</u> 314/1,000
- Edge: <u>No</u> 688/1,000
- Flow: <u>No</u> 935/1,000
- Overlap: <u>Harmonize</u> 492/1,000
- Palette: <u>Forest Whisper</u> 83/1,000
- Size: <u>Rockling</u> 300/1,000
- Special Elements: <u>All</u> 77/1,000
- Traced: <u>No Border</u> 858/1,000

Rarity

- Rarity Rank: #589
- Statistical Rarity: #719
- Single Trait Rarity #352

MintFace Vibe Check

An abstract Pebble that pares back the *Forest Whisper* to its barest forms. Two stick-like shapes dominate the center of the frame, in conversation with the *Bloom* affected orange and verde Pebbles to the west. There is more to be interpreted from the scene by viewing the Pebble 90 degrees clock-wise.

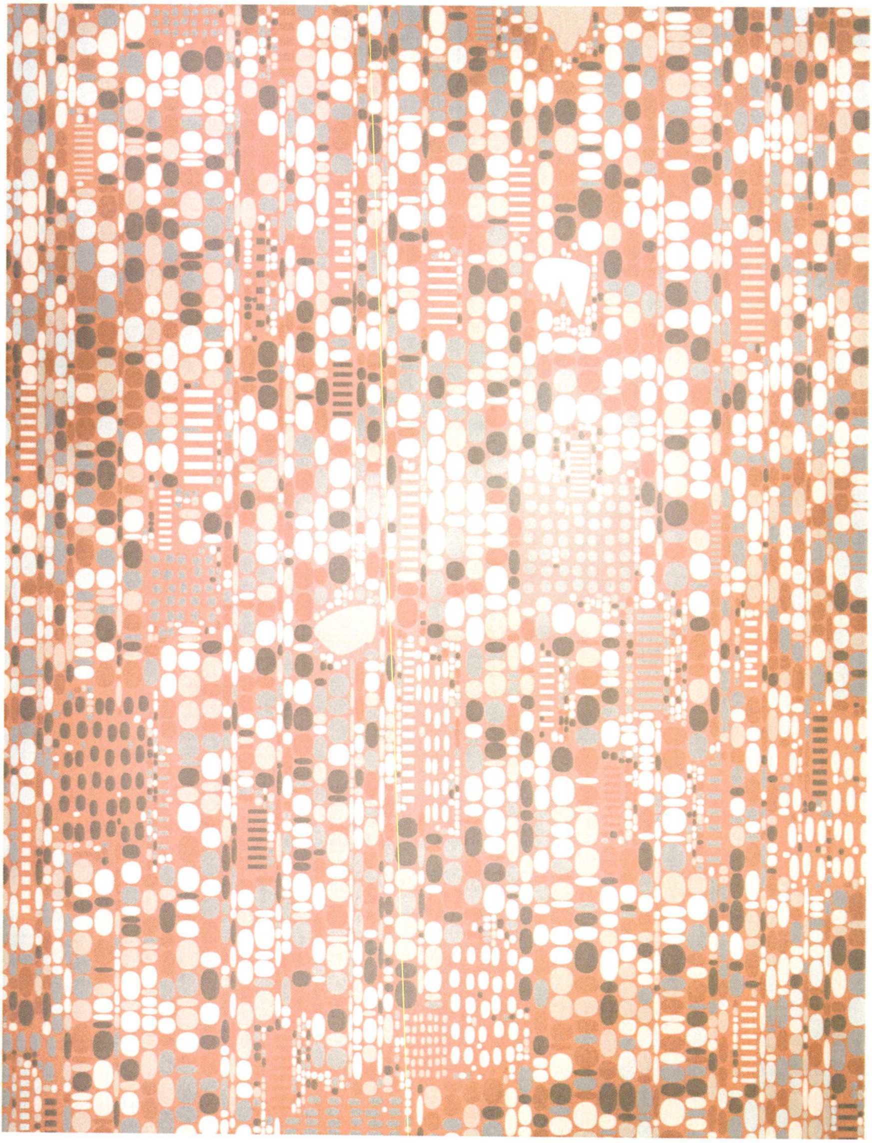

Pebble 14 minted by brookr

"The low token ID is what I like best about it. I'll likely sell it and buy another off the floor if I can get a good price for it." brookr

Pebble 14

- Mint Type - Palettes: MemeMaxis 900 / 1,000
- Color Density: Vivid 349 / 1,000
- Edge: No 688 / 1,000
- Flow: No 935 / 1,000
- Overlap: Harmonize 492 / 1,000
- Palette: Terra Echoes 58 / 1,000
- Size: Boulderette 147 / 1,000
- Special Elements: 3 427 / 1,000
- Traced: No Border 858 / 1,000

Rarity

- Rarity Rank: #900
- Statistical Rarity: #929
- Single Trait Rarity #863

MintFace Vibe Check

Terra Echoes palette dominates when combined with *Boulderette* size. Look for the three *Special Elements*. The rectangular shaped Pebbles; the ladder-like vertical structures; and the sharpened and mis-shapen Pebbles yet to be smoothed out in the storm.

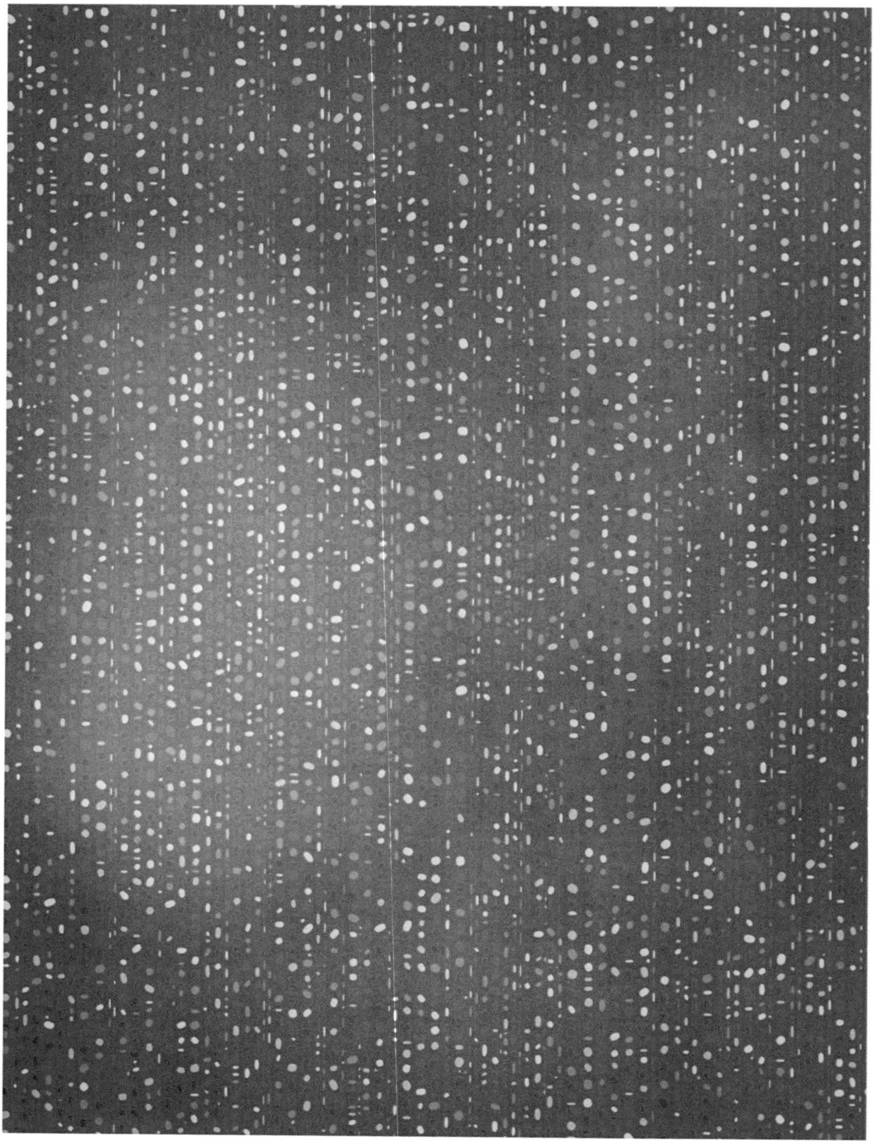

Pebble 15 'Bloodline' minted by Thor

> "Put a HyperMaxi under the microscope and watch Pebbles run through our bloodstream." Thor

Pebble 15

- Mint Type - Palettes: HyperMaxis 50/1,000
- Color Density: Bloom 314/1,000
- Edge: No 688/1,000
- Flow: No 935/1,000
- Overlap: Isolate 99/1,000
- Palette: Salsa Blush 13/1,000
- Size: Craglet 85/1,000
- Special Elements: None 55/1,000
- Traced: Border 97/1,000

Rarity

- Rarity Rank: #4
- Statistical Rarity: #10
- Single Trait Rarity #11

MintFace Vibe Check

Isolate Overlap combined with *Craglet* size creates the illusory effect of a glittery panel on red-dominant *Salsa Blush* background. Looks closer to see the *Border* around every Pebble, in this Pebble with no *Edge* framing.

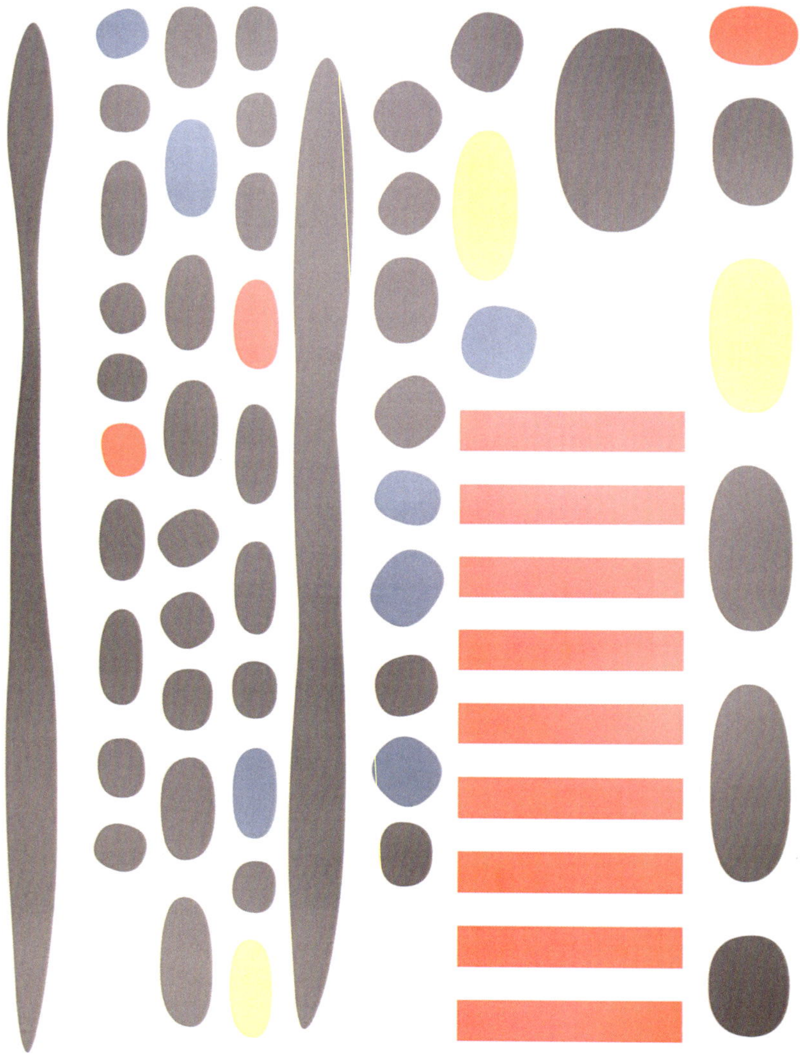

Pebble 23 'Indigenous Journeys' minted by MintFace

"Art that echoes our ancestors desire to explore says something about our shared humanity. Straight lines a metaphor for people, and the pathway, a symbol for travel." MintFace

Pebble 23

- Mint Type - Palettes: MemeMaxis 900/1,000
- Color Density: Bloom 314/1,000
- Edge: Yes 312/1,000
- Flow: No 935/1,000
- Overlap: Disjoin 245/1,000
- Palette: Dino Disco 58/1,000
- Size: Pebbit 151/1,000
- Special Elements: 3 427/1,000
- Traced: Border 97/1,000

Rarity

- Rarity Rank: #281
- Statistical Rarity: #156
- Single Trait Rarity #271

MintFace Vibe Check

'Indigenous Journeys' offers two stick-like symbols that our ancestors may have interpreted as message sticks. The ladder-like pathway on the right, a symbolic representation of a long journey. The most aesthetically pleasing *Dino Disco* palette artwork you will find.

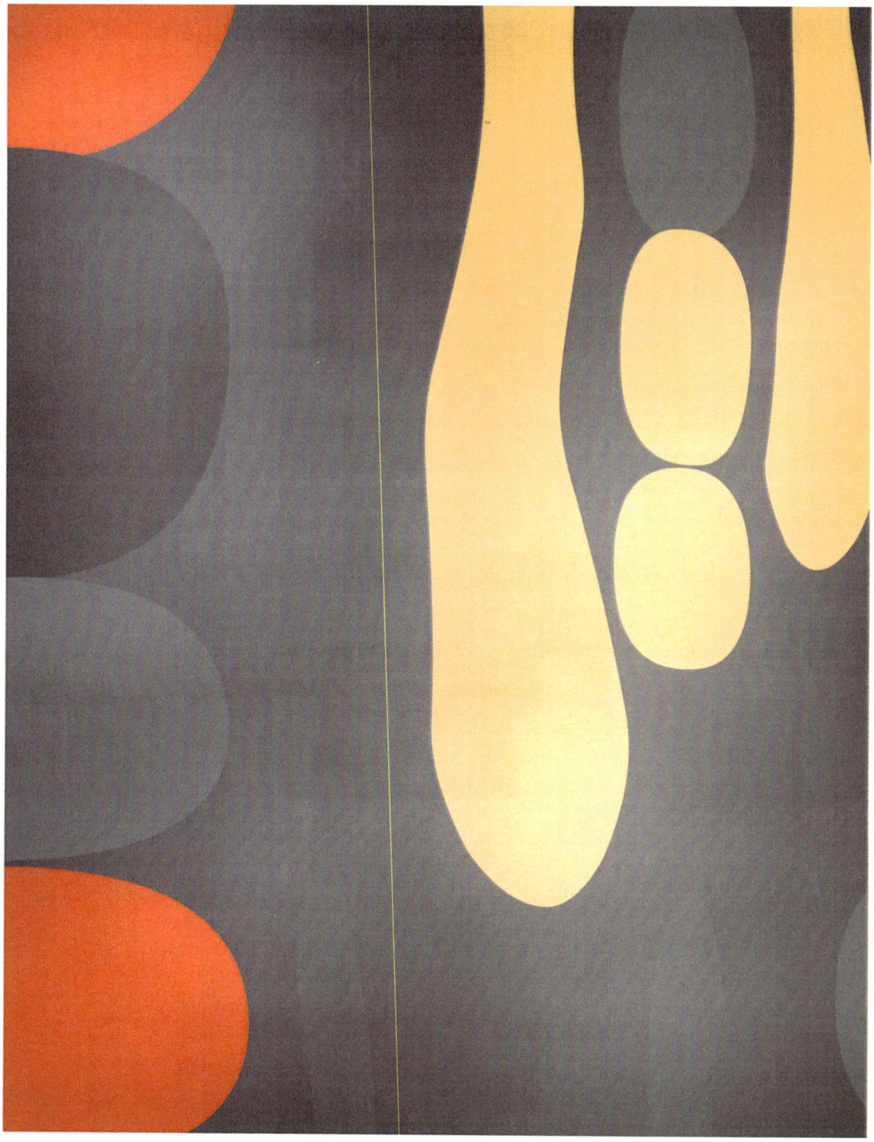

Pebble 28 'A Surrender to Passion' minted by OMDegen

"'A Surrender to Passion' was named by MintFace, the rarest Pebble, as calculated with trait normalization off."
OMDegen

Pebble 28

- Mint Type - Palettes: UltraMaxis 17 / 1,000
- Color Density: Vivid 349 / 1,000
- Edge: No 688 / 1,000
- Flow: Yes 65 / 1,000
- Overlap: Blend 51 / 1,000
- Palette: Magma Mambo 5 / 1,000
- Size: Rockling 300 / 1,000
- Special Elements: 3 427 / 1,000
- Traced: No Border 858 / 1,000

Rarity

- Rarity Rank: #7
- Statistical Rarity: #82
- Single Trait Rarity #1

MintFace Vibe Check

Hands exalted to the sky, 'A Surrender to Passion' expresses one of humanities most craved emotion in a mere four shapes. *Overlap Blend* nudges the Pebbles close enough together for the emergent head and torso to take shape, while the vertical tome of red and black Pebbles provide balance to the drama.

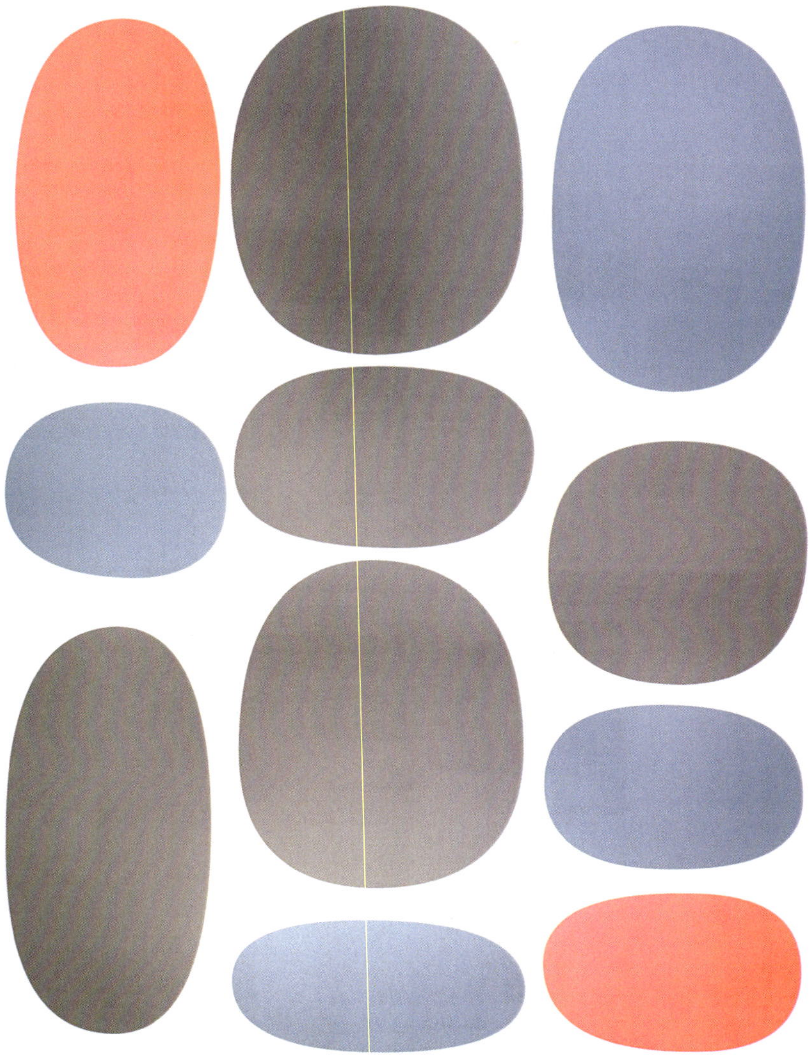

Pebble 35 'Meatballs' minted by Sert

"One of the simplest and more iconic Pebbles, probably you've seen it in a 'RePebble' by artist @toadswiback. *Rockling Size* gives a sense of peace and serenity, enhanced by the colors of *Dino Disco* palette." Sert

Pebble 35

- Mint Type - Palettes: MemeMaxis 900/1,000
- Color Density: Bloom 314/1,000
- Edge: Yes 312/1,000
- Flow: Yes 65/1,000
- Overlap: Harmonize 492/1,000
- Palette: Dino Disco 58/1,000
- Size: Rockling 300/1,000
- Special Elements: 3 427/1,000
- Traced: No Border 858/1,000

Rarity

- Rarity Rank: #161
- Statistical Rarity: #100
- Single Trait Rarity #66

MintFace Vibe Check

'Meatballs' is a tasty dish within the *Dino Disco* palette with a well balanced *Bloom Color Density*. The *Flow* may not have held much sway on the *Rockling* sized Pebbles, instead letting *Harmonize Overlap* serve up a stunning arrangement on the plate.

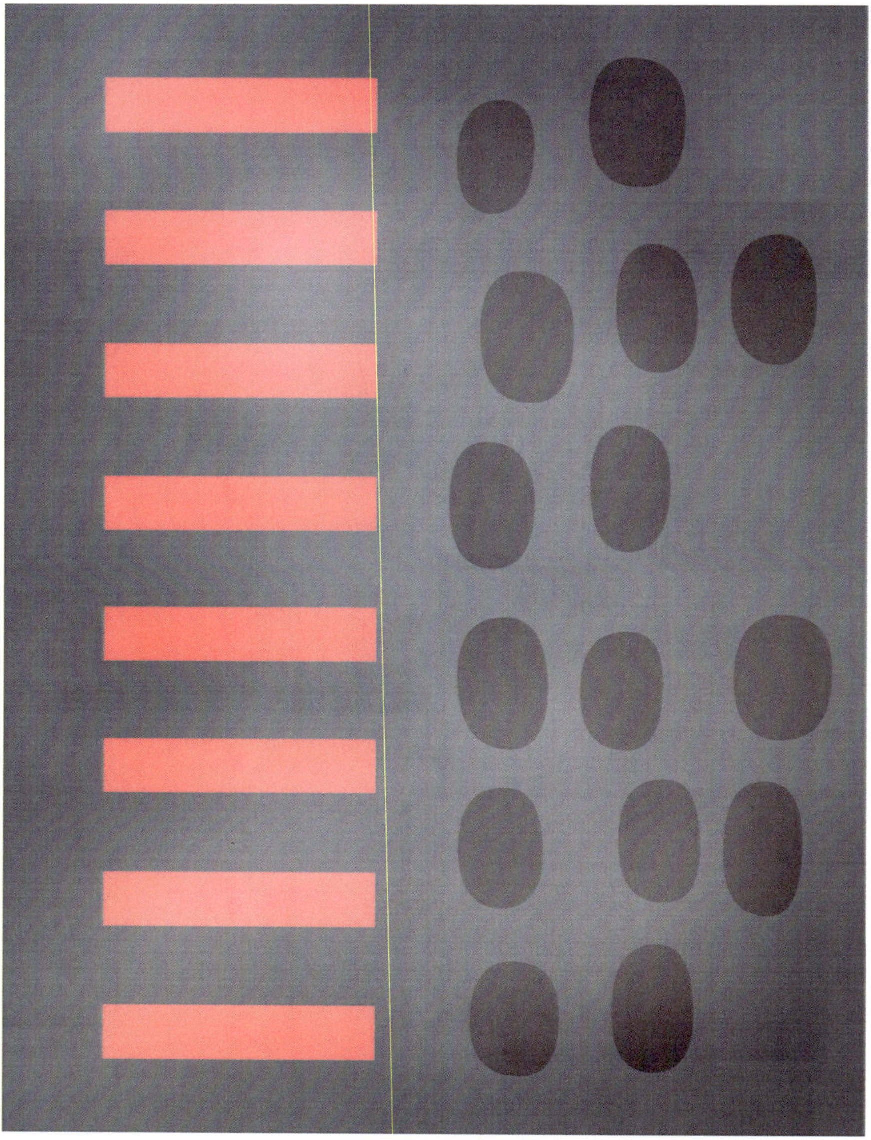

Pebble 41 'Pathway to Disorder' minted by Animated

"'Pathway to Disorder' illustrates the delicate balance between obsession and perfection. A constant focus on perfection may seem like the logical path, but often order dissolves into disorder." Animated

Pebble 41

- Mint Type - Palettes: MemeMaxis 900 / 1,000
- Color Density: Vivid 349 / 1,000
- Edge: Yes 312 / 1,000
- Flow: No 935 / 1,000
- Overlap: Harmonize 492 / 1,000
- Palette: Coral Reef 71 / 1,000
- Size: Rockling 300 / 1,000
- Special Elements: All 77 / 1,000
- Traced: No Border 858 / 1,000

Rarity

- Rarity Rank: #448
- Statistical Rarity: #405
- Single Trait Rarity #352

MintFace Vibe Check

'Pathway to Disorder' won the inaugural Pebble Racing Cup in a series of four knockout rounds. The output is exceptional for its simplicity. A vertical *Coral Reef* pink pathway on the left and grid-like shapes of Pebbles on the right; both derived from *Special Elements*. A champion Pebble to celebrate.

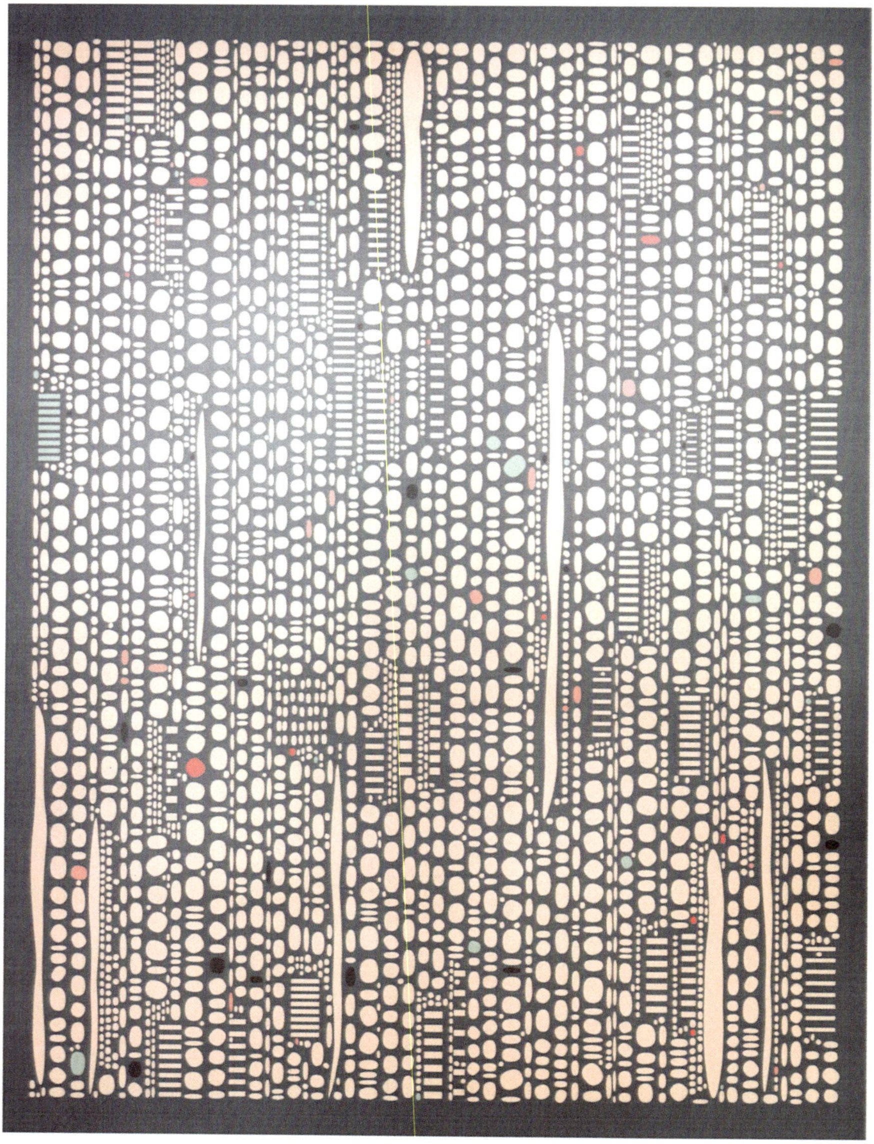

Pebble 43 'Metallic Shine' minted by Animated

A wall of metal
Reflecting the Earth's beauty
Shines down on us all

Pebble 43

- Mint Type - Palettes: MemeMaxis 900/1,000
- Color Density: Faint 153/1,000
- Edge: Yes 312/1,000
- Flow: No 935/1,000
- Overlap: Disjoin 245/1,000
- Palette: Coral Reef 71/1,000
- Size: Boulderette 147/1,000
- Special Elements: 3 427/1,000
- Traced: No Border 858/1,000

Rarity

- Rarity Rank: #516
- Statistical Rarity: #361
- Single Trait Rarity #612

MintFace Vibe Check

Pebble 43 is well-framed in the olive green from *Coral Reef* palette. The *Boulderette* Pebbles are tinted top to bottom as *Faint Color Density* remixes the formal *Coral Reef Palette.* Pebble 43 is a second *Coral Reef* owned by Animated, alongside 41. Compare the two to see how different the same palette can feel.

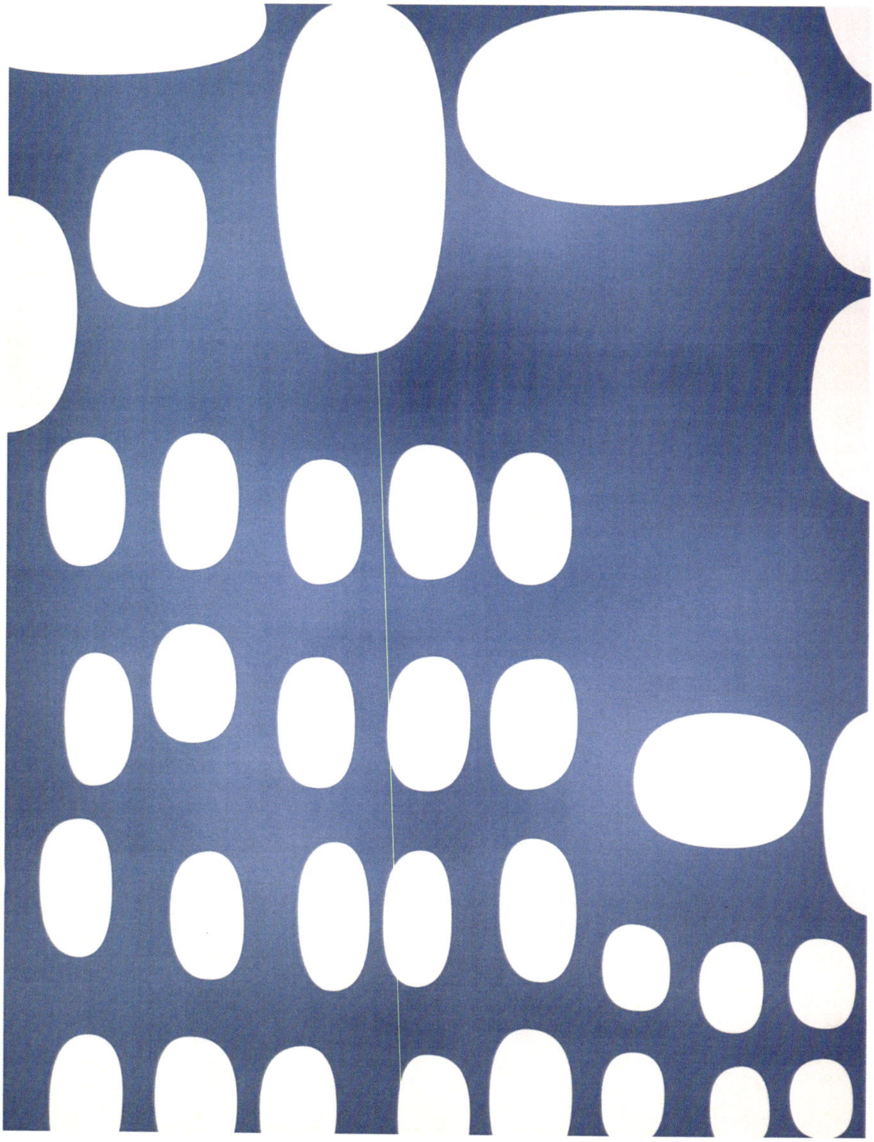

Pebble 71 'Blue Steel' minted by TheMemesMM

Pebble 71

- Mint Type - Palettes: MemeMaxis 900 / 1,000
- Color Density: Faint 153 / 1,000
- Edge: No 688 / 1,000
- Flow: No 935 / 1,000
- Overlap: Harmonize 492 / 1,000
- Palette: Dusk Riverbed 71 / 1,000
- Size: Rockling 300 / 1,000
- Special Elements: 2 291 / 1,000
- Traced: No Border 858 / 1,000

Rarity

- Rarity Rank: #845
- Statistical Rarity: #826
- Single Trait Rarity #817

MintFace Vibe Check

'Blue Steel' reveals the bare minimum of the *Dusk Riverbed* palette, as *Faint Color Density* conceals the color attaché. The *Special Element* intensity is felt most in the white grid of Pebbles in the bottom left hand quadrant. A high performance output from the *MemeMaxis* factory.

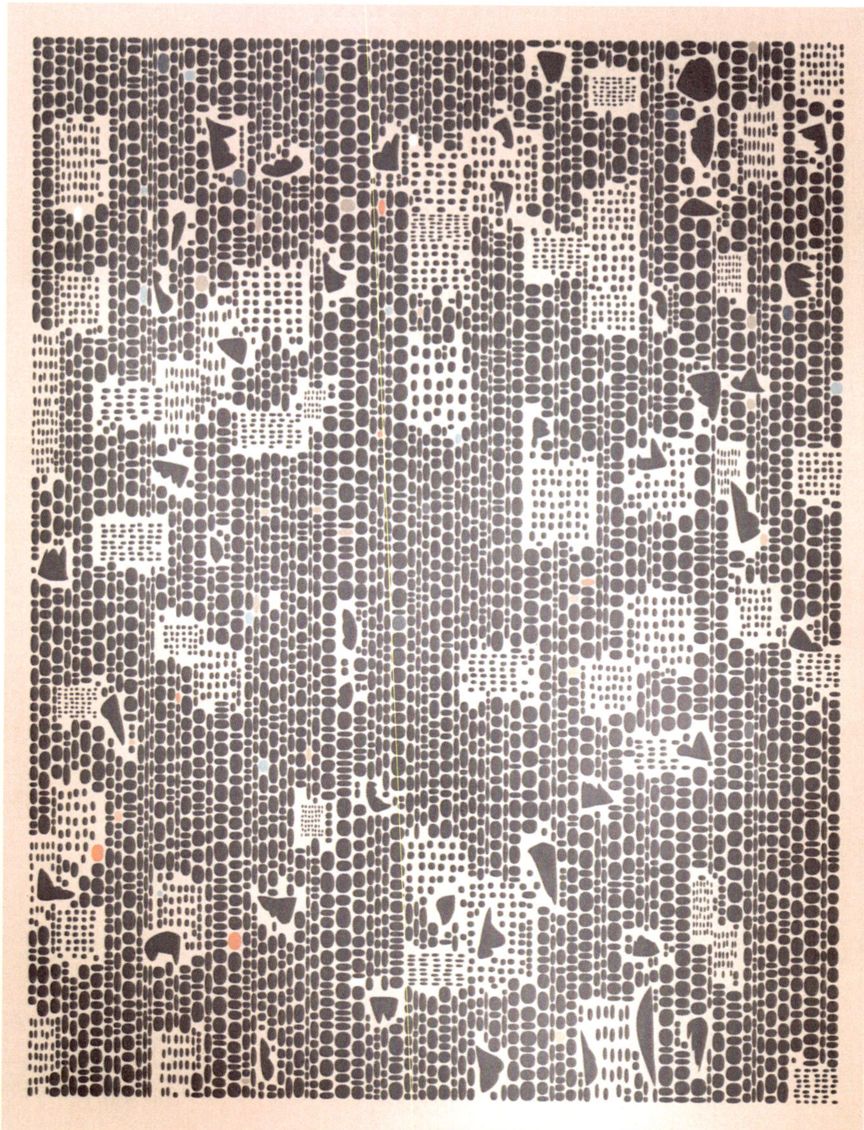

Pebble 81 'Shadow of Satoshi' minted by OMDegen

"'Shadow of Satoshi' - need we say anymore about the legend." OMDegen

Pebble 81

- Mint Type - Palettes: MemeMaxis 900/1,000
- Color Density: Faint 153/1,000
- Edge: Yes 312/1,000
- Flow: No 935/1,000
- Overlap: Harmonize 492/1,000
- Palette: Desert Mirage 79/1,000
- Size: Craglet 85/1,000
- Special Elements: 2 291/1,000
- Traced: No Border 858/1,000

Rarity

- Rarity Rank: #456
- Statistical Rarity: #354
- Single Trait Rarity #578

MintFace Vibe Check

'Shadow of Satoshi' is an 'mfer,' pfp-shaped, Pebble in gold. The eye and mouth attributes can be seen to the right of the canvas, and a circular shaped head can be discerned in grid-like *Special Elements*. The *Desert Mirage* black on gold and *Edge* border only enhance the framed portraiture. Every collection has its #1 loved artwork, and 'Shadow of Satoshi' ran the miles in Pebble Racing to beat out 15 worthy Pebble opponents.

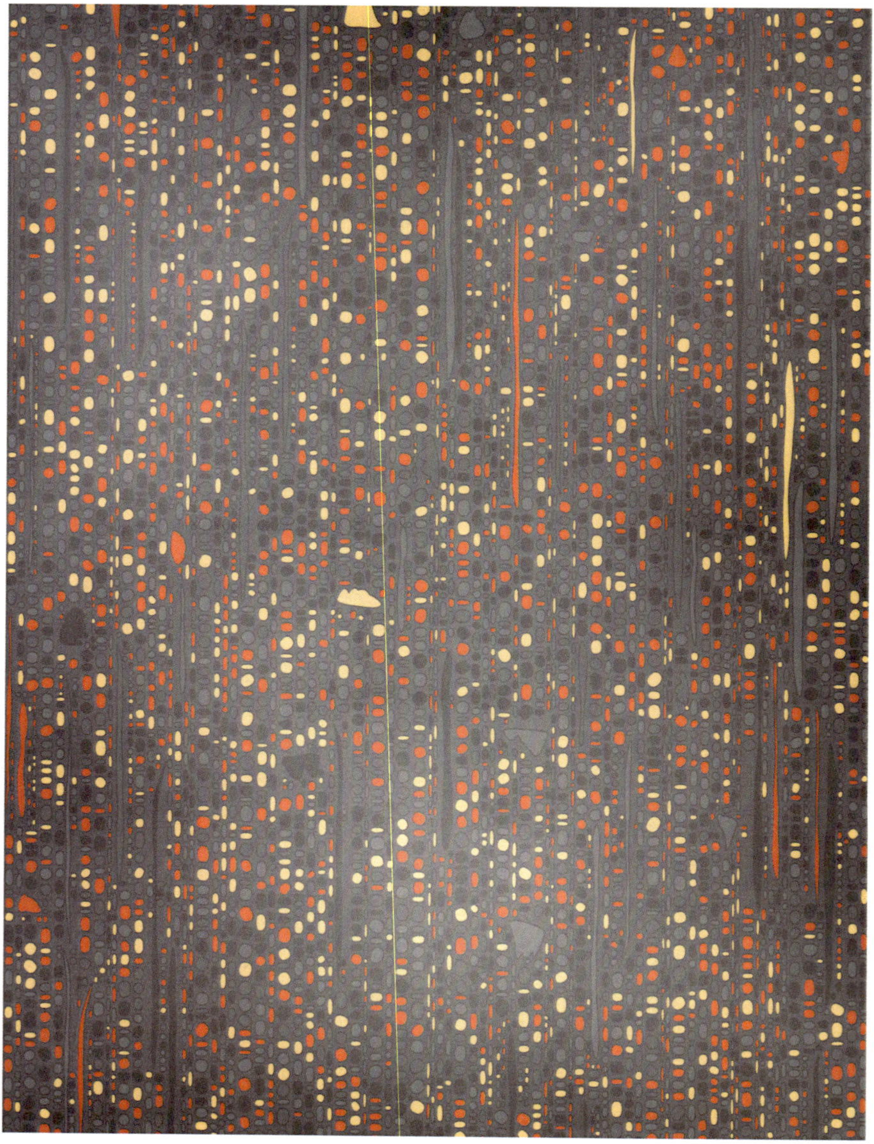

Pebble 83 minted by G9ralt

> One of the rarest Pebbles in existence with Magma Mambo and Border Traced traits." G9ralt

Pebble 83

- Mint Type - Palettes: UltraMaxis 17 / 1,000
- Color Density: Vivid 349 / 1,000
- Edge: No 688 / 1,000
- Flow: No 935 / 1,000
- Overlap: Disjoin 245 / 1,000
- Palette: Magma Mambo 5 / 1,000
- Size: Craglet 85 / 1,000
- Special Elements: 2 291 / 1,000
- Traced: Border 97 / 1,000

Rarity

- Rarity Rank: #34
- Statistical Rarity: #188
- Single Trait Rarity #1

MintFace Vibe Check

UltraMaxis palette was a collectoor reserved palette that could only be generated by minters with a specific selection of 6529 related digital assets. As such, *UltraMaxis* mint type unlocks some unusual combinations such as *Magma Mambo* palette combined with *Craglet*. Zoom in closer and the viewer is rewarded with *Border Traced* around hundreds of *Craglet* sized Pebbles. A treasure.

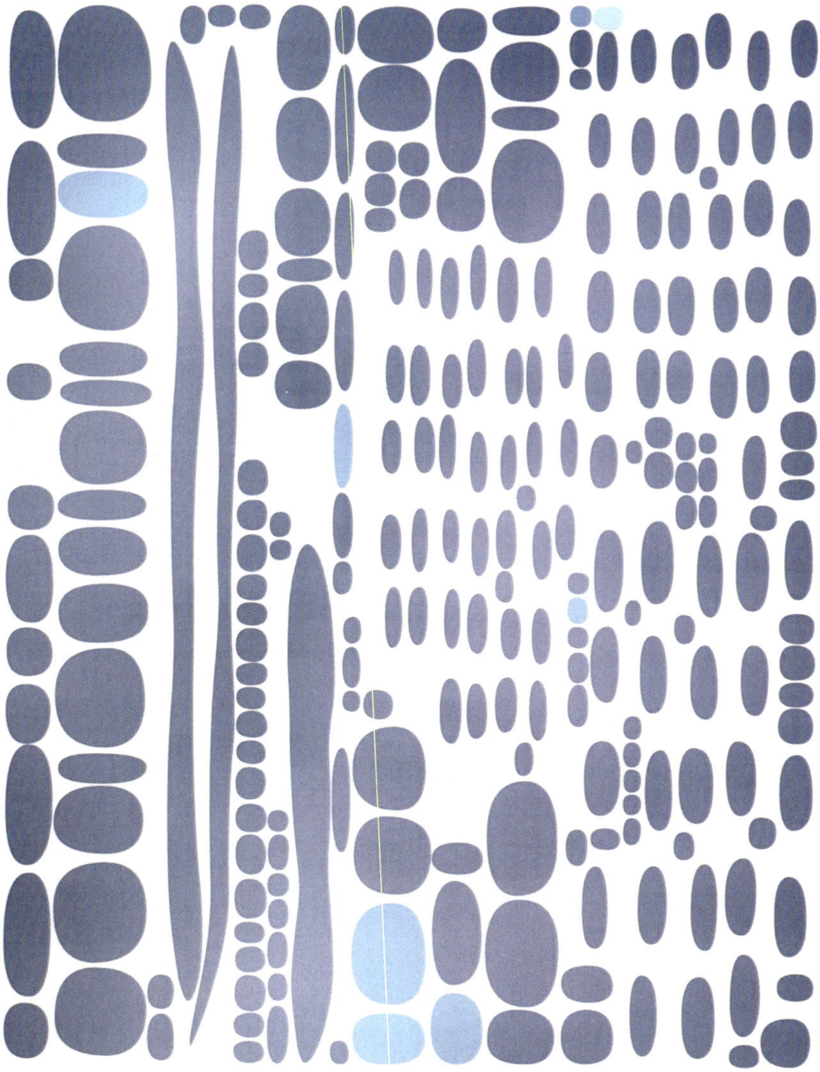

Pebble 94 'Currents of Cobalt Calm' minted by Paul Wilson

"'Currents of Cobalt Calm' features a serene assembly of cobalt blue shapes that evoke the gentle flow of a tranquil river. *Harmonize* balances the scattered elements into a cohesive whole." Paul Wilson

Pebble 94

- Mint Type - Palettes: MemeMaxis 900/1,000
- Color Density: Faint 153/1,000
- Edge: Yes 312/1,000
- Flow: Yes 65/1,000
- Overlap: Harmonize 492/1,000
- Palette: Unigrids 63/1,000
- Size: Crumb 72/1,000
- Special Elements: 2 291/1,000
- Traced: No Border 858/1,000

Rarity

- Rarity Rank: #94
- Statistical Rarity: #57
- Single Trait Rarity #66

MintFace Vibe Check

Unigrids a palette of quiet confidence, often highlighted with a dash of red, not seen here. The pure blues paring back the composition, only enhanced further by the *Harmonize Overlap*. I get a real sense of perspective created by the larger mass Pebbles in the '<' like layout. More than a crumb!

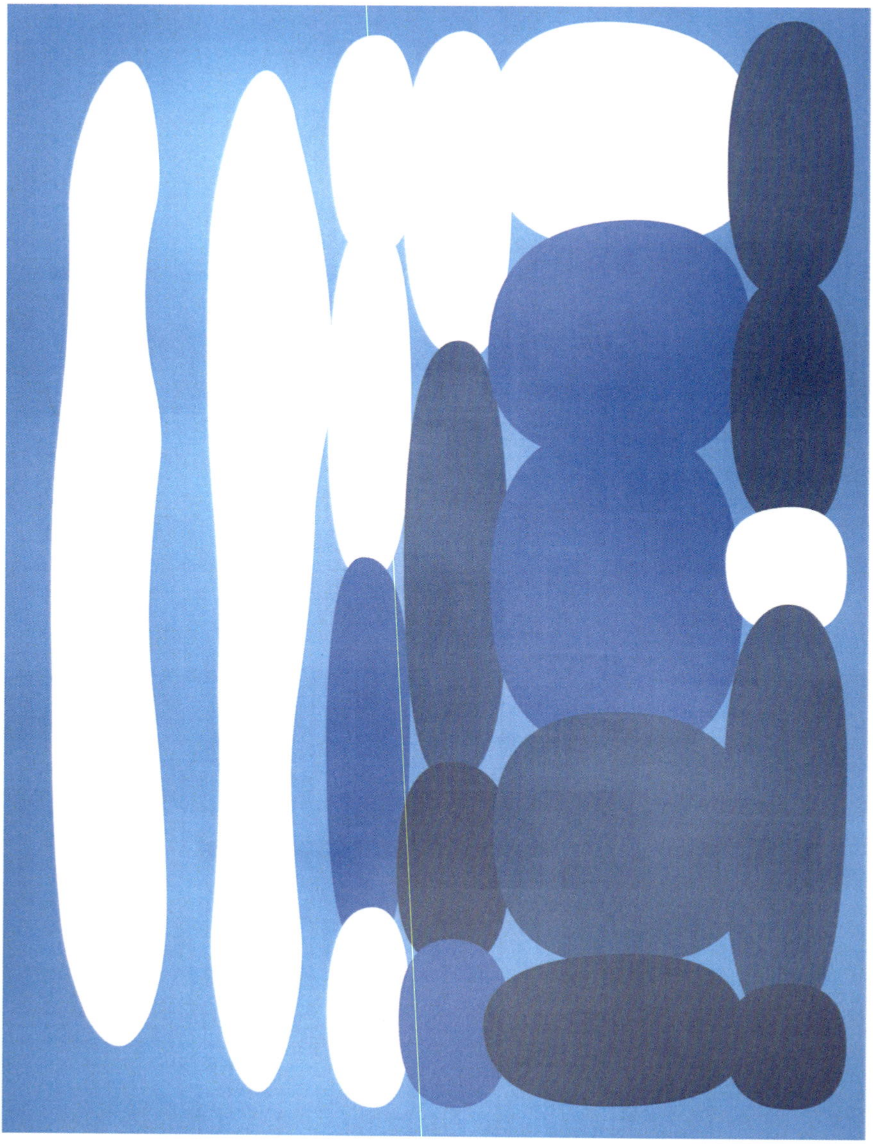

Pebble 96 'Onchain Summer Breeze' minted by DiegoRST

Pebble 96

- Mint Type - Palettes: UltraMaxis 17/1,000
- Color Density: Vivid 349/1,000
- Edge: Yes 312/1,000
- Flow: No 935/1,000
- Overlap: Fuse 113/1,000
- Palette: summer.jpg 7/1,000
- Size: Stonelet 220/1,000
- Special Elements: 2 291/1,000
- Traced: No Border 858/1,000

Rarity

- Rarity Rank: #123
- Statistical Rarity: #280
- Single Trait Rarity #166

MintFace Vibe Check

'Onchain Summer Breeze' is one of two *summer.jpg* palettes that also show *Fuse Overlap* of the Pebbles. *Stonelet Size* coordinates the Pebbles into an almost perfect *Rothko*-like rectangle. A fine *Vivid* that doesn't need the *summer.jpg* neon pink color to speak. Cool summer evenings of 'Onchain Summer Breeze' are on their way.

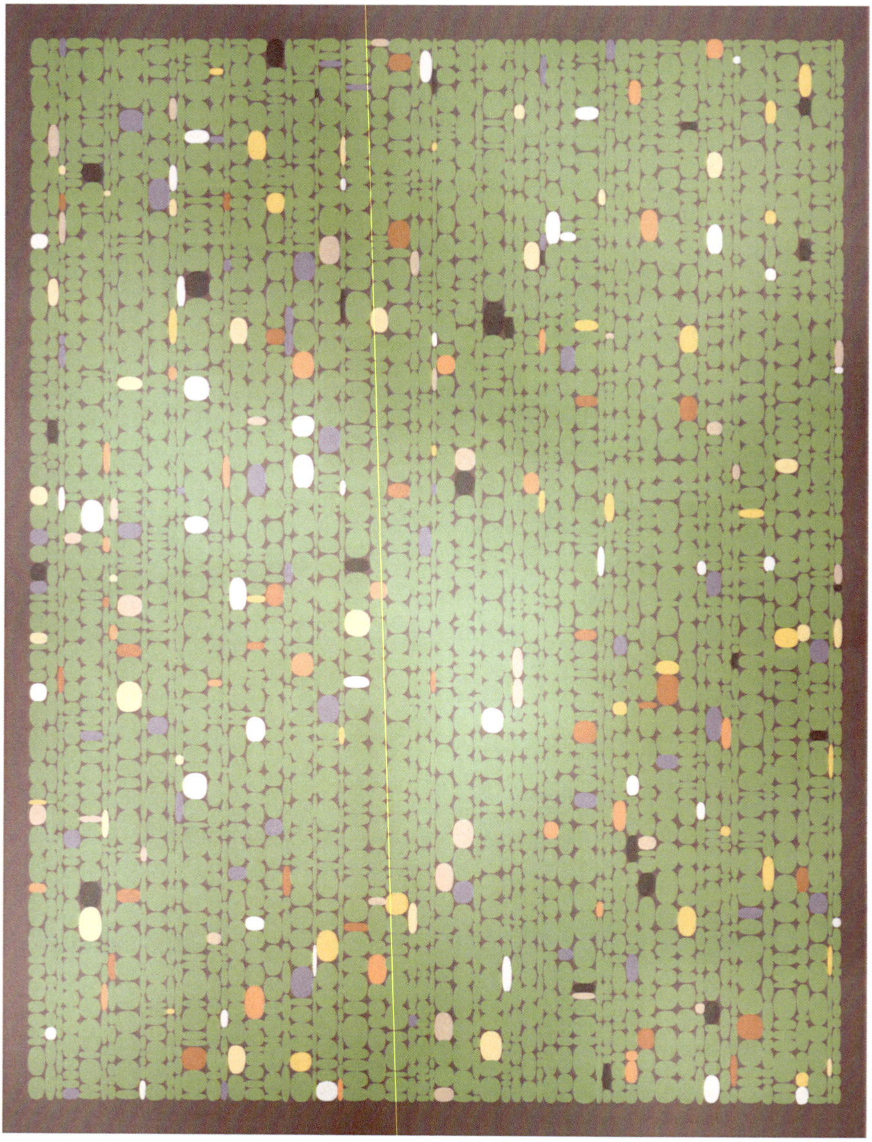

Pebble 98 minted by G9ralt

"I call it 'Water Lillies' because it reminds me of Monet's work. It is the only Sgt.Pepe palette Pebble with a frame."
G9ralt

Pebble 98

- Mint Type - Palettes: Sgt. Pepe 33 / 1,000
- Color Density: Faint 153 / 1,000
- Edge: Yes 312 / 1,000
- Flow: No 935 / 1,000
- Overlap: Blend 51 / 1,000
- Palette: Sgt. Pepe 33 / 1,000
- Size: Boulderette 147 / 1,000
- Special Elements: None 55 / 1,000
- Traced: No Border 858 / 1,000

Rarity

- Rarity Rank: #13
- Statistical Rarity: #11
- Single Trait Rarity #11

MintFace Vibe Check

The *Blend Overlap* connects every green Pebble together in a singular canvas, interspersed with a smattering of the lavenders, canary yellows, whites and pinks from the *Sgt. Pepe* palette. While *Edge* is quite a common feature of the Pebbles collection, 'Water Lillies' is the only Pebble with an *Edge*. Viewers get to see the Pebbles in their purest form with 'Water Lillies' as no *Special Elements* can be seen.

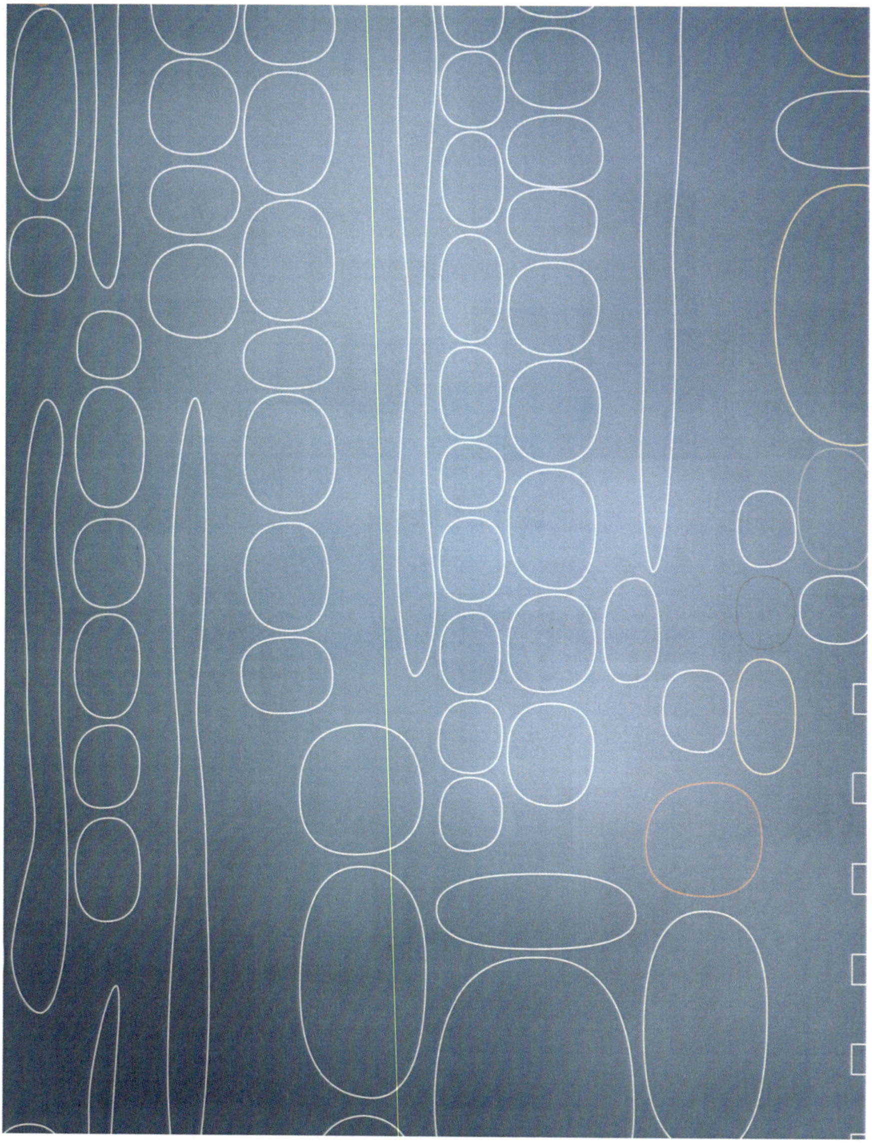

Pebble 99 minted by G9ralt

Gaps mapped with intent,
Structured Emptiness speaks soft,
Order finds its voice.

Pebble 99

- Mint Type - Palettes: MemeMaxis 900/1,000
- Color Density: Hush 143/1,000
- Edge: No 688/1,000
- Flow: No 935/1,000
- Overlap: Harmonize 492/1,000
- Palette: Citrus Slate 72/1,000
- Size: Pebbit 151/1,000
- Special Elements: 3 427/1,000
- Traced: No Fill 45/1,000

Rarity

- Rarity Rank: #155
- Statistical Rarity: #186
- Single Trait Rarity #123

MintFace Vibe Check

No Fill Pebbles continue to be some of the most striking and #99 is an exuberant example. *Citrus Slate* palette pared back to its white outlines. *Special Elements* clearly visible in six vertical stick-like blobs. A ladder-like *Special Element* slightly off the right-hand side of the canvas. *Harmonize Overlap* trait bringing a sense of visual order throughout the work. Bravo!

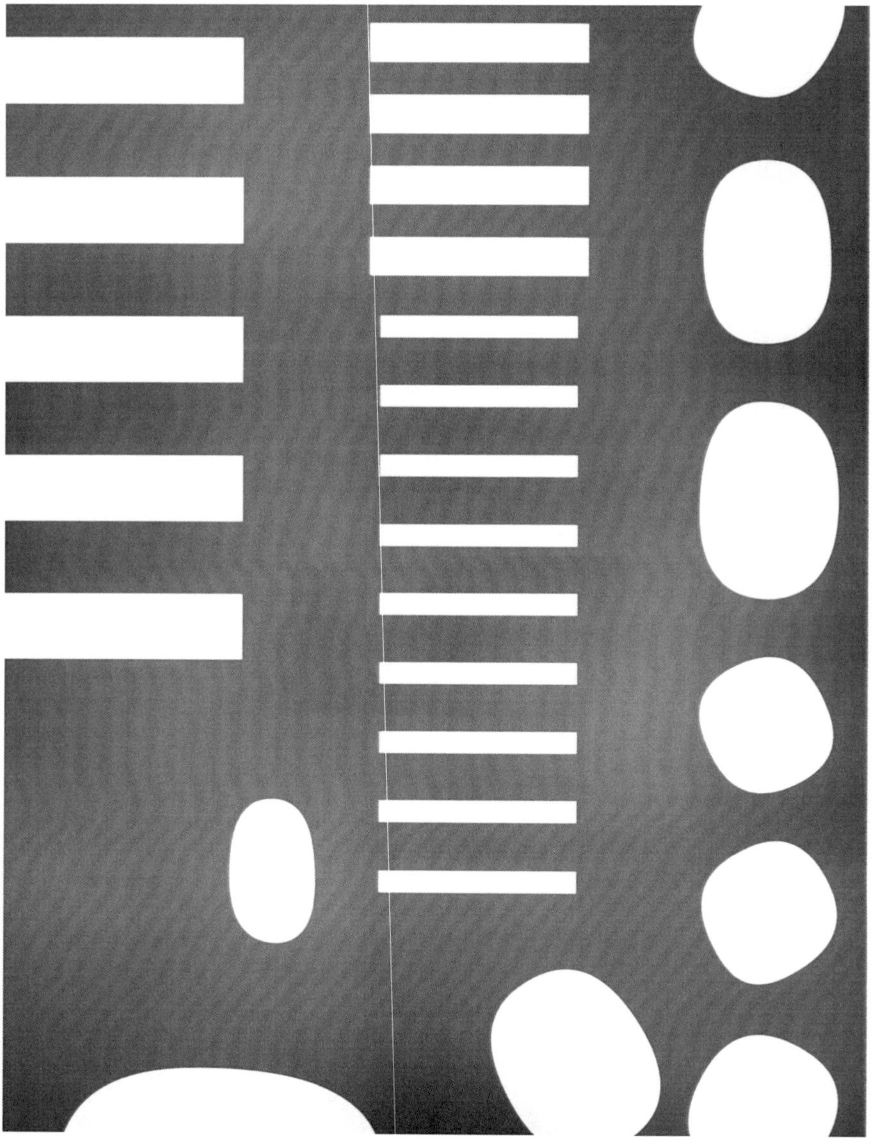

Pebble 114 'Stepping Out' minted by 6529Guardian

"Nothing is black and white in crypto law, but everything is borderless." 6529Guardian

Pebble 114

- Mint Type - Palettes: MemeMaxis 900/1,000
- Color Density: Faint 153/1,000
- Edge: No 688/1,000
- Flow: No 935/1,000
- Overlap: Disjoin 245/1,000
- Palette: Shades of Hey! 55/1,000
- Size: Rockling 300/1,000
- Special Elements: 2 291/1,000
- Traced: No Border 858/1,000

Rarity

- Rarity Rank: #701
- Statistical Rarity: #681
- Single Trait Rarity #817

MintFace Vibe Check

A good example of the *Shades of Hey!* palette with three ladder-like shapes providing clear structure in contrast to the right column of Pebbles. The *Faint Color Density* subtly changes the albescent white to an almost cream color in parts.

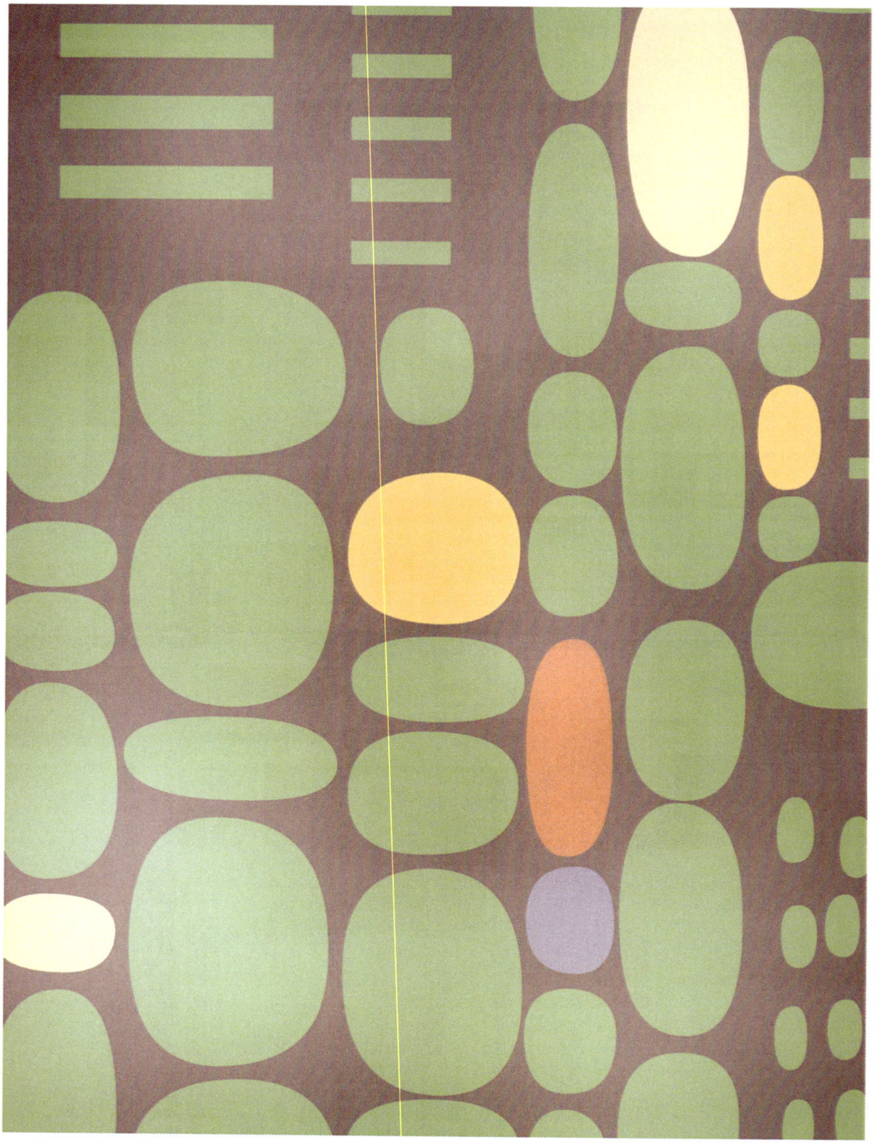

Pebble 116 'Zen Sgt. Pepe' minted by DiegoRST

Pebble 116

- Mint Type - Palettes: Sgt. Pepe 33 / 1,000
- Color Density: Hush 143 / 1,000
- Edge: No 688 / 1,000
- Flow: No 935 / 1,000
- Overlap: Harmonize 492 / 1,000
- Palette: Sgt. Pepe 33 / 1,000
- Size: Pebbit 151 / 1,000
- Special Elements: 3 427 / 1,000
- Traced: No Border 858 / 1,000

Rarity

- Rarity Rank: #585
- Statistical Rarity: #759
- Single Trait Rarity #733

MintFace Vibe Check

'Zen Sgt. Pepe' chills in base colors of lime and burgundy, as the *Hush Color Density* adds a pop of canary yellow, clay and violet. *Harmonize Overlap* is the hero of the *Pebbit Size* Pebble, hitting in the center of our artistic chakras.

Pebble 141 'Talking with God' minted by ricodemus

> 'Talking with God's' claim to fame was winning two rounds in the inaugural Pebble Race, including beating the famed 'Woman with Orange Hat.'" Ricodemus

Pebble 141

- Mint Type - Palettes: MemeMaxis 900/1,000
- Color Density: Bloom 314/1,000
- Edge: No 688/1,000
- Flow: No 935/1,000
- Overlap: Disjoin 245/1,000
- Palette: Serenity 84/1,000
- Size: Rockling 300/1,000
- Special Elements: 3 427/1,000
- Traced: No Border 858/1,000

Rarity

- Rarity Rank: #942
- Statistical Rarity: #906
- Single Trait Rarity #863

MintFace Vibe Check

A solitary figure turns their head upwards praying for crypto redemption. A *Disjoin Overlap* affords the distance to imagine the scene, and the predominance of white Pebbles fade into the background with *Bloom* Color Density. Where the unimagined show up in art, is often not by coincidence.

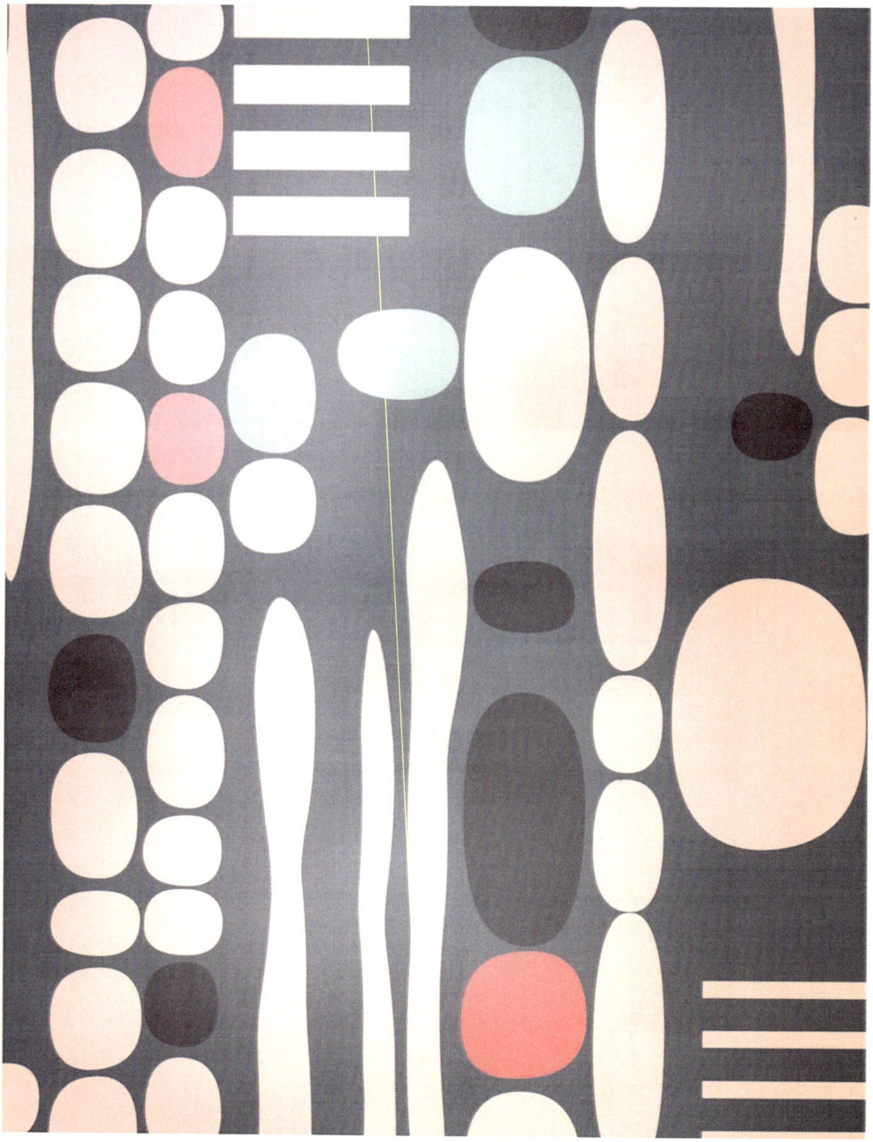

Pebble 144 'Puerta del Sol' minted by pandelic

"The 'Puerta del Sol', named after the historic public square in Madrid, Spain — echoing its bustling crowds, pedestrian crossings, and sun-filled atmosphere year-round. The rare *Coral Reef* palette is immediately striking."
pandelic

Pebble 144

- Mint Type - Palettes: MemeMaxis 900/1,000
- Color Density: Hush 143/1,000
- Edge: No 688/1,000
- Flow: No 935/1,000
- Overlap: Harmonize 492/1,000
- Palette: Coral Reef 71/1,000
- Size: Pebbit 151/1,000
- Special Elements: 2 291/1,000
- Traced: No Border 858/1,000

Rarity

- Rarity Rank: #715
- Statistical Rarity: #722
- Single Trait Rarity #742

MintFace Vibe Check

'Puerta del Sol' connects a well known place in Madrid, Spain with elements of Pebble #144. The flow of people, the pavement and perhaps those who are lingering a little longer. *Hush Color Density* ensures the sun touched cream takes priority, while *Harmonize* arranges each Pebble just so.

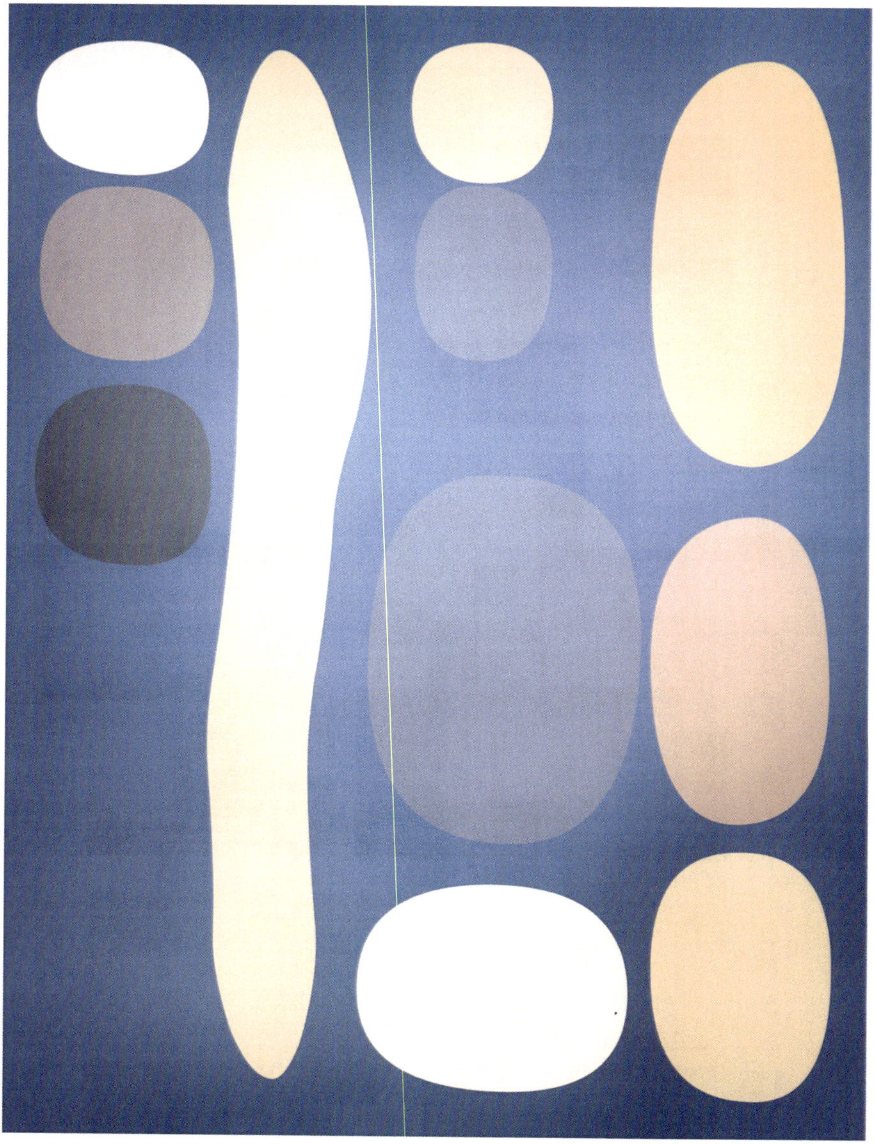

Pebble 145 'Pont du Gard' minted by pandelic

"The 'Pont du Gard', named for the ancient Roman aqueduct constructed in the 1st century CE (current-day France). Its combination of *Dusk Riverbed* palette with *Vivid* color echoes the stones of the river Gardon as well as the cut-outs from the iconic bridge." pandelic

Pebble 145

- Mint Type - Palettes: MemeMaxis 900/1,000
- Color Density: Vivid 349/1,000
- Edge: Yes 312/1,000
- Flow: No 935/1,000
- Overlap: Harmonize 492/1,000
- Palette: Dusk Riverbed 71/1,000
- Size: Rockling 300/1,000
- Special Elements: 2 291/1,000
- Traced: No Border 858/1,000

Rarity

- Rarity Rank: #809
- Statistical Rarity: #620
- Single Trait Rarity #612

MintFace Vibe Check

What a stunningly simple Pebble! Pandelic has truly integrated its provenance with that of one of humanities earliest innovations; the transferring of water across a distance using aqueducts. The vertical *Special Element* symbolic of the waters flow at 'Pont du Gard.'

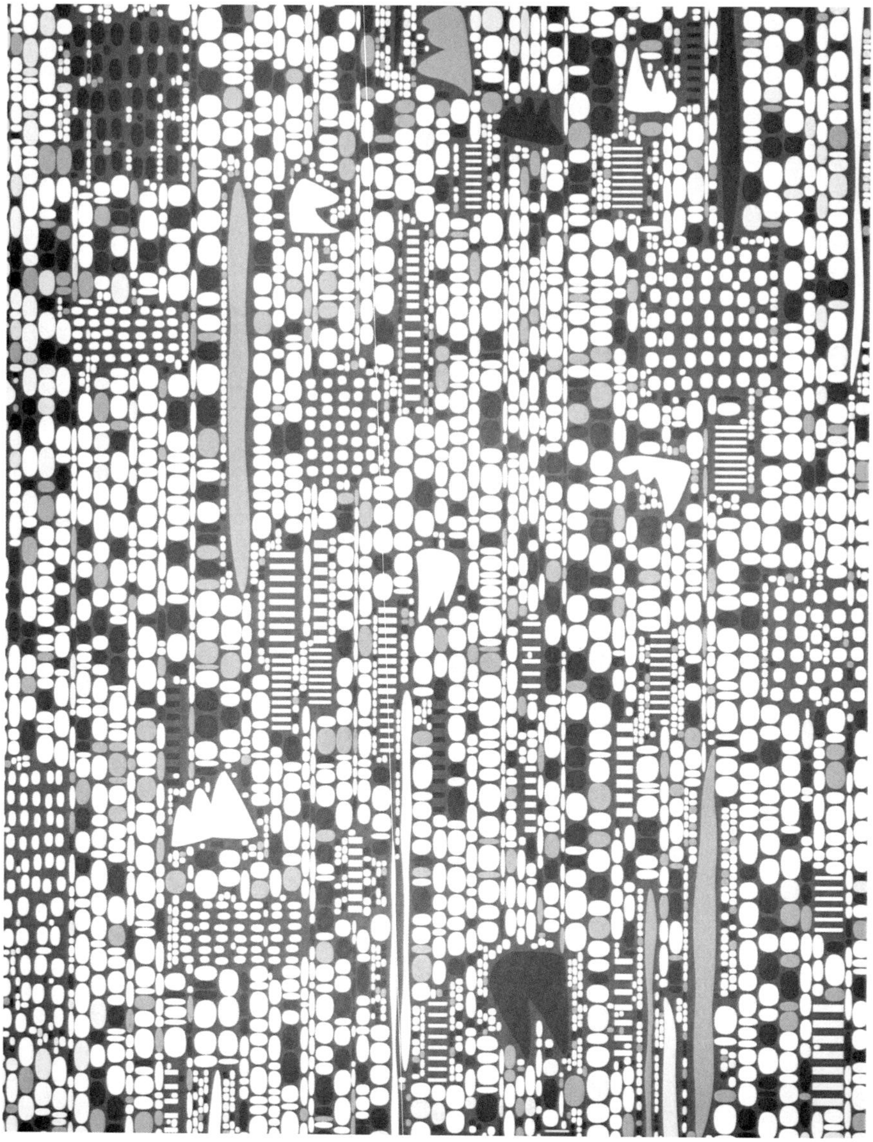

Pebble 155 'Carbon Copy' minted by Regular Dad

> 'Carbon Copy' got its name from the first Pebbles Race. I hope that it will be my legacy to my family and stay with us as long as Ethereum is still making blocks."
> Regular Dad

Pebble 155

- Mint Type - Palettes: MemeMaxis 900 / 1,000
- Color Density: Bloom 314 / 1,000
- Edge: No 688 / 1,000
- Flow: No 935 / 1,000
- Overlap: Harmonize 492 / 1,000
- Palette: Shades of Hey! 55 / 1,000
- Size: Boulderette 147 / 1,000
- Special Elements: All 77 / 1,000
- Traced: No Border 858 / 1,000

Rarity

- Rarity Rank: #468
- Statistical Rarity: #612
- Single Trait Rarity #352

MintFace Vibe Check

'Carbon Copy' imparts a radiance from the *Bloom* Color Density at *Boulderette* Size. The seven sharply pointed *Special Element* Pebbles in black, metallic and white provide interesting break points as do the stick-like lines. The rectangular grid and ladder *Special Elements* integrate well into the scene.

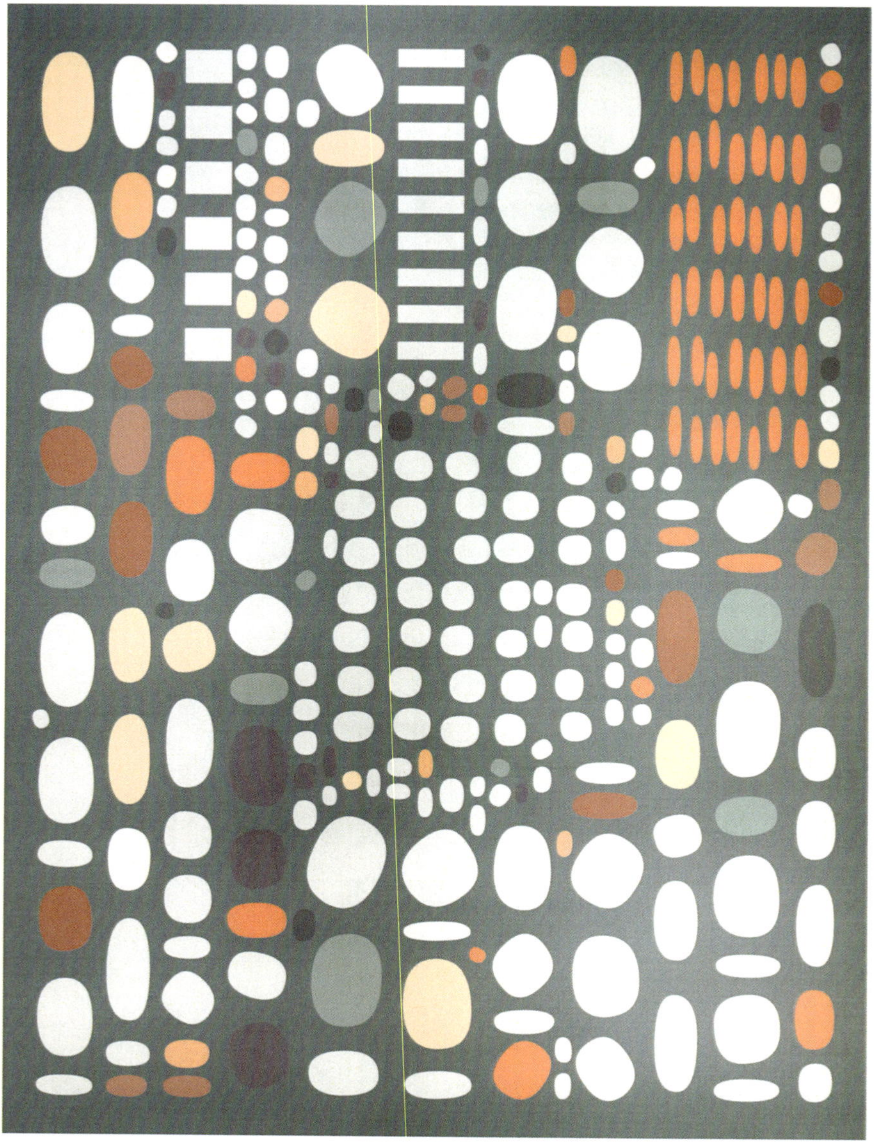

Pebble 169 'A Unified Theory of Everything' minted by Lawtoshi

> 'A unified theory of everything' is a zen garden of traits surrounding an inner courtyard of tranquility. A space for meditative peace in a chaotic world." Lawtoshi

Pebble 169

- Mint Type - Palettes: MemeMaxis 900/1,000
- Color Density: Bloom 314/1,000
- Edge: Yes 312/1,000
- Flow: No 935/1,000
- Overlap: Disjoin 245/1,000
- Palette: Forest Whisper 83/1,000
- Size: Crumb 72/1,000
- Special Elements: 2 291/1,000
- Traced: No Border 858/1,000

Rarity

- Rarity Rank: #453
- Statistical Rarity: #338
- Single Trait Rarity #478

MintFace Vibe Check

A wonderful aerial view of a Japanese zen garden materializes. *Crumb* delivers the ideal size of Pebble to mimic a closer proximity perspective. The *Disjoin Overlap* introduces a healthy amount of negative space around the Pebbles. The centered rectangular Pebble grouping that scarcely creates the number '1811' is a unique *Special Element* example. A lot has been achieved here in memetically numbered Pebble #169.

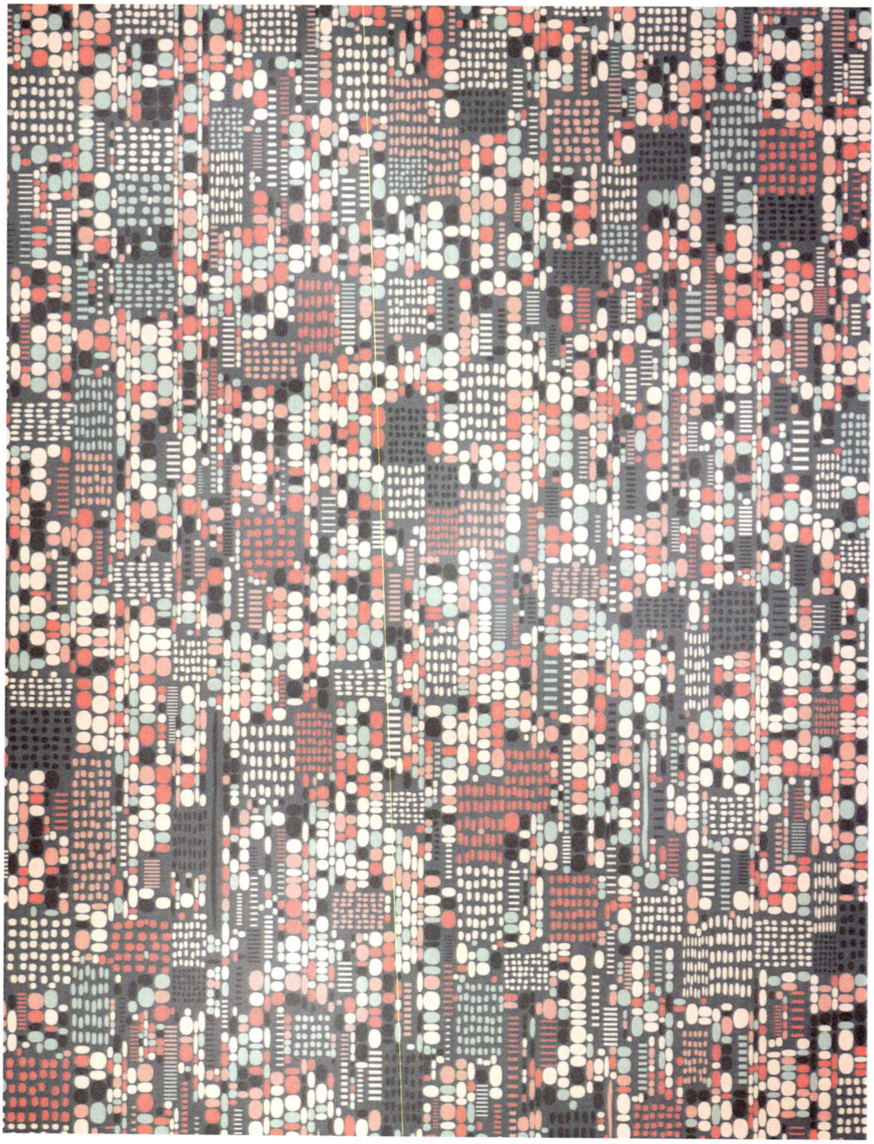

Pebble 206 'Corbita' minted by Mikavert

"A corbita struck the rocks, scattering amphorae across the beach like shattered pottery stars." Mikavert

Pebble 206

- Mint Type - Palettes: MemeMaxis 900 / 1,000
- Color Density: Bloom 314 / 1,000
- Edge: No 688 / 1,000
- Flow: No 935 / 1,000
- Overlap: Harmonize 492 / 1,000
- Palette: Coral Reef 71 / 1,000
- Size: Craglet 85 / 1,000
- Special Elements: 3 427 / 1,000
- Traced: No Border 858 / 1,000

Rarity

- Rarity Rank: #778
- Statistical Rarity: #867
- Single Trait Rarity #578

MintFace Vibe Check

'Corbita' is a blockchain treasure that accrues much of its shine from *Craglet* trait. While many a Pebble turns lopsided with *Special Elements* added, Pebble #206 deftly sprinkles the rectangular grid-like blobs with the fervour of a sailor heading starboard. One mans ruin is another's treasure.

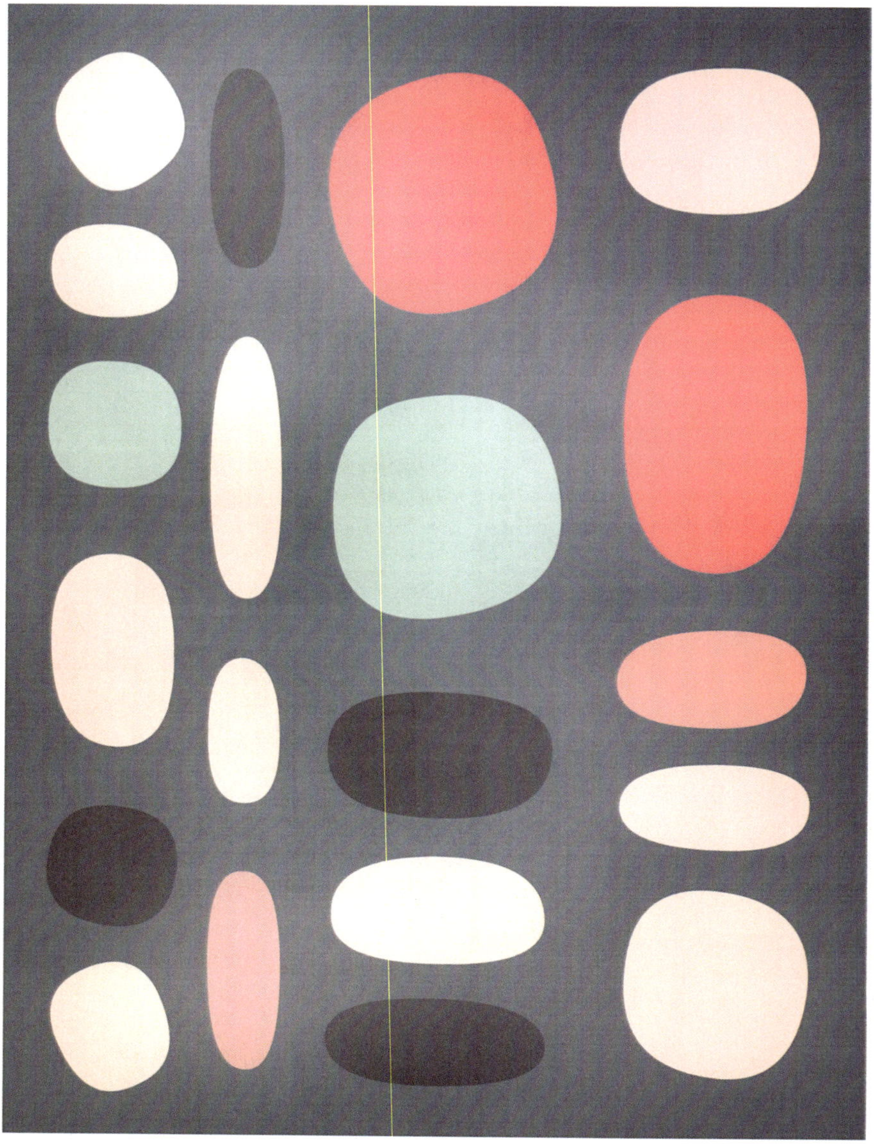

Pebble 222 minted by Maxmyeth

"The *Coral Reef* palette is my favorite in the collection. Once again, I tried to mint a fun number and was successful with this calming beauty." Maxmyeth

Pebble 222

- Mint Type - Palettes: MemeMaxis 900/1,000
- Color Density: Bloom 314/1,000
- Edge: Yes 312/1,000
- Flow: No 935/1,000
- Overlap: Disjoin 245/1,000
- Palette: Coral Reef 71/1,000
- Size: Stonelet 220/1,000
- Special Elements: 2 291/1,000
- Traced: No Border 858/1,000

Rarity

- Rarity Rank: #661
- Statistical Rarity: #445
- Single Trait Rarity #612

MintFace Vibe Check

The absolute delight in a *Disjoin Overlap* that puts faith in each Pebble holding its own across the *Coral Reef* ocean. Maxmyeth minted a beauty that rivals the shores of two busier Pebbles that identify as *Coral Reef* with *Bloom Color Density* at *Stonelet* size.

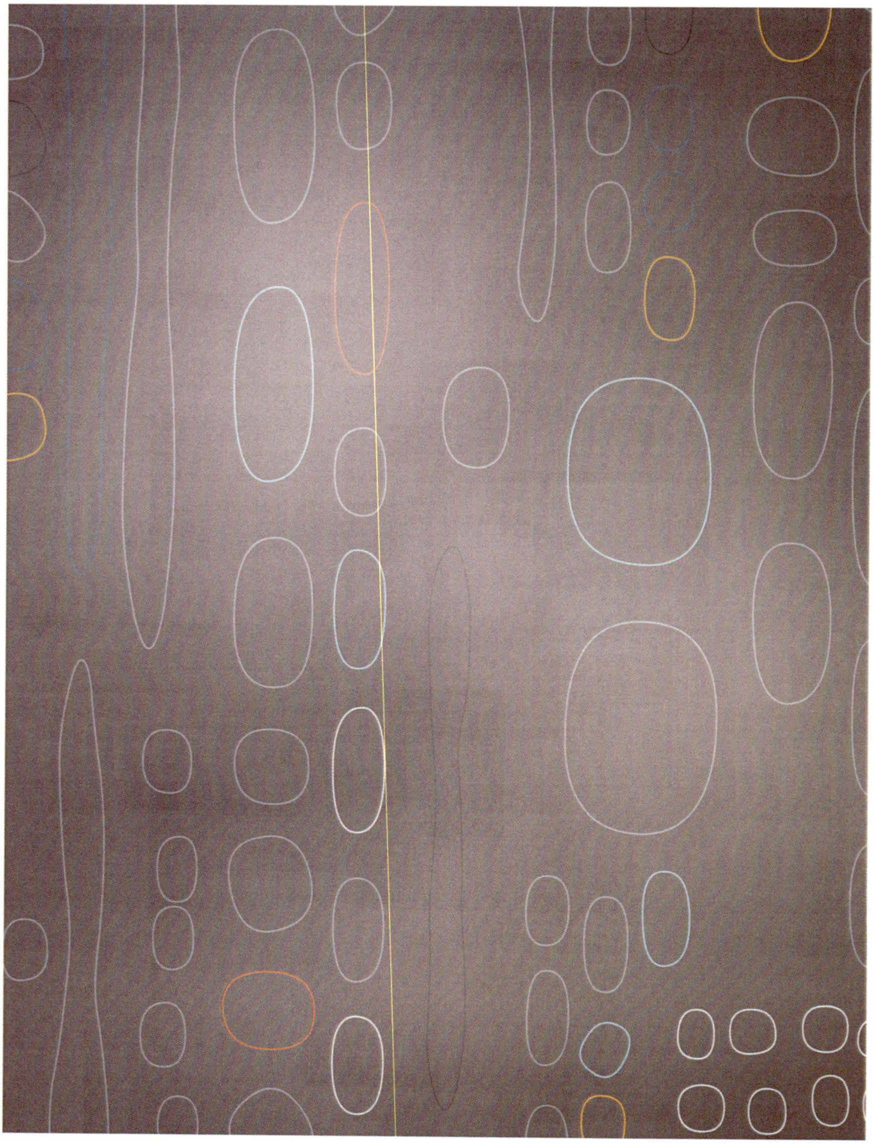

Pebble 223 minted by Maxmyeth

"Coffee is a huge part of my daily routine so it's no surprise this *Galactic Latte* palette is special to me. *No Fill Traced* is my favorite trait in the Pebbles collection." Maxmyeth

Pebble 223

- Mint Type - Palettes: MemeMaxis 900/1,000
- Color Density: Hush 143/1,000
- Edge: No 688/1,000
- Flow: No 935/1,000
- Overlap: Disjoin 245/1,000
- Palette: Galactic Latte 80/1,000
- Size: Pebbit 151/1,000
- Special Elements: 2 291/1,000
- Traced: No Fill 45/1,000

Rarity

- Rarity Rank: #130
- Statistical Rarity: #139
- Single Trait Rarity #123

MintFace Vibe Check

Fill the cup to the brim with *Pebble #223*. A caffeinated banger sporting a combination of *Galactic Latte* and *No Fill* that is found nowhere else.

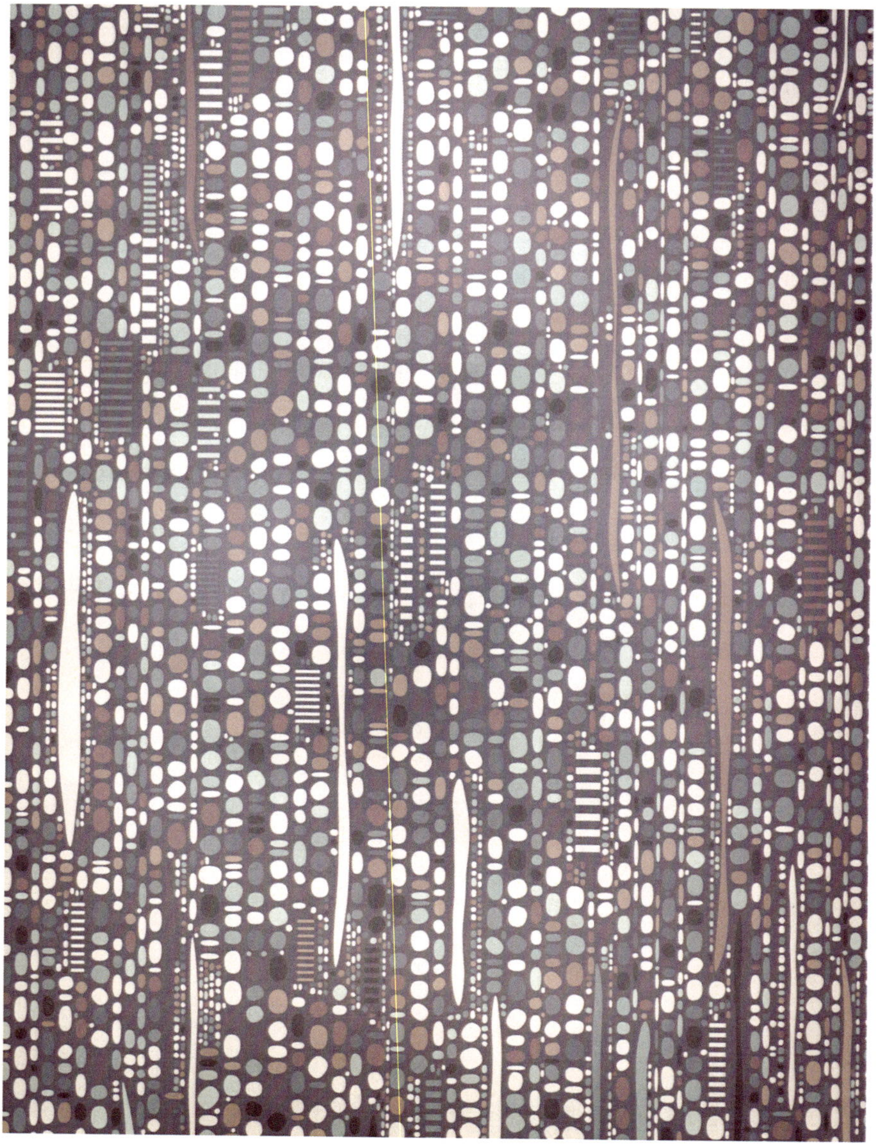

Pebble 250 'Concert Hallucinations' minted by Spritey

"'Concert Hallucinations' creates a mesmerizing effect of Pebbles nested within Pebbles. Featured in the inaugural Pebbles Race." Spritey

Pebble 250

- Mint Type - Palettes: MemeMaxis 900 / 1,000
- Color Density: Bloom 314 / 1,000
- Edge: No 688 / 1,000
- Flow: No 935 / 1,000
- Overlap: Disjoin 245 / 1,000
- Palette: Night Owl Doodles 86 / 1,000
- Size: Boulderette 147 / 1,000
- Special Elements: 2 291 / 1,000
- Traced: No Border 858 / 1,000

Rarity

- Rarity Rank: #817
- Statistical Rarity: #749
- Single Trait Rarity #863

MintFace Vibe Check

Night Owl Doodles traits sets the night-time scene and *Boulderette* transforms the circular shapes into a masses of people one might see at a stadium venue. *Concert Hallucinations* encapsulates the drama of the event.

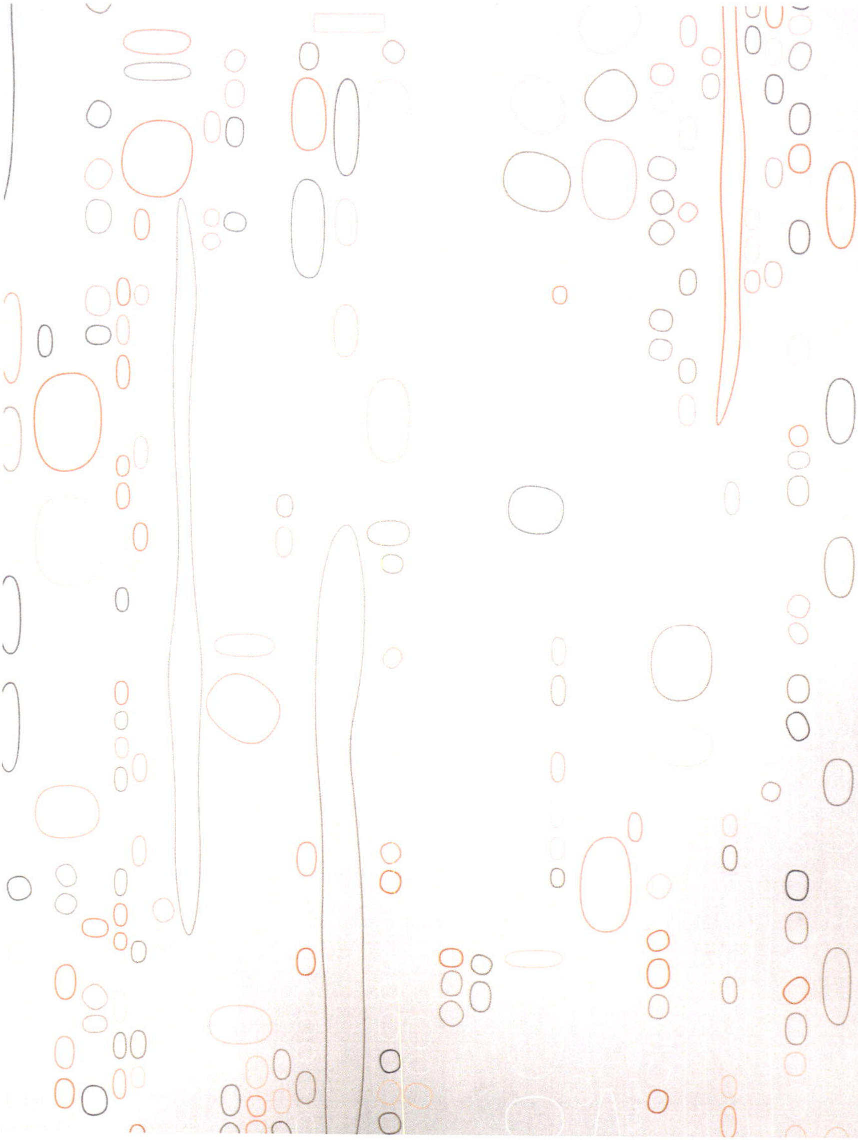

Pebble 271 'SmokeShow' minted by Maybe

"Love how Pebble #271, the 'SmokeShow', hits you over the head with exactly nothing. Love the negative space background shapes." Maybe

Pebble 271

- Mint Type - Palettes: MemeMaxis 900/1,000
- Color Density: Bloom 314/1,000
- Edge: No 688/1,000
- Flow: No 935/1,000
- Overlap: Disjoin 245/1,000
- Palette: Serenity 84/1,000
- Size: Crumb 72/1,000
- Special Elements: 3 427/1,000
- Traced: No Fill 45/1,000

Rarity

- Rarity Rank: #129
- Statistical Rarity: #164
- Single Trait Rarity #123

MintFace Vibe Check

The 'SmokeShow' is mostly hidden from view through its *Traced No Fill* and *Serenity* palette. If there was a Pebble that better demonstrated the saying 'less is more,' we are yet to see it.

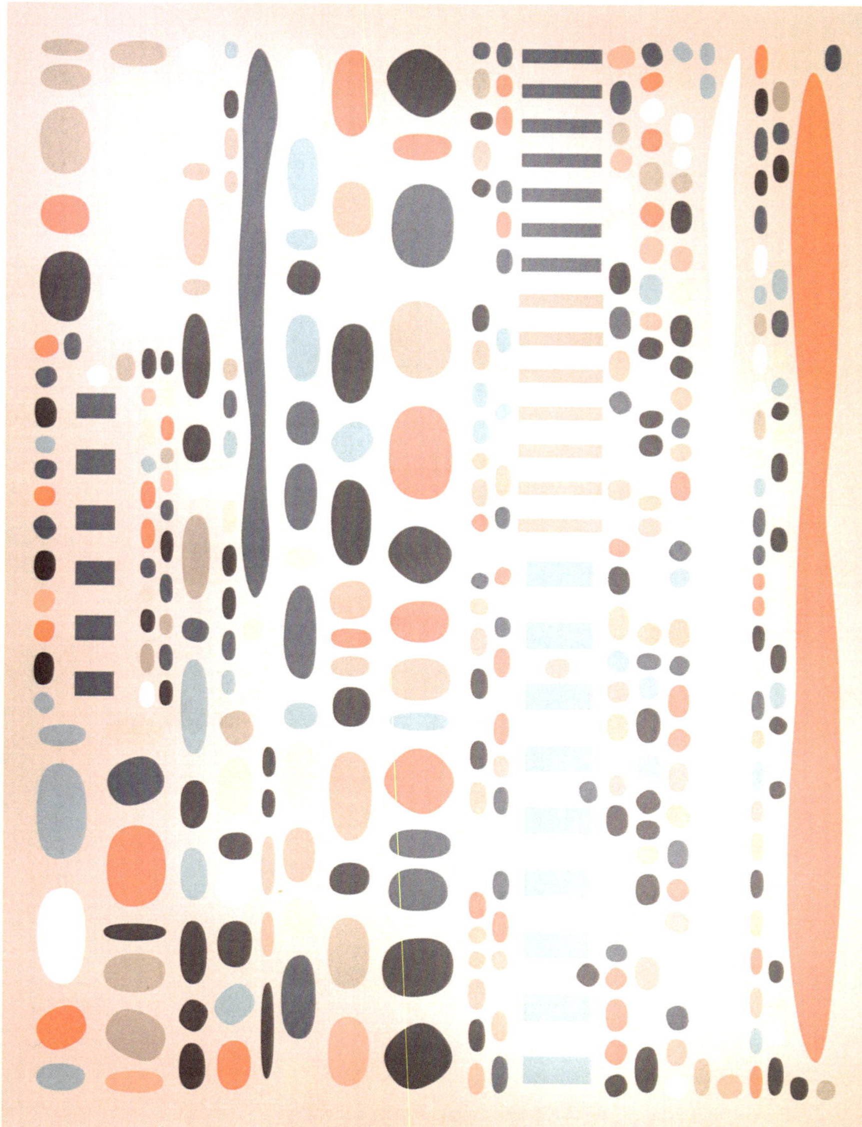

Pebble 275 'DNA Sequencer' minted by Franklin Fit

"Reminds me of DNA sequencing, and how we all are unique in our own right. Favorite traits are *Crumb* and *Desert Mirage* for the time I've spent training in the desert and the solitude and serenity." Franklin Fit

Pebble 275

- Mint Type - Palettes: MemeMaxis 900 / 1,000
- Color Density: Vivid 349 / 1,000
- Edge: Yes 312 / 1,000
- Flow: No 935 / 1,000
- Overlap: Disjoin 245 / 1,000
- Palette: Desert Mirage 79 / 1,000
- Size: Crumb 72 / 1,000
- Special Elements: 2 291 / 1,000
- Traced: No Border 858 / 1,000

Rarity

- Rarity Rank: #462
- Statistical Rarity: #356
- Single Trait Rarity #478

MintFace Vibe Check

Bold elliptical shapes are configured at distance influenced by the *Disjoin Overlap*. The stick-like vertical blobs are in conversation with each other across the vastness of the *Desert Mirage* palette, with the ladder-like *Special Element* forming a platoon of vertical structure.

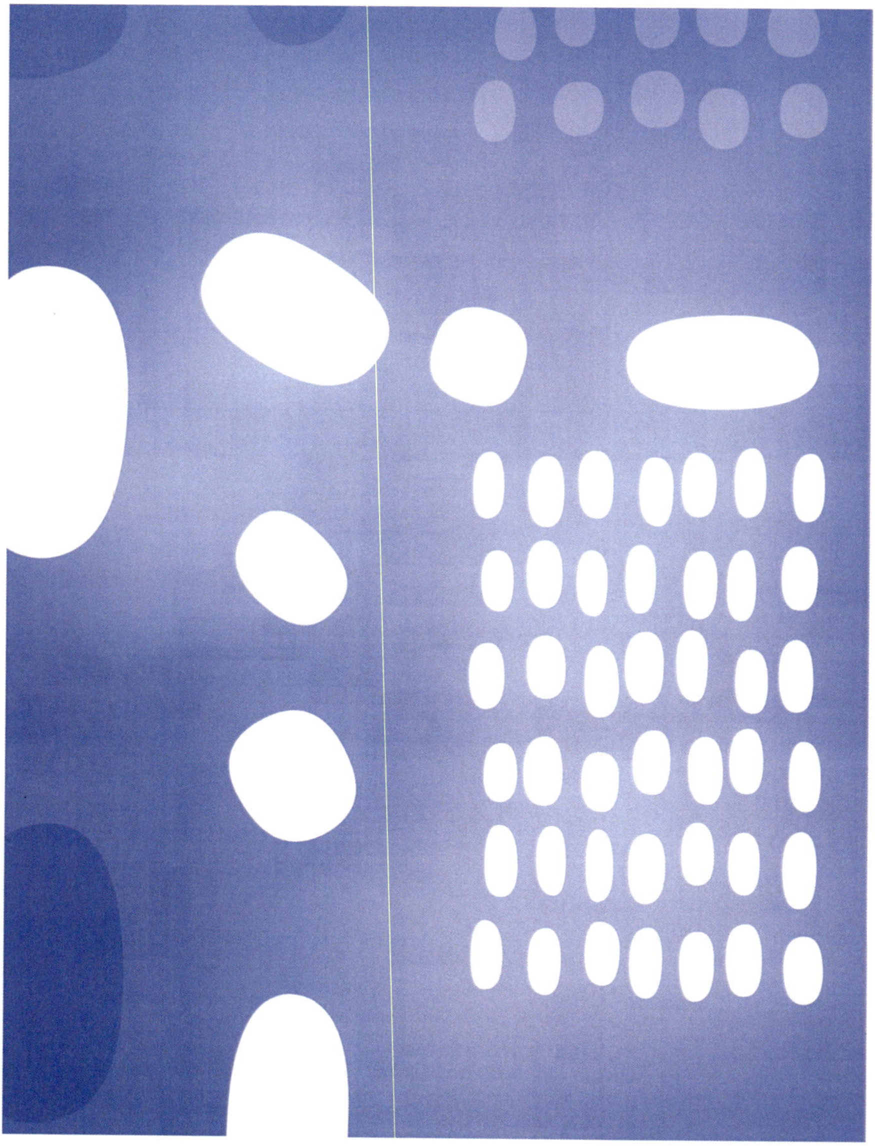

Pebble 281 minted by CaptainDerp

> "I'm attracted to the *Blueprint* palette for its popularity (my bags) but don't feel as much on the aesthetic as I do for Pebble #286." Captain Derp

Pebble 281

- Mint Type - Palettes: HyperMaxis 50/1,000
- Color Density: Hush 143/1,000
- Edge: No 688/1,000
- Flow: No 935/1,000
- Overlap: Isolate 99/1,000
- Palette: Blueprint 21/1,000
- Size: Rockling 300/1,000
- Special Elements: 2 291/1,000
- Traced: No Border 858/1,000

Rarity

- Rarity Rank: #321
- Statistical Rarity: #478
- Single Trait Rarity #406

MintFace Vibe Check

Blueprint palette was made exclusively available to *HyperMaxis Mint Type* people who had attained a recognised amount of Collector Provenance with their wallet. The grid-like Pebbles are a singular *Special Element,* surrounded by *Hush Color Density* Pebbles from the white base layer of *Blueprint.*

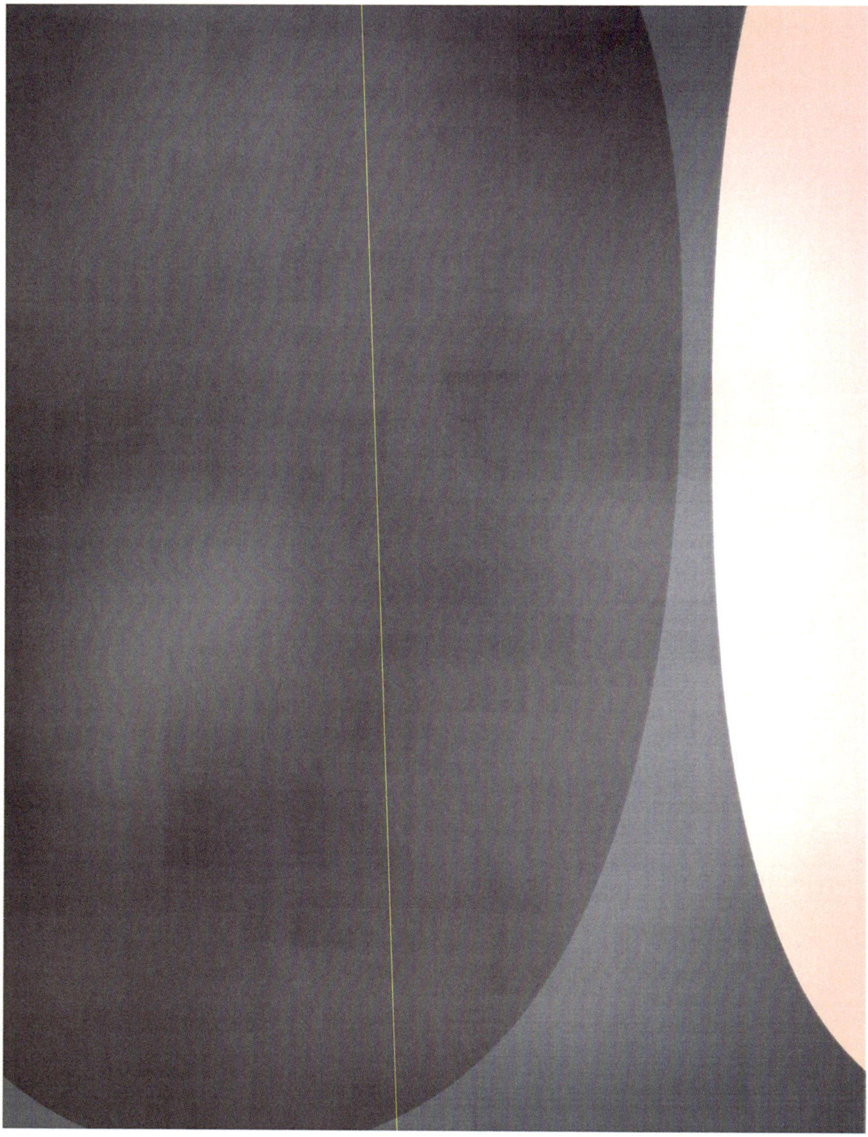

Pebble 286 minted by CaptainDerp

"Indisputably unique. The two massive forms so close together implies intimacy, vulnerability, and potentiality. By far my favorite *Mountlet* for its gravity and tension."
CaptainDerp

Pebble 286

- Mint Type - Palettes: MemeMaxis 900/1,000
- Color Density: Bloom 314/1,000
- Edge: No 688/1,000
- Flow: No 935/1,000
- Overlap: Harmonize 492/1,000
- Palette: Coral Reef 71/1,000
- Size: Mountlet 25/1,000
- Special Elements: 3 427/1,000
- Traced: No Border 858/1,000

Rarity

- Rarity Rank: #259
- Statistical Rarity: #697
- Single Trait Rarity #172

MintFace Vibe Check

A gargantuan *Mountlet* Pebble minted by CaptainDerp. The *Harmonize Overlap* focusses the gaze of the viewer on the confined space between the two behemoths. The opposing forces of charcoal and a gold tinted cream from *Coral Reef* palette further intensifying the on-stage drama.

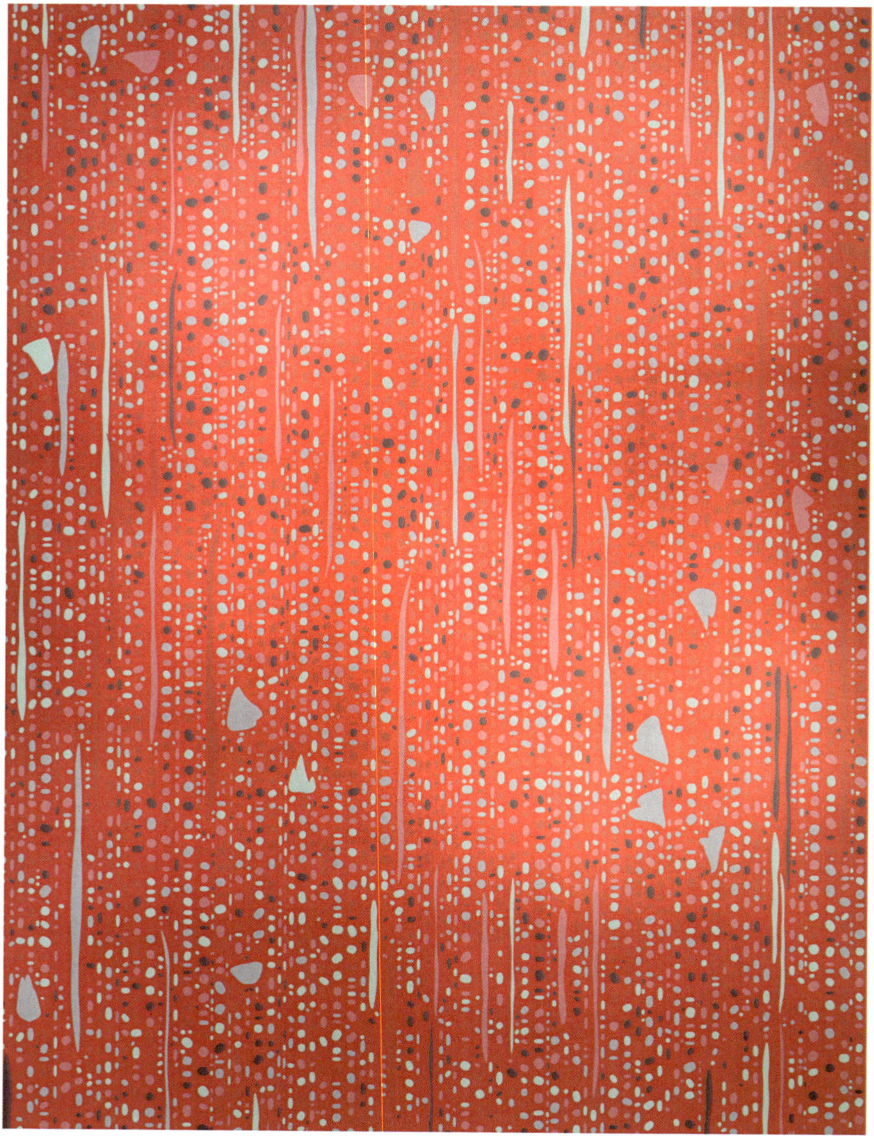

Pebble 295 'Salsa Blush' minted by Northof80

Salsa Blush Pebbles
Craglets and overlaps add flair
Playful and mature.

Pebble 295

- Mint Type - Palettes: HyperMaxis 50/1;000
- Color Density: Vivid 349/1,000
- Edge: No 688/1,000
- Flow: No 935/1,000
- Overlap: Isolate 99/1,000
- Palette: Salsa Blush 13/1,000
- Size: Craglet 85/1,000
- Special Elements: 2 291/1,000
- Traced: No Border 858/1,000

Rarity

- Rarity Rank: #227
- Statistical Rarity: #457
- Single Trait Rarity #262

MintFace Vibe Check

Vivid Color Density dials up the theatrics and doubly so on a red stained *Salsa Blush* palette. The drip-like vertical lines stand in for the entertainment as the confetti like *Craglet* Pebbles dominate the show.

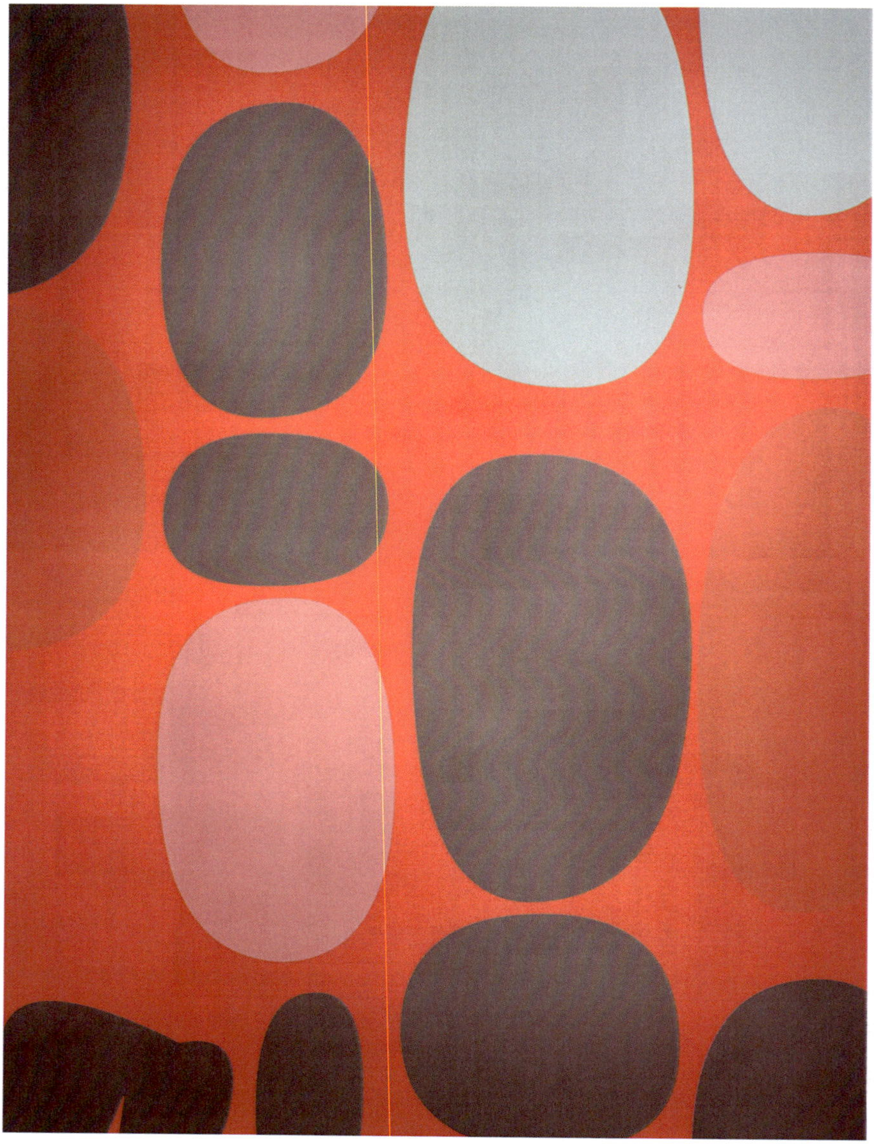

Pebble 299 'The Eruption' minted by Hugo Faz

> 'The Eruption' is the Pebble that blew my heart. Favorite trait is of course the Salsa Blush palette." Hugo Faz

Pebble 299

- Mint Type - Palettes: HyperMaxis 50 / 1,000
- Color Density: Bloom 314 / 1,000
- Edge: No 688 / 1,000
- Flow: No 935 / 1,000
- Overlap: Harmonize 492 / 1,000
- Palette: Salsa Blush 13 / 1,000
- Size: Rockling 300 / 1,000
- Special Elements: 1 150 / 1,000
- Traced: Border 97 / 1,000

Rarity

- Rarity Rank: #201
- Statistical Rarity: #243
- Single Trait Rarity #262

MintFace Vibe Check

'The Eruption' brings the molten energy of *Salsa Blush* palette bubbling up around 12 *Rockling* sized Pebbles and one *Special Element* Pebble on the bottom left corner. The *Traced* Border is not easily seen, due to the immense visual heat from the surrounding lava.

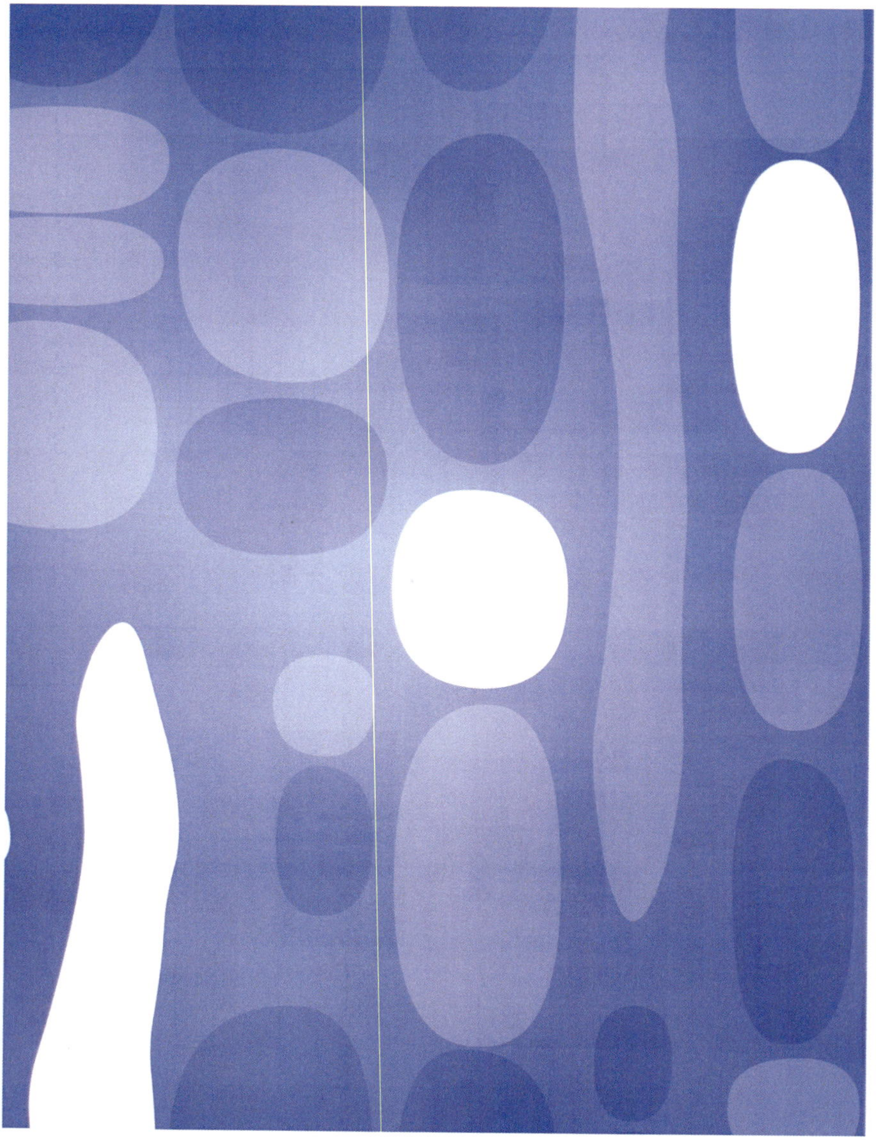

Pebble 302 Freestone River minted by BatSoupYum

"No matter how deep the water gets, keep going."
BatSoupYum

Pebble 302

- Mint Type - Palettes: <u>HyperMaxis</u> 50 / 1,000
- Color Density: <u>Vivid</u> 349 / 1,000
- Edge: <u>No</u> 688 / 1,000
- Flow: <u>No</u> 935 / 1,000
- Overlap: <u>Harmonize</u> 492 / 1,000
- Palette: <u>Blueprint</u> 21 / 1,000
- Size: <u>Stonelet</u> 220 / 1,000
- Special Elements: <u>2</u> 291 / 1,000
- Traced: <u>No Border</u> 858 / 1,000

Rarity

- Rarity Rank: #597
- Statistical Rarity: #885
- Single Trait Rarity #406

MintFace Vibe Check

The river runs swift and freely across 'Freestone River.' Palette #302 inherits a *Stonelet* size that balances the three *Blueprint* color components with the most ease in its class. One of only 21 *Blueprint* palettes reserved for Collector Provenance wallets.

Pebble 321 'Snow Diamonds' minted by DarrenSRS

> "First Generative Art project launched within the 6529 ecosystem. Can't be more O.G. than this!" DarrenSRS

Pebble 321

- Mint Type - Palettes: MemeMaxis 900/1,000
- Color Density: Faint 153/1,000
- Edge: No 688/1,000
- Flow: Yes 65/1,000
- Overlap: Harmonize 492/1,000
- Palette: Serenity 84/1,000
- Size: Rockling 300/1,000
- Special Elements: None 55/1,000
- Traced: No Border 858/1,000

Rarity

- Rarity Rank: #9
- Statistical Rarity: #7
- Single Trait Rarity #11

MintFace Vibe Check

The sparkle of 'Snow Diamonds' shines through the *Faint Color Density*. The *Serenity* palette is redacted back to white, with the terracotta and auburn from the palette not visible. Minimalists can rejoice in 'Snow Diamonds' without having to climb the rarity totem for an *Elephant Pajamas* palette.

Pebble 422 'Monolith Echo' minted by the Complaint Master Blocknoob

> "The 'Monolith Echo,' is a distinguished piece with its striking black monolithic shapes on a serene beige background, it symbolizes timelessness and stability. The essence forged." Blocknoob

Pebble 422

- Mint Type - Palettes: MemeMaxis 900 / 1,000
- Color Density: Hush 143 / 1,000
- Edge: No 688 / 1,000
- Flow: No 935 / 1,000
- Overlap: Disjoin 245 / 1,000
- Palette: Desert Mirage 79 / 1,000
- Size: Rockling 300 / 1,000
- Special Elements: 1 150 / 1,000
- Traced: No Border 858 / 1,000

Rarity

- Rarity Rank: #609
- Statistical Rarity: #573
- Single Trait Rarity #742

MintFace Vibe Check

The four ladder-like structures add weight to 'Monolith Echo.' The *Disjoin Overlap* keeps the larger *Rockling* sized Pebbles at some distance from the structures. The *Desert Mirage* palette places 'Monolith Echo' firmly in the realms of an ancient civilisation, long since overwhelmed by the desert sands.

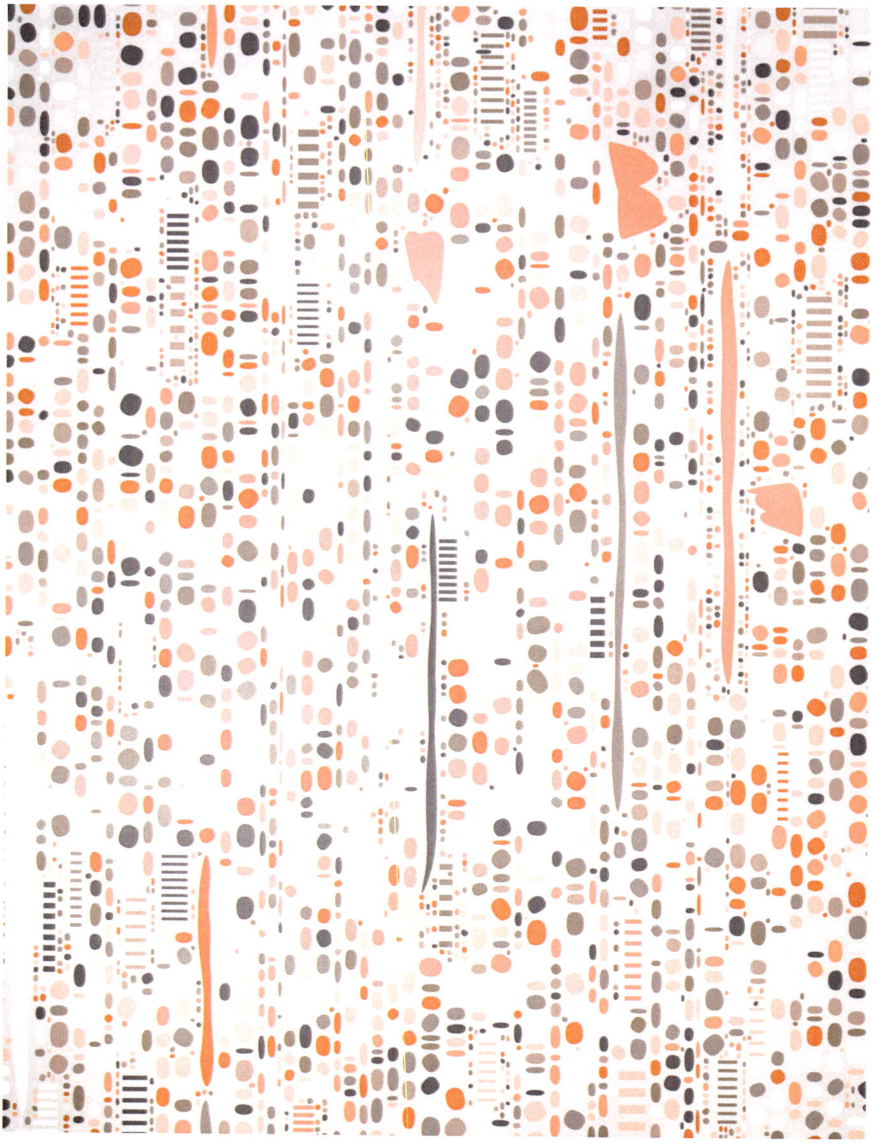

Pebble 426 minted by Prxt0

Pebble 426

- Mint Type - Palettes: MemeMaxis 900/1,000
- Color Density: Vivid 349/1,000
- Edge: No 688/1,000
- Flow: No 935/1,000
- Overlap: Disjoin 245/1,000
- Palette: Serenity 84/1,000
- Size: Boulderette 147/1,000
- Special Elements: 3 427/1,000
- Traced: No Border 858/1,000

Rarity

- Rarity Rank: #879
- Statistical Rarity: #837
- Single Trait Rarity #863

MintFace Vibe Check

A quartet of *Special Elements* play like harp strings from left to right across the *Serenity* lit canvas. The *Vivid Color Density* nature of the work brings a sense of presence further amplified by the vertical ladder-like columns, floating orb-like in *Disjoin Overlap* space. What's not to like?

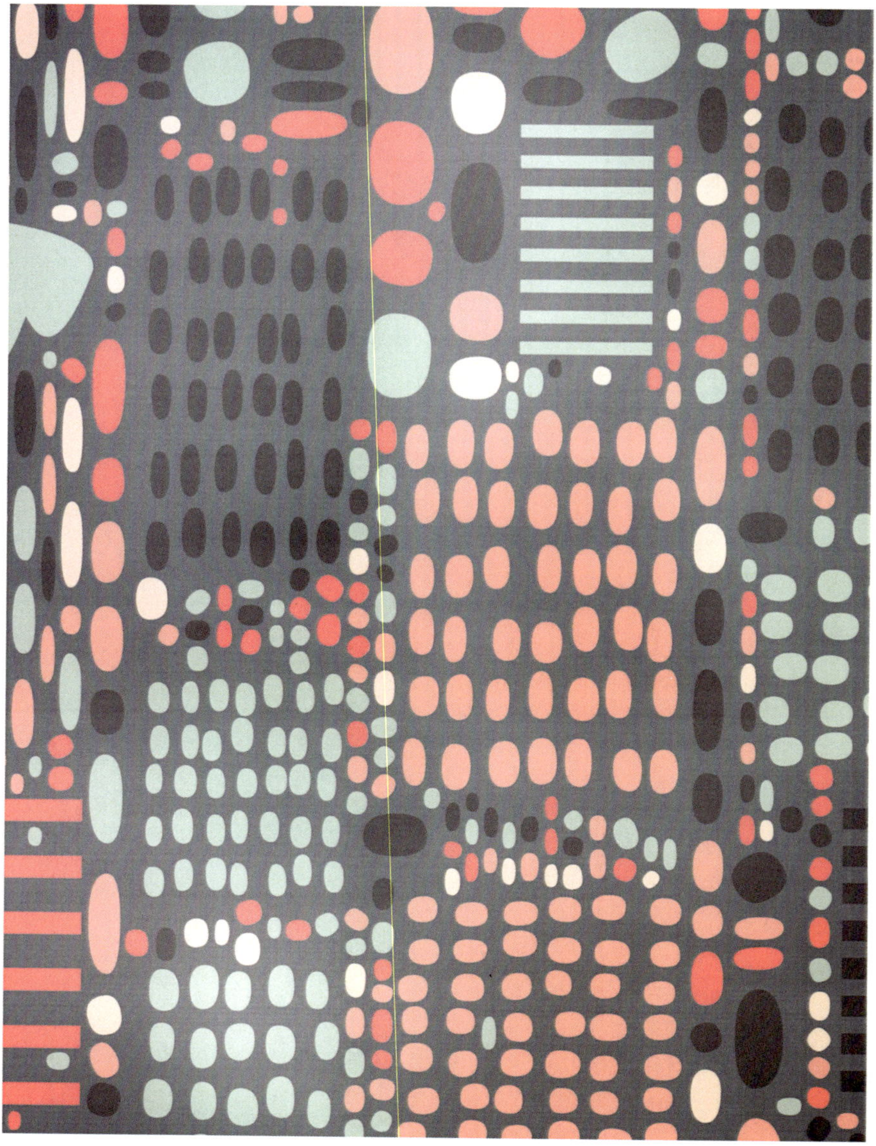

Pebble 431 minted by OMDegen

Pebble 431

- Mint Type - Palettes: MemeMaxis 900 / 1,000
- Color Density: Vivid 349 / 1,000
- Edge: No 688 / 1,000
- Flow: No 935 / 1,000
- Overlap: Disjoin 245 / 1,000
- Palette: Coral Reef 71 / 1,000
- Size: Crumb 72 / 1,000
- Special Elements: 3 427 / 1,000
- Traced: No Border 858 / 1,000

Rarity

- Rarity Rank: #632
- Statistical Rarity: #731
- Single Trait Rarity #478

MintFace Vibe Check

Seven super-sized grids of Pebbles are the hallmark of Pebble #431. There are also three rectangular pathways visible, a second call sign of a *Special Element* making an appearance. The third *Special Element* is most obvious in the craggy-like Pebble in the upper left corner. The best aspects of *Coral Reef* palette on display here.

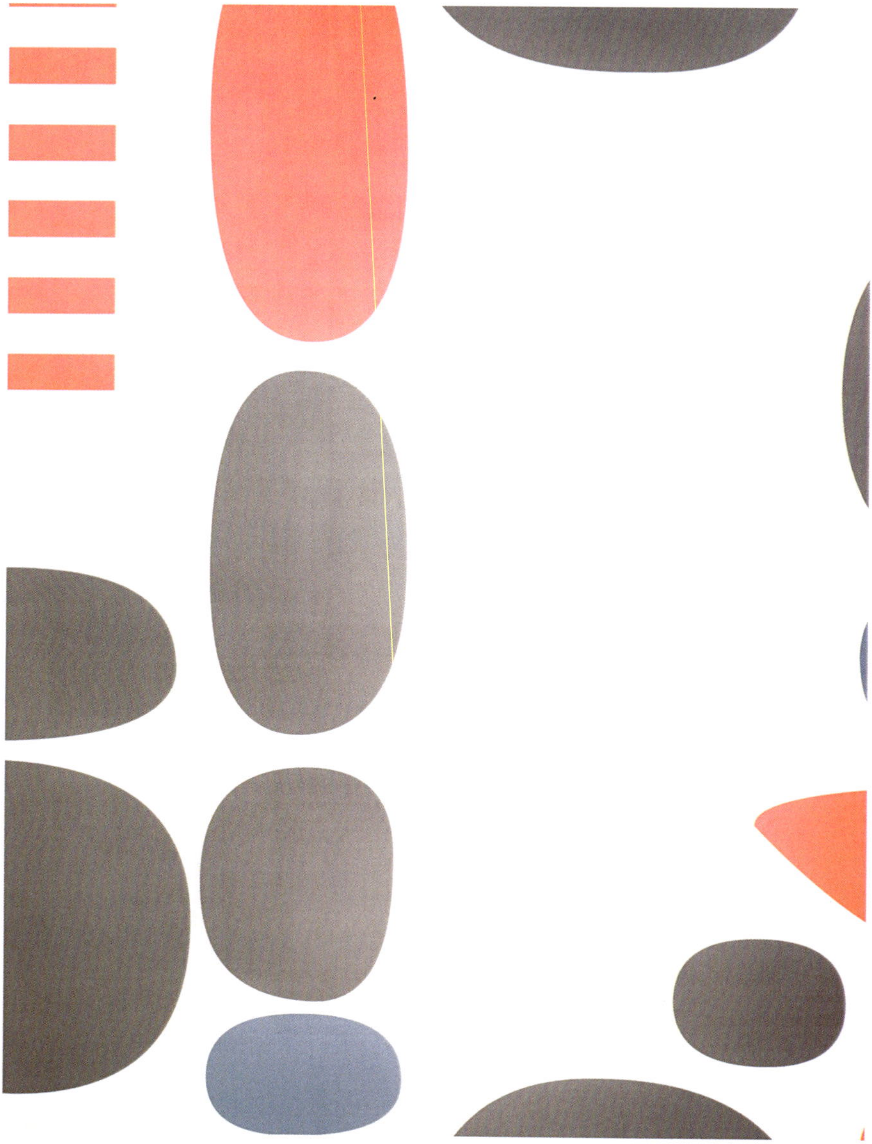

Pebble 448 'Party Cow' minted by clicky2048

"When I stare at this Pebble and let my mind drift, I mainly think of cows and ice cream. I call it 'Party Cow.' I really like the subtle (almost imperceptible) structures lurking in that seemingly blank white area." clicky2048

Pebble 448

- Mint Type - Palettes: MemeMaxis 900 / 1,000
- Color Density: Bloom 314 / 1,000
- Edge: No 688 / 1,000
- Flow: No 935 / 1,000
- Overlap: Harmonize 492 / 1,000
- Palette: Dino Disco 58 / 1,000
- Size: Rockling 300 / 1,000
- Special Elements: 2 291 / 1,000
- Traced: No Border 858 / 1,000

Rarity

- Rarity Rank: #932
- Statistical Rarity: #931
- Single Trait Rarity #863

MintFace Vibe Check

'Party Cow' brings the most optimistic vibes that we embrace in the land of crypto. *Dino Disco* manages to introduce three reds and a blue Pebble from the *Bloom* color density. The ladder-like *Special Element* in the upper left corner leads the viewer's mind thoughtfully beyond the canvas, thanks to the *No Edge* frame.

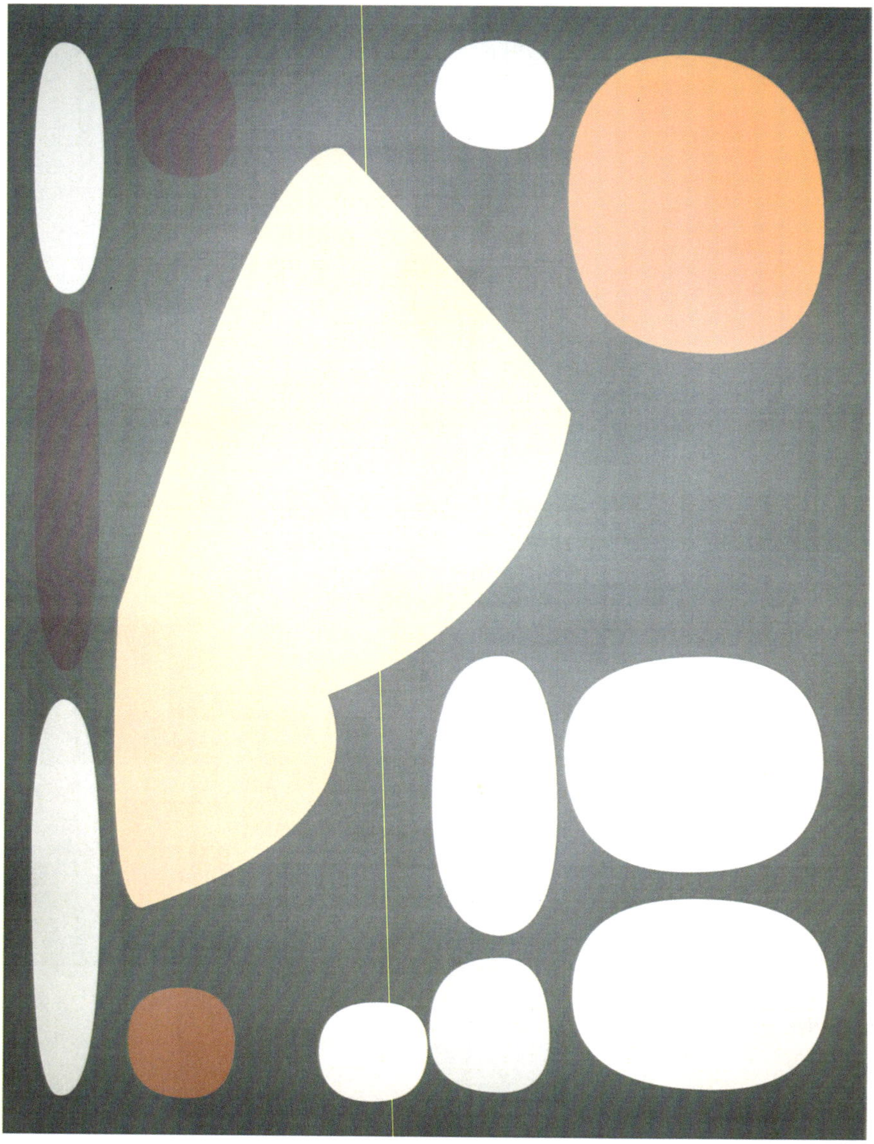

Pebble 457 'Woman with the Orange Hat' minted by MoMO

> "Woman with the Orange Hat. There is a Story in front of her. And there is MoMO at the back of her." MoMO

Pebble 457

- Mint Type - Palettes: MemeMaxis 900/1,000
- Color Density: Bloom 314/1,000
- Edge: Yes 312/1,000
- Flow: Yes 65/1,000
- Overlap: Harmonize 492/1,000
- Palette: Forest Whisper 83/1,000
- Size: Stonelet 220/1,000
- Special Elements: 3 427/1,000
- Traced: No Border 858/1,000

Rarity

- Rarity Rank: #166
- Statistical Rarity: #99
- Single Trait Rarity #66

MintFace Vibe Check

'Woman with Orange Hat' was given her name by MintFace as a re-imagination of Picasso's 'Woman with Blue Hat' (1901). The ownership of the Pebble by MoMO did cause some conjecture and less savoury names such as 'Frog Leg' to be thrown her way by the often ascerbic wit of Bored Surgeon. We are yet to learn from the passage of time how the broader art community will come to be introduced to 'Woman with Orange Hat.'

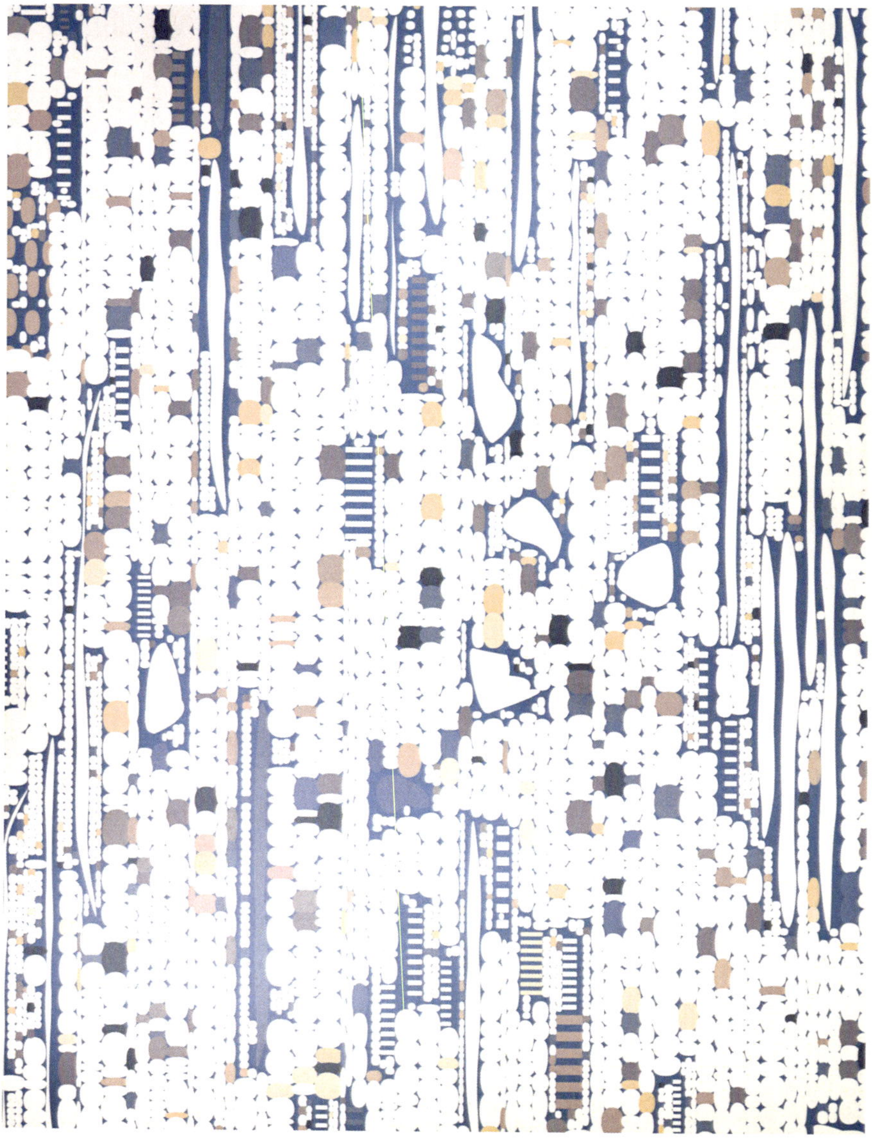

Pebble 480 'The Wave' minted by seizerpunk

> You can't stop 'The Wave' ....just ride it.....it's inevitable."
> seizerpunk

Pebble 480

- Mint Type - Palettes: MemeMaxis 900/1,000
- Color Density: Hush 143/1,000
- Edge: No 688/1,000
- Flow: No 935/1,000
- Overlap: Fuse 113/1,000
- Palette: Dusk Riverbed 71/1,000
- Size: Boulderette 147/1,000
- Special Elements: All 77/1,000
- Traced: No Border 858/1,000

Rarity

- Rarity Rank: #290
- Statistical Rarity: #287
- Single Trait Rarity #352

MintFace Vibe Check

Pebble 480 congeals through *Fuse Overlap* into a wall of camera flashes, as this Pebble struts its stuff. All *Special Elements* are interspersed with particular visual clarity experienced around the ladder-like structures. Like many celebrities, this Pebble is venerated for its quirks.

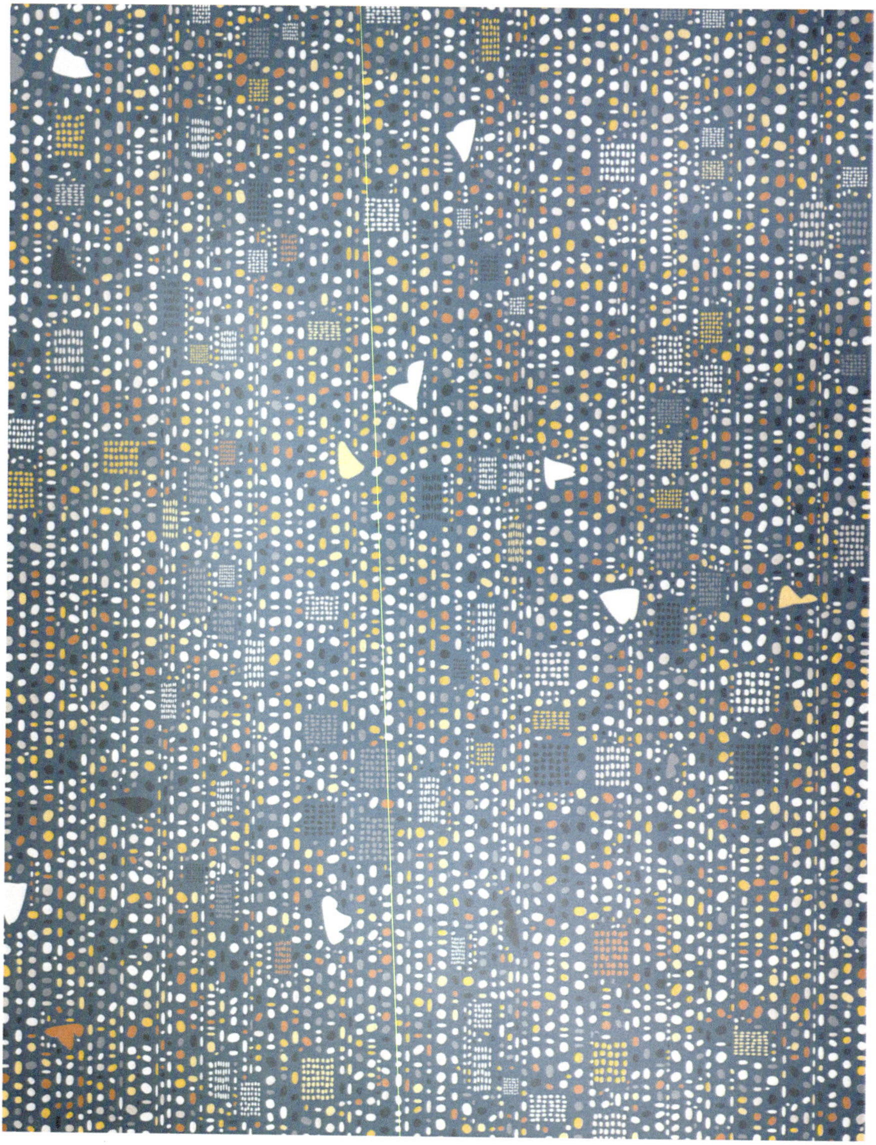

Pebble 510 'Archipelago Novum' minted by PrateekSaraf

"'Archipelago Novum' reflects my life. Lots of hurdles but there are *Special Elements* too." Prateek Saraf

Pebble 510

- Mint Type - Palettes: MemeMaxis 900 / 1,000
- Color Density: Bloom 314 / 1,000
- Edge: No 688 / 1,000
- Flow: No 935 / 1,000
- Overlap: Isolate 99 / 1,000
- Palette: Citrus Slate 72 / 1,000
- Size: Craglet 85 / 1,000
- Special Elements: 2 291 / 1,000
- Traced: No Border 858 / 1,000

Rarity

- Rarity Rank: #440
- Statistical Rarity: #509
- Single Trait Rarity #419

MintFace Vibe Check

An absolute symphony of individual elements that sings off the cryptographic canvas. The yellow highlights of *Citrus Slate* delight in their *Special Element* conjugations. The rectangular Pebble militia are arranged in a dance that lifts the entire piece. You may not see a better Pebble in your life.

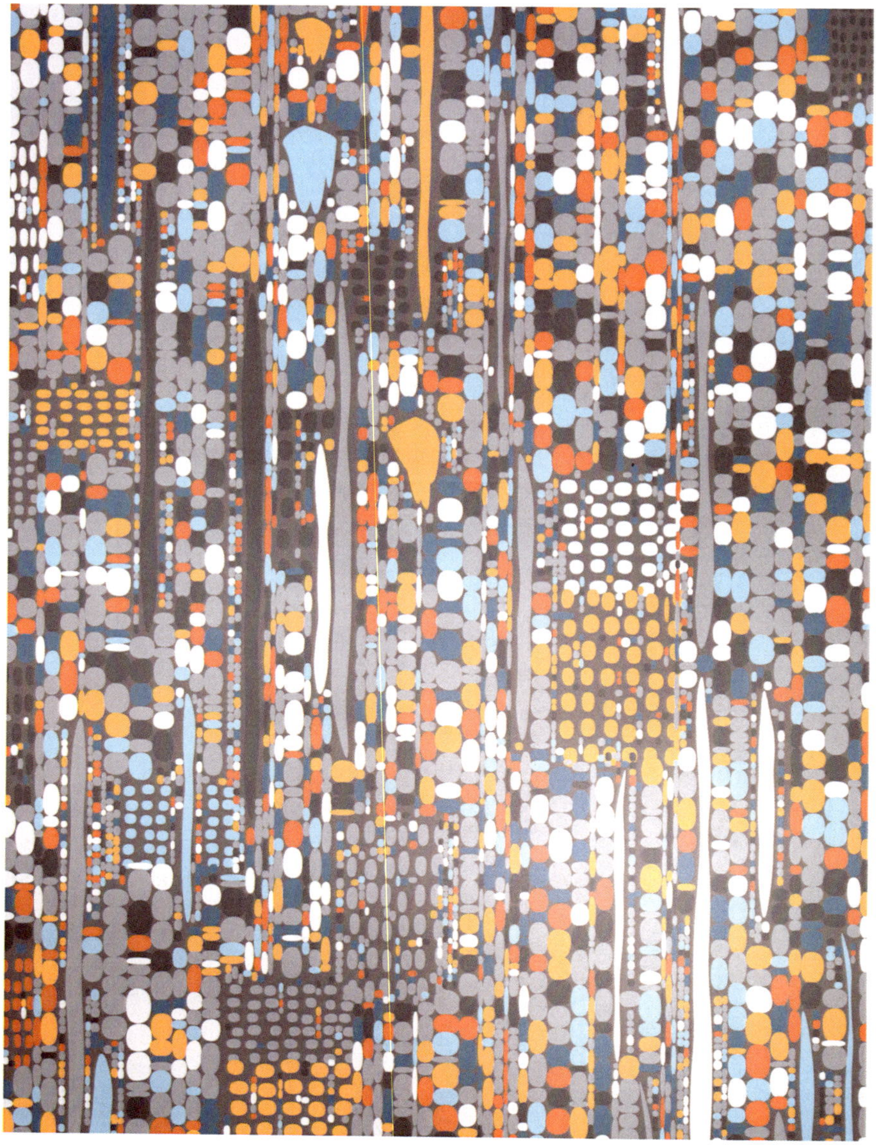

Pebble 513 'Memes & Life' minted by DiegoRST

Pebble 513

- Mint Type - Palettes: MemeMaxis 900 / 1,000
- Color Density: Vivid 349 / 1,000
- Edge: No 688 / 1,000
- Flow: No 935 / 1,000
- Overlap: Blend 51 / 1,000
- Palette: Galactic Latte 80 / 1,000
- Size: Boulderette 147 / 1,000
- Special Elements: 3 427 / 1,000
- Traced: No Border 858 / 1,000

Rarity

- Rarity Rank: #347
- Statistical Rarity: #557
- Single Trait Rarity #224

MintFace Vibe Check

'Memes & Life' connects the *Blend Overlap* dots to position the viewer in an upwards looking gaze. The *Vivid Color Density* brings out the best in the *Galactic Latte* palette, while the *Special Elements* shine across all color permutations.

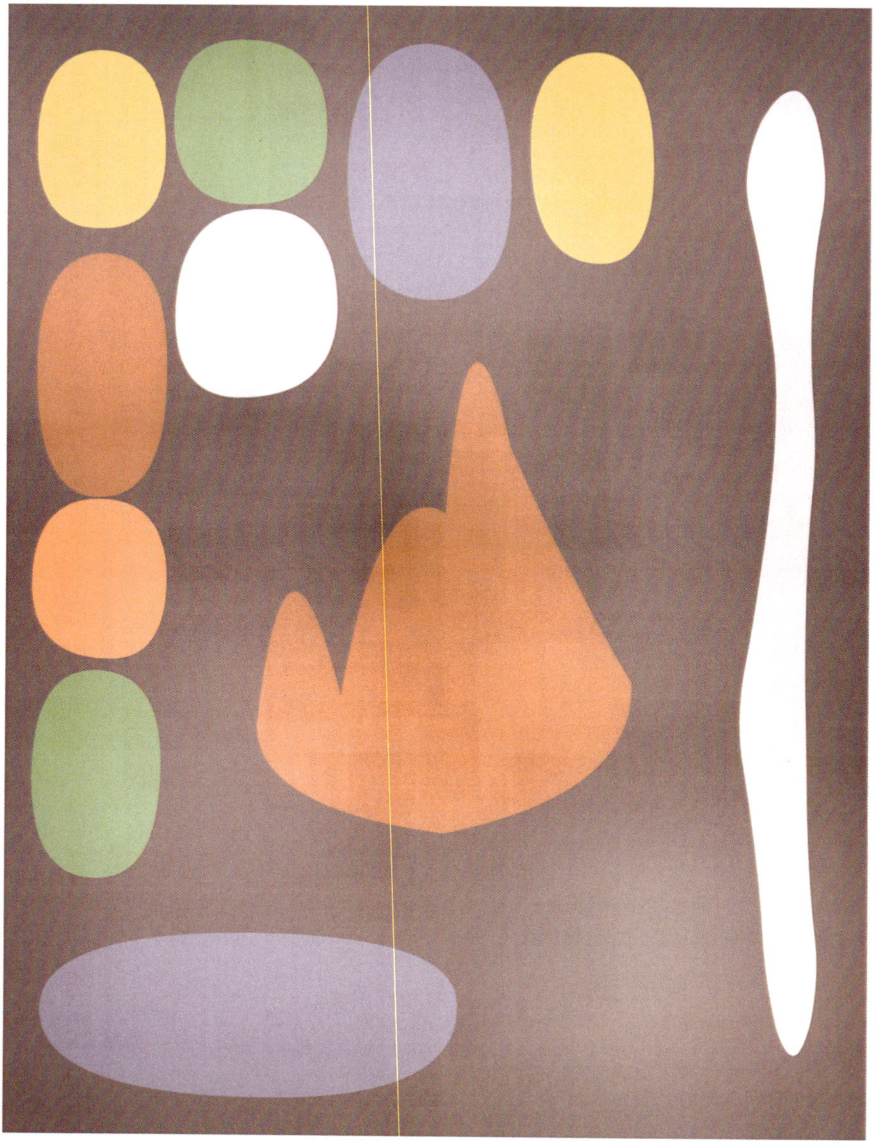

Pebble 529 Sgt. Pepe Campfire acquired on secondary for 6.529 eth by Thor

“Sgt. Pepe palette is legendary and the campfire is a visual metaphor for the Sgt. Pepe community. Super aesthetic with the colours throughout, vibing with the leader on the right.” Thor

Pebble 529

- Mint Type - Palettes: Sgt. Pepe 33/1,000
- Color Density: Vivid 349/1,000
- Edge: Yes 312/1,000
- Flow: No 935/1,000
- Overlap: Harmonize 492/1,000
- Palette: Sgt. Pepe 33/1,000
- Size: Rockling 300/1,000
- Special Elements: 3 427/1,000
- Traced: No Border 858/1,000

Rarity

- Rarity Rank: #669
- Statistical Rarity: #651
- Single Trait Rarity #612

MintFace Vibe Check

The 'campfire-like' shape takes center stage thanks to one of the three *Special Elements* present in the aptly named 'Sgt. Pepe Campfire.' *Harmonize* trait gathers the remaining *Rocklings* in to listen to a story being told, by the long silhouette on the right created by another *Special Element*.

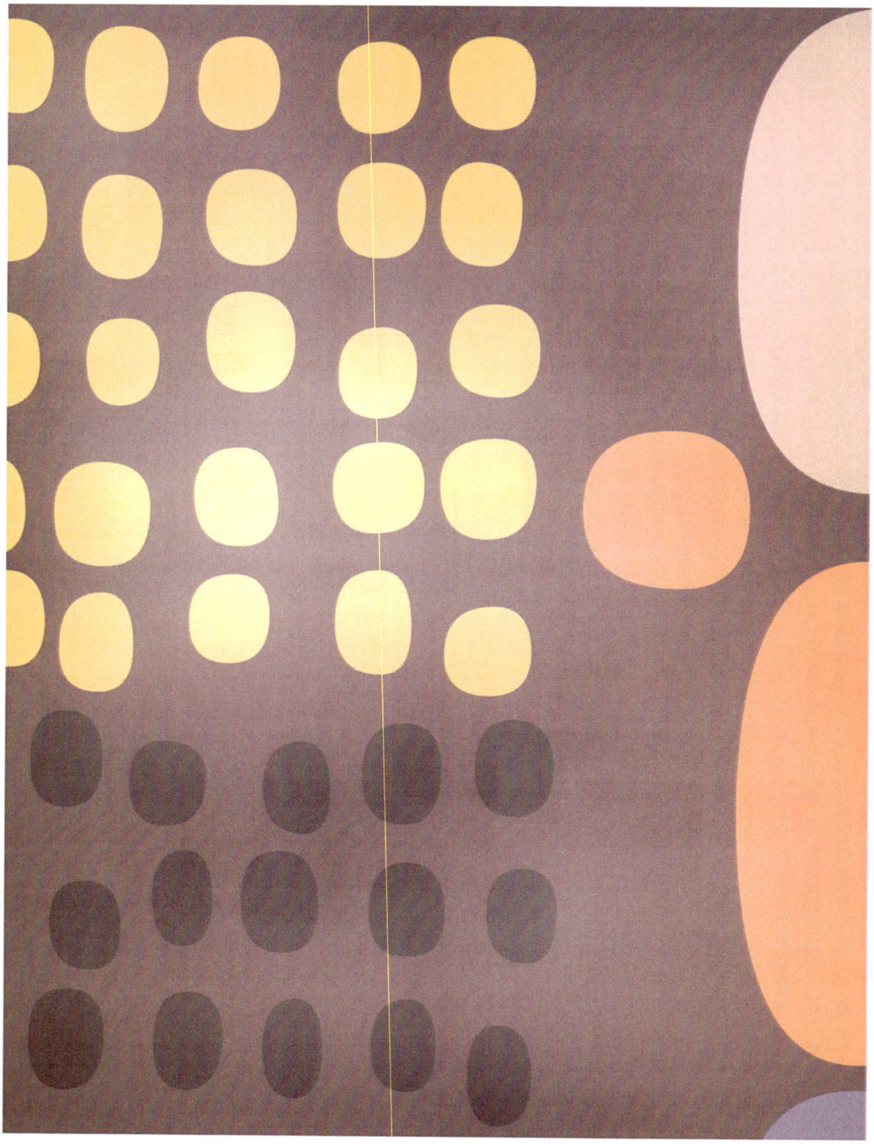

Pebble 551 'Sunset Blvd' minted by GhostPepper

"Sgt. Pepe departs with the setting sun. A hero whose legacy will forever illuminate the path for those who follow." Ghost Pepper

Pebble 551

- Mint Type - Palettes: Sgt. Pepe 33 / 1,000
- Color Density: Drench 41 / 1,000
- Edge: No 688 / 1,000
- Flow: No 935 / 1,000
- Overlap: Harmonize 492 / 1,000
- Palette: Sgt. Pepe 33 / 1,000
- Size: Rockling 300 / 1,000
- Special Elements: 3 427 / 1,000
- Traced: No Border 858 / 1,000

Rarity

- Rarity Rank: #277
- Statistical Rarity: #623
- Single Trait Rarity #190

MintFace Vibe Check

The Sgt. Pepe palette is almost exclusively highly aesthetic Pebbles, yet 'Sunset Blvd' is the only Sgt. Pepe pallete with no green colored Pebbles. 'Sunset Blvd' also has the most sun-drenched yellow goodness of any of the Sgt. Pepe palette. A true gm and gn.

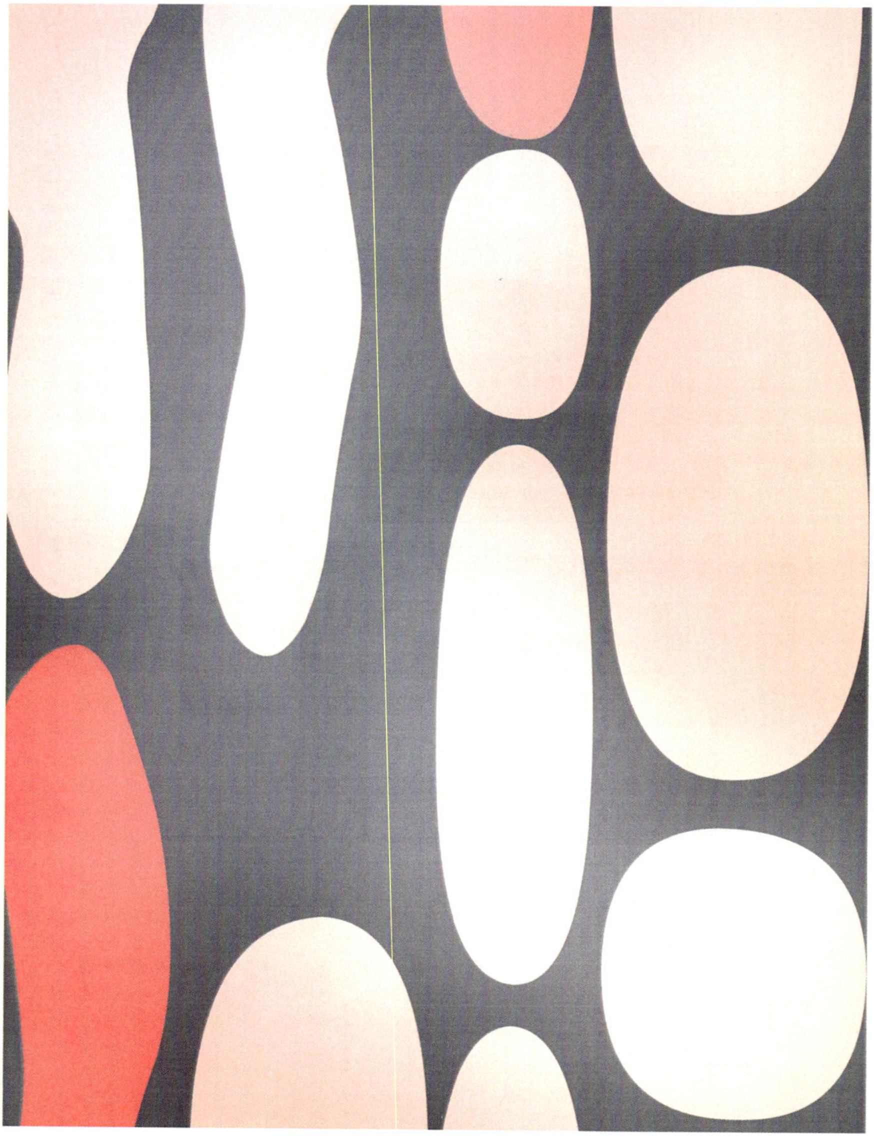

Pebble 558 'Liquid Lava Rain on Glass' minted by Jonny Pickles

"Want to trade. Liquid Lava Rain on Glass is kinda cool. All Pebbles are cool, but I want a different one. Please reach out to JonnyPickles to trade." Jonny Pickles

Pebble 558

- Mint Type - Palettes: MemeMaxis 900 / 1,000
- Color Density: Hush 143 / 1,000
- Edge: No 688 / 1,000
- Flow: No 935 / 1,000
- Overlap: Harmonize 492 / 1,000
- Palette: Coral Reef 71 / 1,000
- Size: Rockling 300 / 1,000
- Special Elements: 3 427 / 1,000
- Traced: No Border 858 / 1,000

Rarity

- Rarity Rank: #871
- Statistical Rarity: #887
- Single Trait Rarity #742

MintFace Vibe Check

Coral Reef palette is more subdued here overall because of the *Hush Color Density*. The viewers attention gets split between the bright pink rain drop and the rest of the view out the window pane.

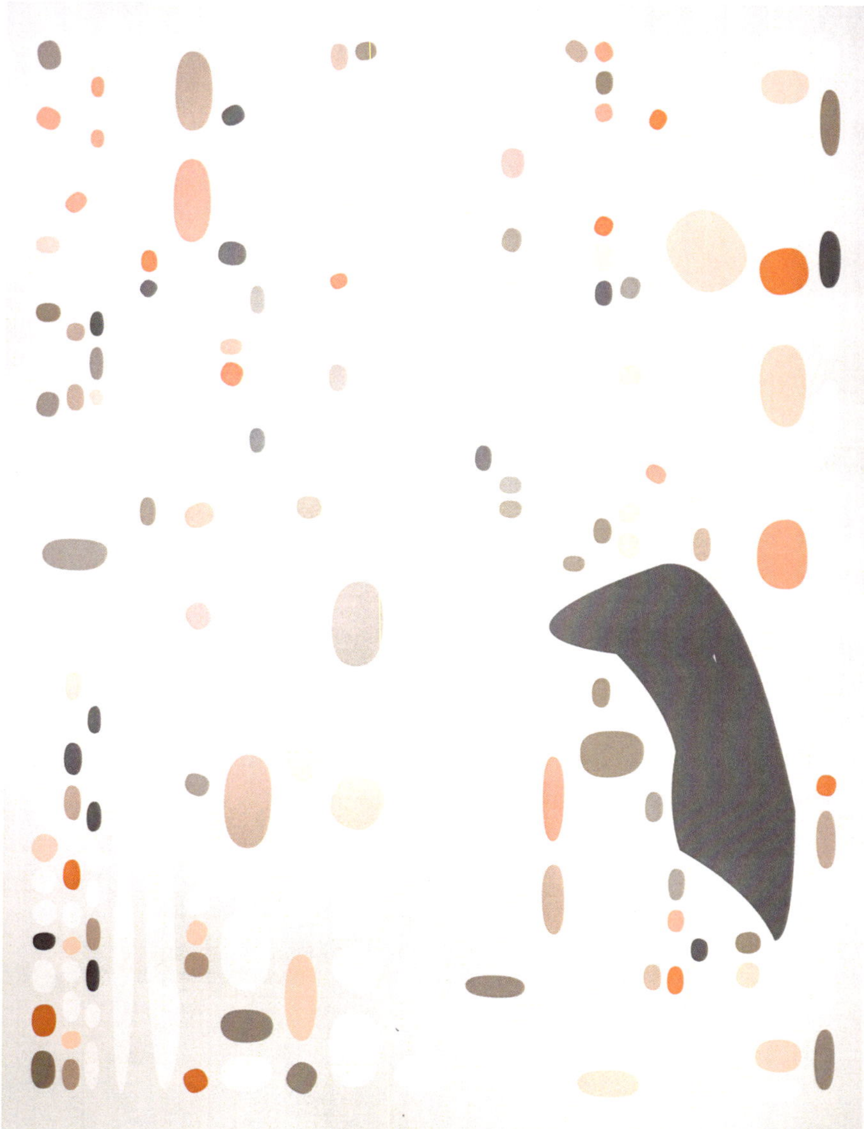

Pebble 563 'The Penguin' minted by Bored Surgeon

> Can you see the penguin? On an avian level, this Pebble rivals The Goose." Bored Surgeon

Pebble 563

- Mint Type - Palettes: MemeMaxis 900/1,000
- Color Density: Bloom 314/1,000
- Edge: Yes 312/1,000
- Flow: No 935/1,000
- Overlap: Disjoin 245/1,000
- Palette: Serenity 84/1,000
- Size: Crumb 72/1,000
- Special Elements: All 77/1,000
- Traced: No Border 858/1,000

Rarity

- Rarity Rank: #287
- Statistical Rarity: #225
- Single Trait Rarity #352

MintFace Vibe Check

'The Penguin' was given its name from the aberrant, Penguin-like shape that arose from a *Special Element*—though some say it looks more like a blob that got lost on its way to a better artwork. This so-called 'Penguin' managed to fluke its way through Pebble Racing, somehow defeating the far superior Pebble #23 'Indigenous Journey'. Perhaps it's a reminder that even in the world of high-tech art, luck sometimes favors the mediocre.

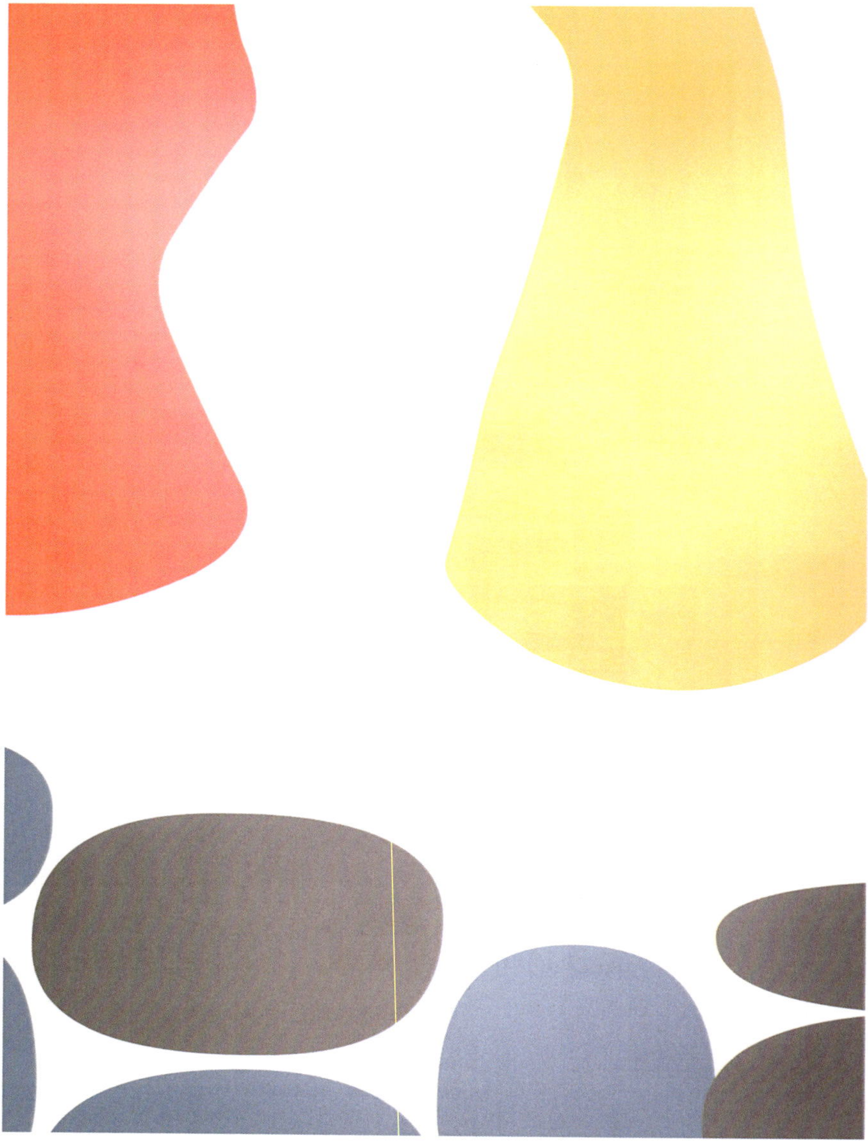

Pebble 586 'Andre the Giant' minted by BatSoupYum

> "The world needs to understand that being different is not a weakness, but rather a unique strength that can inspire others." BatSoupYum quoting Andre the Giant

Pebble 586

- Mint Type - Palettes: MemeMaxis 900/1,000
- Color Density: Vivid 349/1,000
- Edge: No 688/1,000
- Flow: No 935/1,000
- Overlap: Blend 51/1,000
- Palette: Dino Disco 58/1,000
- Size: Mountlet 25/1,000
- Special Elements: 1 150/1,000
- Traced: No Border 858/1,000

Rarity

- Rarity Rank: #109
- Statistical Rarity: #248
- Single Trait Rarity #172

MintFace Vibe Check

'Andre the Giant' bears down on most Pebbles due to its *Mountlet* Size. Drink in the *Dino Disco* palette that is the only one to celebrate all palette colors. If there is a bigger knockout Pebble, it should be tested in the wrestling ring.

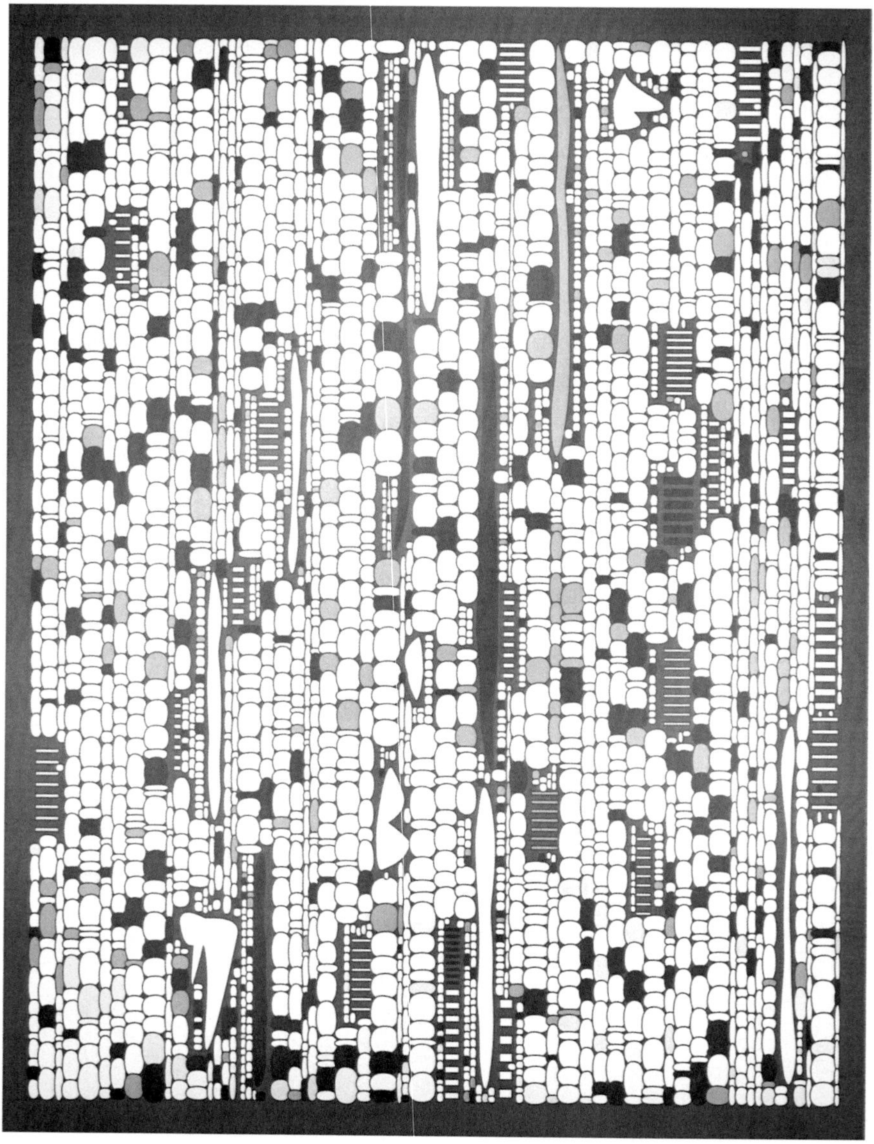

Pebble 617 minted by 696

"I like the color palette and the shapes. It's kinda minimalistic and calm." 696

Pebble 617

- Mint Type - Palettes: MemeMaxis 900/1,000
- Color Density: Hush 143/1,000
- Edge: Yes 312/1,000
- Flow: No 935/1,000
- Overlap: Fuse 113/1,000
- Palette: Shades of Hey! 55/1,000
- Size: Boulderette 147/1,000
- Special Elements: 3 427/1,000
- Traced: Border 97/1,000

Rarity

- Rarity Rank: #211
- Statistical Rarity: #105
- Single Trait Rarity #271

MintFace Vibe Check

Fuse trait lights up Pebble #617 both in form and its glowing radiance. The uniform, tight elliptical formation looks as if the generative algorithm borrowed the layout from strategy game Othello. The *Traced Border* trait encapsulates the white and black Pebbles game with confidence. A brilliant example of a top tier *Boulderette Size* Pebble, demonstrating the successful interplay between traits.

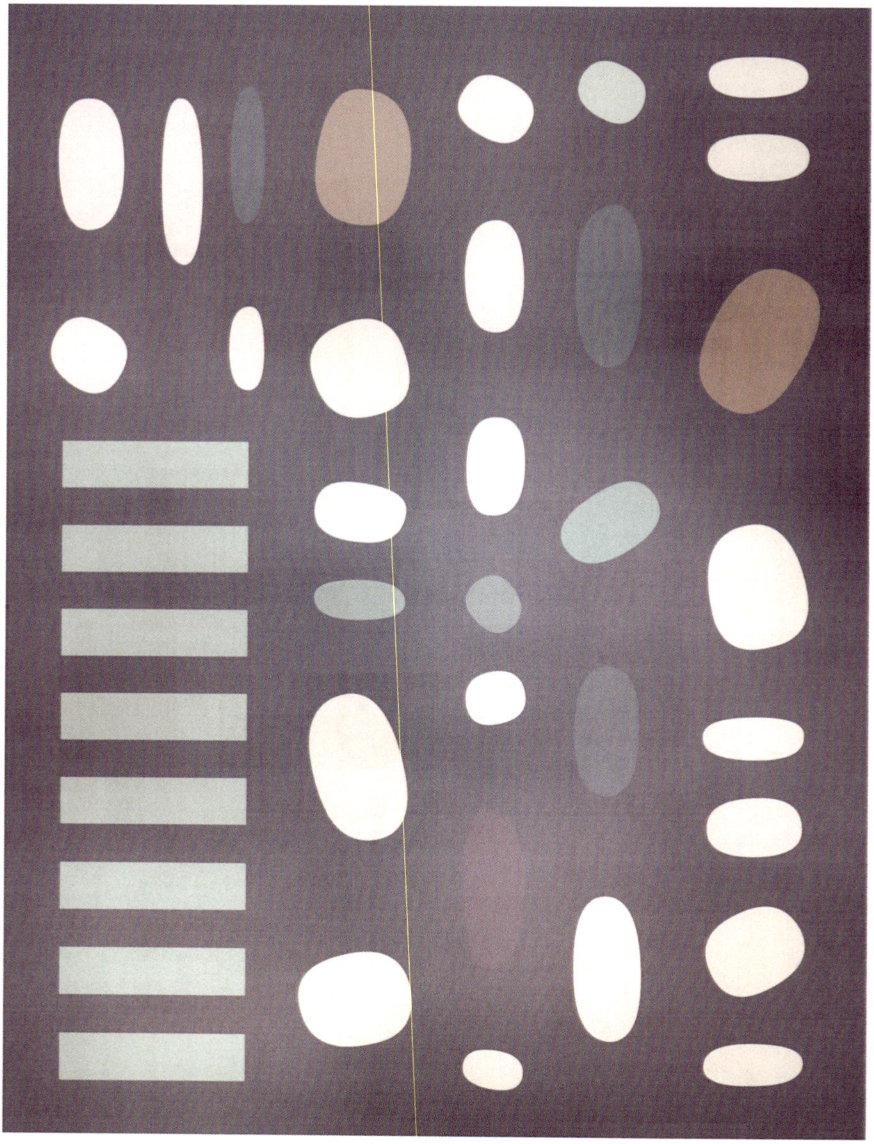

Pebble 683 minted by David

"My Pebble is a universe of little pebbles which contain lots of little pixels. A universe inside a Pebble." David

Pebble 683

- Mint Type - Palettes: MemeMaxis 900 / 1,000
- Color Density: Hush 143 / 1,000
- Edge: Yes 312 / 1,000
- Flow: No 935 / 1,000
- Overlap: Isolate 99 / 1,000
- Palette: Night Owl Doodles 86 / 1,000
- Size: Pebbit 151 / 1,000
- Special Elements: 2 291 / 1,000
- Traced: No Border 858 / 1,000

Rarity

- Rarity Rank: #359
- Statistical Rarity: #234
- Single Trait Rarity #419

MintFace Vibe Check

A well considered *Night Owl Doodles* Pebble where the individual Pebbles move in concert with each other. *Pebbit Size* combined *Isolate Overlap* creates healthy level of proximity between Pebbles and lets the ladder-like *Special Element* ground the entire work.

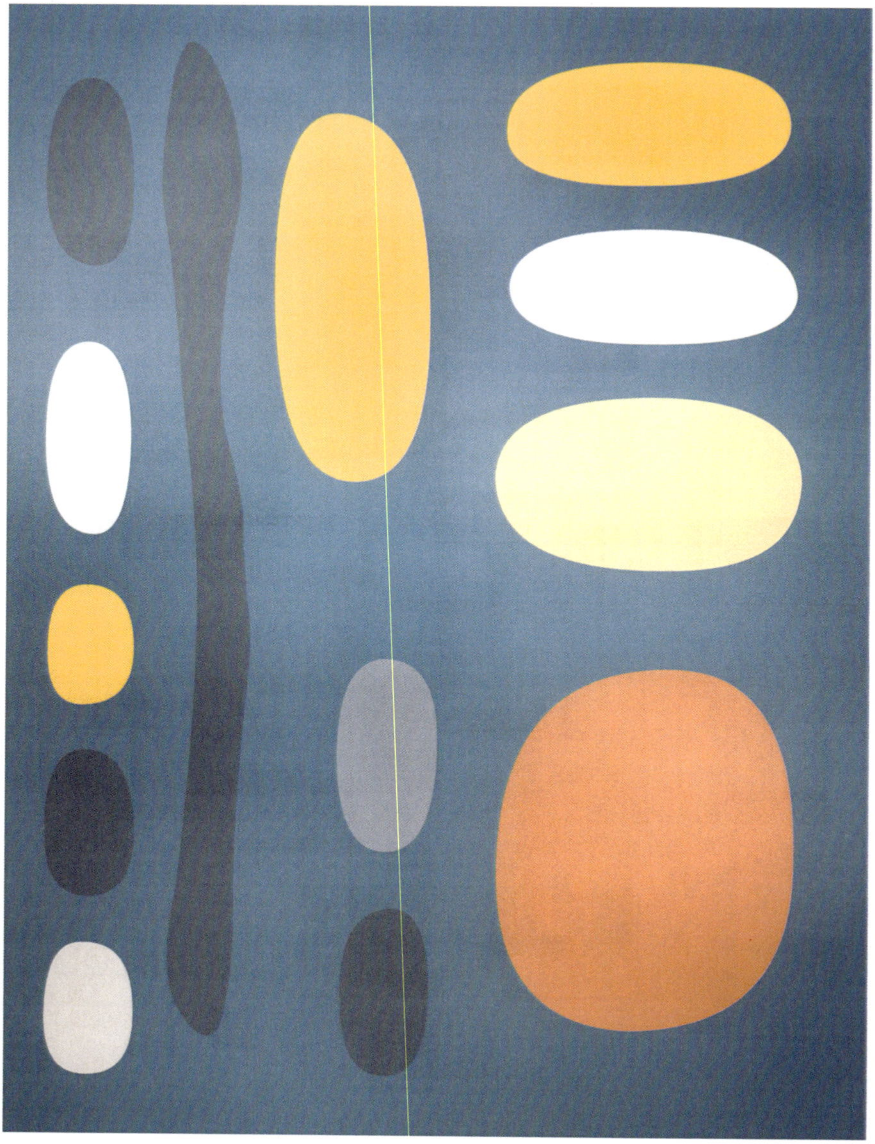

Pebble 687 'Riverside' minted by Stardust

"Riverside is special for the slight bend in the 'stick' created from the rarely seen *Flow* trait." Stardust

Pebble 687

- Mint Type - Palettes: MemeMaxis 900/1,000
- Color Density: Vivid 349/1,000
- Edge: Yes 312/1,000
- Flow: Yes 65/1,000
- Overlap: Disjoin 245/1,000
- Palette: Citrus Slate 72/1,000
- Size: Rockling 300/1,000
- Special Elements: 2 291/1,000
- Traced: No Border 858/1,000

Rarity

- Rarity Rank: #140
- Statistical Rarity: #77
- Single Trait Rarity #66

MintFace Vibe Check

The centrifugal forcefield that draws in surrounding Pebbles to the center is difficult to spot in the larger Pebble sizes such as *Rockling*. Yet here we can see the bending of the stick-like *Special Element* towards the centre of the frame. *Disjoin Overlap* gives every Pebble on the 'Riverside' equal attention.

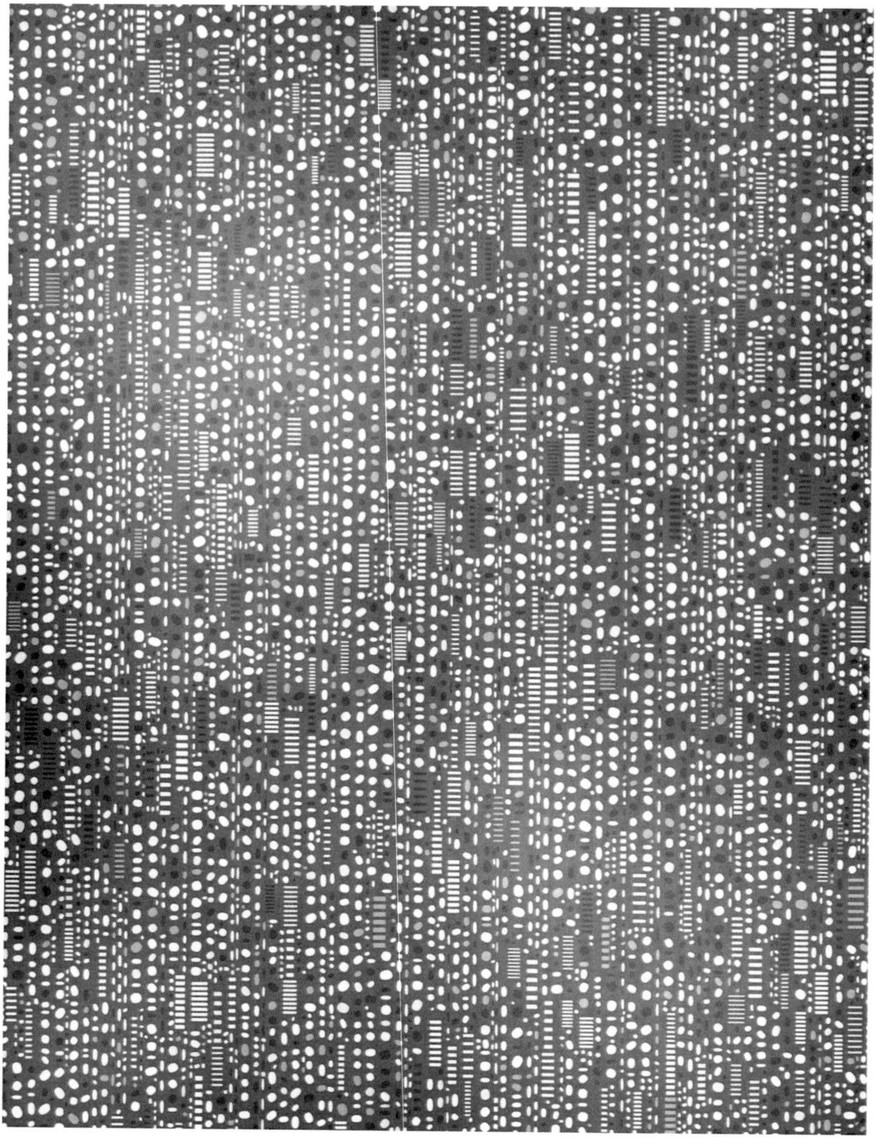

Pebble 689 minted by lapislight

Pebble 689

- Mint Type - Palettes: MemeMaxis 900/1,000
- Color Density: Bloom 314/1,000
- Edge: No 688/1,000
- Flow: No 935/1,000
- Overlap: Isolate 99/1,000
- Palette: Shades of Hey! 55/1,000
- Size: Craglet 85/1,000
- Special Elements: 1 150/1,000
- Traced: No Border 858/1,000

Rarity

- Rarity Rank: #346
- Statistical Rarity: #399
- Single Trait Rarity #419

MintFace Vibe Check

Stark city contrasts of *Shades of Hey!* black and white are packed together by *Craglet* size with a little breathing room afforded by *Isolate Overlap*. The city spreads beyond our field of vision with *No Border Traced*. A stunning Pebble for the contemporary collectoor.

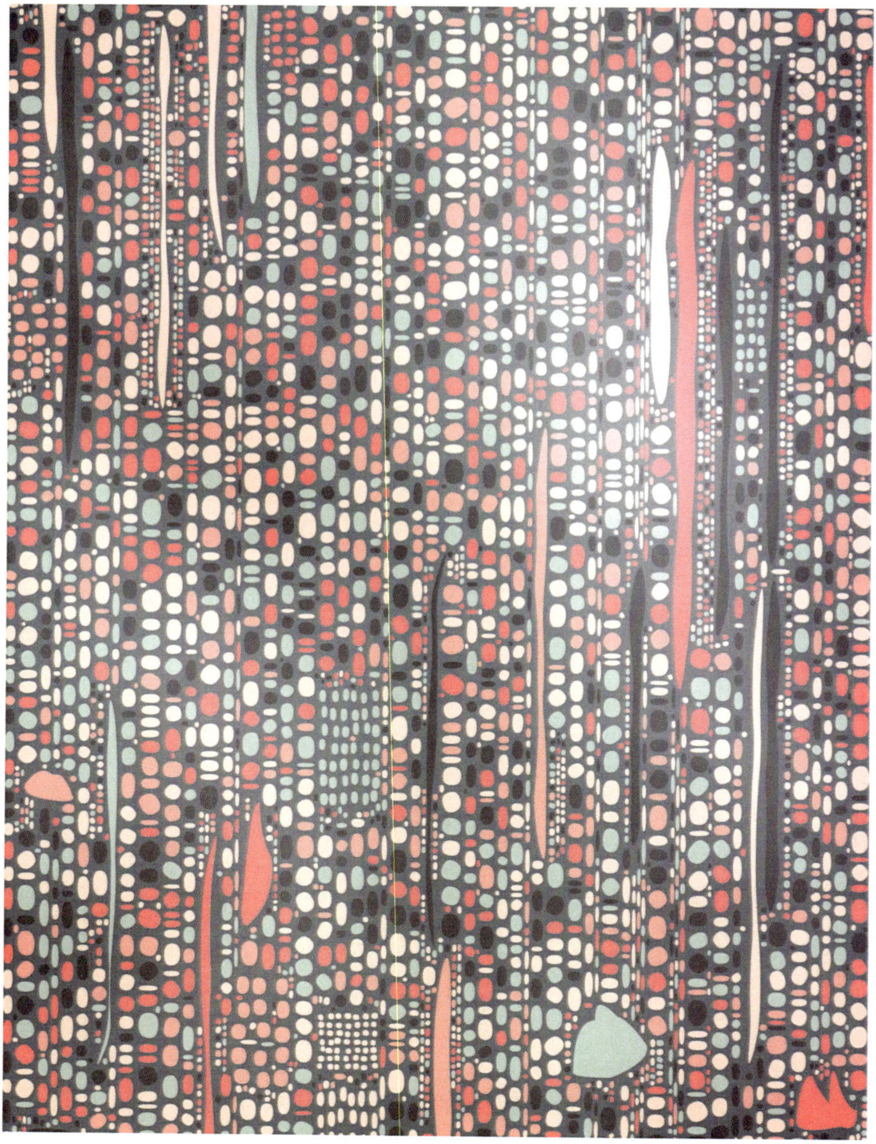

Pebble 690 minted by lapislight

Pebble 690

- Mint Type - Palettes: MemeMaxis 900 / 1,000
- Color Density: Vivid 349 / 1,000
- Edge: No 688 / 1,000
- Flow: No 935 / 1,000
- Overlap: Disjoin 245 / 1,000
- Palette: Coral Reef 71 / 1,000
- Size: Boulderette 147 / 1,000
- Special Elements: 3 427 / 1,000
- Traced: No Border 858 / 1,000

Rarity

- Rarity Rank: #854
- Statistical Rarity: #827
- Single Trait Rarity #863

MintFace Vibe Check

Meme numbered artworks are afforded an elite status by collectoor communities and the applause for minting Pebble #690 goes to lapislight. A *Vivid Color Density* Pebble with plenty of exquisite details to be discovered throughout the *Boulderette* size array.

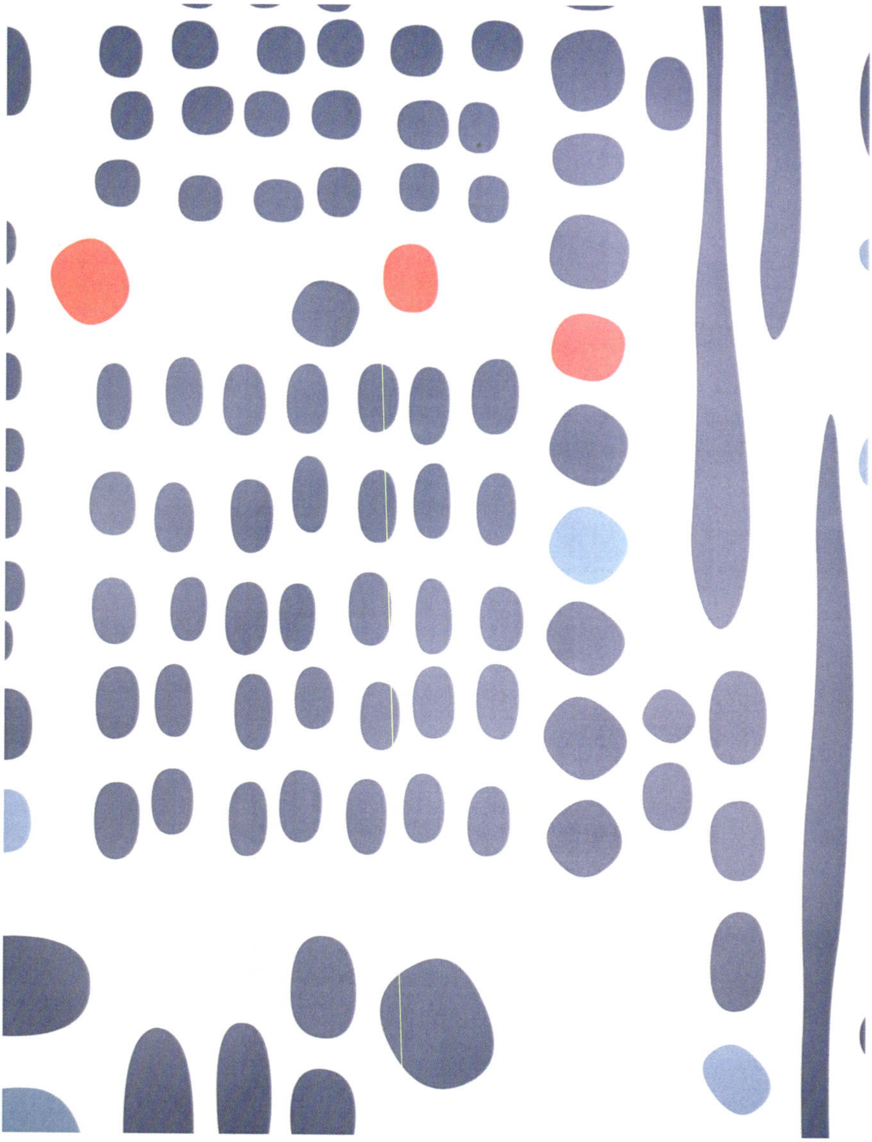

Pebble 714 'Cribbage' minted by MoonFront

> 'Cribbage' is a top one hundred rarity because it is one of three *Flow Pebbles* that also contains all *Special Elements.*" MoonFront

Pebble 714

- Mint Type - Palettes: MemeMaxis 900/1,000
- Color Density: Bloom 314/1,000
- Edge: No 688/1,000
- Flow: Yes 65/1,000
- Overlap: Disjoin 245/1,000
- Palette: Unigrids 63/1,000
- Size: Pebbit 151/1,000
- Special Elements: All 77/1,000
- Traced: No Border 858/1,000

Rarity

- Rarity Rank: #98
- Statistical Rarity: #79
- Single Trait Rarity #66

MintFace Vibe Check

Disjoin Overlap creates some space beyond the demanding trio of red 'lights' shining through the *Unigrid* palette. *Flow* trait is present yet we may not fully comprehend what its role is in Pebble #714.

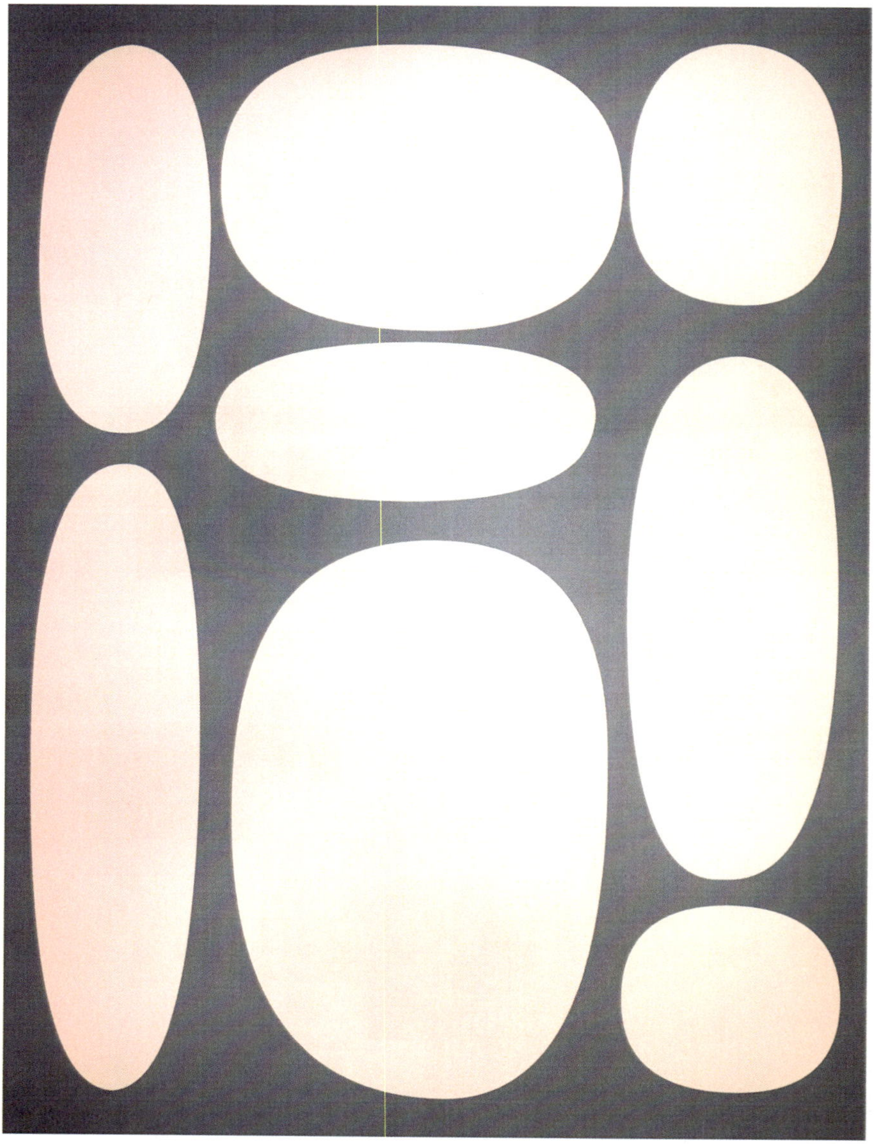

Pebble 715 'Genesis Eggs' minted by MoonFront

"Pebble 715 is named 'Genesis Eggs' that will hatch into the holder's Aigents wen OM100." MoonFront

Pebble 715

- Mint Type - Palettes: MemeMaxis 900/1,000
- Color Density: Faint 153/1,000
- Edge: Yes 312/1,000
- Flow: No 935/1,000
- Overlap: Harmonize 492/1,000
- Palette: Coral Reef 71/1,000
- Size: Rockling 300/1,000
- Special Elements: 1 150/1,000
- Traced: No Border 858/1,000

Rarity

- Rarity Rank: #524
- Statistical Rarity: #377
- Single Trait Rarity #612

MintFace Vibe Check

Harmonize Overlap creates a sense of delicate poise amongst the larger sized *Rockling* Pebbles. One gets a sense of the artwork as a whole and its strength emanating towards the viewer cannot be looked away from.

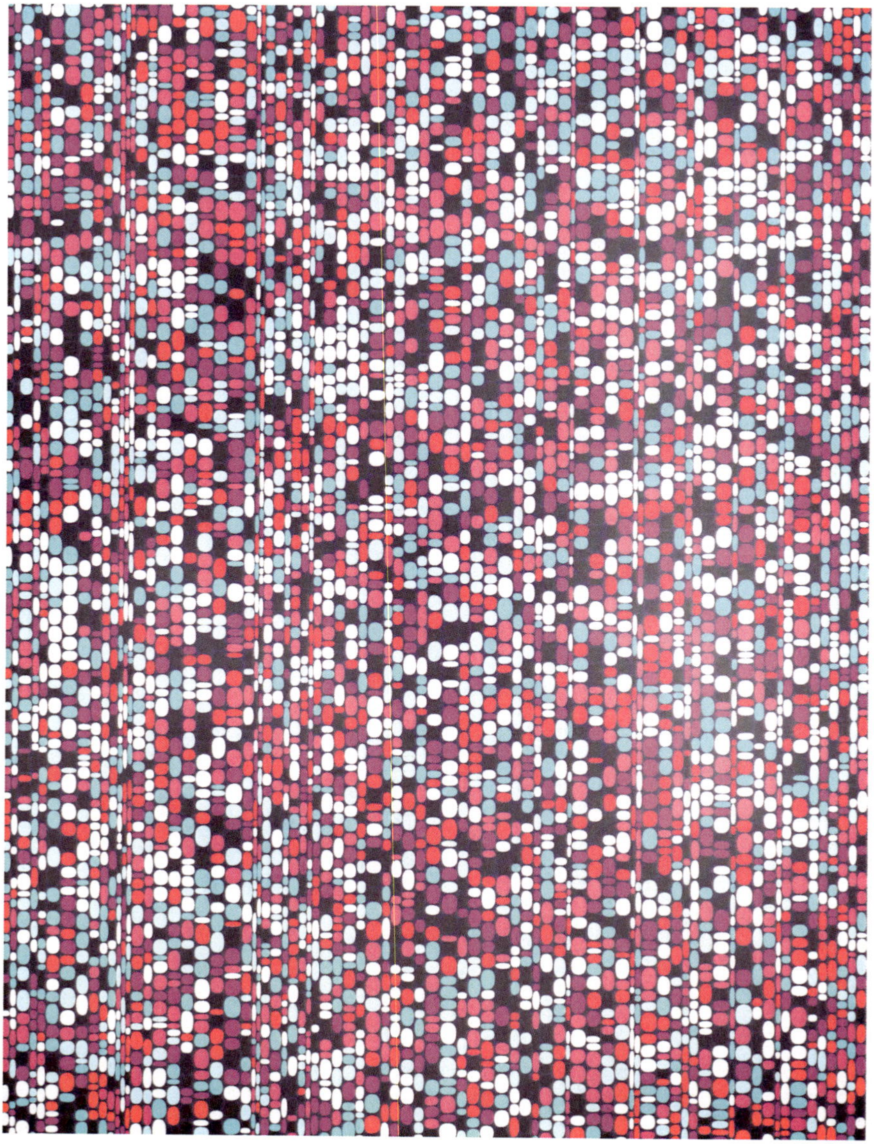

Pebble 716 'The Matrix' minted by MoonFront

> 'The Matrix' holds a top 50 rarity position for its clean (no *Special Elements*) and flowing *Craglet* and *Beatbox* vibes."
> MoonFront

Pebble 716

- Mint Type - Palettes: MemeMaxis 900 / 1,000
- Color Density: Vivid 349 / 1,000
- Edge: No 688 / 1,000
- Flow: No 935 / 1,000
- Overlap: Harmonize 492 / 1,000
- Palette: Beatboxes 40 / 1,000
- Size: Craglet 85 / 1,000
- Special Elements: None 55 / 1,000
- Traced: No Border 858 / 1,000

Rarity

- Rarity Rank: #45
- Statistical Rarity: #69
- Single Trait Rarity #11

MintFace Vibe Check

Beatboxes palette brings the party to a future dominated by a *Craglet* sized view. There is a purity to 'The Matrix' Pebble revealed only to those who realise there are no *Special Elements* to be seen.

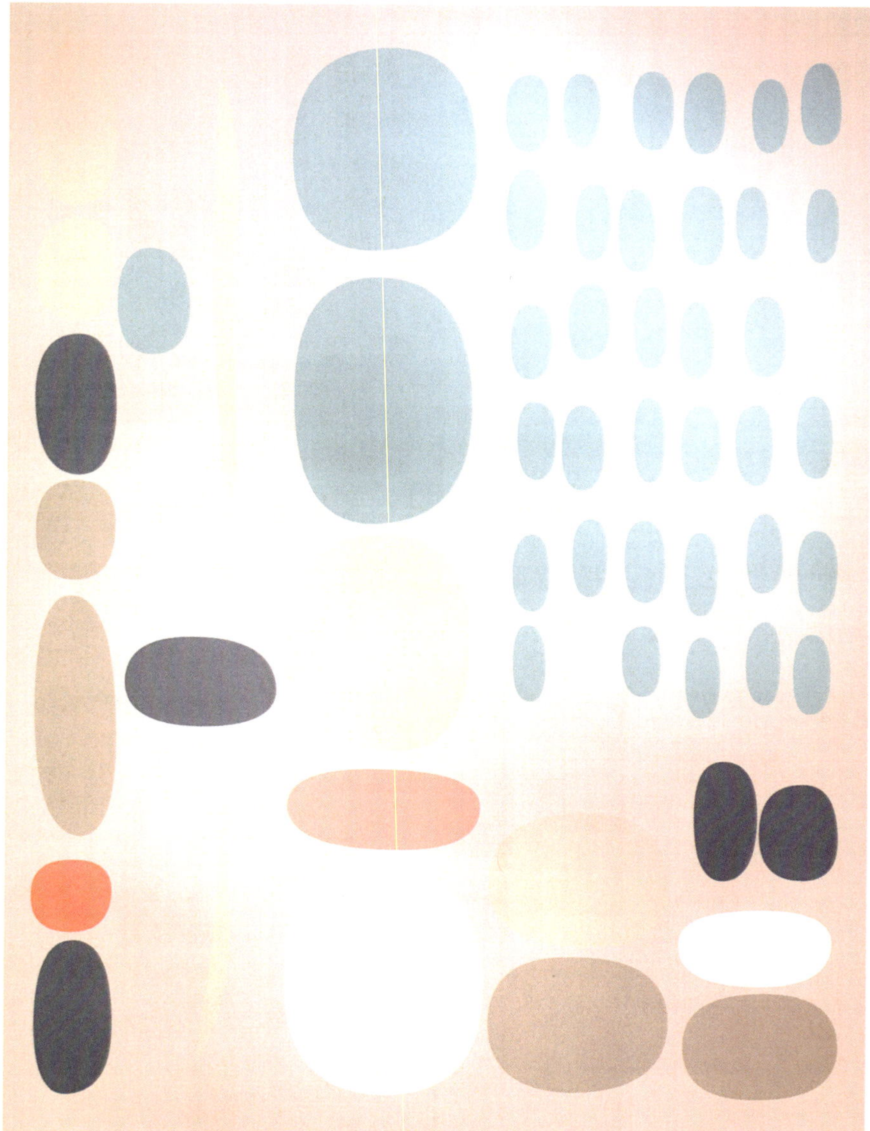

Pebble 724 minted by Prxt0

Pebble 724

- Mint Type - Palettes: MemeMaxis 900/1,000
- Color Density: Drench 41/1,000
- Edge: Yes 312/1,000
- Flow: No 935/1,000
- Overlap: Harmonize 492/1,000
- Palette: Desert Mirage 79/1,000
- Size: Pebbit 151/1,000
- Special Elements: All 77/1,000
- Traced: No Border 858/1,000

Rarity

- Rarity Rank: #179
- Statistical Rarity: #185
- Single Trait Rarity #190

MintFace Vibe Check

The shimmering gold canvas gets lit up in the *Desert Mirage* landscape with *Drench Color Density* placing a varied range of colored *Pebbit* sized Pebble to relish. All *Special Elements* are present, some more easily spotted than others.

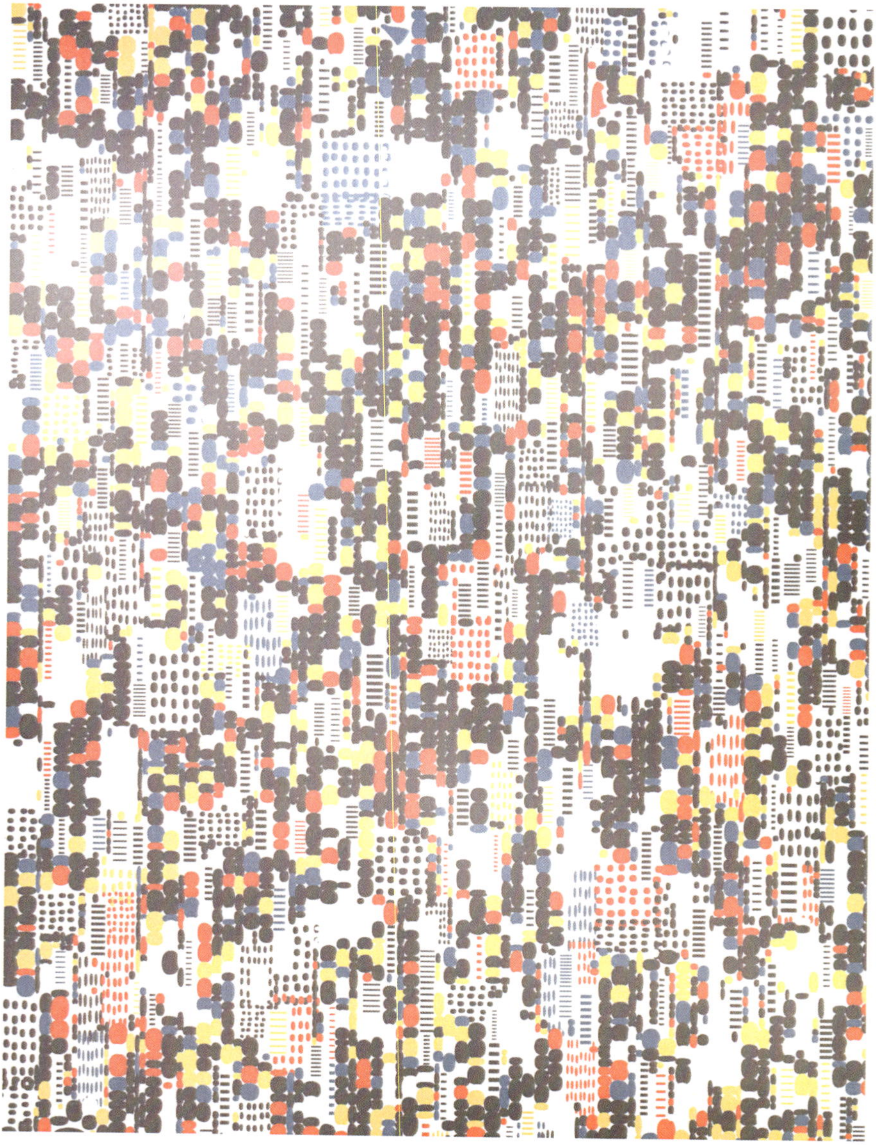

Pebble 752 'Dense City' bought on secondary by Vanto

> 'Dense City' represents the vibrancy and vivaciousness of *Craglets*. Rhythms of city life captured in the red, yellow and blue *Dino Disco* palette; the Piet Mondrian of Pebbles."
> Vanto

Pebble 752

- Mint Type - Palettes: MemeMaxis 900/1,000
- Color Density: Bloom 314/1,000
- Edge: No 688/1,000
- Flow: No 935/1,000
- Overlap: Fuse 113/1,000
- Palette: Dino Disco 58/1,000
- Size: Craglet 85/1,000
- Special Elements: 3 427/1,000
- Traced: No Border 858/1,000

Rarity

- Rarity Rank: #478
- Statistical Rarity: #587
- Single Trait Rarity #513

MintFace Vibe Check

The *Dino Disco* palette elaborates the vastness of a city beyond when paired with *Craglet* size and *Fuse Overlap*. A combination that gives 'Dense City' an instantly recognisable place on the blockchain.

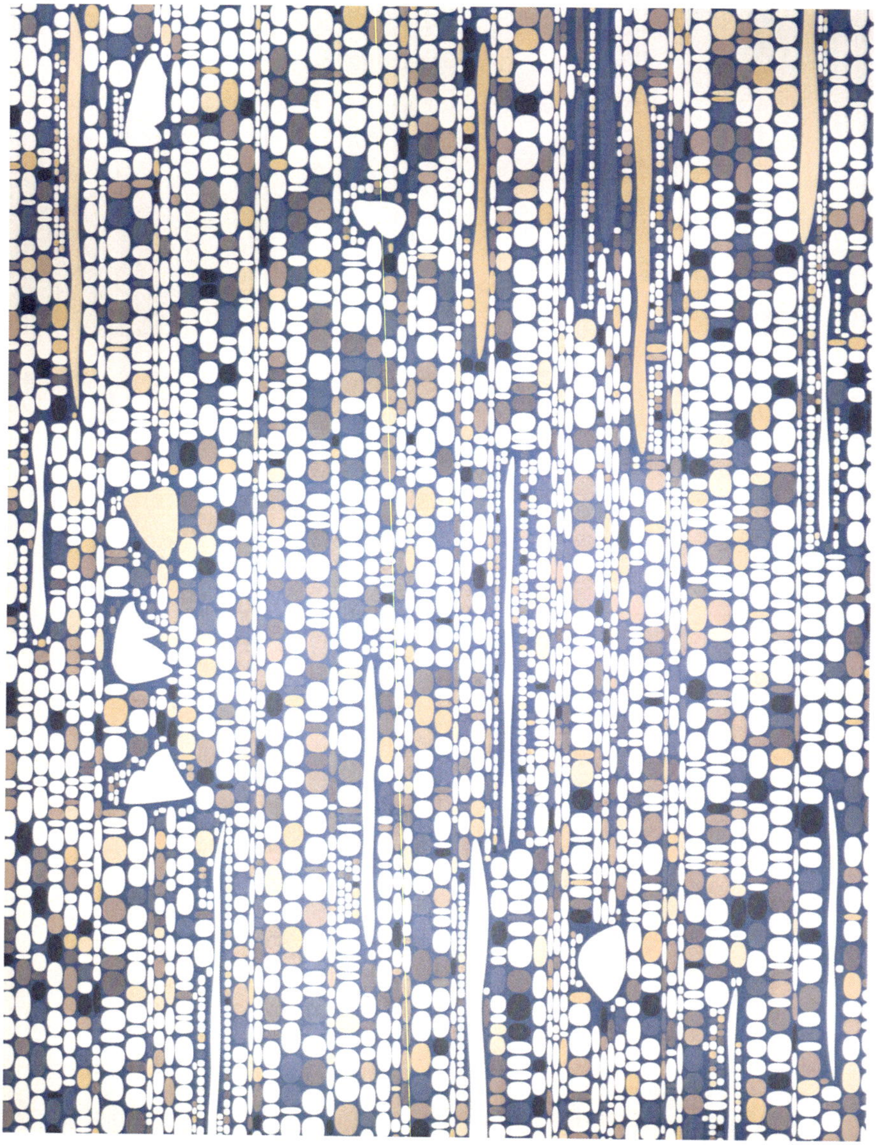

Pebble 781 bought on secondary by Sir Winston

"Sold my original Pebble 315 due to an emergency. I missed owning the collection so much, I went back and picked up this one after emergency. I believe I was meant to own this one!" Sir Winston

Pebble 781

- Mint Type - Palettes: MemeMaxis 900 / 1,000
- Color Density: Hush 143 / 1,000
- Edge: No 688 / 1,000
- Flow: No 935 / 1,000
- Overlap: Harmonize 492 / 1,000
- Palette: Dusk Riverbed 71 / 1,000
- Size: Boulderette 147 / 1,000
- Special Elements: 2 291 / 1,000
- Traced: No Border 858 / 1,000

Rarity

- Rarity Rank: #706
- Statistical Rarity: #717
- Single Trait Rarity #742

MintFace Vibe Check

An integrated Pebble that hits all the notes of form, subtlety and rhythm. The *Special Elements* of both stick-like blobs and random shaped Pebbles introduce a vivacious spirit. To top it off, *Dusk Riverbed* palette does justice to the entire score. Encore!

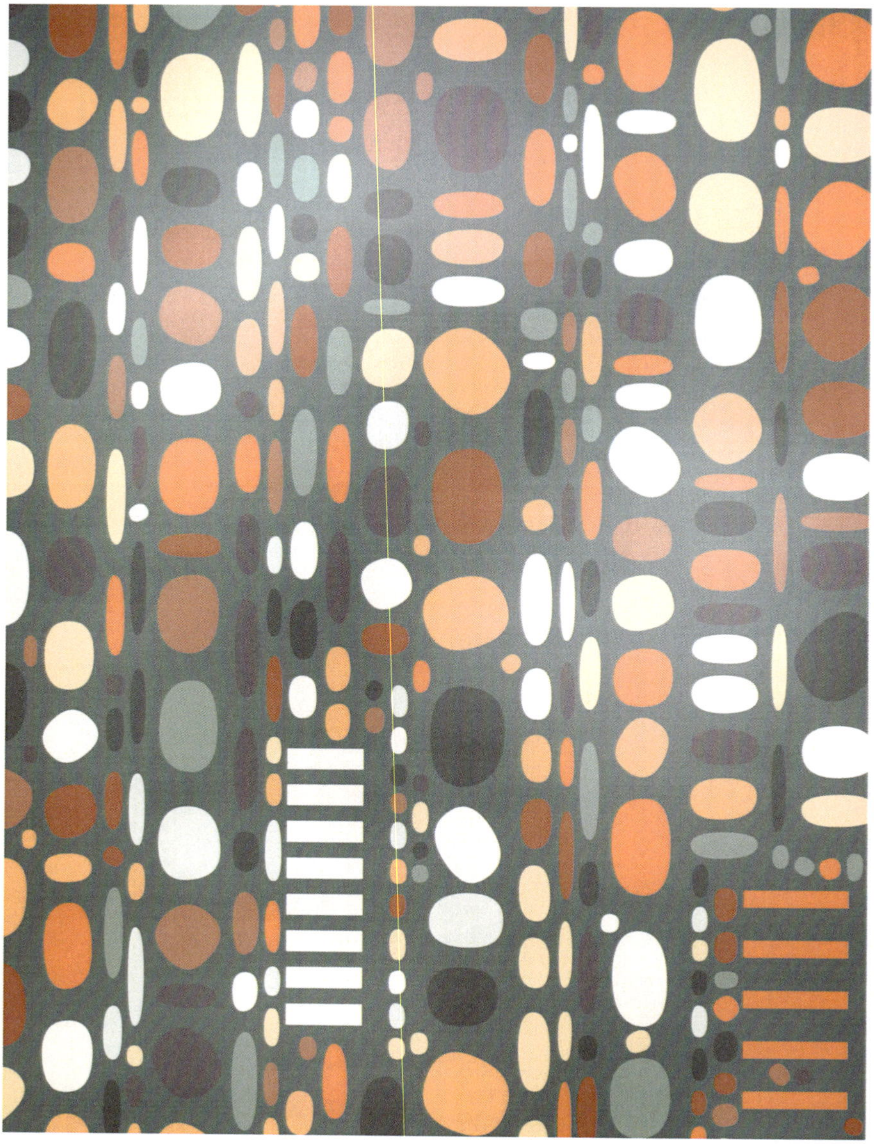

Pebble 805 'Pebbles' minted by Pakal

"'Pebbles' embodies the serene beauty of natural formations with its meticulously arranged ovals and rectangles." Pakal

Pebble 805

- Mint Type - Palettes: MemeMaxis 900 / 1,000
- Color Density: Vivid 349 / 1,000
- Edge: No 688 / 1,000
- Flow: No 935 / 1,000
- Overlap: Disjoin 245 / 1,000
- Palette: Forest Whisper 83 / 1,000
- Size: Crumb 72 / 1,000
- Special Elements: 1 150 / 1,000
- Traced: No Border 858 / 1,000

Rarity

- Rarity Rank: #487
- Statistical Rarity: #562
- Single Trait Rarity #478

MintFace Vibe Check

Absolutely stunning Pebble through the *Vivid Color Density* energy that transforms *Forest Whisper* into a full spring bloom. *Crumb Size* places this Pebble nearer the top of the rarer *Size* trait charts.

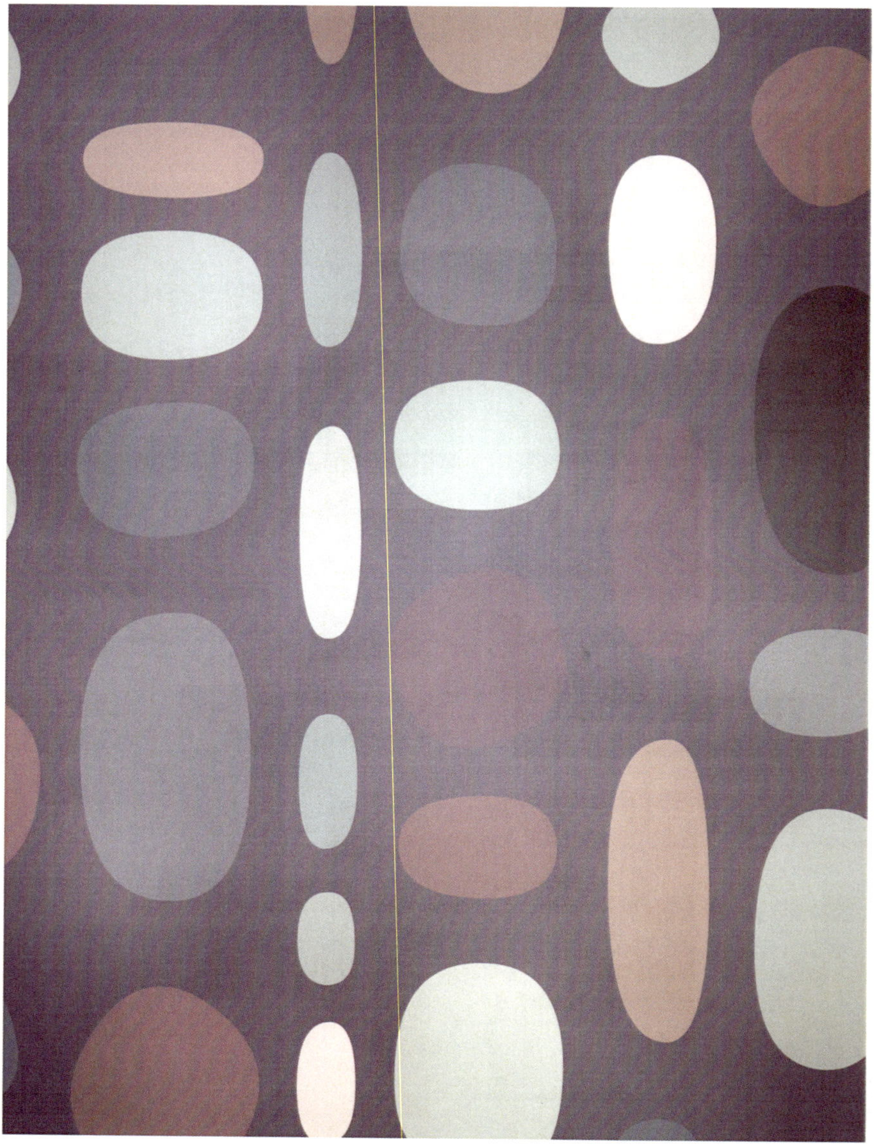

Pebble 816 'Pathway Home' bought on secondary by Articulate

"Can I get back to you on the Pebble name? I'm still shaking." Articulate

Pebble 816

- Mint Type - Palettes: MemeMaxis 900/1,000
- Color Density: Drench 41/1,000
- Edge: No 688/1,000
- Flow: No 935/1,000
- Overlap: Disjoin 245/1,000
- Palette: Night Owl Doodles 86/1,000
- Size: Stonelet 220/1,000
- Special Elements: None 55/1,000
- Traced: No Border 858/1,000

Rarity

- Rarity Rank: #20
- Statistical Rarity: #34
- Single Trait Rarity #11

MintFace Vibe Check

'Pathway Home' lights the way across the *Night Own Doodles* palette. Each Pebble inherits a subdued range that is shown in its highest *Color Density* with *Drench* variant. 'Pathway Home' is one of 55 'pure' Pebbles with no *Special Elements* necessary to communicate its message.

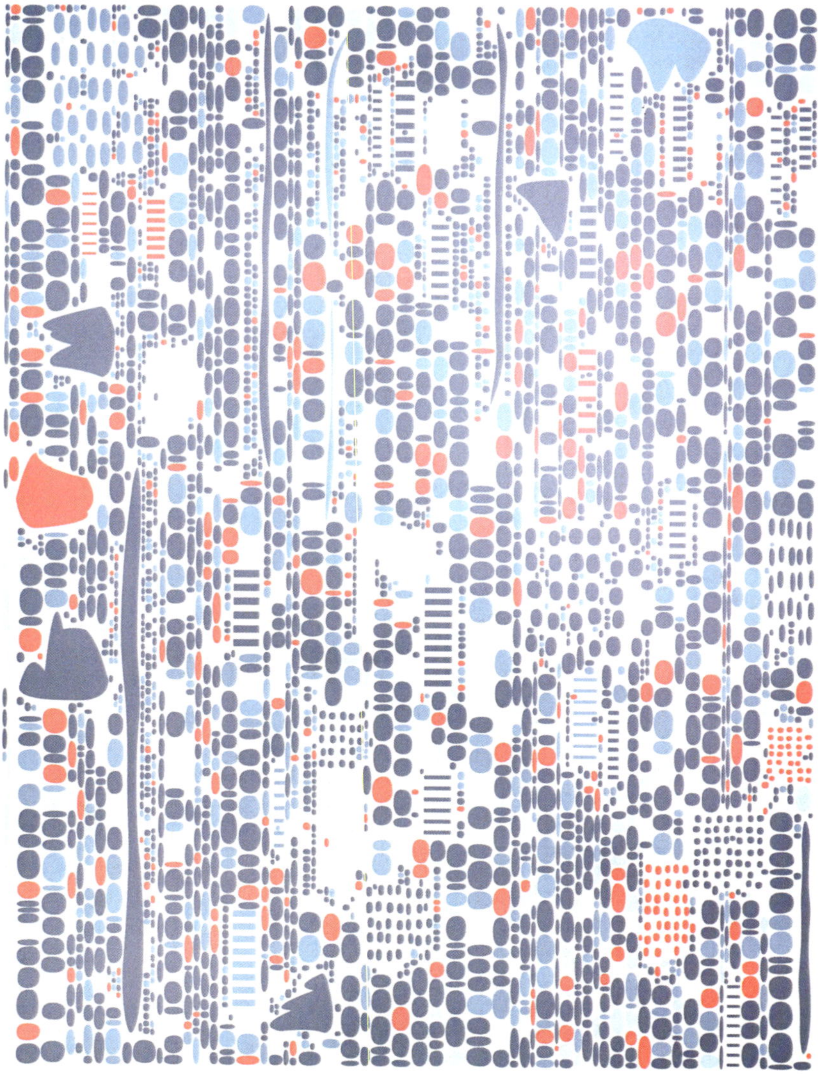

Pebble 854 'Sweet Dreams' minted by Ghost Pepper

"'Sweet Dreams' makes me think of colorful candies. Yum!"
GhostPepper's daughter

Pebble 854

- Mint Type - Palettes: MemeMaxis 900/1,000
- Color Density: Bloom 314/1,000
- Edge: Yes 312/1,000
- Flow: No 935/1,000
- Overlap: Harmonize 492/1,000
- Palette: Unigrids 63/1,000
- Size: Boulderette 147/1,000
- Special Elements: All 77/1,000
- Traced: No Border 858/1,000

Rarity

- Rarity Rank: #380
- Statistical Rarity: #319
- Single Trait Rarity #352

MintFace Vibe Check

'Sweet Dreams' is a refreshing Pebble combining the style of *Unigrids* with the poise of *Boulderette*. The delightful craggy *Special Elements* in red and blue are a focal point. The generous presence of *All Special Elements* interspersed by Pebbles ties the entire work together.

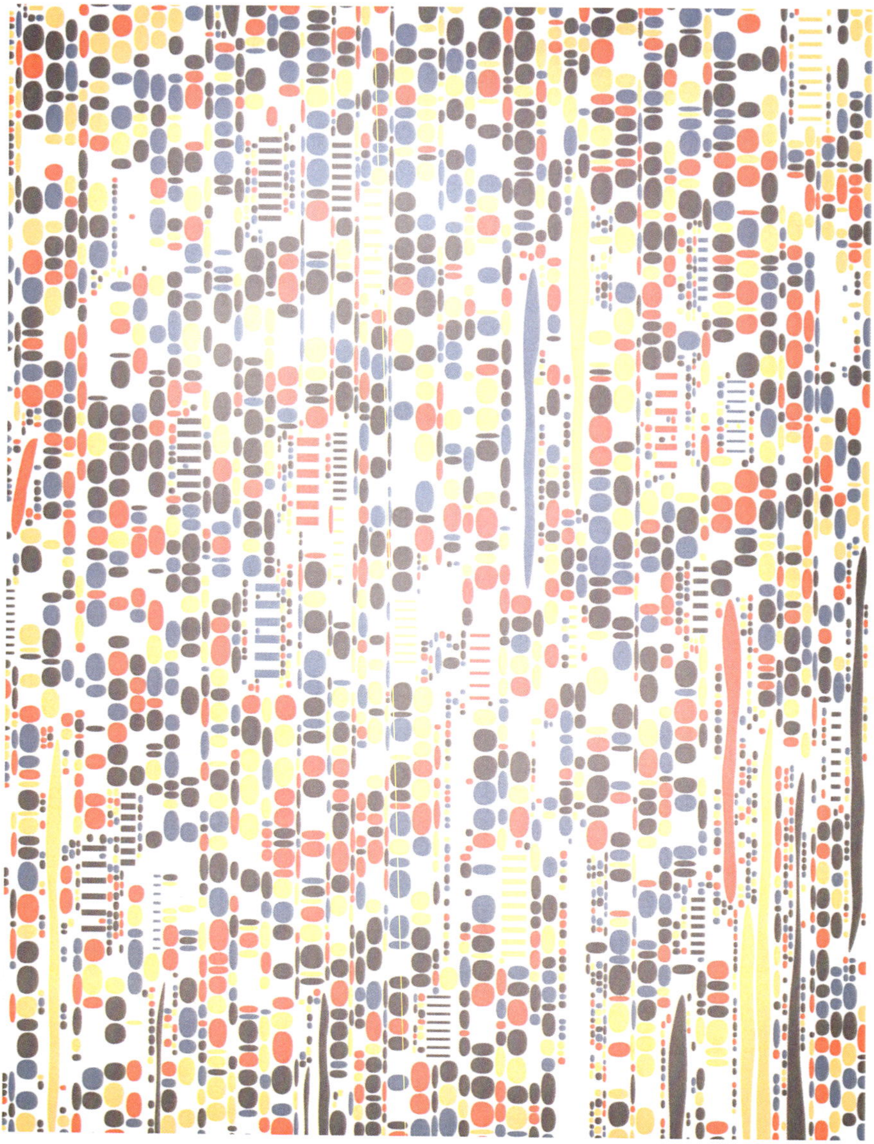

Pebble 863 'The Dance Floor' minted by Casa NUA

"'The Dance Floor' with *Vivid* and *Harmonic* traits is crowded with three *Special Elements*. The *Dino Disco* palette on Pebbles 863 brings us back to the 70's dance halls."
Hugo Faz

Pebble 863

- Mint Type - Palettes: MemeMaxis 900/1,000
- Color Density: Vivid 349/1,000
- Edge: No 688/1,000
- Flow: No 935/1,000
- Overlap: Harmonize 492/1,000
- Palette: Dino Disco 58/1,000
- Size: Boulderette 147/1,000
- Special Elements: 3 427/1,000
- Traced: No Border 858/1,000

Rarity

- Rarity Rank: #900
- Statistical Rarity: #929
- Single Trait Rarity #863

MintFace Vibe Check

Party! Party! Party! Nothing says fun like a streamer filled room of brightly colored fun. 'The Dance Floor' is one of just three brightly lit *Dino Disco* palettes that do not dominant with the 'lights out' grey in the palette. The party never stops with Pebble #863.

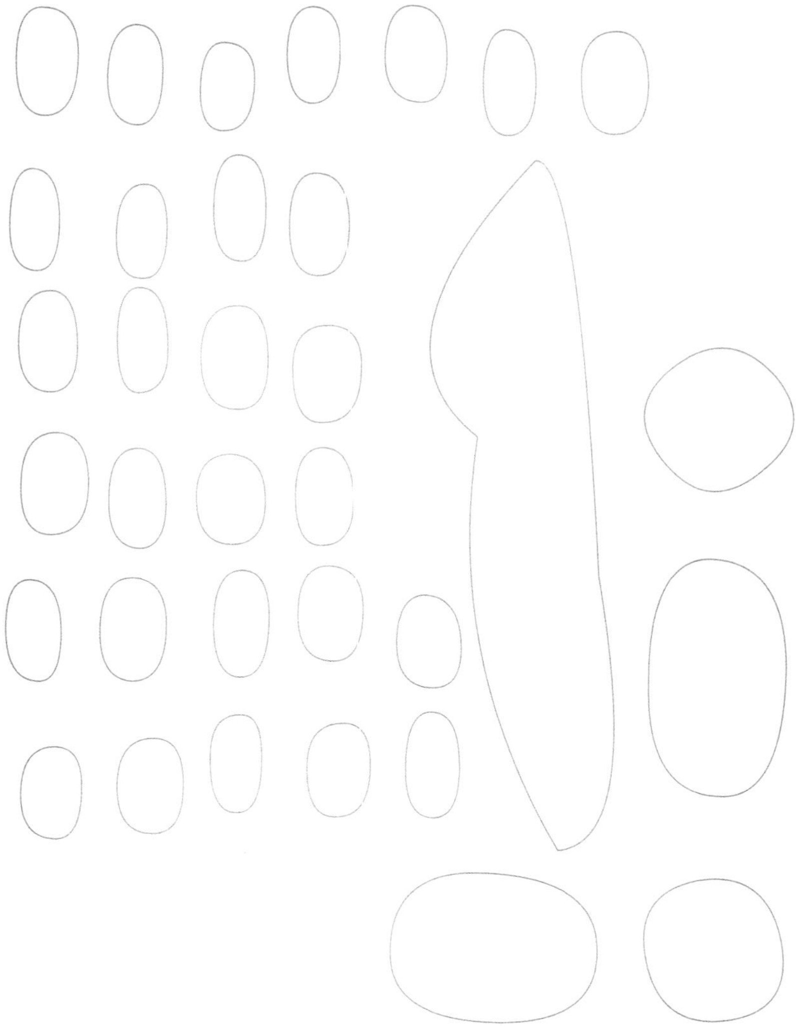

Pebble 886 'Beeple Tower' acquired on secondary for 6.529 eth by Thor

"'Beeple Tower' is a nod to Beeple the artist who kickstarted the NFT art revolution by selling an NFT for $69,000,000. A rare *Mountlet* in the most phallic of shapes."
Thor

Pebble 886

- Mint Type - Palettes: <u>MemeMaxis</u> 900/1,000
- Color Density: <u>Faint</u> 153/1,000
- Edge: <u>Yes</u> 312/1,000
- Flow: <u>No</u> 935/1,000
- Overlap: <u>Disjoin</u> 245/1,000
- Palette: <u>Dino Disco</u> 58/1,000
- Size: <u>Mountlet</u> 25/1,000
- Special Elements: <u>All</u> 77/1,000
- Traced: <u>No Fill</u> 45/1,000

Rarity

- Rarity Rank: #18
- Statistical Rarity: #38
- Single Trait Rarity #123

MintFace Vibe Check

The large vertical mass has given Pebble #886 the moniker 'Beeple Tower'. *Mountlet*s are the 'Bold Squiggles' of Pebbles for their bombastic nature, yet with Pebble #886 we are treated to a *Mountlet* anomaly. The *Traced No Fill* trait excavates weight felt through the mass of color on the artwork to create a refined exception.

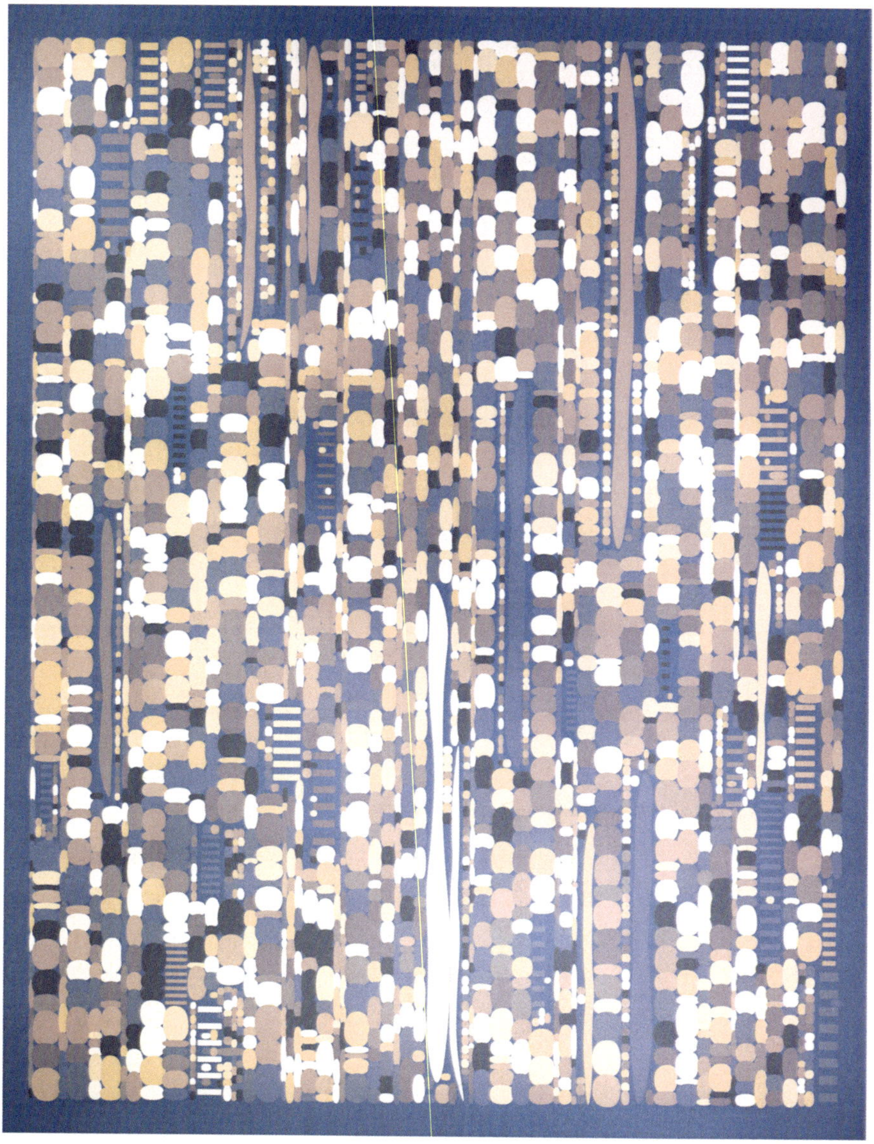

Pebble 888 minted by Burnasso

> "Each Pebble is a unique grail in itself including Pebble 888!" Burnasso

Pebble 888

- Mint Type - Palettes: MemeMaxis 900/1,000
- Color Density: Vivid 349/1,000
- Edge: Yes 312/1,000
- Flow: No 935/1,000
- Overlap: Fuse 113/1,000
- Palette: Dusk Riverbed 71/1,000
- Size: Boulderette 147/1,000
- Special Elements: 2 291/1,000
- Traced: No Border 858/1,000

Rarity

- Rarity Rank: #458
- Statistical Rarity: #317
- Single Trait Rarity #513

MintFace Vibe Check

The *Fuse Overlap* trait merges these *Boulderette*-sized Pebbles inwards. *Vivid Color Density* lifts the *Dusk Riverbed* palette from sea blue towards an inkier shade. The ladder *Special Elements* overlay texture to deliver an interesting contrast that shapes the overall piece.

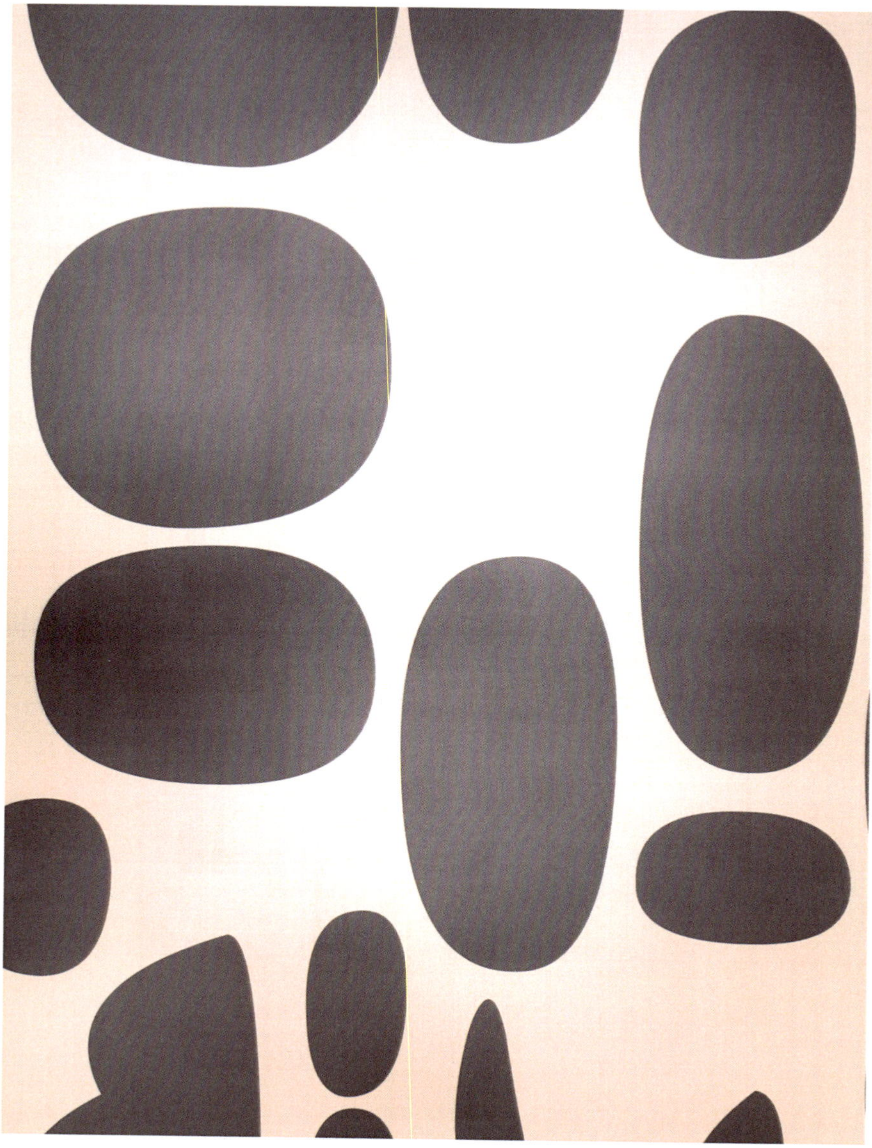

Pebble 896 'The Sun is Always Shining' minted by Angol

> “This one has the *Desert Mirage* palette. The white Pebble is like the sun. In the desert, the sun is always shining :-)”
> Angol

Pebble 896

- Mint Type - Palettes: MemeMaxis 900 / 1,000
- Color Density: Faint 153 / 1,000
- Edge: No 688 / 1,000
- Flow: No 935 / 1,000
- Overlap: Harmonize 492 / 1,000
- Palette: Desert Mirage 79 / 1,000
- Size: Rockling 300 / 1,000
- Special Elements: 3 427 / 1,000
- Traced: No Border 858 / 1,000

Rarity

- Rarity Rank: #899
- Statistical Rarity: #900
- Single Trait Rarity #817

MintFace Vibe Check

The expected five color palette of *Desert Mirage* evaporates to black, white and sand, adding to the feeling of a mid-day scorcher. *Harmonize* adjusts the space between each Pebble, as the white solar glare beats down.

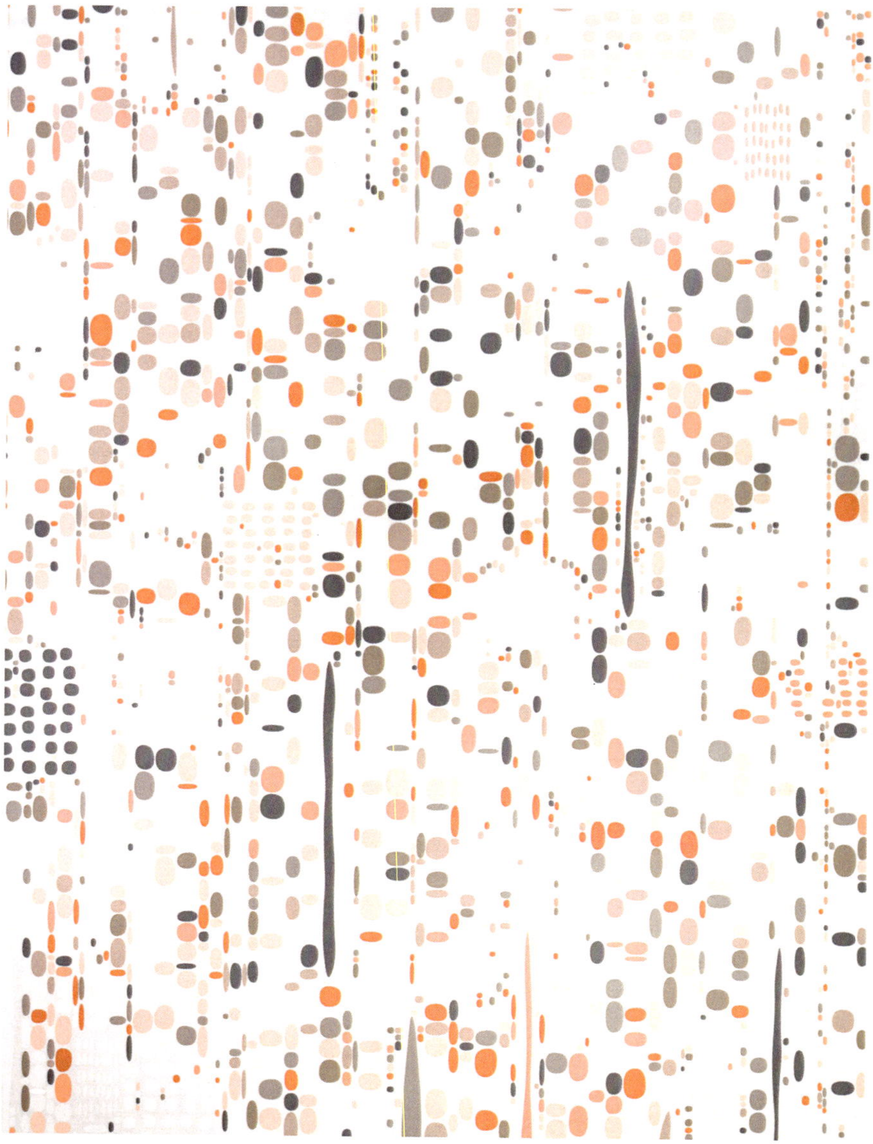

Pebble 909 'Running with the Devil' minted by BatSoupYum

"The *Boulderette* and *Serenity* traits are a perfect fit for 'Running with the Devil.'" BatSoupYum

Pebble 909

- Mint Type - Palettes: MemeMaxis 900/1,000
- Color Density: Bloom 314/1,000
- Edge: No 688/1,000
- Flow: No 935/1,000
- Overlap: Harmonize 492/1,000
- Palette: Serenity 84/1,000
- Size: Boulderette 147/1,000
- Special Elements: 2 291/1,000
- Traced: No Border 858/1,000

Rarity

- Rarity Rank: #898
- Statistical Rarity: #880
- Single Trait Rarity #863

MintFace Vibe Check

'Running with the Devil' is an energetic work, as *Boulderette* size combined with *Harmonize Overlap* creates enough negative space for the rouge Pebbles to glow. The white grid *Special Elements* fade into the background, while charcoal *Special Elements* tempt us into the darkness.

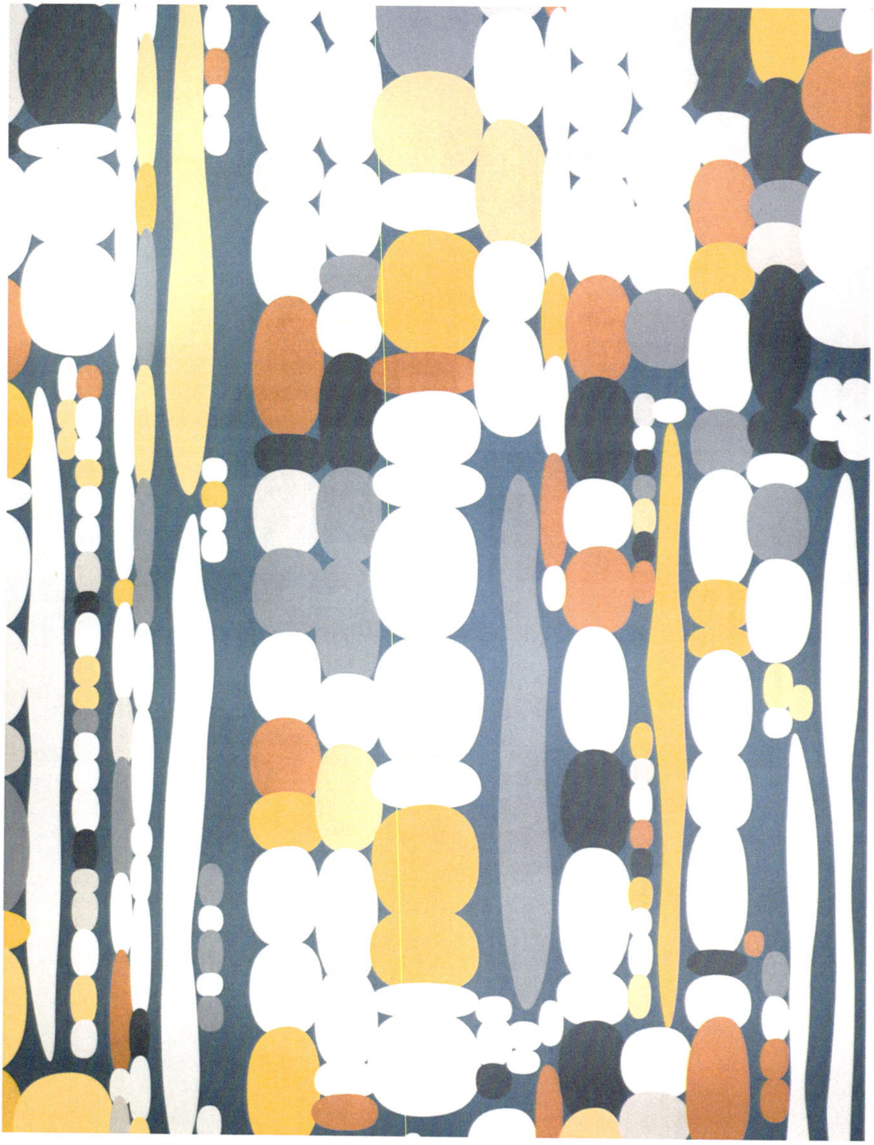

Pebble 954 minted by WintermuteGAN

“Everything, everywhere all at once. A fused citrus immersion of a cascade in full bloom.” WintermuteGAN

Pebble 954

- Mint Type - Palettes: MemeMaxis 900 / 1,000
- Color Density: Vivid 349 / 1,000
- Edge: No 688 / 1,000
- Flow: No 935 / 1,000
- Overlap: Disjoin 245 / 1,000
- Palette: Coral Reef 71 / 1,000
- Size: Crumb 72 / 1,000
- Special Elements: 3 427 / 1,000
- Traced: No Border 858 / 1,000

Rarity

- Rarity Rank: #99
- Statistical Rarity: #81
- Single Trait Rarity #66

MintFace Vibe Check

The seven stick-like blobs provide a north to south directional quality to Pebble #954. With *No Border* present, the eye imagines beyond the frame where these Pebbles might be travelling to. What is unusual about Pebble #954 is the fused nature of the Pebbles not usually a quality of *Disjoin* overlap. Perhaps *Crumb* size has overruled the overlap trait on this occasion.

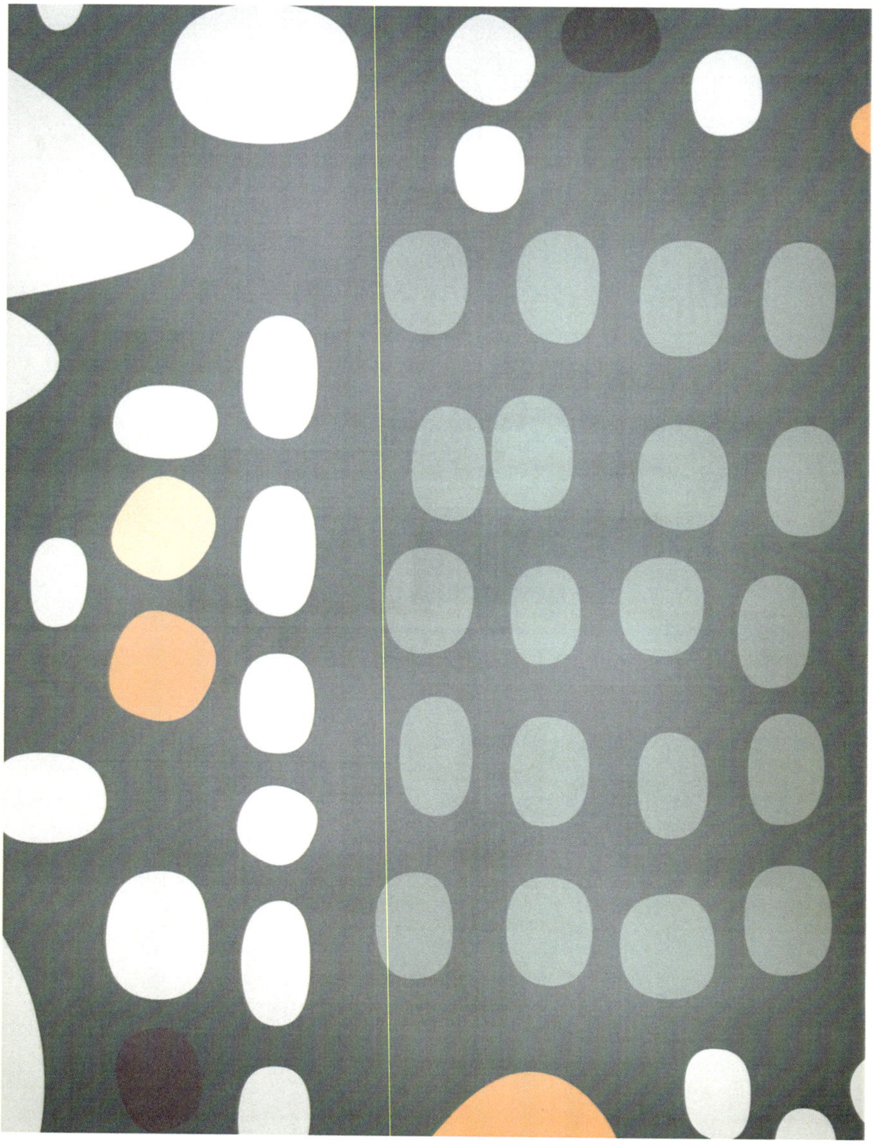

Pebble 958 'The Dolphin' minted by smpsmyth

"Occasionally, the dolphin pops it's head out to feed..."
smpsmyth

Pebble 958

- Mint Type - Palettes: MemeMaxis 900/1,000
- Color Density: Hush 143/1,000
- Edge: No 688/1,000
- Flow: No 935/1,000
- Overlap: Disjoin 245/1,000
- Palette: Forest Whisper 83/1,000
- Size: Stonelet 220/1,000
- Special Elements: 3 427/1,000
- Traced: No Border 858/1,000

Rarity

- Rarity Rank: #769
- Statistical Rarity: #720
- Single Trait Rarity #742

MintFace Vibe Check

'The Dolphin' derives its name from the marine mammal-like shape swimming into the frame in the upper left corner. A deliberate grid of light green circles dominates the canvas without commanding attention, providing plenty of space for 'The Dolphin' to happily swim through the bubbles.

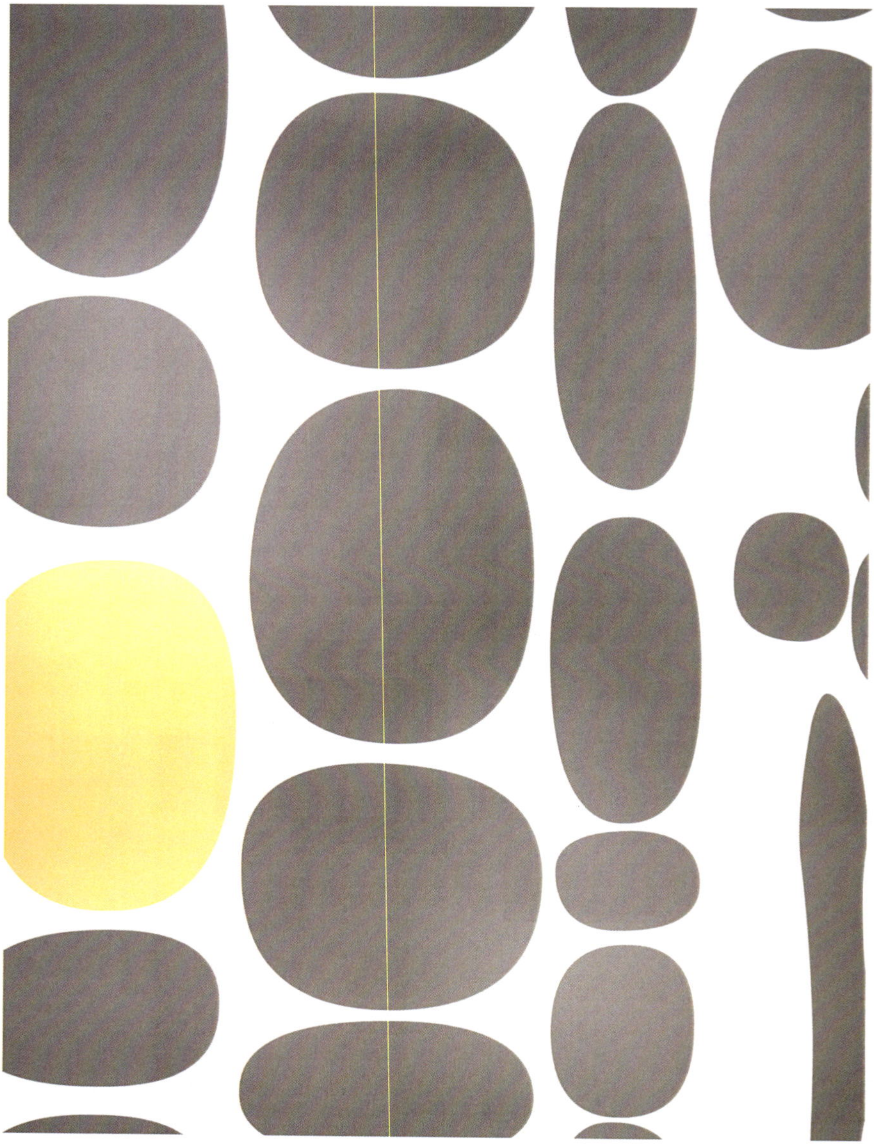

Pebble 960 'The Goose Egg' bought on secondary by gmmoney

“ 'The Goose Egg' was first.” gmmoney who bought on the secondary market.

Pebble 960

- Mint Type - Palettes: MemeMaxis 900 / 1,000
- Color Density: Faint 153 / 1,000
- Edge: No 688 / 1,000
- Flow: No 935 / 1,000
- Overlap: Harmonize 492 / 1,000
- Palette: Dino Disco 58 / 1,000
- Size: Stonelet 220 / 1,000
- Special Elements: 2 291 / 1,000
- Traced: No Border 858 / 1,000

Rarity

- Rarity Rank: #776
- Statistical Rarity: #775
- Single Trait Rarity #817

MintFace Vibe Check

One of the most memetic Pebbles on mint day for its instant connection to 'The Goose' Ringer collected by 6529 Museum with support from 6529 Funds. The emergent forms that code makes possible makes us question whether the very fabric of reality may be a simulation. Few.

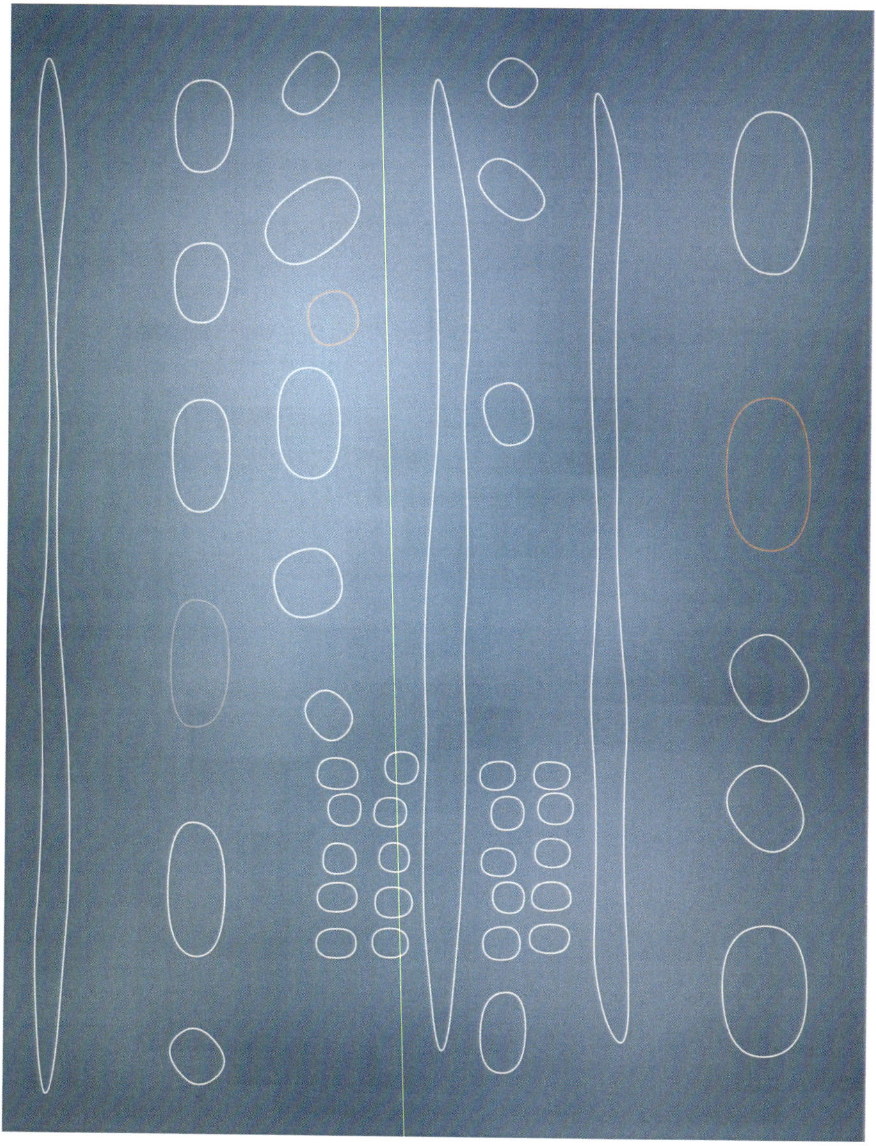

Pebble 962 'Empty Threats' minted by 4lteredBeast

"'Empty Threats' is a play on words. 'Sticks and Stones' alongside the *No Fill* trait makes the threats of violence empty." 4lteredBeast.

Pebble 962

- Mint Type - Palettes: MemeMaxis 900/1,000
- Color Density: Faint 153/1,000
- Edge: Yes 312/1,000
- Flow: No 935/1,000
- Overlap: Isolate 99/1,000
- Palette: Citrus Slate 72/1,000
- Size: Pebbit 151/1,000
- Special Elements: 3 427/1,000
- Traced: No Fill 45/1,000

Rarity

- Rarity Rank: #93
- Statistical Rarity: #75
- Single Trait Rarity #123

MintFace Vibe Check

Traced No Fill continues to thrill us with an outline of almost entirely chalk white Pebbles, in contrast to most of the *Citrus Slate* Pebble peers. *Overlap Isolate* lets every Pebble breath as if it were a bubble in a carbonated glass of panaché.

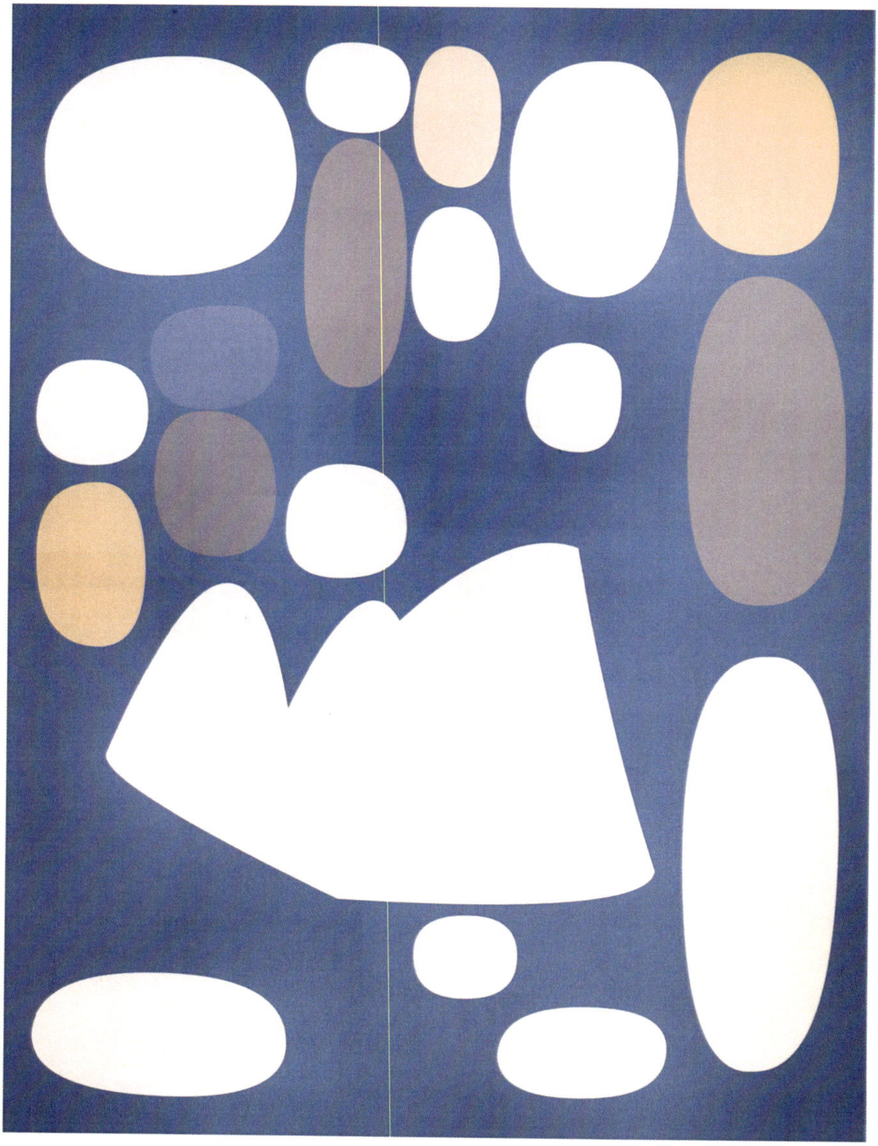

Pebble 986 'The Antidote' minted by Giopetto

"'The Antidote.' Long story, maybe I will tell it in full someday. It wasn't the Pebble of choice but it helped when it was needed." Giopetto

Pebble 986

- Mint Type - Palettes: MemeMaxis 900/1,000
- Color Density: Hush 143/1,000
- Edge: Yes 312/1,000
- Flow: No 935/1,000
- Overlap: Harmonize 492/1,000
- Palette: Dusk Riverbed 71/1,000
- Size: Stonelet 220/1,000
- Special Elements: 2 291/1,000
- Traced: No Border 858/1,000

Rarity

- Rarity Rank: #588
- Statistical Rarity: #435
- Single Trait Rarity #612

MintFace Vibe Check

The strong centering of a sharp edged rock in Pebble #986 is the result of one of the two *Special Elements.* Dusk Riverbed delivers a calm and soothing palette as close as one might get to swimming in a deep clear river.

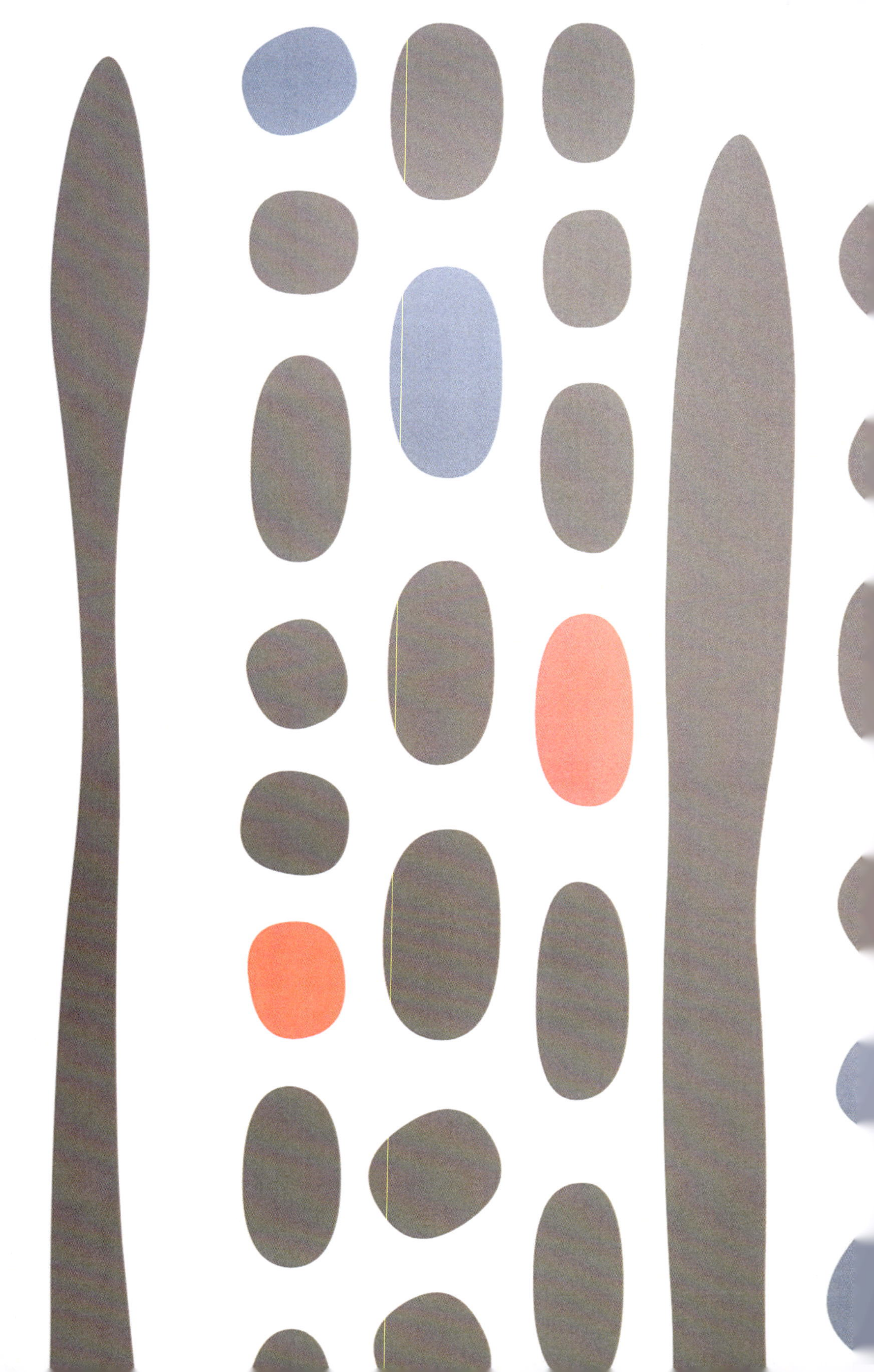

PART IV

6529 CONTRIBUTIONS

PEBBLES IN 6529 MUSEUM

The NextGen art contract that the Pebbles collection was minted on is the contribution of Punk6529. The 6529 Museum holds many Pebbles that were minted, and are included here in their entirety.

We explore which Pebbles were acquired on the secondary market by Punk6529, as they might represent interesting outputs or Trait Set gaps in the initial 6529 Museum allocation that needed filling. Yes, some people collect entire Trait Sets.

A Trait Set is a collection of each generative art output. A collectoor might decide to collect all the Pebble *Palette* traits, *Size* traits, or try something more audacious such as the Ultimate Pebble Set of all *Palette, Size,* and *Traced* types. How far along is the 6529 Museum in collecting Trait Sets?

- 85% of all 20 palettes collected (2nd to punksladsmemes)
- 100% of all 7 Pebble *Sizes* collected (1 of 3 collectoors)
- 100% of all 3 *Traced* collected (1 of 10 collectoors)

Two of the 52 Pebbles in the 6529 Museum were acquired on the secondary market. Pebble #904 with the *Dino Disco* palette was acquired for 2.54 eth to assist in Trait Set completion, and Pebble #688, one of five

Pebbles with *Craglet* Size and *No Fill* Traced combination, was acquired for 10 ETH.

Pebble #13 is notable for its *summer.jpg* palette, *Traced Border,* and *Mountlet* Size. Any of those traits on their own would be considered a collection rarity. Pebble #85, colloquially known within the community as 'The Gooch,' is a meme in its own right. Pebble #467 is a scintillating concerto of *Citrus Slate* at *Crumb* size with a well-defined *Traced Border* around every Pebble. The stick placements create a sense of perspective.

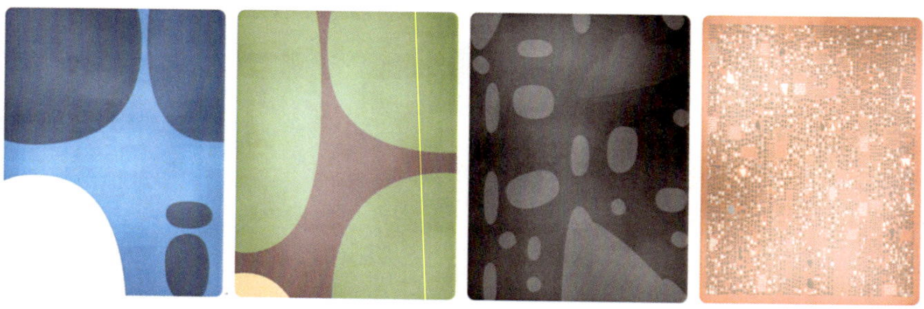

Pebble 13, 85, 331, 437

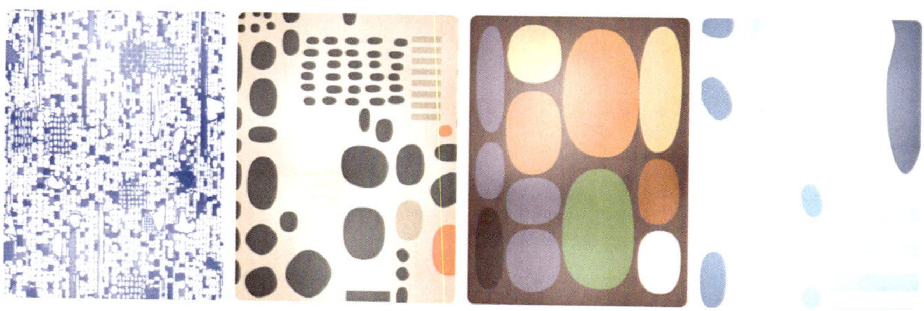

Pebble 438, 454, 455, 466

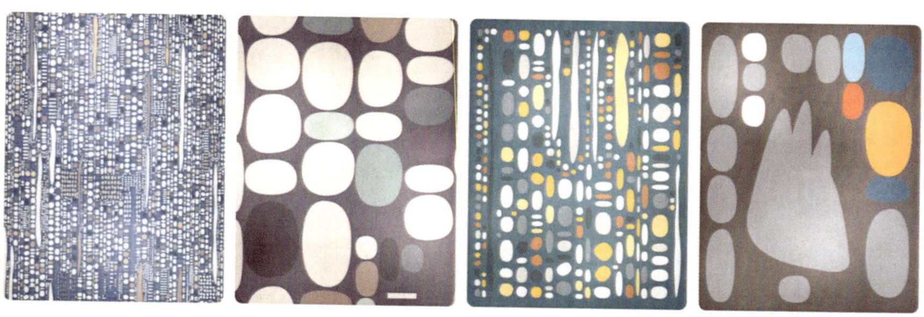

Pebble 465, 464, 467, 532

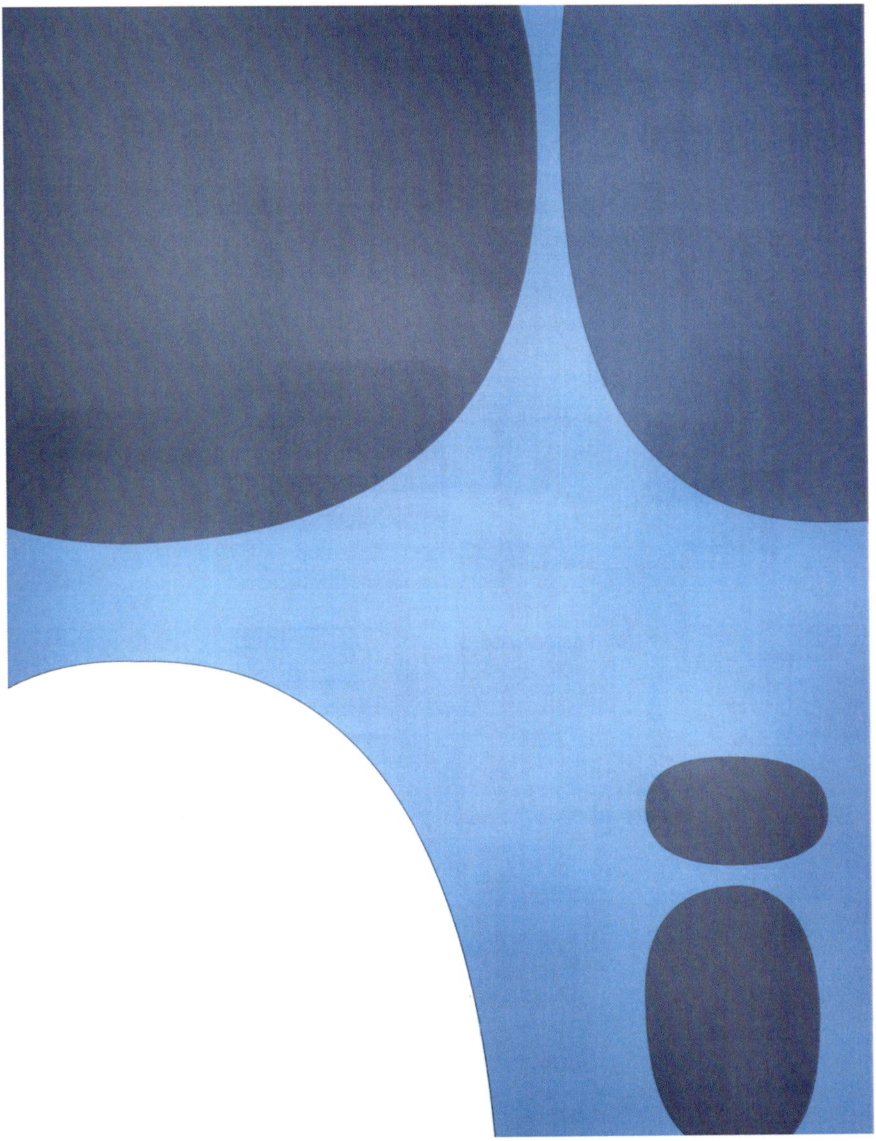

Pebble 13 with summer.jpg palette, Traced Border and Mountlet size minted by 6529 Museum

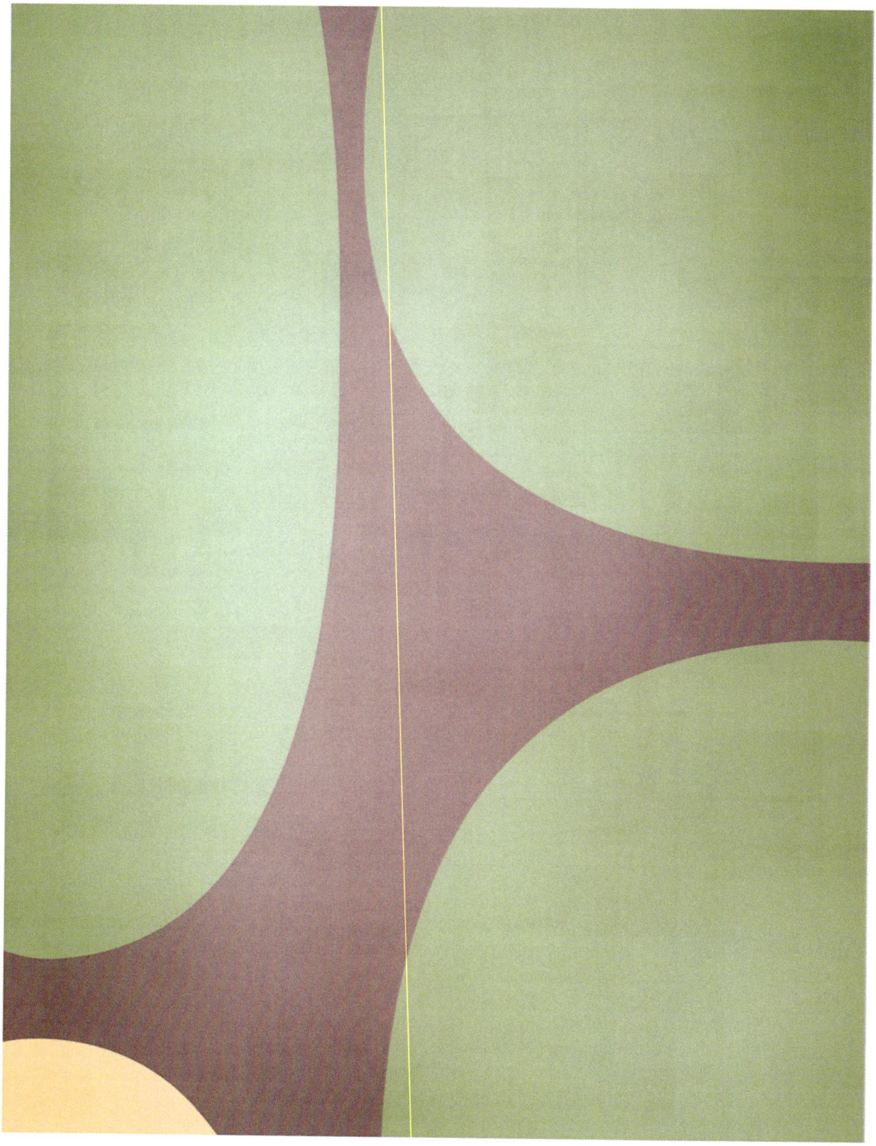

Pebble 85 'The Gooch' with Sgt. Pepe palette minted by 6529 Museum

Pebbles #531 and #538 are a pair of twins. Both from *Desert Mirage* and *Vivid Color Density* lineage, yet each with their own personality. Pebble #531 enjoys a *Border Traced* and lives with *No Special Elements,* while Pebble #538 is more outgoing with three *Special Elements* and an *Edge frame.* Pebble #688 was acquired on secondary, and if there is a Pebble that looked like the 6529 Museum aesthetic, then Pebble #688 is the one.

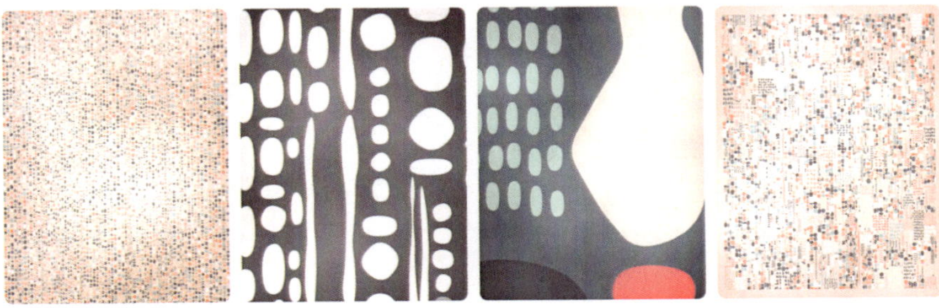

Pebble 531, 534, 533, 538

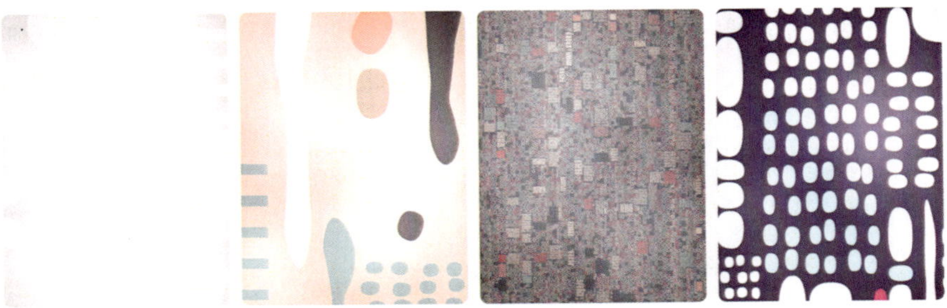

Pebble 539, 616, 688, 727

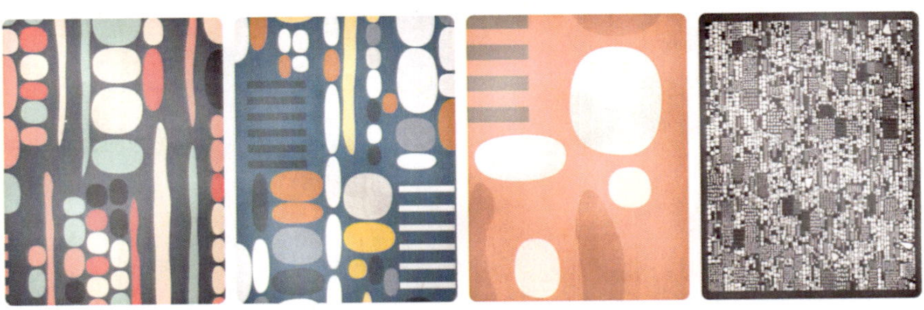

Pebble 728, 730, 732, 729

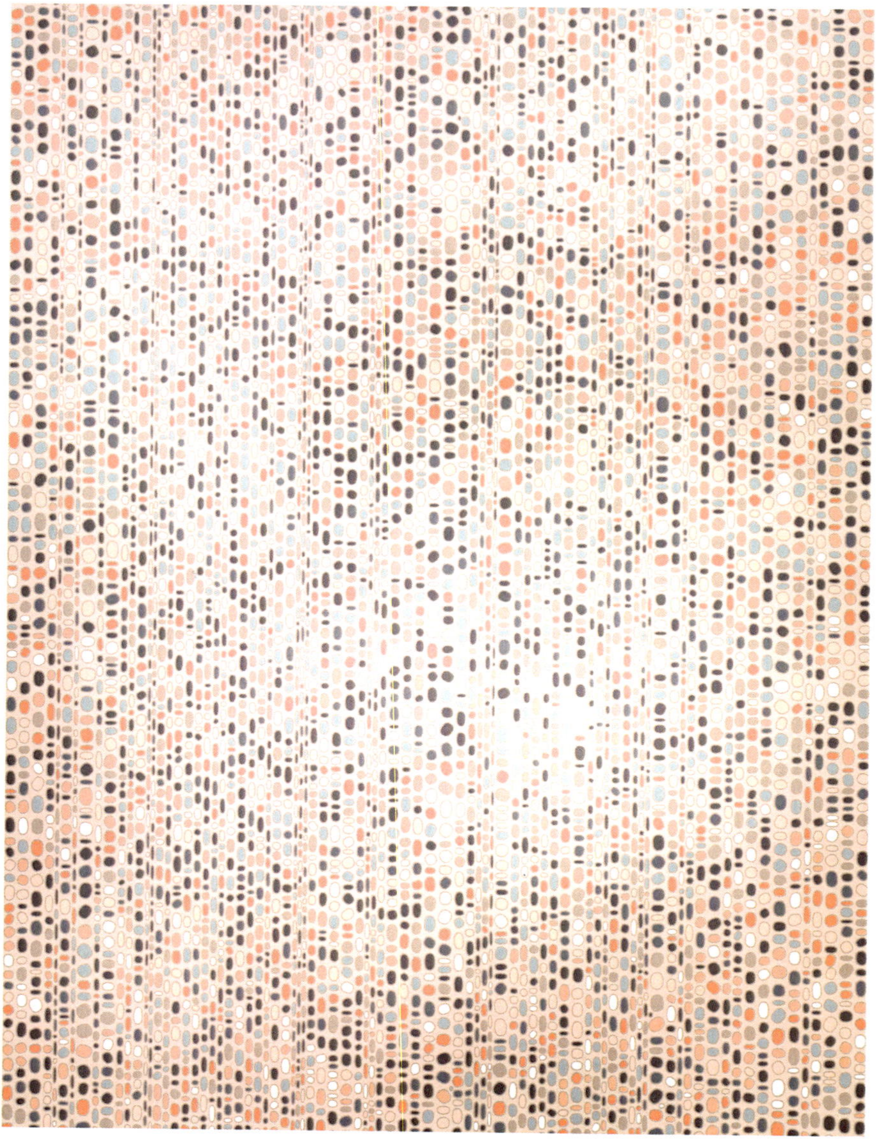

Pebble 531 'Desert Mirage Twin I' minted by 6529 Museum

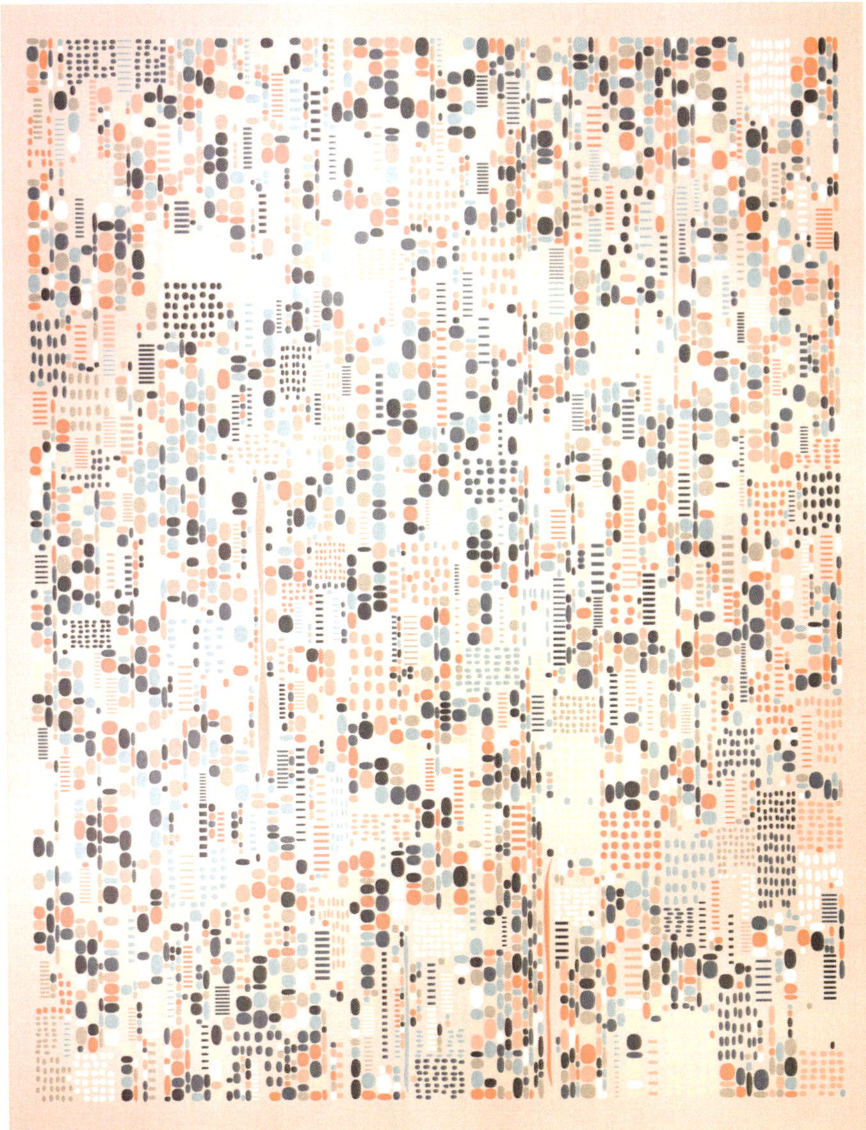

Pebble 531 'Desert Mirage Twin II' minted by 6529 Museum

Pebble #777 steals the show for the smaller *Boulderette*-sized Pebble appreciators while Pebble #778, minted immediately after, owes much of its character to the *Fuse Overlap* on *Serenity* palette. There is much detail in Pebble #778 suggesting further magnificence may await in printing a substantially-sized print. Before turning the page, take in the striking 'typewriter-like' composition of Pebble #776 in the *Forest Whisper* palette.

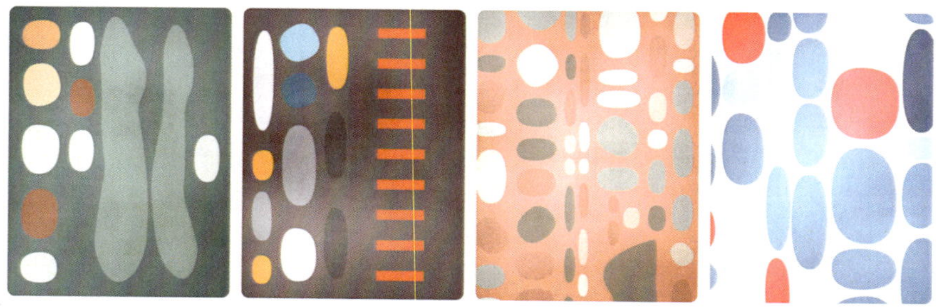

Pebble 738, 737, 731, 741

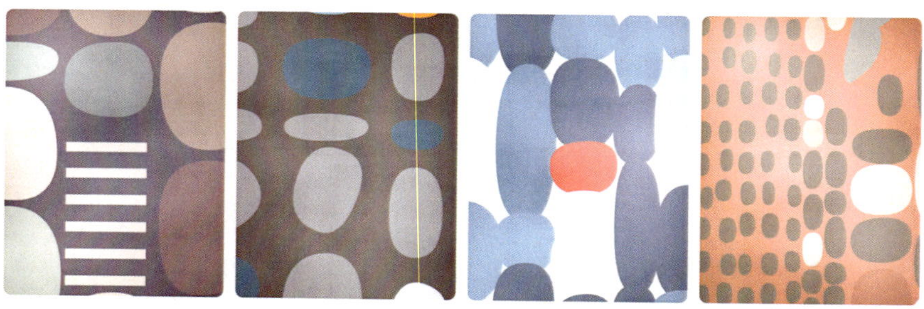

Pebble 740, 742, 739, 743

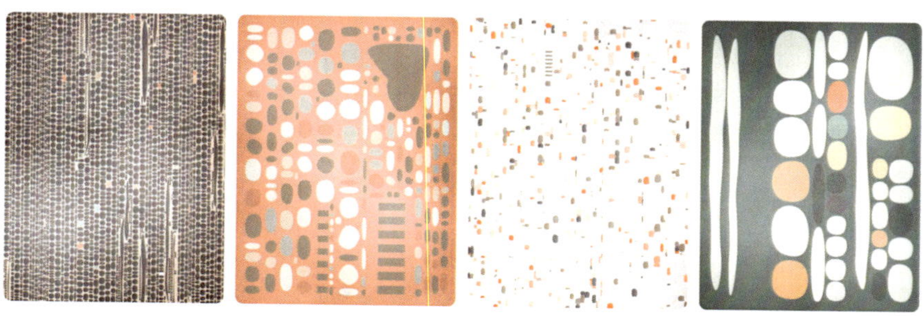

Pebble 777, 779, 778, 776

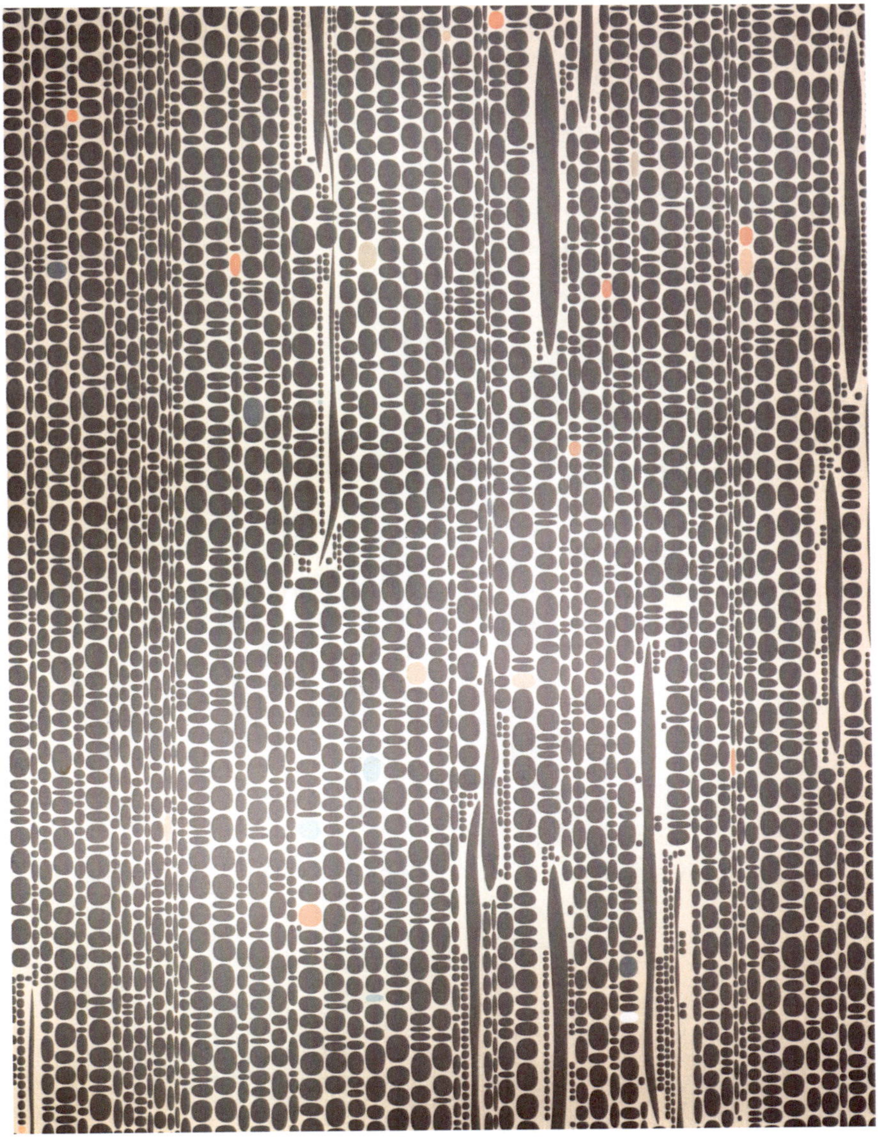

Pebble 777 with Boulderette size minted by 6529 Museum

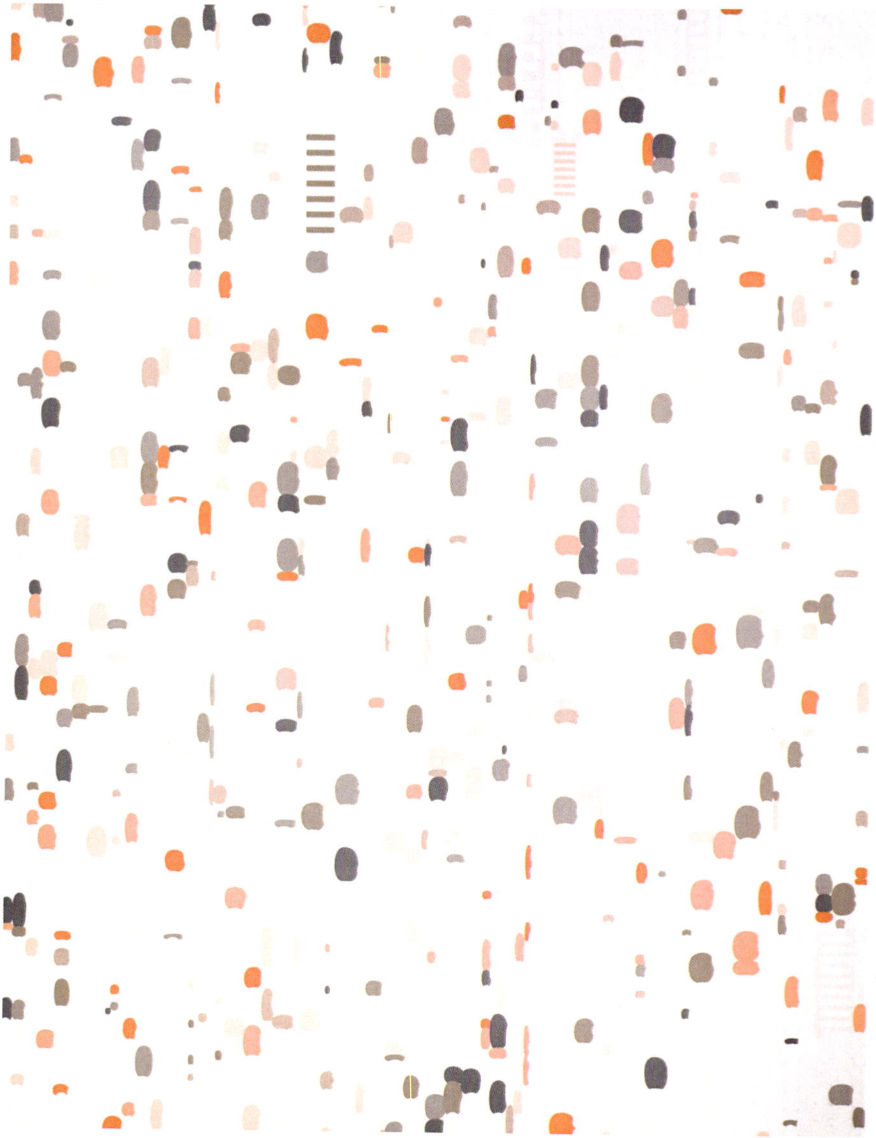

Pebble 778 with Serenity palette and Fuse Overlap minted by 6529 Museum

Pebble #788 cannot be ignored for its *Rockling*-sized audacity yet don't overlook the subtlety of Pebble #787. Sitting in quiet *Serenity* with a series of *Vivid,* larger-sized interlinking *Stonelet* Pebbles, Pebble #787 illustrates what *Blend Overlap* is capable of when paired with *Traced No Fill*. Pebble #791 successfully represents the randomly-shaped Pebbles often found in *Special Elements,* outputted in a *Vivid Unigrid* palette.

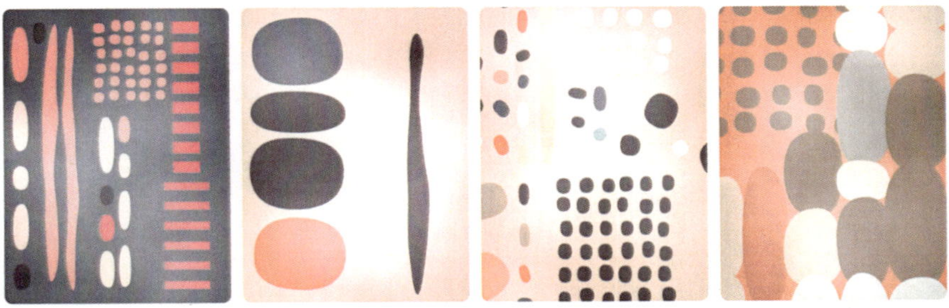

Pebble 783, 788, 785, 786

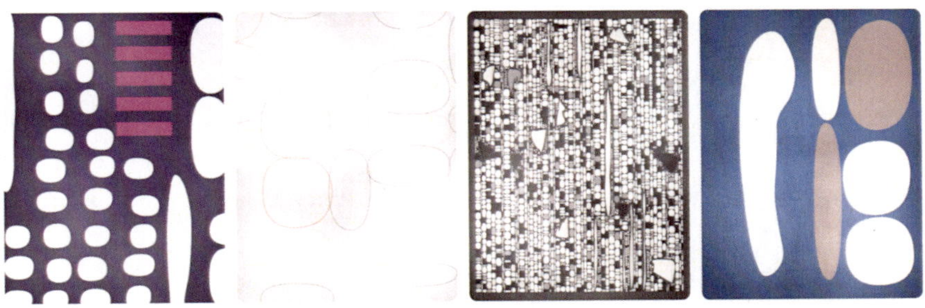

Pebble 784, 787, 789, 790

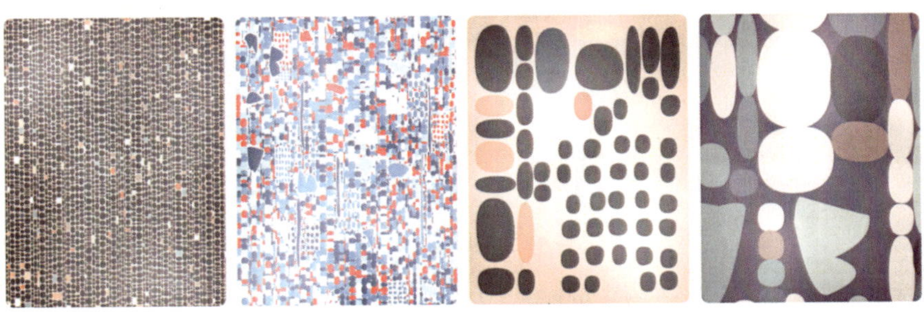

Pebble 794, 791, 795, 793

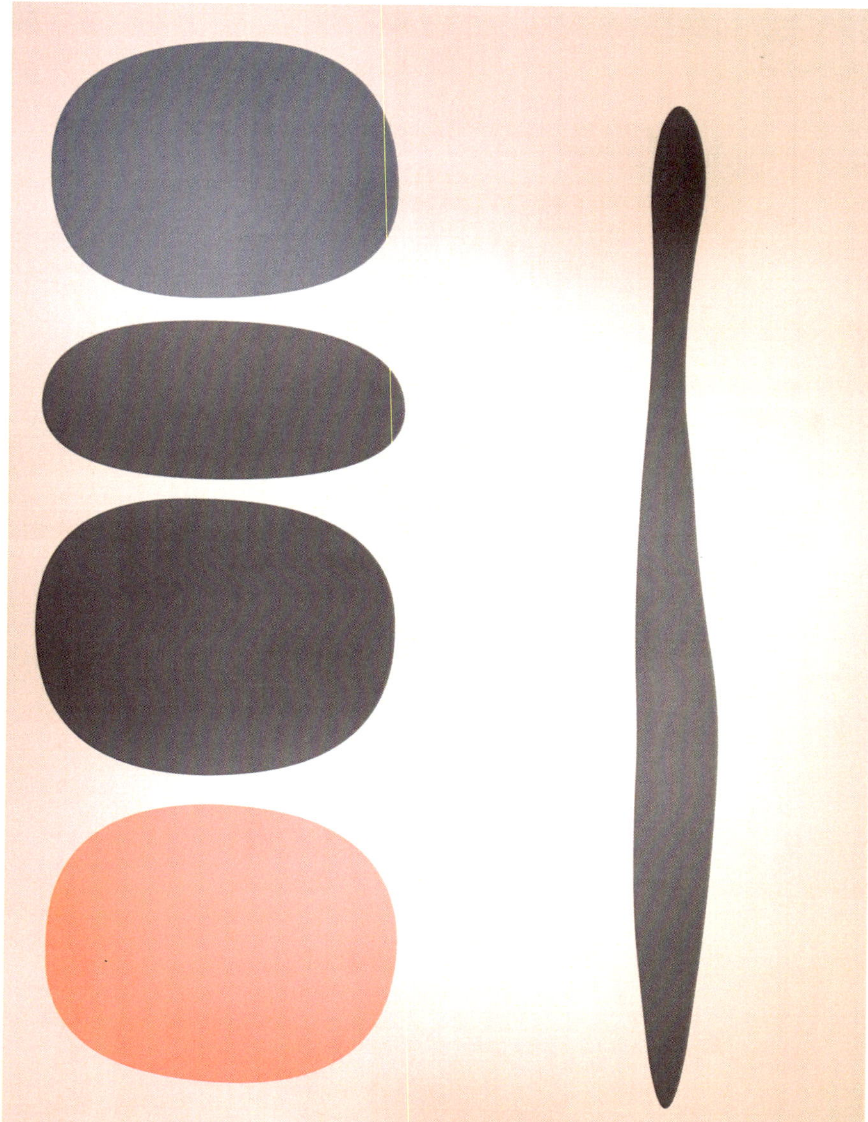

Pebble 788 with Rockling size minted by 6529 Museum

Pebble 787 with Blend Overlap and Traced No Fill minted by 6529 Museum

The last four Pebbles in the 6529 Museum by minted token number are Pebble #796, #792, #797, and #904. While the eye may immediately be drawn to the Mondrian-like *Dino Disco* palette of Pebble #904, a real hero lives next door in Pebble #792. The *Mountlet* size of Pebble #792, that extend beyond the *Edge*, gives a strength that one would recognize from the *Bold* Chromie Squiggle trait.

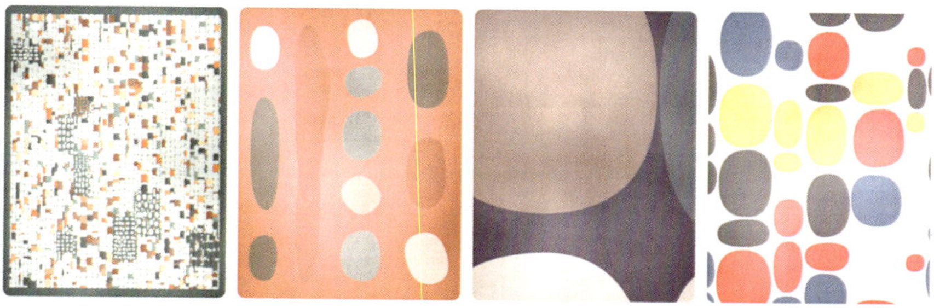

Pebble 796, 797, 792, 904

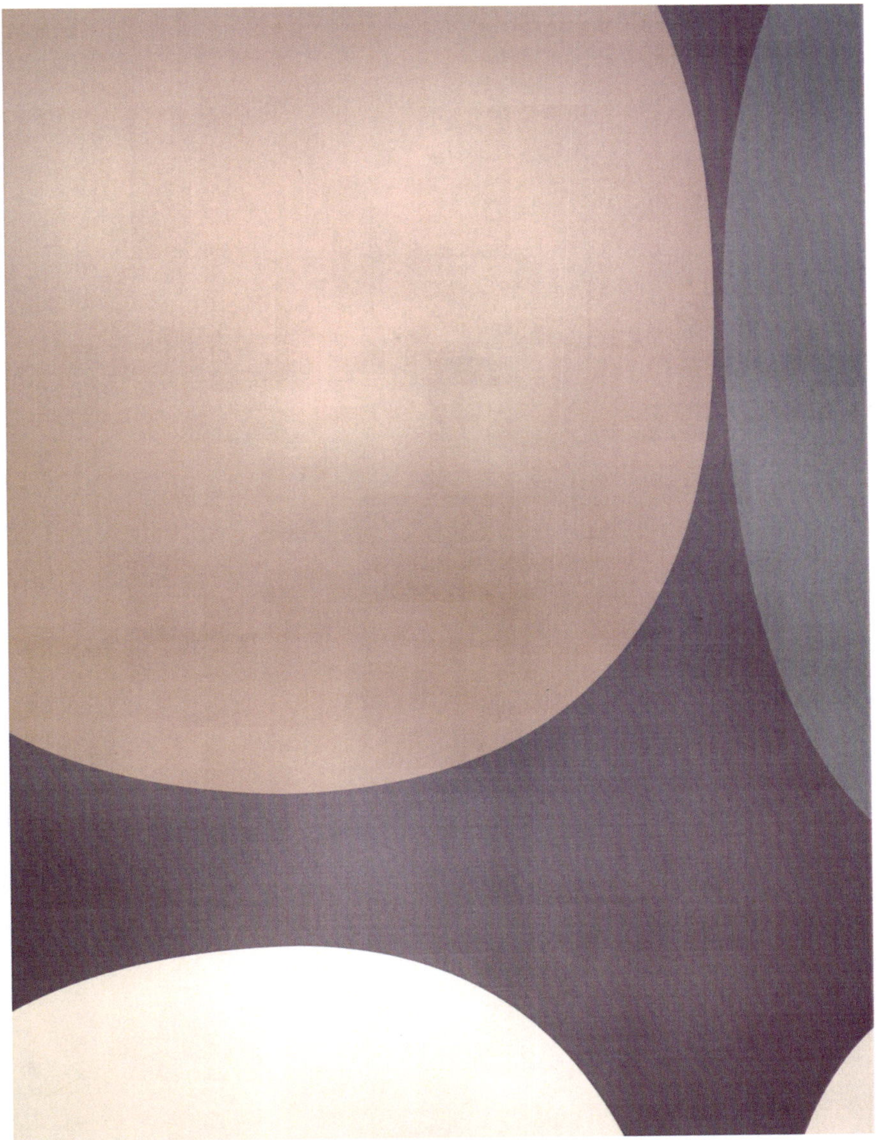

Pebble 792 with Mountlet size and Edge minted by 6529 Museum

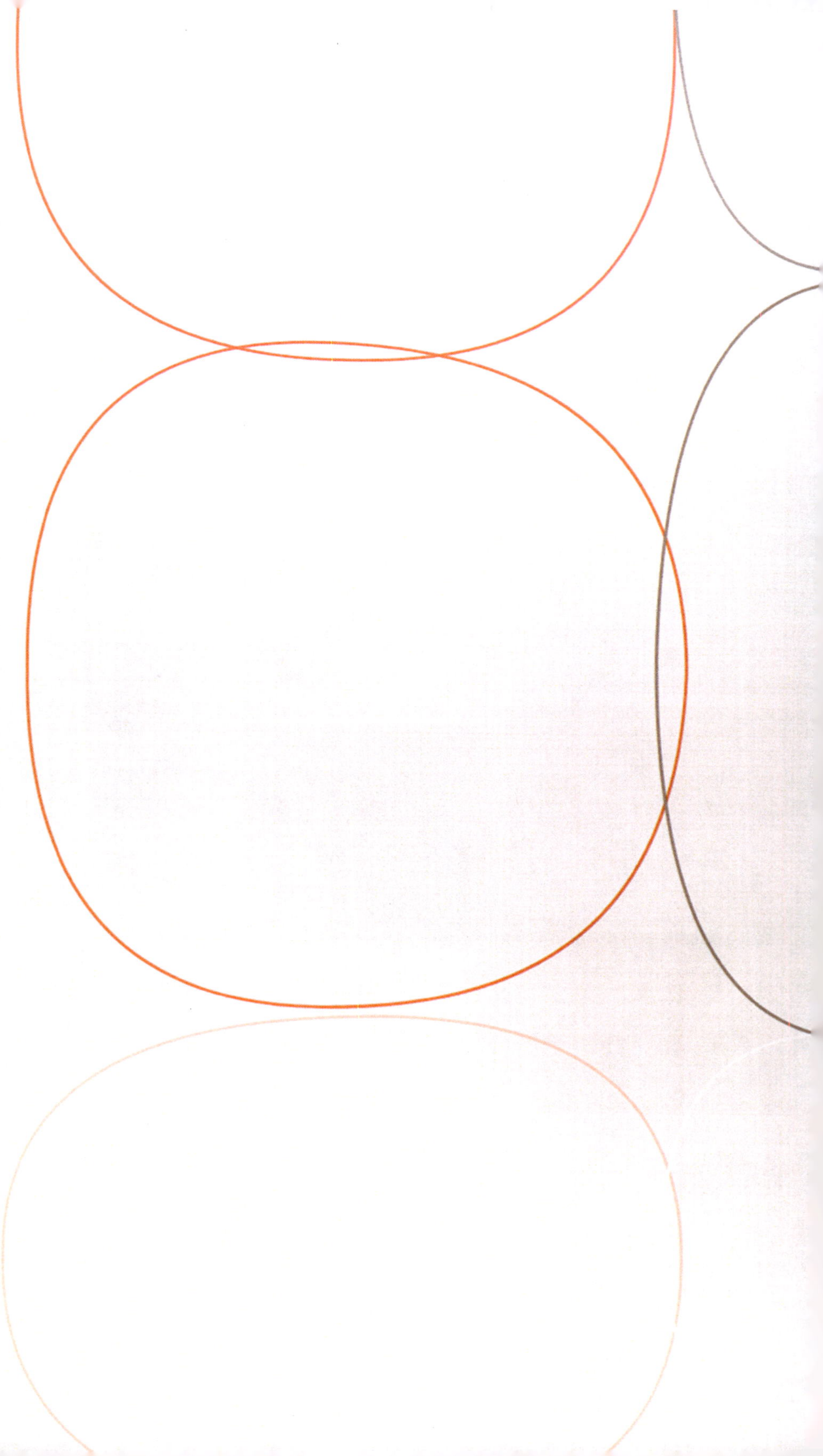

THE NEXT GEN ART CONTRACT

WRITTEN BY PUNK6529

NextGen is an on-chain generative art NFT contract. It is also a tool supporting the ambitious aspirations of the 6529 community in the areas of art experimentation and decentralized social organization. The central 6529 thesis is that, with the popularization of NFTs, we now have the complete toolkit available to create decentralized, open and transparent social and economic systems.

We believe that the classic values of liberal democracies such as human rights and public goods/commons should apply in the digital domain as well, and that it is important that the digital domain is not exclusively corporate-led.

We often call this end-state an 'open metaverse,' but other names for it could include 'a network state focused on decentralization' or 'a decentralized social system'.

Whatever it is called, the desired end-state is 100,000 or 1M, or 10M, or 100M people organizing some meaningful part of their societal activities through decentralized systems (blockchains and smart contracts).

This is what we are trying to build, and NextGen is another piece of the infrastructure we consider important for this mission.

. . .

Overall Approach

The fundamental structure of the NextGen contract follows the overall approach pioneered by Art Blocks in 2020-2021.

- A single core contract (with various supporting contracts) with custom token number spaces to separate different collections by different artists
- On-chain storage of the generative script and the seed / hash used to generate the image
- Randomized traits at mint

Given that the above structure is generally well-understood, we would like to focus on a few areas where we have adjusted the standard approach to support our specific goals and needs.

Native Allowlists

We believe that allowlists are the best approach for most in-demand mints. They support fairness and transparency in minting allocations, reduce gas costs, and permit both artists and projects to remain in control of their mint prices and distribution approaches.

NextGen natively supports complex allowlists, across multiple minting phases.

Native Delegation

We have been a leading voice for wallet safety for a long time designing all our systems to encourage 6529 collectors and community members to use safe practices when interacting with our website and smart contracts. To support this objective, we launched NFTDelegation.com in Spring 2023 and have been using it within the community to support address consolidation and delegation.

NextGen is the first NFT contract to support NFTDelegation natively. Allowlist members will be able to mint using any active delegates they have at the time of mint.

. . .

Personalization, Customization and Collector Provenance

The classic approach to a generative mint is that the algorithm is fully randomly (or pseudo-random, to be precise) determined at the time of mint. This is a good practice and we are supportive of it.

We believe, however, that there are both art and non-art use cases that could benefit from the output being influenced by information about the collector or minting address. This is most easily explained with two examples:

- Pebbles will pass some collector information for certain mints and adjust the output to reflect their provenance in a small way.
- The NextGen contract has also been deployed by the University of Nicosia to deploy student generative art certificates with on-chain student information (grade and name).

We believe this area is largely unexplored and potentially very fruitful.

Extra On-Chain™

Most generative collections, even the on-chain ones, serve an off-chain URI with metadata and potentially rendered images, to easily interoperate with marketplaces and galleries.

NextGen mints will start off working in this model, but the NextGen contract has the ability to switch metadata and rendering data to be 100% on-chain.

This removes even the smallest dependency from off-chain systems and, more importantly, makes the metadata composable on-chain. The combination of the ability to personalize the output and then serve the data on-chain is extraordinarily interesting to us.

It unlocks the ability to have a form of permanent Art Oracles on-chain. We can't wait to see what people come up with.

. . .

Artist Provenance

NextGen allows the artist to cryptographically sign a NextGen collection from an Ethereum address or ENS of their choice. As our protocol for community-verified identity improves, we hope the combination of the two will be able to provide assurances of 'who the artist was' over decades and even centuries.

Multiple Randomization Methods

NextGen supports three different randomization methods with the capacity to integrate more approaches in the future. Strictly speaking, all commonly used randomization methods are, scientifically, pseudorandom methods, but the differences have no practical effect in this context. For the purposes for which they are used, they are effectively random.

Phases / Periodicity

NextGen supports a wide range of phased and periodic minting approaches, from simple mints to periodic mints that can span for decades.

Minting Sales Models

NextGen supports all widely used (and some not-widely used) minting sales models

- Airdrops
- Fixed price mints
- Phase priced mints
- Linear descending auction
- Exponentially descending auction
- Linear ascending mint
- Burn-to-mint (internal or external collection)
- Swap-to-mint (internal or external collection)
- Mint-to-auction

The combination of Minting Sales Models and Phases can be used to create interesting and experimental minting dynamics.

On-Chain Libraries

NextGen supports the ability for collections to reference on-chain libraries to have no off-chain dependencies in rendering.

More Information

Additional technical information can be found here: https://seize-io.gitbook.io/nextgen/

NextGen Collections Model

We do not have a fixed plan in place following the genesis Pebbles collection and will develop and refine our approach over time.

This is what we currently believe will be our direction:

- We do not anticipate a large number of NextGen collections in the short-term.
- Generative collections require a lot of work to be done correctly, and we only would like to make interesting drops.
- We are under no pressure to mint NextGen collections, so we will mint a collection whenever it feels right.

We are broadly interested in three categories of collections:

- Collections that support our decentralization objectives
- Collections that explore interoperability or composability on-chain
- Collections that are unusual or interesting aesthetically or technically

We have a strong bias towards all NextGen collections being released under a CC0 license.

- The NextGen contracts are available under an Apache 2 open-source license
- Anyone who would like to take advantage of the work and time we have invested in the contracts is welcome to deploy their own instance of the contracts and mint their own collections.
- You do not need to ask our permission, but we will surely appreciate hearing about what you are doing with the contracts.

If you have an interesting idea along the lines above, please get in touch with us. We would love to brainstorm with you and see if it is a fit.

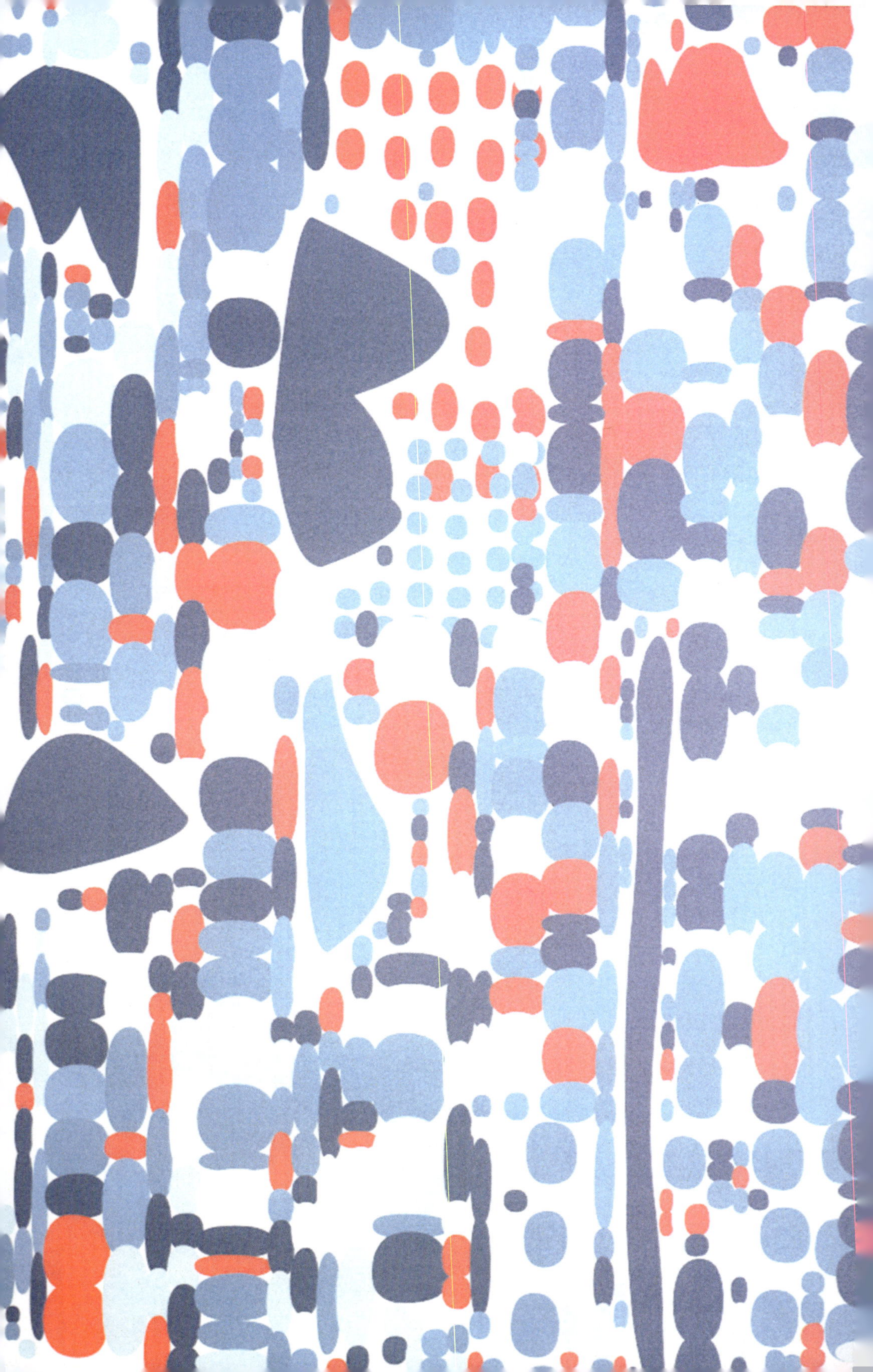

COLLECTION PARAMETERS

WRITTEN BY PUNK6529

About Pebbles

Pebbles aims to explore the order that can emerge from a small set of organically inspired elements of points, lines, textures, and light.

History of Technical Innovation

ZeBlocks prides itself on technical innovation in its generative mints and on-chain work. Most ZeBlocks projects, including Pebbles, are 100% on-chain, and do not use any external libraries.

Pebbles follows in the tradition of prior ZeBlocks projects:

- Unigrids: SVG-based generative art & music project
- Beatboxes: First fully immersive VR audiovisual generative art
- Senisthesia: Audio-sensitive generative art NFTs

Pebbles: Matched To The Human Eye

Pebbles is one of the highest-resolution generative collections ever released.

. . .

The Challenge:

With the exception of SVG-based collections (that typically have simpler structures), most generative collections do not, in practice, have unlimited scalability in terms of resolution. An output can be scaled up and rendered to a higher resolution, but if the underlying data point density does not exist in the algorithm, render quality will typically start to suffer above 4K

The Goal

Pebbles aims to provide sufficient resolution to match or exceed the acuity of the human eye, even in a world of wall-sized TVs or AR devices. Under typical large-screen TV viewing distances, 4K or 8K is more than sufficient to exceed the acuity of the human eye.

If wall-sized TVs become common in the future, the limit of human vision to discern differences in resolutions, under normal conditions, will move up to somewhere between 8K and 16K.

Pebbles is designed to have no loss of resolution up to 12.5K and continue to provide extraordinary detail at 16K and beyond. In practice, and under the majority of future display conditions, every Pebble has more resolution than the human eye can discern

The Approach

The Pebble algorithm addresses this issue in two ways:

- Very dense number of data points
- Matches the data points to the exact pixels available at each render, regardless of resolution
- This makes it computationally expensive to render. Pebbles does not use p5.js or other processing libraries to improve rendering performance, particularly at large sizes.

NextGen x Pebbles

NextGen will take the following approach to support Pebbles extraordinary resolution:

- On mint day, NextGen rendered Pebble mints in 1K. This allowed a first look at the outputs.
- Post-mint, the base image was re-rendered in 2K for online viewing.
- NextGen provides 4K, 8K and 16K renders for download and printing. We can't wait for people to dig into these super high quality renders.
- Though NextGen can serve collection renders 100% on-chain, the switch to on-chain rendering for the Pebbles Collection will be delayed until GPU improvements allow for reasonable real-time rendering times. This does not impact other NextGen collections, which can go fully on-chain independently.

Key Collection Parameters

- Collection Size: 1,000
- Orientation: Vertical
- Aspect Ratio: 1:1.294
- Script: Javascript
- Script Size: 17Kb
- External libraries used: None
- License: Creative Commons 0 (CC0)
- Prints: An official ZeBlocks approved printing process

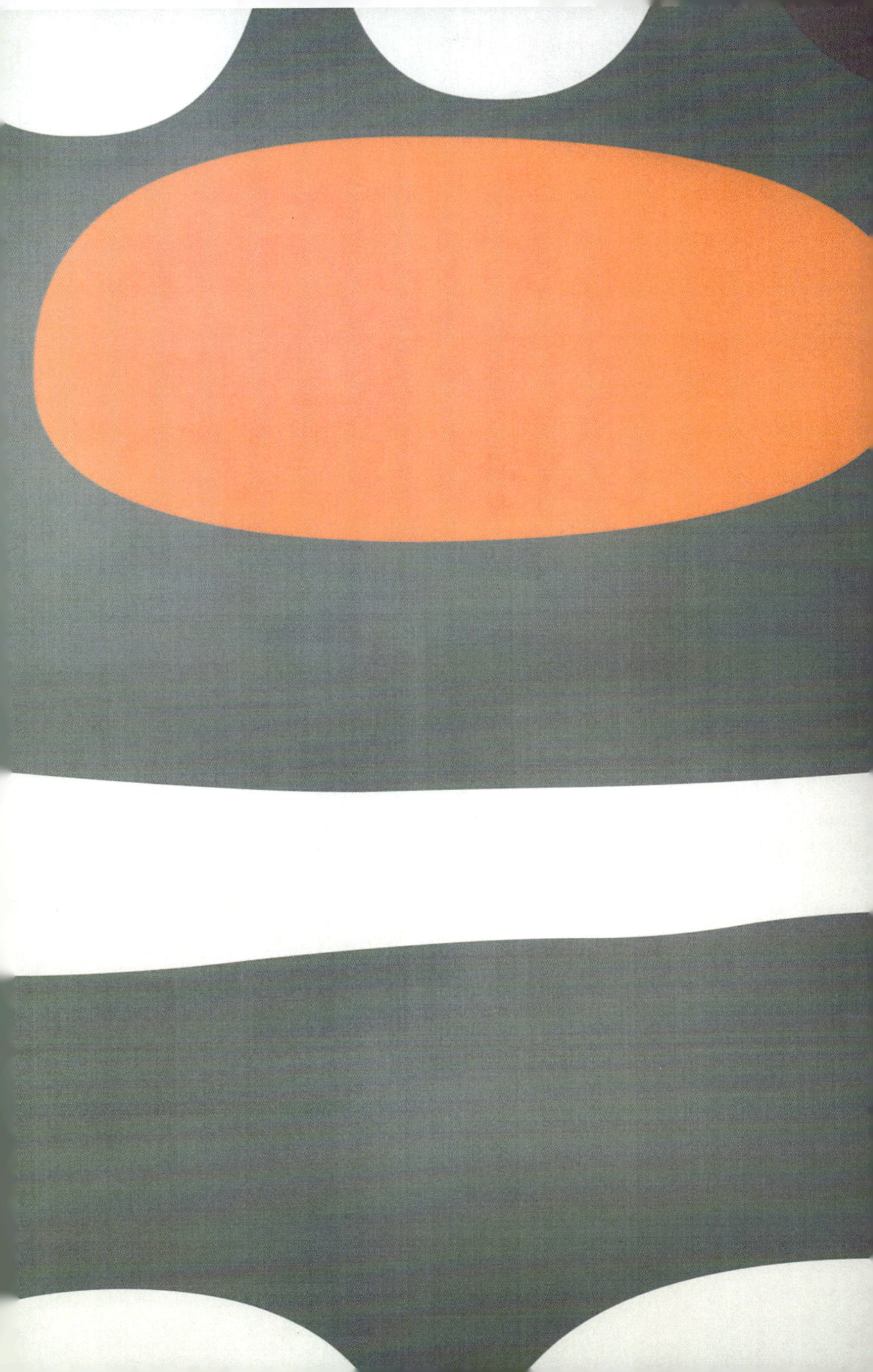

AFTERWORD

MintFace (@mintfaced on X) published the Pebble book for art collectoors to understand the generative art collection and for Pebble collectoors to understand the traits that influenced the output of each artwork. The book is not financial advice to buy Pebbles; you can, of course, buy Pebbles if you like. The full Pebbles collection is available to browse as part of the NextGen collection on seize.io.

Pebbles | A MintFace Generative Art Guide

Published by:

UmPrint Publishing

New Zealand

ISBN Hardcover: 978-1-0670257-0-0

ISBN Softcover: 978-1-0670257-1-7

420p 3.17cm

First Edition: June 2024

Cover Design by: MintFace

Edited by: ChatGPT4.0

For permissions, please contact: @mintfaced

ALSO BY MINTFACE

MINTED | Artists on the Blockchain 2021

Nouns Almanac | Every day a new Noun is born 2022

www.ingramcontent.com/pod-product-compliance
Lightning Source LLC
LaVergne TN
LVRC080752160926
848054LV00065B/890/J

* 9 7 8 1 0 6 7 0 2 5 7 0 0 *